Java Gently for Engineers and Scientists

INTERNATIONAL COMPUTER SCIENCE SERIES
Consulting Editor: A D McGettrick University of Strathclyde

Java Gently for Engineers and Scientists

Judith M Bishop
Department of Computer Science
University of Pretoria

Nigel T Bishop
Department of Mathematics, Applied Mathematics and Astronomy
University of South Africa

An imprint of **Pearson Education**

Harlow, England · London · New York · Reading, Massachusetts · San Francisco
Toronto · Don Mills, Ontario · Sydney · Tokyo · Singapore · Hong Kong · Seoul
Taipei · Cape Town · Madrid · Mexico City · Amsterdam · Munich · Paris · Milan

Pearson Education Limited
Edinburgh Gate
Harlow
Essex CM20 2JE
England

and Associated Companies throughout the world

Visit us on the World Wide Web at:
http://www.pearsoneduc.com

First published 2000

ISBN 0-201-34304-5

British Library Cataloguing-in-Publication Data
A catalogue record for this book is available from the British Library

Library of Congress Cataloging-in-Publication Data
A catalog record for this book can be obtained from the Library of Congress

10 9 8 7 6 5 4 3 2 1
05 04 03 02 01 00

Typeset by 43
Printed and bound in Great Britain by
T.J. International Ltd., Padstow, Cornwall

To our parents in France, Françoise and Michael

And in memory of Jean, Yvonne, Francis and Irene
who were always so interested in our scientific careers

Contents

Example programs and Case studies

Preface

Java Gently for Engineers and Scientists aims to introduce programming through examples of problems that engineers or scientists may encounter. Some of these are numerical in nature, while others are concerned with handling data derived from a wide variety of sources. The whole of the Java language is covered, and the standard of programming is based firmly in the modern style of object-oriented, well-structured, readable, maintainable and visually attractive programs.

Why Java?

We believe that Java is an excellent teaching language, and that it is in a different class to C, which is much favoured by engineers; to Fortran, which is still used by professional scientists; and to Pascal, which it is rapidly replacing in computer science communities. Java provides:

- a small and efficient core language;
- objects as the basic means of structuring a program;
- full graphics, event-driven programming and multimedia (sound, image and animation);
- genuine platform independence and the ability to transmit and run programs over the Internet;
- facilities for parallel programming and for communicating on the network in a variety of ways.

It can be argued that engineers and scientists only need a C-like core of Java. It is our belief, however, that Java is a very well-designed language, and as such is well within the capabilities even of students whose main focus is not programming, but scientific understanding. By using all that Java has to offer, students can explore and reveal more about the physical world, and the excitement engendered thereby will spur them on to learn more. For that reason, we teach Java properly, with graphics, objects and exceptions coming in right at the beginning.

Approach to programming

The approach to programming used in the book hinges on Java's main selling points: it is small, but very powerful. In order to show the power, we start off with a program that shows how the web is used, but then move straight into covering the basic concepts. Because Java has a smaller number of constructs than Pascal or C++, we can spend *less time* here, and therefore can spend time on the numerical methods and scientific problem solving which are the main focus of the book.

After trying several alternatives, we found that the following multi-faceted approach presented students with the most leverage in their programming tasks:

- **Graphics** and **interactive interfaces** from the start via three, small, self-contained classes, which themselves form Case studies in the book.
- **Object orientation** as a means of structuring programs, thus avoiding global methods and variables, and excessive parameter passing.
- **Creation of library classes** based on the numerical methods discussed in each chapter, and the construction of a Java package as a result.
- **Web**, **distributed** and **parallel** processing receiving first-class status in the book.

Graph, Display and Text

The three classes developed for this book are Graph, Display and Text. Graph is used to draw sketch graphs of x–y values and is both versatile and simple to use. Only three methods are needed to produce a decent representation of a program's output. Display is a class that manages a window with input and output shown side by side. This arrangement is unique, and has already proved popular with users, as it facilitates programs being run and rerun with different data, a very common requirement in scientific processing. The Text class comes from *Java Gently* and serves to make input of bulk data from files straightforward, as well as simplifying Java's real number formatting options.

In order that students are not 'hooked into' these classes for ever, as soon as their programming skills are mature enough (starting at Chapter 7) we take them inside the classes, as Case studies in themselves, and show how customized user interfaces, graphs and text output can be created from scratch in Java.

Object orientation

Deciding how to formulate scientific programs in Java was quite a challenge. The typical numerical program consists of an iterative algorithm, such as a Newton–Raphson root finder, which uses a function supplied by the user, and receives and returns several values. In Java, one cannot return several values via a method call, so the interface between the user's program and the algorithm would be either via global variables or objects. Objects are the modern and obvious choice. However, we had to make it easy for novices to incorporate objects even into early programs, otherwise they would learn bad habits, which are notoriously hard to unlearn.

Therefore, in Chapter 3, we introduce the technique of a local class as a means of grouping the numerical algorithm along with the data it needs. The main program instantiates the class, and can transfer values in and out of the object so created. Later on we tackle the second issue, that of having the algorithm work on a user-defined function. Here abstract methods are the obvious choice. They are introduced in Chapter 6, and used without fuss thereafter. Abstract methods were slightly easier to deal with than Java's interfaces, and had the added advantage that the concept would transfer across to other object-oriented languages such as C++ (virtual functions).

Creating a library

It is both satisfying and useful for students to know how to create libraries of reusable software. The scientific community is well known for its pre-eminence in this field. Both the programming skills required to create self-contained software and the mechanics of getting it into a package are important skills for engineering and science students to acquire.

Web, distributed and parallel processing

One of Java's outstanding successes was its use in a simulator which ran as an applet during the time of the landing of the Rover on Mars in July 1997. Java revolutionized the access scientists had to such expensive equipment. By downloading an applet from NASA, it was possible to see how the Rover was moving and to pretend to control it. In 1997, this was a simulation, but NASA is planning online access for the next Mars mission. Thus how to use Java on the web is very important, even for students. By teaching the writing of GUI programs from the start (via the `Display` class), anything that the students produce can be made into an applet with minimal changes and shared with other scientists.

It is certainly true that scientists need processing power. While a full treatment of parallel programming is beyond the scope of this book, it is possible to give students a taste of how it works. The two aspects of connecting up several computers via the Internet and of synchronizing processes via threads are covered in Chapter 9.

Learning by example

Throughout the book, new concepts are illustrated with small copy-book programming extracts. Then each new feature is fully explored in a genuine worked example. There are over 60 complete, fully worked examples, together with test data and output. Each example has been carefully chosen so that it both illustrates the feature that has just been introduced and solves a real problem in the best possible Java style. As soon as a new feature is introduced, it becomes part of the repertoire of the programmer, and will re-emerge in subsequent examples when needed. As the book progresses, the examples get longer and more challenging.

These examples serve as more than simple illustrations of concepts: they are also Case studies in problem-solving, programming methodology and, of course, scientific techniques. Each follows the steps of problem, solution, program design and testing, with digressions along the way, so that students realize that the programming process may not always give the best and correct solution first time.

Approach to numerical methods

Numerical methods are an essential part of the toolbox of a scientist or engineer interested in getting the most out of a computer. In many cases, with modern computer libraries, it may be possible simply to use a package to solve the numerical part of a physical problem. Nevertheless, as a programmer, one still has to have an elementary knowledge of the kinds of methods that exist, and an idea of how they work.

We have chosen to include a selection of methods and examples as the discussion on Java unfolds. These provide excellent Case studies and reinforce the idea that a computer is a really useful tool. Moreover, it is hoped that by making numerical methods easy for students, they will not be seen as a dry or obscure adjunct to scientific programming, but rather as part and parcel of the programming process.

As with programming, we take an integrated approach to numerical methods. Many of these result in fairly simple programs, so instead of putting all the methods and accompanying examples at the end of the book, we introduce two or three per chapter as the Java constructs make them feasible.

Since this is a programming textbook and not a numerical methods one, the emphasis is on describing the method to a level at which it can be converted into a program. Nevertheless, the background to the methods is covered, and mention is made of other numerical methods in the category. As the book progresses, methods result in the development of a standalone Java class which is then used in the example that follows, and often in other examples later on. The reader is shown how the Java class can be added to a library for this purpose.

Range of problems

There are over 60 worked examples in the book, all of them resulting in complete listed programs and output, often graphical in nature, and making use of pictures and sound where appropriate.

In choosing the problems, we have tried to maintain a balance between the classic computing examples which illustrate Java's features so well (finding the HCF, sorting) and a range of simple applications in the problem domain of our expected audience. Since the fields of science and engineering cover a very wide spectrum, we have chosen to concentrate on applications in elementary circuit analysis (finding steady-state charges, identifying the saturation point of an amplifier), basic mechanics (springs and accelerating trains), chemical processes and heat flow . We have tried not to let the application intrude into the programming insight which it is meant to provide, and in all cases the numerical problems should be within the capabilities of the reader who has taken, or is taking, a basic course in calculus.

For those familiar with our earlier books, it may be interesting to note that *Java Gently for Engineers and Scientists* is descended from *Pascal Precisely for Engineers and Scientists* which was first published in 1990 and is still being reprinted, and *Java Gently (2nd edition)*, now in its third printing in 1999. However, like inherited classes, *JGES* adds much that is new, and does not use everything that the other books offered. True to its name, the examples come mainly from *PPES*, and some of the programming sections from *JG*, but the approach to programming, as already explained, is totally different to both its parent texts.

Who the book is for

The book is intended for science or engineering students learning to program for the first time in Java. Students would normally be in their first year at a university or college, and be proficient in mathematics to the level of a first course in calculus. The book does not require mathematical manipulation: rather, it emphasizes the translation of mathematics into programs. Thus the book would certainly be accessible to school pupils taking science in senior years. Because there is an emphasis on facts and examples, rather than long discussions, the book would also be suitable for experienced programmers or hobbyists who wish to pick up Java quickly.

Students should have access to the Java Development Kit from Sun, running on PCs, Macs or Unix. There is no reliance in the book on any of the myriad of development environments that are available.

The book is based on many courses given in Java since 1996, and on courses in other languages presented to science and engineering students at first-year university level since 1980. Included are many of the class-tested examples and exercises from these courses. All examples have been tested on Java Platform 2 on Windows NT, 95 and Linux. The browsers used for the applets were Netscape Communicator 4.6 and Sun's HotJava, which often performed more reliably. Microsoft's Internet Explorer should also, of course, run any of the applets.

Because technology, and especially Java, is advancing at a rapid rate, it may be that a new version of Java becomes available after the book is completed. Consult our web site for the latest information and for program updates.

Learning aids and the web site

There is a whole range of these! Specifically, the book offers:

- over 60 worked **examples** with complete Java programs;
- ten-point **quizzes** after each chapter, with solutions at the end of the book;

- five large **Case studies** of real physical problems;

- over 100 set **problems** to suit a wide range of abilities and interests;

- **answers** at the web site to a selection of the problems, and full answers available to instructors;

- special `Graph`, `Display` and `Text` **classes** to get students started on visually pleasing programs;

- an accessible way of presenting Java **syntax** to the novice programmer;

- an active **web site**, with a team of helpers to answer questions from readers around the world.

All examples have been tested and run and are available on our web site which is actively maintained and regularly updated. The web site at

www.booksites.net/bishop-jges

also contains:

- web pages which introduce the book;

- all the examples for downloading, either individually or in chapters or one go;

- frequently asked questions (FAQs);

- error list;

- discussion board;

- future plans for the book;

- e-mail contact with the authors and the *Java Gently* team.

Acknowledgements

We have been very fortunate in having the assistance of an amazingly talented group of students at the Computer Science Department, University of Pretoria. Tony Abbott, Alwyn Moolman, Johnny Lo and Basil Worrall worked on the programs with us over several years. Daniel Acton prepared the web site with help from Graeme Pyle and Vafa Izadinia. Louis Botha and Reinette Grobler gave invaluable technical advice. The TechTeam of Edwin Peer, Eric Clements, Dieter Schutte and Jacques van Gruenen solved numerous small problems of compatibility and Java. We thank the department for the equipment provided, and for the non-stop dial-in service which enabled us to work late into the night. JMB would also like to thank the Computer Science Department at the University of Victoria, Canada, for the excellent facilities provided during the final stages of the book's production.

The software we used came from Sun, Microsoft and Apple and we pay tribute to these giants in the computer industry for the ease of use and stability that we so often take for granted. The book was prepared on an iMac and the programs developed on a Windows NT workstation, both a pleasure to work with. The Addison-Wesley team in the UK once again showed its professionalism. Thanks are due to

Emma Mitchell and Michael Strang for starting this, their third *Java Gently* project, to Kate Brewin and Karen Sutherland for taking it over so ably, and to David Harrison and Bridget Allen for their production skills.

Finally, as always, we thank our dear sons William and Michael for their understanding and patience with our months of preoccupation with the book. They are still learning Pascal, but we hope that when they enrol at university as scientists and engineers, they will reap the benefits of their forbearance, and enjoy Java as we do.

Judith M. Bishop, Nigel T. Bishop
Pretoria, South Africa
August 1999

CHAPTER 1

Introduction

1.1 Welcome to Java

Welcome to Java! Here is an example of what Java can do:

The Orbits of the Planets Project

As part of its schools outreach programme, the country of Savanna (situated on the grasslands of Africa) is funding a project to make information about planets available on the web to school children. Rather than just finding an electronic book, visitors to the web site will be able to make enquiries about planets that they have spotted, and to see how the orbits move. Consider the web pages from the first version of the site, shown in Figures 1.1 and 1.2. It all looks pretty interesting, and even impressive, but where is the Java?

The fact that it is not obvious is a tribute to Java's usefulness and power. The first web page (Figure 1.1) announces the project and gives links to some of the proposed planet pages. (They may not all be ready yet.) If we click on the Mars link, we get Figure 1.2. This page has a picture and some text on the left and some corres-

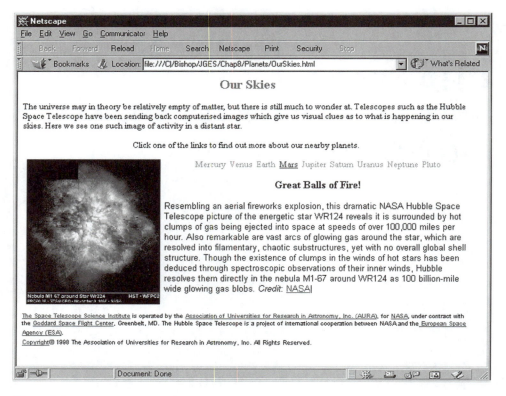

Figure 1.1 *The first page of the web site, showing links to the planets*

ponding data on the right. In the centre is a diagram of the orbit of the planet. Although we cannot show this in the book, the orbit actually moves, and the values in the two boxes at the bottom, indicating the orbit and the time elapsed in Earth years, change as time goes by.

This is the applet at work, running quietly on your machine. There is more about this applet in Chapter 8, and enhancements are suggested as part of the exercises there. One of the features of the orbit animation is that the dotted lines reflect speed. For a planet with a high eccentricity making its orbit more of an ellipse than a circle, the dots closer the Sun will be longer, indicating that the planet travels further in the same time step. Further from the Sun they will be shorter. After Pluto, Mercury has the highest eccentricity, at 0.21, whereas Mars is at 0.09, as Figure 1.2 shows.

Of course, Java is not just a means for moving information around on the web: it is a real programming language, of the stature of C++, Pascal, Ada and Modula-3. Learning to use Java is what this book is all about, but it also serves as a general introduction to the principles of programming, and most of all, an introduction to the classical methods of scientific problem solving. By the end of the book, you will be able to program Java applications and applets to perform such diverse tasks as solving circuit equations, finding complex roots of equations, process control and manufacturing

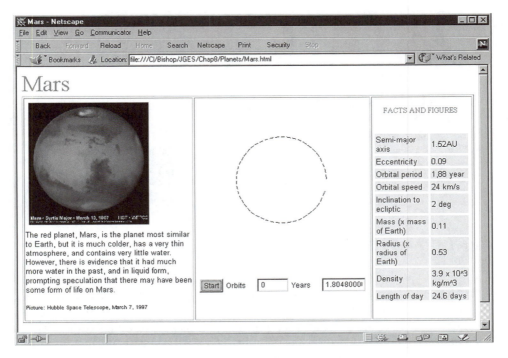

Figure 1.2 *The second web page, showing images, text and an applet*

output, Mars landers and nuclear reactors, tagging pets, converting currencies and chatting on the Internet. Most of the problems are scientific in nature, and rely on a mathematical formulation, but several are just based on real world information processing.

How Java works

Java is unlike any other language that has gone before. It is designed to work easily within the World Wide Web of computers through commonly available, user-friendly software called **browsers**. All computers these days have a browser – be it Netscape, Explorer, HotJava or Mosaic – and all browsers are now **Java-enabled**. This means that you can scan through documents stored all around the world, and at the click of a link, activate a Java program that will come across the network and run on your own computer. You do not even have to know that it is a Java program that is running.

The key advantage of being Java-enabled is that instead of just passive text and images appearing on your screen, calculations and interaction can take place as well. You can send back information to the **host** site, get more Java programs, more documents, and generally perform in a very effective way. Figure 1.3 sums up the circle of activity that takes place with a Java-enabled browser. Java programs that run on the web are actually called **applets** (short for 'little applications'), and we shall use this term from now on.

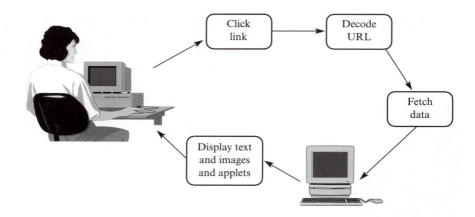

Figure 1.3 *Browsing the World Wide Web with Java applets (URL = Uniform Resource Locator)*

Another important property of Java is that it is **platform independent**. This means that it is independent of the kind of computer you are using. You may have a Macintosh, or a Pentium, a Silicon Graphics or a Sun workstation. Java applets do not mind. They are stored on a host site in such a way that they can run on any computer that has a Java-enabled browser.

So what does Java-enabled mean? It means that inside the browser there is a program known as a **Java Virtual Machine** (JVM) which can run Java for that particular computer. The Java that comes over the net is in a standard form known as

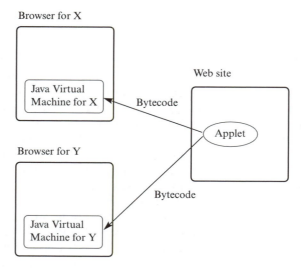

Figure 1.4 *Java applet going to two different computer types X and Y*

bytecode. Your JVM can understand the applet in bytecode and make it work properly on your particular computer. That is why if you get an applet when running under Windows, it will have a Windows 'look and feel' to its buttons and layout. If you pull the same applet down onto a Macintosh, it will look like a typical Mac program. Figure 1.4 sums up this process.

1.2 Software development

Computers consist of hardware and software. When one buys a computer, or uses it in the laboratory, the tendency is to focus on the hardware: how much memory does it have, what is the speed of the processor and so on? These are factors in using a computer, but they are not the most important. If is of course annoying if, for example, one runs out of disk space, but at least a plan can be made to store some of the information somewhere else, or even delete it, to make room.

We would claim that the software that the computer comes with is what really detemines its quality. In this section, we shall briefly run through the software components that are necessary for programming in Java, and show how they interact. The description is intended to be a general one, not specific to any particular make or supplier of software. Then we shall outline the stages of software development. The next section shows how these are tackled in this book.

The programming process

The programming process is the activity whereby programs are written in order to be stored and made ready for execution or running. The programs can be run on the same computer on which they were written, or they can be fetched over the web in the manner we have already described. Programming these days needs the support of many software packages, themselves programs developed by others. Some of the software comes with the computer you buy, some you can purchase later, and some you can get as freeware, shareware or applets over the web. In order to develop your own programs, you will need at least an operating system, an editor and a compiler.

Operating systems

The core software loaded onto a computer is its **operating system**. Some operating systems are specific to certain types of computers – for example, MacOS is intended for Macintosh computers – and others are designed to run on a variety of different designs. Windows, Unix and its derivative, Linux, are examples here. The operating system provides the necessary interfaces to the hardware: reading from disk, writing to the screen, swapping between tasks and so on. It also looks after files and provides commands for the user to move files, change their names, etc. Through the operating system, we activate the next level of software.

Editors and compilers

The programming process involves creating a sequence of instructions to the computer, which are written down in the particular programming language. The creative process is expressed through an **editor**, of which there are many on the market. Once ready, the program is submitted to a **compiler**. The function of the compiler is twofold. In the first instance, it makes a thorough check on the validity of what has been written. If there are any errors (called compilation or syntax errors) then these must be corrected and the program resubmitted for compilation. Activating the Java compiler can be done at a simple level by typing in the following to the operating system, where Welcome.java is the file we created through the editor:

```
javac Welcome.java
```

Once the program is free of compilation errors, the compiler enters a second phase and translates the program into a form that can run on a computer. For compilers for most other languages this form will be the native machine instructions of the particular computer's processor. For Java, though, it is the JVM that is the target of compilation, no matter what the computer is that will ultimately run the translated program.

Although the compiler checks the grammar of the program and can look for quite a range of potential errors, it cannot detect errors in the logic. For example, in the applet shown in action in Figure 1.2, it would be quite possible for a careless programmer to display orbits and years in the wrong boxes by mistake. These are known as **logic** errors.

Logic errors can be avoided by:

● carefully structuring the program in the first place;

● following good programming guidelines; and

● actually reusing existing pieces of program instead of rewriting everything from scratch each time.

However, sometimes the only way to detect a logic error is to run the program and see what happens. This is the second-last stage of the software development process. The program is **executed** or **run** by activating it through the operating system. In Java we would activate an ordinary program by a command such as

```
java Welcome
```

Some logic errors can be detected by carefully testing the program with well-chosen test data. After finding and correcting an error, the test should be rerun because it is very easy to introduce some other error while fixing the first. All of these topics are covered in this book. The programming process is summed up in Figure 1.5.

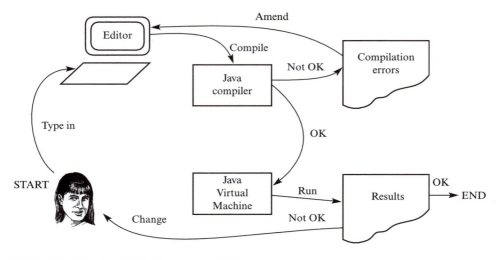

Figure 1.5 *The programming process in Java*

Development environments

Because the edit–compile cycle repeats itself over and over again in the programming process, software exists which combines editing and compiling and enables one to switch between them at the touch of a button. Examples of such Java systems are Java Workshop, JBuilder, Kawa, Visual J++ and Symantec Café. An integrated development environment (IDE) also includes facilities for managing large projects, perhaps involving several programmers. Another feature is an enhanced editor for creating user interfaces by designing them on the screen.

An advantage of some Java IDEs is that, like Java itself, they are platform independent, so that you can continue working in the same environment even if you change computers. A disadvantage of IDEs is that they are not always intuitive and sometimes take a while to learn to operate effectively.

Maintenance

It is surprising, but true, that Figure 1.5 represents in industry terms only about 30% of the programming process. The real hard programming starts after the product has been delivered and it begins its useful life. Then it has to be **maintained**, an activity which is similar to the maintenance on an aircraft – essential and sometimes costly. Maintenance for software includes fixing errors, making user-required changes and adding enhancements. A primary aim of a programmer even when learning to program should be to make maintenance as easy as possible. Throughout the book we shall mention ways of achieving this goal.

Examples

Java Gently for Engineers and Scientists teaches programming by example. There is a tried and tested progression of examples which leads you from first principles through to the more complex constructs in the language. Each example is carefully chosen so as to use only those features that have been covered, and each example uses the features correctly. Achieving this balance means that the order of topics covered has been carefully thought out. Because the target audience of this book is not necessarily computer science majors, the scientific methods and examples govern the sequence of topics to quite a large extent.

Each example follows a sequence of steps which is usually:

- a problem or an opportunity;
- a solution or an approach;
- program design and techniques employed;
- an example, including expected screen layout;
- the complete listing of the program;
- testing with real values and proper screen output.

The problem is a short statement in the user's terms of what needs to be done. The solution starts to give an idea as to what approach should be followed to solve the problem, including what software can be reused from elsewhere. The algorithm forms the nub of the problem-solving process. The program is a complete, running Java program and each of them can be found on our web site **www.booksites.net/bishop-jges**. The example and testing help to make the programs realistic.

Program design

Java is an object-oriented language, which means that a program in Java is composed of interrelated objects. *Java Gently for Engineers and Scientists* uses object orientation right from the beginning, building up programs in terms of their objects and the relationships between them. Specifically, we concentrate on objects for reuse so that by the end of the book, we have built up a really useful library of routines from Simpson's rule to the predictor–corrector method. It is quite a challenge to integrate scientific routines into Java programs in a simple way so that data and functions can be specified where needed. *Java Gently for Engineers and Scientists* has met this challenge and you can be assured that you will be led into programming in the best possible style.

In *Java Gently (2nd edition)* we used class diagrams to describe the inter-relationships within programs. In this book, a standard model of class interrelationship is developed in Chapter 3, and many of the programs follow this pattern. They can therefore be understood from the listings quite easily, and class diagrams are not used.

Programs

Programs are written in programming languages. There are many such languages, but relatively few are available on all kinds of computers. Those that have achieved more or less universal use include Pascal, Delphi, Ada, Fortran, Cobol, Basic, VB, C++, Lisp, Prolog, Modula, Perl, Tcl and now, of course, Java. Java was developed in 1993 under the name of Oak, and achieved popularity in 1996 when Sun Microsystems launched its Java compilers free on the web.

Java programs look like stylized English, and examples can be found on any page of this book. The form of a program is important: any mistakes will cause the compiler to reject your efforts. It is therefore necessary to learn the syntax of the language precisely. To assist you in this endeavour, when a new construct is introduced, its syntax is shown precisely in a **form** that not only explains how a feature is constructed, but also gives an indication of how it should be laid out in a regular way. An example of a simple form is

```
if-statement

if (condition)
    then-part;
else
    else-part;
```

The meaning of the bold face and italics will become clear as we start introducing Java statements.

1.3 Scientific computing

The advent of computers in the 1940s and 1950s was largely due to the efforts of scientists at the time who needed to solve more and more problems to a greater degree of accuracy. In order to use the computer, scientists had to express their mathematical models and solutions in numerical form. The branch of study on which they relied is called numerical analysis, and from it we have the numerical methods which are the mainstay of any computationally oriented engineer or scientist.

A **numerical method** is an expression of a mathematical solution in a form which produces numerical answers, rather than symbolic ones. Mathematicians typically manipulate symbols and produce symbolic answers. Engineers are concerned, in addition, with the physical properties of the mathematics, fitting actual values to equations, and expecting numbers as results.

The mathematical techniques that can be expressed numerically include:

- differentiation;
- integration;

- finding roots of equations;
- solving differential equations;
- solving simultaneous equations;
- curve fitting and interpolation;
- matrix manipulation.

Thus we can differentiate x^2 symbolically to give $2x$, but we can also apply a numerical technique which for a given value of x will produce the appropriate value for the differential. The value of the numerical methods is that they can be applied in cases where the symbolic answer is hard to find.

The above list contains techniques which are now very well understood, and many can be explained at a simple algorithmic level. They therefore provide an excellent vehicle for the novice programmer to practise new-found skills.

In this book we shall present one or two methods in most of the above categories, and then follow this with an example of their application, drawn from a real engineering problem. In addition, we will show in each case how the routine that we develop can be generalized and placed in a library for later use by ourselves or others.

An example

For example, in Chapter 3 we present a simple differential equation for the current variation in an *RL* circuit, i.e.

$$\frac{\mathrm{d}I}{\mathrm{d}t} = \frac{E}{L} - \frac{R}{L}I$$

and show how it can be solved using a predictor–corrector algorithm:

```
double dbydt (double c) {
  return E/L - R*c/L;
}

void solve () {
  double currentp;

  // The predictor-corrector loop
  for(int i = 1; i <= imax; i++) {
    currentp = current + h * dbydt(current);
    current += h * (dbydt(current) + dbydt(currentp)) / 2;
    t += h;
  }
}
```

Later on, in Chapter 6, we use abstraction and inheritance – two well-known object techniques – to generalize this technique and place it in a library for reuse.

Understanding formulas?

The formulas involved both in the methods themselves and in their applications can look quite intimidating. Nevertheless, it is a programmer's job to be able to interpret formulas, and to present them in a form acceptable to the computer. With sights set on learning to program, it is not essential that the meaning of the formulas be understood. Such understanding will add to the fulfilment that programming a solution brings, but the methods and examples should still be accessible to those who are not familiar with the particular branch of engineering or science under discussion.

Graphics

The ability to express results graphically is one of the most attractive features of today's computers. The advent of good graphical hardware is a 1980s' phenomenon, and Java is a language of the 1990s. There is therefore nothing holding it back from producing an attractive graph, such as in Figure 1.6.

    The problem is that producing a graph like this is not simple and tends to hinder one in the focus of the task, which is to get the results out. To ease matters, we have devised a `Graph` class especially for this book. The class enables simple graphs with

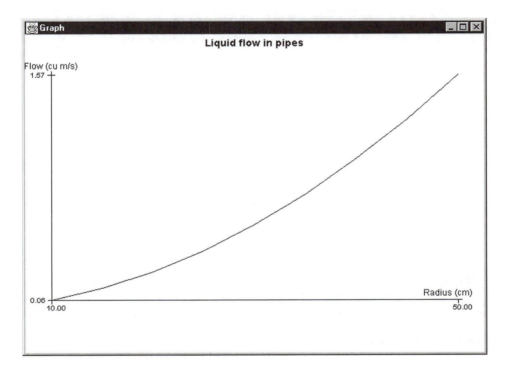

Figure 1.6 *An example from the* `Graph` *class*

axes and labels to be drawn with just a few statements, while at the same time providing for sophisticated options when required. The use of the class is introduced right from Chapter 3, and is used in virtually every example. We also use the class itself as a Case study in Chapter 7.

User interaction

While output is very important, in scientific programming the ease of input should have an equal priority. There are two kinds of input: parameters which drive the program, and bulk data which has to be processed. While we can envisage the bulk data coming from a file, the inputting of parameters has always been difficult. In this book, we have created a unique class which enables input and output to appear on a screen display together. The Display class is used through the book, and is investigated as an example in its own right in Chapter 9. Figure 1.7 shows the display associated with liquid flow in pipes.

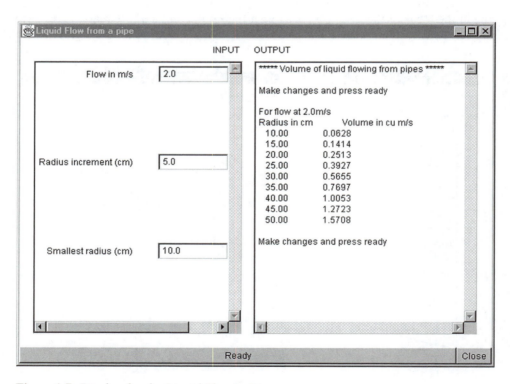

Figure 1.7 *Display for the Liquid Flow in Pipes program*

Packages

Numerical analysis is one of the more mature branches of computing and, as such, is fortunate in having a wealth of techniques which are already written up as programs, or more precisely, as **packages**. The practising engineer or scientist who wishes to use a numerical technique as part of the solution to a problem will in many cases find the package he or she needs in the computer's library. As some of the methods are fairly complex, this is an obvious advantage. Fortunately, Java provides a straightforward way of creating and using libraries.

In this book, we are primarily concerned with mastering the rudiments of programming in a particular language, and cannot at the same time reflect real world practices exactly. Nevertheless, wherever possible, we have expressed the methods as self-contained classes, with tightly controlled interfaces, and have shown how they can be used and reused in different circumstances in different programs, without change.

Examples where this is done extensively are the predictor–corrector method, which is used in Example 3.8 and again in Case study 2 in Chapter 6; the statistical functions used in the light bulb analysis and rainfall calculations in Chapter 5; the SOR method, which is used in program examples 5.8 to 5.10 and Case study 1; and the secant method which is used in Example 6.5 and Case study 2.

Finding out more

This book does not intend to do more than present a selection of good numerical methods that have a wide applicability in science and engineering. To find out about more methods, and about their derivation and limitations, the reader will need to consult a textbook specifically on numerical methods or numerical analysis.

1.4 Getting started with Java

If you do not have Java development facilities where you are studying or working, then you will want to set them up for yourself. The Java Development Kit (JDK) is Sun's free gift to the Java programming community. You can download, install and use it as freeware. The JDK gives you a full compiler and interpreter for the very latest version of Java. There is also a directory on documentation for all the Java libraries (known as APIs or Application Programming Interfaces) and a directory called the Java tutorial. Both of these are worth downloading if you have time and space. The JDK, the API documentation and the tutorial each occupy about 10 Mbytes on disk, so you are looking at about 30 Mbytes all together.

The following instructions regarding acquiring and installing the JDK are correct at time of writing.

Downloading the JDK

To download the JDK, first don't. In other words, find out whether it is available locally on your server or on CD-ROM form in your organization. If you cannot get the system you want nearby, go to Sun's site:

www.javasoft.com

Here, choose the 'Products and APIs' from the list of options, and then look from there for the JDK. You will be asked about your machine and operating system, and then you can download. You should also print out the web page associated with the download, which tells you how to install and test the system.

Once you have got the JDK, you will need to install it. Follow the instructions carefully, especially such things as setting paths and classpaths.

Testing the system

To test whether you have installed the system correctly, use a simple text editor of your choice to type in the first Java program shown in Example 2.1 and save it in a file called `SIUnits.java`. (The file name and capitalizing are important.)

Keep your editor open while opening up a command line window as well (Unix or Windows). Make sure that the current directory of the command window is the one that contains file `SIUnits.java`. Now type in

```
javac SIUnits.java
```

The JDK compiler will take the file and compile it. If you made no typing errors, the command prompt will be returned. If there are error messages, go back to the edit window, fix the Java program accordingly, then recompile.

Once you have a clean compilation, the compiler will have created a file called `SIUnits.class`. To run the program, type in

```
java SIUnits
```

(Note: do not add the word 'class' here.) The program should produce output on the next line in the command window.

Installing the `javagently` package

Once you get started with Java, you will encounter the need to interact with your program, and an easy way to do this is provided by special `Text`, `Display` and `Graph` classes in the `javagently` package written for this book. Full listings of these classes are given in sections 7.4, 9.2 and 10.2. You do not have to type them in if you can fetch them from the web.

These useful classes are stored in a package called `javagently` and in order to access it, a suitable import-statement must be added to the program, i.e.

```
import javagently.*;
```

Since javagently is our own package, it does not come precompiled with the JDK or with the Java IDE you may be using. We therefore have first to create it before the import-statement will work. Follow these easy steps:

1   At a level above that where you are working, create a directory called javagently.

2   Download the Display.java, Graph.java, Text.java and List.java files from the web site into this directory. (List is used by Graph.)

3   In the directory created in step 1, compile the four files.

4   There will now be the class files for each in the javagently directory.

5   Using the method particular for your machine, add the directory immediately above javagently to your classpath (not to the path). In Windows, this involves going into the Environment section of the System settings and adding the directory to the CLASSPATH environment variable.

6   Put

```
import javagently.*;
```

at the start of your program.

Figure 1.8 summarizes the result of these steps for a typical situation on a PC.

An import-statement in a Java class causes a look-up process via the classpath. Thus we include the C:\COS110 directory in the classpath, because that is where javagently resides. We don't include C:\COS110\javagently in the classpath, because the package is not in that directory! Any and all of the Java classes under myprograms or any other directory on the same or a lower level, or anywhere else, can make use of javagently in this way.

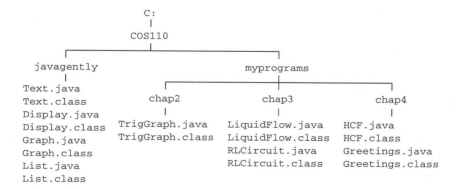

Classpath includes C:\COS110\

Figure 1.8 *Example of a directory structure for using the* javagently *package*

The documentation and tutorial

The additional information supplied with the JDK is invaluable. The documentation gives a hypertext view of all Java's libraries, with detailed descriptions and examples of each method. This is the Java programmer's 'help'. The tutorial consists of a collection of articles by different people at different times and at different levels. It is not comprehensive, in that it is not intended to cover all of Java or to replace textbooks, but it does give insight into how and why certain parts of Java were developed, and the sample programs form a good addition to those in a book.

Java integrated development systems

Although the JDK is free and many people use it solely, there are more elaborate systems on the market, as described in section 1.2. These IDEs fall into two classes: those that come with their own built-in Java compiler, and those that make use of the JDK for compilation.

The first kind includes Sun's Java Workshop, Microsoft's Visual J++, Symantec Café, Borland JBuilder and Metrowerks CodeWarrior (available from your local computer store or computer representative). The advantage of these systems is that some of the compilers can outperform the JDK in speed. The disadvantage is that when the Java language is upgraded, as it is at intervals, you have to upgrade your IDE (at a cost) as well.

All the above are available for PC platforms using Windows 95 or NT or later. In addition, Java Workshop runs under Solaris on Sun workstations and CodeWarrior is available for the Macintosh.

The second kind of system includes the Kawa system from Tek-Tools, which we have found to be really very user-friendly, with good performance. Kawa is available electronically from **kawa@tek-tools.com** at reasonable cost. It runs only on PC platforms. Once you have Kawa, you can continue to download new versions of the JDK and link them into your IDE immediately. Thus you are able to take advantage of new Java features even in beta releases.

Web sites for Java

Java is a web language and there are several excellent sites which discuss Java issues and have Java articles and Java resources for downloading. Four in particular are worth watching:

www.javasoft.com – Sun's Java site, regularly updated with topical articles and news about Java products and use.

www.gamelan.com – an incredible collection of Java resources, information and applets.

www.javaworld.com – a monthly online magazine devoted to Java.

www.booksites.net/bishop-jges – the web site for this book.

1.5 The web site

Java Gently for Engineers and Scientists is part of a set of *Java Gently* books which have linked web sites. The first edition of *Java Gently* came out together with a web site whose initial purpose was as a repository for the programs in the book. Since May 1997, the site has grown into an active web site, with readers from all over the world contributing to the discussions, making suggestions, and informing us of their ideas about Java and the book. The number of hits is over 50000 and growing daily.

On the special web site for this book, **www.booksites.net/bishop-jges**, you can find the following:

- About the book
- Summary of the chapters
- List of institutions using *Java Gently for Engineers and Scientists* for teaching
- All the examples for individual viewing or downloading in bulk
- Answers to frequently asked questions
- A discussion board, watched over by the authors and the *JG* team
- Messages about Java of immediate interest
- Other material available from the authors on Java
- List of known errors in the book
- Plans and dates for future versions and editions of *Java Gently for Engineers and Scientists*
- Link to the publisher's site

In addition to providing a great deal of information, the web site can be used in two innovative ways. Firstly, for lecturers with access to online facilities in the classroom, the programs can be displayed and viewed directly from the site. We have used this method in teaching, and have found it more effective than copying the programs onto transparencies first. The ability to move rapidly between programs, to save, compile and run very quickly, makes for a dynamic teaching environment.

The second innovation of active web sites like *Java Gently for Engineers and Scientists'* is that you can interact with a team who can answer questions and discuss Java issues. This team started at one of the author's institutions, the University of Pretoria, but ultimately includes all the *Java Gently for Engineers and Scientists* readers who access the web site and are prepared to share their expertise. In other words, you are not alone out there.

The web site is updated regularly and comments and suggestions are always welcome. All queries are answered and contributions acknowledged.

QUIZ

1.1   What does a compiler do?

1.2   What is the difference between a compilation error and a logic error?

1.3   What is the clock speed of the computer you are using?

1.4   How much memory does your computer have?

1.5   What is the capacity of the disks you are using?

1.6   Would this textbook (including all the spaces) fit on your disk, assuming one printed character per byte of memory?

1.7   List all the computer applications that you come into contact with in the course of an ordinary week.

1.8   Have you ever been on the wrong end of a computer error? If so, could you tell whether the mistake was in the program or was caused by the data that was read in?

1.9   Find out the name, version and creation date of the computer, operating system and compiler that you will be using.

1.10   Get into *Java Gently for Engineers and Scientists'* web site and try out the Planets system. The address is **www.booksites.net/bishop-jges**.

CHAPTER 2

Simple programs

2.1 Two starter programs

To start our study of scientific programming in Java, we shall look at two small programs. The first is a simple text-based program, and the second uses graphics and colours. We shall not go into the details of the programs, but just use them as a starting point for introducing programming in Java, and for enabling you to start using the computer straight away. There are several amendments you can make to the programs, which will give you a reason to get to grips with your programming environment.

EXAMPLE 2.1   SI units

The aim of our first program is to display some unusual SI units. The program is

```
class SIUnits {

  /* SIUnits program            by J M Bishop Dec 1998
```

```
    *  ---------------
    * Illustrates a simple program displaying output.
    */

  public static void main (String args []) {
    System.out.println("Resonant frequency    hertz");
    System.out.println("Inductance            henries");
    System.out.println("Capacitance           farads");
  }
}
```

and it does indeed, if run, display the required output on the screen as follows:

```
Resonant frequency    hertz
Inductance            henries
Capacitance           farads
```

At this stage we shall note only a few points about the program. Firstly, the text between /* and */ is called a **comment** and is there to help explain to the reader what the program does. It is not **executed** (or **run**) by the computer. Secondly, text in quotes in the println lines is known as a **string** and is what is actually displayed. The rest of the lines and the closing braces (or curly brackets) are part of the outline which always accompanies a Java program. We shall learn more about them soon.

Exercise   Run the SIUnits program as described in section 1.4. Change it so that it includes a heading, e.g. 'SI Units'. Change it again so that it prints out some more units of your choice, or underlines the heading using hyphens. Experiment and use the opportunity to become familiar with your programming environment.

EXAMPLE 2.2   Sine and cosine graphs

One of the advantages of Java is its built-in facilities for graphics, colour, animation, sound and so on. Here is a very simple program to display two graphs on the same axes in a window:

```
import javagently.*;

class TrigGraphs {

  /*  Simple Trig Graph drawing program      N T Bishop
   *  ==================================      July 1999
   *
   *
   * Draws two trig graphs on the same axes.
   * Illustrates the use of the Graph class
   * and its symbol and colour facilities
   */

  public static void main ( String args []) {
    Graph g = new Graph("Sine and Cosine","x","y");
    double x;
```

```
// The first graph - y=sin(x)
g.setSymbol(true);
g.setColor(g.blue);
g.setTitle("Sine");
for (int i = 0; i <= 100; i++) {
  x = i / 10.0;
  g.add(x, Math.sin(x));
}

// The second graph - y=cos(x)
g.nextGraph();
g.setColor(g.red);
g.setTitle("Cosine");
for (int j = 0; j <= 100; j++) {
  x = j / 10.0;
  g.add(x, Math.cos(x));
}
g.showGraph();
System.out.println("Type CTRL-C to end");
  }
}
```

The output produced by the program is shown (not in colour, unfortunately) in Figure 2.1.

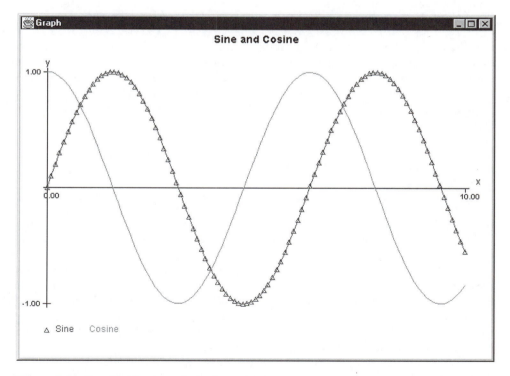

Figure 2.1 *Graphical output from the* TrigGraphs *program*

TrigGraphs is a longer program than SIUnits, but the substance of the program repeats itself for each graph, so only half is new. The effect of certain lines of the program can be seen. In the first graph,

```
g.setSymbol(true);
```

causes the sine graph to have triangles plotted at every point. This line is missing from the part of the program that draws the cosine graph, and therefore, the cosine is just a smooth line.

Being able to program in a graphics environment is an essential skill for today's programmers, but there is a lot of detail to learn, much of which is repetitive and can be looked up when needed. To avoid being too distracted by graphics when we need to concentrate on programming and science, we have devised a special easy-to-use graph system, which is used in Example 2.2 and throughout this book. In order to establish that there is nothing really hidden behind the scenes, we shall examine the system itself as a Case study to show how graphics is done at the raw Java level in Chapter 7.

The program in Example 2.2 also illustrates the use of Java's second type of comment: the one-liner, introduced by //. Either kind of comment is acceptable. The advantage of // is that it is automatically ended by the end of a line. On the other hand, many programmers regard the /* */ pair as more elegant. The convention for using the paired comment symbols is to have the closing */ underneath the /*, as shown in these programs.

Exercises Run the TrigGraphs program and check that the graphs come out in the right colours as specified in the program (blue for sine and red for cosine). Alter the formulas used to calculate each point so that the program displays other graphs such as $\frac{1}{2}\sin(x)$ or $\cos(2x)$. Also experiment with the effect of the counter 100 (which gives the number of points) and the dividing by 10.0. What happens if we divide by a smaller number?

2.2 Java basics

In this section we give a broad overview of the most central parts of a Java program and how they fit together. The concepts that we cover are summarized in the figure at the end of the section.

A Java **program** consists of a set of one or more interdependent classes. **Classes** are a means of describing the properties and capabilities of the objects in real life that the program has to deal with. For example, the program described in Chapter 1 could well have a class for the Planets. A simple Java program will consist of one class with a method called main, as we can see in the two examples above, and then maybe use some other classes, such as Graph, as in Example 2.2.

Within the class we define its properties and capabilities, which are known as **fields** and **methods**, respectively, in Java. Jointly they are known as **members** of the class. For `Planets`, an example of a field might be its `diameter` and of a method might be `startOrbiting`, which would set the planet orbiting on the screen.

Declarations

Data is stored in fields of a class, and declarations are used to establish the name and type of each field. The simplest type is an integer number. In Java terms, we refer to an integer as `int`. Therefore, as part of the `Planets` class, we would have the declaration

```
int noOfEnquiries;
```

Real numbers in Java are called double, so in `TrigGraphs` we had

```
double x;
```

Names in computer languages are called identifiers. An **identifier** in Java consists of letters and digits (and some special characters such as underscore, but we shall not use them in this book), but must start with a letter. Spaces are not allowed, and capital and small letters are considered to be different so that `noOfEnquiries` is not the same as `Noofenquiries`. Unlike `x`, `noOfEnquiries` consists of more than one word, so to make it easier to read, the convention is to use capitals for the inner words.

A declaration sets aside storage in the computer's memory for the field, and the amount of storage depends on the type. An integer, for example, occupies 4 bytes. There is more about types and storage in section 2.5. In `TrigGraphs`, we have defined five fields – `g`, `x`, `i`, `args` and `j` – as well as one method, `main`.

Methods and statements

The capabilities of a class are expressed in one or more methods. A **method** is a named sequence of instructions to the computer, written out in the language we are using, in this case Java. The instructions are properly called **statements**, and fall into the following five categories:

1   **invocation** – causing a method to be performed;
2   **assignment** – changing the state of a field by using another value of the same kind;
3   **repetition** – performing certain statements over and over again;
4   **selection** – deciding whether to perform certain statements or not;
5   **exception** – detecting and reacting to unusual circumstances.

Most languages have a similar set of options. In the `TrigGraphs` program there are examples of the first three in this list: several methods (such as `setSymbol`) are called, values are assigned (notably to `x`), and statements are repeated 100 times. See if you can find out where these statements occur in Example 2.2. By the end of this chapter you will be able to write them yourself.

Invoking a method

At this point, we wish to examine how we cause the method to perform its statements. In simple terms, when we mention the name of a method, control within the program is transferred to that method, which then progresses through its statements until it reaches the end. The method then passes control back to where it was called from. This process is called method invocation, and we talk about **invoking** or calling a method.

If the method is declared in our own class, we can just call it by giving its name: for example, the `Planets` class could say

```
startOrbiting();
```

if that was one of its own methods. When we refer to a method in another class, we prefix it with the name of the class or the object we created from it. For example, `Math` is a class and `sin` is a method in that class, so we can invoke

```
y = Math.sin(x);
```

Recalling that `g` is a `Graph` object, we can also invoke

```
g.setSymbol(true);
```

The distinction between whether we are calling a method from a class or an object will become clear as we go along. Suffice it to say that unless the method is in our class, its name consists of two parts: the place where the method is declared and the method identifier itself.

Finally, we note that in the calls above, the method name was followed by brackets and in some cases these brackets had names of fields in them. This process is termed calling a method with a **parameter**. Parameters enable us to customize the action of methods, as we saw in the two calls

```
g.setColor(g.blue);
g.setColor(g.red);
```

Methods are revisited in section 3.4.

The form of a program

Now we note precisely how to write down the instructions that introduce a Java program. The following pattern gives the format we must use for a simple program. In this book, Java's syntax is explained by means of **forms** and examples.

The top line of the form gives the name of the Java concept being defined. The contents of the box give the syntax of the concept, in the usual layout that would be used for it.

Simple program

```
class classname {
  public static void main (String args []) {
    declarations of fields and methods
    intermingled with statements
  }
}
```

There are three kinds of words in a form, with the following meanings:

1   bold text – Java keywords that must be there, e.g. **class** or **void**;
2   italics – identifiers and other parts that we fill in, e.g. *classname*;
3   plain words – words that have to be in these positions but are not keywords, e.g. main and String.

Keywords are those identifiers that are reserved for Java's use and may not be used by the programmer for anything else. Thus we cannot call a variable 'static'. Keywords are introduced in forms as they become relevant.

The curly backets of a program must match for each class and method. In the form, the outer set refers to the class and the inner set refers to the main method. The words in italics describe parts of the program that must be supplied by the programmer. The class name is compulsory, but the declarations and statements are optional. Thus the following is a valid Java program which does nothing:

```
class DoNothing {
  public static void main (String [] args) {
  }
}
```

When there are statements, each ends with a semicolon. In this way, there can be several statements to a line, but most of the time Java programmers stick to one statement per line.

Following on from the discussion in this section, we can interpret what is meant by each of the lines of the program. The introduction of the class name is clear. Thereafter, we have a single method called main. It is a void method, and will be called by the outside world as DoNothing.main. Who calls it? When the JVM is activated, as described in Chapter 1, it must be given the name of a class. It then looks for a method called main in the class of that name, and starts running it from there.

Because the method has to be accessed by the virtual machine, it must have an additional modifier, public. The rest of our methods for the moment do not need this modifier, nor its opposite, private, and we shall discuss the need for them in more detail in Chapters 6 and 10.

Finally, the parameter in the form is there so that information can be transmitted to the program when it starts up. The square brackets indicate that the parameter is going to be an array – a computer term used for several fields, all with the same name and indexed by numbers. Arrays are fully covered in Chapter 5. Often we do not use the `main` method's parameter, but it is still necessary to include it when the method is defined.

Declaring and accessing objects

Objects are fundamental to a language such as Java. Throughout the next few chapters we shall see how objects impact on the way we design even the simplest programs. In Chapter 6 we shall cover all the more powerful aspects of object-oriented programming. Creating an object from a class is called **instantiation**. The form for instantiating an object is

---

Object instantiation

Classname objectname = **new** *Classname (parameters)*;

For example, in `TrigGraphs`, we had

```
Graph g = new Graph("Sine and Cosine","x","y");
```

The available fields and methods of the object are then accessed in one of two ways:

Object member access

```
objectname.membername
classname.membername
```

The first form is used for most members. The second form is used for members which have specially been designated as occurring once only per class. They are known as

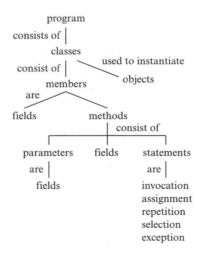

Figure 2.2 *Terminology for the parts of a program so far*

class members and are identified by the keyword **static**. So far the class members that we have encountered include Math.sin and the main method, which as we have already noted will be called by the system by its class name, e.g. SIUnits.main or TrigGraphs.main.

The concepts we have covered so far are summarized in Figure 2.2.

2.3 Beginning with output

Having covered the fundamental structure of a Java program in terms of its most important constituents, we can now consider how to write a simple program that displays something on the screen. In programming parlance, what goes to the screen is called **output**, but programmers often use the terms write, print, output and display interchangeably. If we refer to the previous section, we shall see that there is no special statement group for output in Java. All input and output are handled by methods in classes supplied by the language. Thus in order to print, we have to know *which* methods to call: we already know *how* to call them from section 2.2.

Output methods

The methods we are looking for are called println and print. They are found in a built-in Java class called PrintStream. They are called through a special object, out, defined as a field in the universally available class called System. The object out is automatically connected by Java to the screen of your computer. Therefore from these three components,

1   the class System,
2   the object out, and
3   the methods print and println,

we can construct the correct method call statements for displaying output. Because these method calls will be used so often, we refer to them as output statements as a shorthand. The simple form of Java statements to display a piece of text is

Output statements

```
System.out.println (items);
System.out.println ();
System.out.print (items);
```

String output

The first kind of items we consider for printing are strings. A **string literal** is any sequence of characters enclosed in quotes, e.g.

```
"Mary Jones"
"hertz"
"kilometres per sec"
```

Although string literal is the correct term, much of the time we just use the word string. If a quote itself is needed in the string then a backslash \ precedes it. The backslash is called an **escape character**: it does not form part of the string, but enables the next character to do so. An example is

```
"He said \"No\""
```

which is the string *He said "No"*. Calling the `println` method displays the string given as a parameter and ends the line of printing. (The 'ln' in `println` is short for 'line'.) Thus, the statements

```
System.out.println("kilometres per sec");
System.out.println("He said \"No\"");
```

will cause the following to be displayed:

kilometres per sec
He said "No"

(In examples from now on, Java statements are given in plain type, and the corresponding output is shown in bold.)

The `print` method works in a similar way except that it does not end the line, so that a subsequent `print` or `println` will continue on the same line from the last point reached.

The string is optional for the `println` method. If `println` is called on its own, then it will finish off the current line. This facility can also be used to obtain a blank line, as in

```
System.out.println ("kilometres per sec");
System.out.println ();
System.out.println ("He said \"No\"");
```

which would give as output:

kilometres per sec

He said "No"

Remember that any Java method call that does not provide parameters (the items in brackets) must still have the brackets. To obtain several blank lines, we can use several `println` calls in a row, as in

```
System.out.println();
System.out.println();
System.out.println();
```

Alternatively, we can make use of another escape character, \n, standing for 'new line', as in

```
System.out.println ("\n\n\n");
```

Concatenation

One final point about strings and printing. What happens should a string be too long to fit on a single line of a screen when we are writing a program? We cannot go onto the next line. We have to end the string and start a new one, joining the two together with a plus operator. This is known formally as **concatenation**. An example of concatenation would be

```
System.out.println ("The next total eclipse of the sun " +
    "as seen from Northern Europe will take place on " +
    "24 December 2003");
```

There are many more examples of long strings in the programs that follow.

EXAMPLE 2.3   Displaying a warning

Problem   Display a warning message on the screen that the computer might have a virus.[†]

Program   This program is very simple, and similar to that in Example 2.1. It has a class and a `main` method, followed by several output statements which when executed will display the box shown below.

```
class DisplayWarning {

    /* Displaying a warning program      by J M Bishop  Aug 1996
     * ---------------------------      Java 1.1 October 1997
     * Illustrates the form of a program and the use of println.
     */

    public static void main(String args []) {
        System.out.println("----------------------------");
        System.out.println("|                          |");
        System.out.println("|       W A R N I N G      |");
        System.out.println("|  Possible virus detected |");
        System.out.println("|   Reboot and run virus   |");
        System.out.println("|     remover software     |");
        System.out.println("|                          |");
        System.out.println("----------------------------");
    }
}
```

† A virus is a program that can infect your computer and cause damage to files on the disk and so on. This program does not itself detect a virus: it just prints out the warning message.

Testing The output produced by this program would be

```
-----------------------------
|                           |
|        W A R N I N G      |
|   Possible virus detected |
|   Reboot and run virus    |
|      remover software     |
|                           |
-----------------------------
```

Here we use dashes and bars for effect, but in Chapter 7 we shall see how to make use of the graphics facilities of a computer screen to obtain smarter-looking output.

Layout

How the program is written down, in terms of lines and spaces, does not have an effect on how the output appears. Only what is inside the quotes is actually displayed when the program executes. When the output statements display strings, there is no gap in the output if the string in the program had to be split into different pieces joined by +. In the same way, blank lines or comments in the program do not have any effect on the output. Therefore, the following statements will cause the same output as above:

```
System.out.println("kilometres per sec");

                  System.out.println();
   System.out.println("He " +
"said \"No\"");
```

The point is that the instructions given to the computer do not *have* to be in any special layout. We usually write them neatly one underneath each other, and we also use **indenting** to make groups of statements stand out, but there is no formal rule that says this should be so. Other points about the layout of the program which we can make right now are:

- more than one statement can be written on a line;
- statements can be split over several lines (but strings cannot);
- statements are ended by semicolons.

2.4 Expressions and assignment

Computations in progamming involve evaluating **expressions**. Expressions can be mathematical formulas, but can also be the result of a condition (such as $i<=100$) or the concatenation of two strings (as we saw in the previous section). Expressions can be stored in fields that we have declared. This process is called **assignment** and the field into which we assign something is known as a **variable**. Assignment is the first real statement that we shall consider from the five groups mentioned in section 2.2. There is quite a lot involved in getting ready for an assignment, and we shall tackle it in the following steps:

- what a type is;
- how to declare a variable and a constant;
- how to compute values from expressions;
- assignment itself;
- how to print the values of variables and expressions;
- several examples.

Types

Java, like most modern languages, is what is known as **strongly typed** and also **strongly classed**. This means that every field and expression has a type or a class, and only those of the same types or classes can be used together. Put in simple terms, this means that we cannot mix strings and numbers, nor could we mix planets and birds, for example. Java has eight built-in types, known as the **primitive types**, but the three that are commonly used in calculations are:

1   **int** for ordinary positive and negative integer numbers in a range extending over two thousand million;

2   **long** for even longer integer numbers or for the results of integer calculations;

3   **double** for numbers with fractional parts (i.e. real numbers) or for the results of calculations involving at least one real number.

The other types are `boolean`, `byte`, `char`, `float` and `short`, and we shall introduce them as they are needed in the next chapters.

A type governs how much storage is made available for the values that are stored in variables of that type. Thus `int` uses 32 bits (4 bytes), and `long` and `double` each 64 bits (8 bytes). The full table of numeric types and their storage is given in the next section.

Declarations of variables and constants

Objects store their data in variables. Variables may be declared anywhere in a Java class or method, but usually most of them are grouped at the start or end. The form of a variable declaration is one of the following:

Variable declaration
type *name;*   **type** *name1, name2, name3;*   **type** *name = value;*

The declaration introduces one or more variables of the given type. The last form can be used to initialize a variable at the same time as declaring it. Examples of declarations of variables are

```
int     temperature;     // in degrees Celsius
int     frequency;       // in kilohertz
double  salary;
double  tax = 25;        // initially 25%
long    k, m, n;         // integer unknowns
double  x, y, z;         // real unknowns
```

It is worth while keeping declarations neat and tidy, with the identifiers and types lined up. It is also a useful habit to indicate what the variables are to be used for, if this is not immediately obvious from their identifiers, as well as to give some supporting information regarding the units that are intended, as shown in some of the examples.

In the real world, many values acquire names. For example, 3.141592 is known as pi, and a decade is 10. Giving names to quantities makes them easier to remember and use. In Java, named entities whose values are not going to change are known as **constants**. They are declared in declarations of the form

---

Constant declaration

`static final type` *name* = *value*;

Examples of constant declarations are

```
static final int speedLimit = 120;
static final int retirementAge = 65;
static final double kmperMile = 1.609;
```

We noted above that the declaration modifier `static` indicates a class field. Thus constant declarations can occur only at the class level, and not inside methods, even inside `main`. The second modifier, `final`, indicates that the contents of the field cannot be changed during the program; in other words, it is constant.

When variables are declared we have the option of specifying an initial value or of receiving a **default initialization**. For the numeric types, the default is zero. How does a variable declaration with initialization differ from a constant declaration? The fundamental difference is that once constants are set, they cannot be changed again. With variables, the values can change through assignment.

Expressions

Expression is the term given to formulas in programming languages. The way in which expressions are written in programming languages is somewhat different from the normal way of writing them. The main differences are that:

● multiplication is indicated by an asterisk *;

- division is indicated by a slash /;
- denominators follow numerators on the same line.

For example, consider some very simple formulas and their Java equivalents:

$$\frac{1}{1.25}$$ `1/2.5`

$$\frac{y(x-3)}{x-1}$$ `y*(x - 3)/(x - 1)`

The implication of the last point – writing on one line – is that we use more brackets in Java expressions than we would in ordinary arithmetic or mathematics. Division that would usually be written as a fraction has to be split into two bracketed parts separated by a slash, as shown in the second example.

As another example, to print a temperature, t, converted to Fahrenheit, using the formula

$$\frac{9t}{5} + 32$$

we would say

```
System.out.println (9 * t / 5 + 32);
```

which, assuming $t = 15$, would print out

59

An important consideration is that in Java the division operator / works at two levels: integer and real. If both the values are integer, it performs integer division, otherwise it performs real division. Integer division is not usually what one wants so that often one of the values must be made real explicitly. For example, 1/2 will produce 0, whereas 1.0/2 will give 0.5. However, integer division does have its uses, as shown in Example 2.5 later on in this section.

As well as the usual four operators (or five, if we regard / as having two meanings), use is often made in programming of finding the remainder after integer division. The operator used to represent this **modulus** is %. Examples of its use are

```
23 % 2        → 1
6 % 6         → 0
81 % 11       → 4
```

In Java, the normal **precedence** rules apply, with brackets coming before division and multiplication, which are performed before addition and subtraction. There is more on precedence in the next section.

While we are on the subject of writing out formulas, we note that the trigonometric functions are called with brackets like this:

```
sin x   →   Math.sin(x)
```

`Math` is a built-in class which supplies methods for trigonometry, exponentiation and other operations. Going back to the 'all on one line' restriction, we see that to raise to a power, we have to call a method, as in

x^4 →   `Math.pow(x,4)`

Another useful method in the `Math` class is that for rounding a real[†] number to an integer. Examples are

```
Math.round (6.6)    →   7
Math.round (6.3)    →   6
```

There is more to expressions than this short introduction reveals, but the more advanced features will be added as we need them in the next few chapters. There is also a full list of the `Math` functions in the next section. To end, here are some more formulas written in Java:

$$\sqrt{b^2 - 4ac}$$ `Math.sqrt(Math.pow(b,2) - 4 * a * c)`

$$\frac{1}{2}mv^2$$ `0.5 * m * Math.pow(v,2)`

$$\sqrt{2gE\left(\frac{1}{W_1} + \frac{1}{W_2}\right)}$$ `Math.sqrt(2 * g * E * (1/W1 + 1/W2))`

$$\frac{L_1 + L_2 + \sqrt{M}}{L_1 + L_2 - 2M}$$ `(L1 + L2 + Math.sqrt(M))/(L1 + L2 - 2 * M)`

$$\frac{1}{2\pi\sqrt{LC}}$$ `1/(2 * Math.PI* Math.sqrt(L * C))`

Assignment

Having declared a variable, we can now use an assignment statement to give it the value of an expression. The assignment statement has several forms:

Assignment statement
`variable = expression;` `variable op= expression;`

The effect of an **assignment statement** is to evaluate the expression and to assign the resulting value to the variable indicated by the identifier. The equals sign which indicates the assignment is read 'becomes'. Thus we can write

```
temperature = 24;
```

† The term real number has its usual meaning in this book, and includes both the `double` and `float` types that Java provides for expressing real numbers.

and read it 'temperature becomes 24'. The value of the expression is 24, and this is assigned to the variable temperature. In the next sequence

```
oldWeight = 65;
newWeight = oldWeight - 5;
```

oldWeight is assigned the value 65, and is then used to calculate the value for the variable newWeight, which is 60.

Assignment requires that the types of the expression and the variable are the same. Thus we cannot assign something of type int to a Planet, or even a double variable to an int variable. However, bearing in mind that even in mathematics the real numbers encompass the integers, we *can* assign integers to reals. So the following is permissible:

```
double rate;
rate = 10;
```

The second form of the assignment statement includes an operator and is used as a shorthand where the value of the variable is also the first operand. A classic example is

```
i += 2;
```

which will add two to i. It has exactly the same effect as

```
i = i + 2;
```

but is actually quicker for the computer to execute.

Printing expressions and variables

The examples so far have used calls to the print and println methods to print **strings**. It is also possible to print **numbers** and, indeed, to print the results of calculations. For example, to print 4 times 5 less 2 we would have

```
System.out.println (4 * 5 - 2);
```

which would print out

```
18
```

Similarly, we can print out the values of expressions involving variables or constants, e.g.

```
static final double kmperMile = 1.609;
System.out.println (100 * kmperMile);
```

which would print

```
160.9
```

What if we want to print more than one value out, or a mixture of numbers and strings? We said in the previous section that several strings can be printed out in one print call if they are joined by a plus operator. The same applies here. However, we have now to understand what is going on behind the scenes.

The concatenate operator joins strings. When it finds something else to its left or right – for example, a number – it looks for a `toString` method defined by the class, which can convert that value to a string. All the built-in types have `toString` methods. The + operator can then perform the concatenation on the string versions and the printing proceeds. For example, we can say

```
System.out.println (100 + " miles is "
                    + 100 * kmperMile + " kilometres");
```

which would print

100 miles is 160.9 kilometres

Both numbers were converted to strings and joined up with the other two to make the full message. Note that it is important to include spaces in a string that is adjacent to a number, since such spaces are not otherwise inserted.

EXAMPLE 2.4   Effective resistance

Problem   In a particular circuit, there are three resistances connected in parallel as follows:

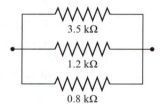

We want to calculate the effective resistance through this section of the circuit.

Solution   The formula for the effective resistance, R, of n resistors in parallel is

$$\frac{1}{R} = \frac{1}{r_1} + \frac{1}{r_2} + \dots + \frac{1}{r_n}$$

Using this formula, R itself is found by dividing 1 by the result of the calculation on the right hand side.

Program   We can write a program with this formula as an expression, using the three values in the diagram above.

```
class Resistance {

  /* The Resistance program       J M Bishop 1990
   * ---------------------        Java version A Moolman 1997
   * Calculates effective resistance of three resistors in parallel
   * Illustrates expressions and printing
   */

  public static void main (String args []) {

    System.out.println("For resistors connected in parallel\n");
    System.out.println("       |------ 3.5 kohms ------|");
    System.out.println("----|------ 1.2 kohms ------|----");
    System.out.println("       |------ 0.8 kohms ------|");
    System.out.println();
    System.out.println("The effective resistance is " +
        (1 / (1/3.5 + 1/1.2 + 1/0.8)) + " kohms");
  }
}
```

Testing   Running the program produces the following output:

```
For resistors connected in parallel

       |------ 3.5 kohms ------|
----|------ 1.2 kohms ------|----
       |------ 0.8 kohms ------|

The effective resistance is 0.4221105527638191 kohms
```

The output is actually a bit of a surprise. Why was the answer printed with such a long fractional part? The short answer is because that is how it is stored. When the calculation was done, the result was stored as a real number. Real numbers are not stored as fractions but as decimals, and there is a great deal of space to store them. In this case, there were 17 digits. So the second question is: why did Java print all of them? We consider the answer in the next section.

2.5 Numerical computing

Since this book is designed for use in a scientific or engineering environment, one thing we have to be careful about is the accuracy of the numbers we produce. In all computer languages, there are aspects which help in ensuring that answers are both correct and accurate. We shall consider some of these in Java, and also continue our exploration of the numeric types begun in the previous section.

More on printing integers and reals

As we have said earlier, when a number is to be printed, Java calls its `toString` method which returns the string version, and this is passed to the `print` method.

`toString` has no information about how many digits it should produce, so it gives all of them. `long` integers may yield as many as ten digits and double real numbers up to 17, as we have seen above. If the real number's value lies outside the significance of 17 digits, Java resorts to printing the number as a fraction and an exponent raised to the power of ten. There is one digit before the point and between an additional 1 and 16 digits (as required) after it. The resulting required decimal exponent comes after an E. This format is known as **scientific format**, or **E-format**. So, how would Java print the following numeric expressions?

Declaration	Printed as
10	10
650	650
2001	2001
14.75	14.75
-1.6213	-1.6213
1/1.6213	0.6167889964843027
123456789	123456789
0.000000005	5.0E-9
1.0/2	0.5
1/2	0

Only the last one is surprising, but remember that Java regards / as an integer operator if both the values are integers. In integer terms, the result of 1 divided by 2 is 0.

Clearly, the problem with the above scheme is the long real numbers. In order to achieve finer control, we have devised a special package for the book, described at the end of this section. Java also has its own, but rather hard to use, formatting classes in the `java.text` package and we shall delve into these in Chapter 10.

Numeric types

The six numeric types are shown with their properties in Table 2.1. `byte` is typically used in programs that are dealing with data at the level of the machine. `short` can be a way of saving space, but is not often used in Java programs. `int` is the usual type for declaring integers, but `long` also frequently appears as it is the default for the result

Table 2.1 *Details of the numeric types*

Type	Representation	Initial value	Storage	Maximum value
byte	signed integer	0	8 bits	127
short	signed integer	0	16 bits	32767
int	signed integer	0	32 bits	2147483647
long	signed integer	0	64 bits	over 10^{18}
float	floating point	0.0	32 bits	over 10^{38}
double	floating point	0.0	64 bits	over 10^{308}

of an integer expression, as we shall see in Example 2.5. `float` would be the natural choice for real numbers, except that `double` is the default type for the result of real expressions. That is why we introduced `int`, `long` and `double` in the previous section.

The numeric types have access to the operators mentioned already, and can be output in a rough sort of way as explained in section 2.4. Both the operators and the output can be extended, though.

Each of the primitive types has a companion class which provides, among other things, two useful constants. These are

---

Numeric constants

```
typeclass.MIN_VALUE
typeclass.MAX_VALUE
```

The typeclass is a companion to the type, e.g. `Long` for `long`, `Double` for `double`. These classes, called envelopes, are discussed in section 6.1.

Numeric operators

We have mentioned five operators so far: +, −, *, / and %. There are two more that apply to the integer types. In programming, a common operation is to add one to a counter. For example, we might have the assignment

```
int total;
total = total + 1;
```

It seems wasteful to have to type the variable's name twice in every case. Thus there are two special operators defined to abbreviate common increments and decrements. These are shown in the next form:

Increment and decrement operators

```
variable ++;        // add one to variable
variable --;        // subtract one from variable
```

The example above becomes

```
total++;
```

In fact ++ is a shorthand for +=1, as in

```
total += 1;
```

This form would not be used for one, though. Its use is for adding other values or full expressions. For example, if we were always adding five, then we would use

```
total += 5;
```

One way to remember that the increment operator is += and not =+ is that the latter, in an assignment, could be misinterpreted as assigning a positive value, not adding it. That is,

```
total =+ 5;
```

would treat +5 as a constant and assign it to total.

The Math class

We have already alluded to the Math class which Java provides for the standard arithmetic and trigonometric functions one would expect even on a good calculator. Math belongs to the package java.lang which is the only one that is automatically imported into every program. Therefore we can use Math functions at any time. The following form summarizes the main ones.

```
Math class methods

final double E
final double PI
double exp (doublevalue)
double log (doublevalue)
double pow (doublevalue, doublevalue)
double sqrt (doublevalue)
double acos (doublevalue)
double asin (doublevalue)
double atan (doublevalue)
double cos (doublevalue)    // in radians
double sin (doublevalue)    // in radians
double tan (doublevalue)    // in radians
... abs (...)            // int, long, float, double
... max (..., ...)       // int, long, float, double
... min (..., ...)       // int, long, float, double
... round (...)          // int from float
... round (...)          // long from double
```

These methods will be used in many of the examples that follow. Math.round is used in the next one.

EXAMPLE 2.5   Fleet timetables

Problem   Savanna Deliveries Inc. has acquired new vehicles which are able to travel 15% faster than the old vehicles (while still staying within the speed limit). The company would like to know how this will affect journey times.

Solution   Times are represented in a 24 hour clock, such as 0930 or 1755. We need to find out how an arrival time will change, based on the reduction in the total journey time. Therefore, we need to be able to subtract times to find the journey time and multiply the result by 0.85, representing a 15% reduction. The question is how to do arithmetic on times.

Algorithm Times consist of two parts: hours and minutes. In order to do subtraction and multiplication on times, we have to convert them to minutes first, perform the calculation, then convert back. Assuming we can do this, the overall algorithm is

> **New fleet**
> Read in the departure and arrival times
> Calculate journey time
> Reduce journey time by 15%
> Add to the departure time to get the new arrival time
> Print out new journey time and arrival time.

The first conversion involves splitting an integer into two parts. To do this, we need to divide by 100, giving the hours, and get the minutes by taking the remainder. The algorithm together with an example is

> **Convert to minutes**
> | | |
> |---|---|
> | Time is | 0715 |
> | Find hours from time/100 | 7 |
> | Find minutes from time modulo 100 | 15 |
> | Set minutes to hours*60 + minutes | 435 |

Converting back is similar. The algorithm is:

> **Convert to hours and minutes**
> | | |
> |---|---|
> | Minutes are | 435 |
> | Set hours to minutes/60 | 7 |
> | Set minutes from minutes modulo 60 | 15 |
> | Set time to hours*100 + minutes | 715 |

Program The program to handle one journey is quite simple. The departure and arrival times of a particular vehicle are set as constants. In the next chapter we shall see how to read them in instead. Remember that division of integer values yields an integer result, so that the algorithms above have a direct translation into Java.

```
class NewFleet {

    /* The New Fleet Program           by J M Bishop  Aug 1996
     * --------------------            Java 1.1 October 1997
     * Works out the new arrival time for vehicles that are
     * 15% faster than before.
     *
     * Illustrates constants, expressions and assignment.
     * Includes use of the modulo operator %
     */
```

```
static final double reduction = 0.85;
static final int depart = 900;
static final int arrive = 1015;

public static void main(String args []) {

   long newArrive,              // 24 hour clock time
        newJourneyTime,
        newArriveM;             // in minutes in a day
   int  departM,
        arriveM,
        oldJourneyTime;

   System.out.println("***** Train travel *****\n");
// convert the initial times to minutes
   departM = (depart / 100)*60 + depart % 100;
   arriveM = (arrive / 100)*60 + arrive % 100;

// calculate the old and new times
   oldJourneyTime = arriveM - departM;
   newJourneyTime = Math.round(oldJourneyTime*reduction);

// create the new arrival time in minutes and
// then in a 24 hour clock time
   newArriveM = departM + newJourneyTime;
   newArrive = (newArriveM / 60)*100 + newArriveM % 60;

// Report on the findings
   System.out.println("Departure time is "+depart);
   System.out.println("Old arrival time is "+arrive);
   System.out.println("Old journey time is "
     +oldJourneyTime+" minutes");
   System.out.println("New journey time is "
     +newJourneyTime+" minutes");
   System.out.println("New arrival time is "+newArrive);
   }
}
```

Notice that we use six different variables to keep all the values relevant at any one time. They are also given names which indicate their meaning well.

An interesting point in the above program is why three of the variables were declared as long. Java uses long and double as the default types for the result of integer and real expressions respectively. Thus the expression

```
oldJourneyTime * reduction
```

which involves a real number will produce a double result. The version of Math.round that takes a double parameter produces a long result. In order to keep the types the same across the assignment, newJourneyTime must be declared as long. There is actually a way of changing from one type to another – called casting – as we shall see next.

Testing   Testing the program gives

```
***** Train travel *****

Departure time is 900
Old arrival time is 1015
Old journey time is 75 mins
New journey time is 64 mins
New arrival time is 1004
```

Conversions between types

We have hinted on several occasions that it is possible to convert between numeric types. Why would we wish to do this? A common example is that of calculations which result in real values, but which then should be displayed as integers for ease of understanding. So far, two specific conversions have been discussed:

1   Rounding a `double` number to a `long` using `Math.round`.

2   Assigning an `int` to a `double` number.

Another kind of conversion applies across the board to the numeric types in order of size, which means we can assign

```
byte => short => int => long => float => double
```

or any combination of these in the same direction. For example, `byte` to `long` is allowed, and `short` to `double`. But what about the other direction? Suppose we want to 'downsize' a `double` to a `float`. In this case we have to use a **type cast**. The type cast takes the form

Type cast
(**type**) *expression*

For example,

```
float kilograms;
double estimate;
kilograms = (float) (estimate * 1.2);
```

The proviso is that the value of the expression must be applicable to the values that can be stored by the type. Referring to Table 3.1, we could not cast a `short` value of 1000 into a `byte`, since it would not fit. Java will report a compilation error (if the value is deducible at compile time) or otherwise a run-time error. In the case of real to integer type casts, however, any fractional part is discarded. For example,

```
(int) 6.3       gives 6
(int) 6.8       gives 6
```

Finally, we note that type casting is allowed only between numeric types. Unlike other languages, there is no facility in Java for casting characters and booleans into numbers and vice versa. (See section 4.2 for these types.)

Precedence

Java divides operators into precedence groups, and the ones we have studied so far are grouped thus:

Group	Operators	Comment
1	++ -- (typecast) + -	plus and minus are unary
2	* / %	% is for modulo
3	+ - +	plus is for add and concatenation
4	= x=	where x is one of + - * / %

From the table, we can deduce some important relationships. Type casts are done before anything. Therefore in

```
(int) x + 7.5
```

the cast applies only to the x. If we want it to include the 7.5, brackets must be employed. Then string concatenation is at the same precedence level as arithmetic plus. So

```
System.out.println("Start with " + temp + 32);
```

where `temp` is, say, 50, will produce the unexpected result of

```
Start with 5032
```

To get

```
Start with 82
```

as probably required, we must break the precedence again, as in

```
System.out.println("Start with "+ (temp + 32));
```

Java Gently's formatting methods

In order to give more control over how values are printed, Java provides formatting classes, but they are not easy to use and can make a simple program look rather complicated. What we do, in the company of many other authors, is to define a class which provides a simpler interface to these somewhat basic facilities. The class defined for the *Java Gently* books is called `Text` and it provides the output methods shown in the following form. There are also methods for input and opening files, which we cover later in Chapter 4.

The `Text` class – format methods

```
// Formatting class methods
String format (int number, int align)
String format (double number, int align, int frac)
```

The two methods provide a means for controlling numeric output. The `align` parameter specifies the minimum number of characters that should be used to print the number. Thus if the number is 123 and the `align` parameter is 6, there will be three spaces in front of 123 when output. In this way, numbers can be neatly lined up in columns. Both `format` methods have the property that if the number will not fit in the gap given, the gap will be expanded to the right, and the digits before the decimal point will be printed in full anyway. For real numbers, the `frac` parameter is definite: there will always be that number of digits in the fractional part. Any further digits are truncated or zeroes added as needed.

The methods do not output anything themselves but serve as conversions from numbers to strings; these strings can then be included in a `println` statement in the usual way. For example, suppose we say

```
System.out.println(Text.format(x, 9, 4));
```

then for various values of *x* we get

```
Value of x          123456789 Column
-1234.5678          -1234.567
1234.56789          1234.5678
4.56789             4.5678
0                   0.0000
45.67               45.6700
4                   4.0000
123456789           123456789.0000      expanded out to 14 columns
777777.88888        777777.8888         expanded out to 11 columns
```

How to compile, store and access the `javagently` package was explained in section 1.4. Other methods associated with it are added in the next chapters. The `Text` class is not at all long, and is discussed in full in Chapter 10. Now we look at an example that uses the outputting features of `Text` to good advantage. There will be many more examples as we go along.

EXAMPLE 2.6   Accelerating train

Problem   A train starts with an acceleration of 0.5 m/s^2, which decreases uniformly to zero in 2 minutes. It then travels with uniform speed for another 3 minutes, after which it is brought to rest by the brakes with a constant deceleration of 1 m/s^2. This sequence is shown in the diagram:

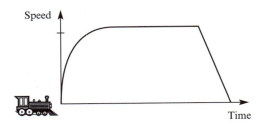

We want to find out how far the train travelled in km. In the next chapter, we shall see how to vary the figures suggested above.

Solution Although we have been given precise figures for this journey, the problem could well come up again with different values, so we shall generalize, and refer to the various times, distances, velocities and accelerations as follows:

$r_a r_b$ – the acceleration and deceleration rates;

$t_1 v d_1$ – the time, velocity and distance achieved at the point when acceleration stops;

$t_2 d_2$ – the time and distance achieved at the point when deceleration starts;

d_3 – the distance achieved during the deceleration phase.

Given this, we can use the usual equations of motion to get to the velocity and distance over the period of acceleration as

$$v = \frac{r_a t_1}{2}$$

$$d_1 = \frac{r_a t_2^2}{3}$$

The distance d_2 covered at constant speed depends on the velocity reached, and is simply vt_1. For the final distance of deceleration, we have

$$d_3 = \frac{v^2}{2r_d}$$

Algorithm Armed with these equations, we simply have to calculate the three distances and add them up. In Java, though, it is considered good practice to use meaningful, albeit longer, names. The algorithm would therefore look like this:

Train travel
  Calculate the velocity and distance1 based on the acceleration and time1.
  Calculate distance2 based on the velocity for time2.
  Calculate distance3 based on the velocity and deceleration.
  The distance is the sum of the three.

Because distance2 depends on the velocity, and just to make things clearer, we declare variables for each of the distances and do the calculations step by step.

Program   The four given values are set up as constants. However, we do not want to tie the program down to these in the future, and should make allowance for any particular length of real numbers. Thus we choose to format with `Text.format` `(x,3,1)`, indicating that there will be three spaces and one after the decimal point. As we explained above, the `Text` class will expand the printing if necessary, not just cut the number off. In order to use the `Text` class, we need an import statement, which is the first one in the program.

```
import javagently.*;

class TrainTravel {

  /* The Train Travel Program        J M and N T Bishop
     ========================        1990, 1999
   *
   * Calculates the distance travelled under acceleration,
   * constant speed and deceleration.
   * Illustrates constants, variables, expressions and printing
   */

  static final double startAcceleration = 0.5;   //  m/s/s
  static final double deceleration = 1.0;         //  m/s/s
  static final double time1 = 2;                  //  min
  static final double time2 = 3;                  //  min
  static final double kilo = 1000;
                    // metre to km conversion factor

  public static void main (String args []) {
    System.out.println("******* Train travel *******\n");
    System.out.println(startAcceleration +
                    " m/s/s decreasing to 0 in " +
                    time1 + " mins,");
    System.out.println("constant speed for " + time2 + " mins,");
    System.out.println("and " + deceleration + " m/s/s to rest\n");

  // Perform the calculation in simple steps, saving
  // each partial result

    double secs1 = time1*60;    // time1 in secs
    double secs2 = time2*60;    // time2 in secs
    double velocity = 0.5 * startAcceleration * secs1;
    double distance1 = (startAcceleration * secs1 * secs1) / 3;
    double distance2 = velocity * secs2;
    double distance3 = velocity * velocity / (2 * deceleration);
    double totalDistance = (distance1 + distance2 + distance3)
                    / kilo;
    System.out.println
          ("The journey covers " +
            Text.format(totalDistance,5,2) + " km");
  }
}
```

Testing   Running the program gives

```
******* Train travel *******
0.5 m/s/s decreasing to 0 in 2.0 mins,
constant speed for 3.0 mins,
and 1.0 m/s/s to rest

The journey covers   8.25 km
```

We can verify by calculation that the answer is correct.

QUIZ

2.1   In the form of the introduction to the `main` method, which is the one identifier which the user can change?

2.2   What would be the difference in the values produced by the following three expressions?

      `Math.round(5.8)`   `(int) 5.8 + 1`   `(int) (5.8 + 1)`

2.3   Could we use an `int` variable to store the number of seconds in a millennium (1000 years)?

2.4   Give two ways of printing your name and address in a neat label (a) using only one statement, and (b) using several statements. Explain why concatenation will almost certainly be necessary in (a).

2.5   What would be printed out on your computer from the following expressions?

```
52 % 10
9000009
Math.pow(4,3)
21 / 7
22 / 7
4 - 3 / 4 - 2
```

2.6   The `Math` class has a `sqrt` method. Give a statement to assign to `x` the value of

$$\sqrt{\frac{b^2 - 4ac}{2a}}$$

2.7   What will be the value of `total` after the following statements?

```
total =0;
total ++;
total -=7;
total +=20;
total %=10;
```

2.8   Set up suitable declarations for the following variables: a distance in track events in the Olympics, the mass of bags of flour sold in a supermarket, the age of a child in a school, minutes in an hour, a bank balance in dollars.

2.9   Referring to Example 2.5 on fleet timetables, classify each of the following as a keyword, variable, constant, method, class, object or package.

main	newArrive	Math	round
final	NewFleet	class	100
System	out	println	arrive

2.10 Given the following declarations in the same class, which ones would cause the compiler to report errors and why?

```
integer i, j, k;
max = 10;
double x = 1;
double K = 1,000;
int Prize = G50;
int 2ndPrize = G25;
int homeTime = 4.30;
double x = 6;
```

PROBLEMS

2.1 **Areas of shapes.** A firm of engineers is interested in knowing the area of different shapes with the same basic measurement. Specifically, the engineers would like to compare the area of a square, circle, equilateral triangle and rhombus (angle 45°) with the measurement r used as follows:

Write a program to print these values (in m²) for r equal to 20 metres.
Hint: the area of a circle is πr^2, of an equilateral triangle $(\sqrt{3}/4)r^2$, and of the rhombus $r^2/\sqrt{2}$.

2.2 **Printing investigation.** Perform a thorough investigation of the behaviour of your Java system in printing integer and real numbers using `Text.format` and without it.

2.3 **Fencing a paddock.** A farmer wishes to build a fence around an irregular paddock. The farmer has measured the position of the four corners as (x,y) distances in km relative to the farmhouse as follows:

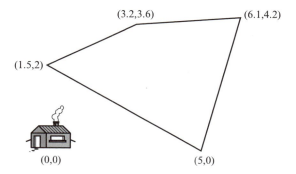

Write a program to print out the perimeter of the paddock, using the formula for the distance between two points as

$$\sqrt{(x_1 - x_2)^2 + (y_1 - y_2)^2}$$

2.4 **Weighted averages.** A programming course has three parts to it, a test, an assignment and an examination, which are weighted at 20%, 30% and 50%, respectively. Write a program which will set marks for the three components (out of 100) and print the final mark using the weightings.

2.5 **Fuel consumption.** A motor car uses 8 litres of fuel per 100 km on normal roads and 15% more fuel on rough roads. Write a program to print out the distance the car can travel on a full tank of 40 litres of fuel on both normal and rough roads.

2.6 **Factory shifts.** At a factory, the 24 hour day is divided into three shifts as follows:

Shift 1   from 00.00 to 07.59
Shift 2   from 08.00 to 15.59
Shift 3   from 16.00 to 23.59

Write a program which calculates from a time (supplied as a constant real number) the remaining length in hours and minutes of the appropriate shift.

CHAPTER 3

Structuring

3.1 Properties of a good program

The structure of a program indicates how its parts are connected together, and how sound those connections are. One can think of the structure of a bridge: each strut and rivet plays its role, and the whole performs a defined function efficiently. Bridges can even look pleasing. So it is with programs. When we create them we aim to achieve a structure that in the first instance achieves the required purpose, but then is also readable, reusable and efficient. These are the properties of a good program.

Correctness

It seems obvious that a program when complete should be correct but we all know that the two properties can diverge widely. Much software these days is released to the world with errors remaining (called bugs). In defence of such software, one must say that programming is one of the most complex engineering tasks that we know, and it is also one of the newest (genetic engineering is perhaps more recent). It is only since the mid-1980s that codified books on software engineering started to appear, and standards of software reliability began to be set by international bodies. So how do we program to achieve correct software? There are two golden rules:

1   Follow good programming practice while writing a program.
2   Test the program thoroughly throughout its development.

This book aims to instil good practice by example, and by motivating guidelines that can be followed in any programming activity. Interestingly enough, these are frequently not Java specific.

Testing is very important, as no matter how hard we try, we cannot always imagine all possibilities that might occur when the program starts running. With simple programs, we can read through the logic and reason about what will happen. With more complex programs (extending over more than two pages, say) and, in particular, programs where the user can alter the course by supplying data, the task is very much harder. Here the careful design of test data pays off.

Readability

In order to reason about a program, we have to be able to read it, and perhaps even discuss it with others. Some of the factors which aid readability are:

- use of meaningful identifiers, e.g. `kmperMile` instead of `k`;
- careful layout, especially indenting and blank lines;
- comments to explain the function of statements that follow.

One can also take readability further by starting to develop a **style** of writing which enables you to find what you are looking for quickly, and to communicate effectively within a group of programmers. For example, you may organize your classes so that their methods always appear before the fields, at the front. Another suggestion is to arrange the methods of a large class alphabetically by name (as the Java APIs do). Software organizations will often set up such guidelines – and expect them to be followed by employees.

Within the Java community, there are some agreed style guidelines with respect to identifier names. To some extent their aim is to obviate the confusion that can arise because Java is case sensitive. The guidelines are simple, and can be applied to the statement:

```
System.out.println(Text.format(expenditureToDate, 8, 2));
```

1   variables start with a small letter, e.g. `out`;
2   methods start with a small letter, e.g. `println`;
3   inner words in an identifier start with a capital letter, e.g. `Date`;
4   class names start with a capital letter, e.g. `Text` or `System`;
5   package names start with a small letter, e.g. `javagently`.

Reusability

While some might say that the inaccuracy of software is a major crisis in the industry, of equal concern is the inability of firms to produce software on time. One of the ways in which we aim to alleviate this position is to reuse software that has been tried and tested before. Java's packages are a classic example of reusability: instead of each of us writing a class to store and manipulate dates, one is provided. In the same way, in this book we have written three very useful classes which give leverage in the learning of the language.

Reusability works both ways: when writing a new program, we look around for existing classes that can be used or even adapted, and at the same time, we try to write our own classes so that they have a general appeal, without compromising their efficiency or readability in their primary program. Java has specific class constructs which aim to assist with reusability, and these are covered from Chapter 6 onwards.

Efficiency

There is nothing more frustrating than a program which is too slow or too big. Of course, a complex task might require time, memory and disk space, but simple tasks should not. There are many small ways in which we can start out by programming thriftily, while once again not compromising our other goals. Just a few ideas for keeping a program compact are:

- declare variables as needed, do not overdo it;
- maximize the use of methods, thus avoiding copies of common statements;
- do common calculations once and store the result.

As we progress in programming maturity, more of these will be mentioned. The next sections show different ways in which we can group statements to aid readability, reusability and efficiency. These include blocks, loops, methods and classes. In section 3.4 we tackle program design and devise a standard way of dividing up a program which works for the rest of the book.

3.2 Repetition with for-loops

Computers, like all machines, are very good at doing the same thing over and over again. In a program, such repetition can be formulated as a **loop**. There are two kinds of loops possible in Java, as in most languages: **counting loops** and **conditional loops**. In this section we look at counting loops; the conditional ones are introduced in Chapter 4.

The form of a for-loop

Counting loops in Java are introduced by the keyword **for**, and are therefore commonly known as for-loops. A basic Java for-loop is specified in the following form:

Simple for-statement

```
for (start; check; update) {
   body ;
}
```

The for, brackets and body form the compulsory structure of the loop, and the italicized parts have to be expanded. The **start** part introduces one or more **loop variables** which are to be tested and updated. If there is more than one loop variable then their starting statements are separated by commas. The **check** is a comparison which gives the condition for the loop to end, based on the current value of the loop variables. The **update** part consists of assignments to change the values of the loop variables each time round the loop. The **body** of the loop consists of statements. If there is only one statement, then the braces can be omitted.

Usually, there is only one loop variable. Loop variables must be numbers, and by convention they are usually integers. It is possible, but this is considered bad practice, to have a loop variable which is a real number. The reason is that a comparison on real numbers is inexact at the limits, and a loop may execute for one more or less than the number of times expected.

Consider the following example to print out five rows of stars (asterisks):

```
for (int i=0; i<5; i++)
    System.out.println("**********");
```

Are we sure that five and not six rows are printed? One way to verify that five rows are printed is to reason that i takes on the values 0 to 4, but not 5. Another way is to look at the statement operationally. Once the initialization has been completed (and it happens only once) the sequence in which the other three parts of the loop are executed is

- check
- body
- update

Taking it slowly, i starts at 0. It is checked against 5, a line of stars is printed and i is incremented to 1. When i gets to 3, the stars are printed, i is incremented to 4, checked against 5, more stars are printed, and i is incremented to 5. Now it is checked that it is *less than* 5 and fails. The loop then ends and control continues after the final brace. We can therefore verify that five rows are printed.

It is good practice to have a standard way of writing simple for-loops. If we want to run a loop n times, we can choose between

```
for (int i=1; i<=n; i++)
for (int i=0; i<n; i++)
```

The first version is perhaps easier to understand. However, many related sequences in Java, especially arrays (as discussed in Chapter 5), use zero as a starting point. It has therefore become conventional to start loops at zero, and the second form is therefore preferred.

EXAMPLE 3.1   Multiple labels

Problem   A technician at Savanna Chemicals Inc. would like to print out lots of cautionary labels, which can then be photocopied onto sticky labels.

Solution   We checked with the technician and confirmed that for the time being, it is alright to have the labels one underneath each other. The solution is to take the body of the DisplayWarning program in Example 2.3 as a model and put it in a loop.

Program   The program follows on quite easily. Note that we follow each label by two blank lines to separate them, and use a constant, nLabels, to specify how many labels there must be.

```
class LotsofLabels {

  /* The Lots of Labels program      by J M Bishop July 1996
   * ------------------------        Java 1.1 November 1997
   * Prints labels one underneath each other.
   * Illustrates a simple for-loop.
   */

  static final int nLabels = 8;

  public static void main (String args []) {

    for (int i=0; i < nLabels; i++) {
      System.out.println ("--------------------");
      System.out.println ("|                  |");
      System.out.println ("|   C A U T I O N  |");
      System.out.println ("|                  |");
      System.out.println ("| Highly Flammable |");
      System.out.println ("|     Chemicals    |");
      System.out.println ("|                  |");
      System.out.println ("--------------------");
      System.out.println ("\n\n");
    }
  }
}
```

Testing   As expected, the output would be eight of the following, one underneath each other:

```
-----------------------
|                     |
|   C A U T I O N     |
|                     |
| Highly Flammable    |
|     Chemicals       |
|                     |
-----------------------
```

Using the loop variable

The loop variable serves to record the current iteration of a loop and its values can be used in various ways, some of which are:

- in an output statement;
- in simple arithmetic;
- as part of the bounds of another loop.

Together, these three facilities make looping much more interesting. Take the first use. We can number the star lines printed earlier as follows:

```
for (int i=0; i<5; i++) {
  System.out.print((i+1));
  System.out.println(" **********");
}
```

which would print

```
1 **********
2 **********
3 **********
4 **********
5 **********
```

Notice that the loop variable, i, runs from 0 to 4, but we print out $(i + 1)$ giving 1 to 5. If we had not put the $(i + 1)$ in brackets, then it would have been misinterpreted as the value of i plus a string concatenation with the value 1, giving 01 11 21 31 41. Check it and see.

Now consider how to print out the first ten even numbers. There are actually two ways. We can have a loop from 0 up to and not including 10 and write out double the loop variable, as in

```
for (int number = 0; number < 10; number++)
  System.out.print((number * 2) + "   ");
System.out.println();
```

which will produce

```
0 2 4 6 8 10 12 14 16 18
```

The other way is to do the doubling in the update part, which would be

```
for (int number = 0; number < 20; number+=2)
  System.out.print(number + "  ");
System.out.println();
```

To print the first ten odd numbers requires a bit of thought. If `number*2` is an even number, then `number*2+1` or `number*2-1` is an odd number. Choosing one of these expressions, we have

```
for (int number = 0; number < 10; number++)
  System.out.print((number * 2 + 1) + "  ");
System.out.println();
```

which will produce

```
1 3 5 7 9 11 13 15 17 19
```

EXAMPLE 3.2   Flow of liquid in a pipe

Problem   An engineer is responsible for recommending certain sizes of pipes for a new plant. The radius of the pipes can vary between 10 cm and 50 cm, in intervals of 5 cm. The flow of liquid in the pipe is constant at 2 m/s. The decision as to the sizes of pipe required will be made on the basis of volume of liquid flowing out of the pipe, measured in cubic metres per second. Graphically, we have

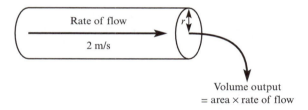

Volume output
= area × rate of flow

Solution   The volume is given by the area of the pipe's cross-section multiplied by the rate of flow. We can write a program to loop through the possible radius sizes, calculating the volume and printing it out.

Algorithm   The loop is to go from 10 cm to 50 cm, in multiples of 5 cm. If we start r at 10, then we are looking at calculating the volume for radii

        10
        10 + 5
        10 + 10
          .
          .
          .
        10 + 40

This sequence can be rewritten as $r + ih$, where $r = 10$, $h = 5$ and i goes from 0 to 8. Thus to print out the radii, we would use the sequence-printing loop:

```
for (int i = 0; i < 8; i++)
  System.out.println((radius + increase * i));
```

However, we must not forget to convert the radius given in centimetres to metres by dividing r and h by 100 when calculating the volume. To ensure that we keep track of these values, we declare them as named constants, i.e.

```
static final double  flow = 2;        // m/s
static final double  radiusCm = 10;   // smallest radius (cm)
static final double  increaseCm = 5;  // radius increment (cm)
```

Units are very important in scientific programming, of course. π is also needed in the calculation, but its value is already available in Java as the constant `Math.PI`.

The column width for the tabulation can best be worked out from the headings required, giving 8 for the radius and 16 for the volume.

Program

```
import javagently.*;

class LiquidFlow {

  /*  Program to calculate liquid flow in a pipe     N T Bishop
   *  ===========================================     1990, 1999
   *
   * Prints a table of the radius vs the flow rate
   * Illustrates a for-loop with a body that uses the
   * the loop variable.
   *
   */

  static final double  flow = 2;        // m/s
  static final double  radiusCm = 10;   // smallest radius (cm)
  static final double  increaseCm = 5;  // radius increment (cm)

  public static void main (String args []) {
    System.out.println("***** Volume of liquid flowing "+
                    "from pipes *****\n");
    System.out.println("Speed is constant at " + flow + " m/s\n");

    // Get ready to print the table
    System.out.println("Radius in cm\tVolume in cu m/s");

    double radiusM   = radiusCm / 100;    // smallest radius (m)
    double increaseM = increaseCm / 100;  // radius increment (m)
    double volumeFlow;
    for (int i = 0; i < 9; i++) {
      volumeFlow = Math.PI *
            Math.pow((radiusM + increaseM * i), 2) * flow;
```

```
        System.out.println(
                Text.format(radiusCm + increaseCm * i,8,2) +
                Text.format(volumeFlow, 16, 4) );
      }
    }
  }
}
```

Testing   The output from the program will be as follows:

```
***** Volume of liquid flowing from pipes *****

Speed is constant at 2.0 m/s

Radius in cm    Volume in cu m/s
    10.00           0.0628
    15.00           0.1414
    20.00           0.2513
    25.00           0.3927
    30.00           0.5655
    35.00           0.7697
    40.00           1.0053
    45.00           1.2723
    50.00           1.5708
```

Other looping options

1   **Backwards.**   We note that loops can also count backwards using `- -`. Thus, to print the sequence

```
    10 9 8 7 6 5 4 3 2 1 0 -1 -2 -3 -4 -5 -6
```

we could say

```
    for (int n = 10; n >=-6; n--)
      System.out.print(n + "  ");
    System.out.println();
```

2   **Empty.**   It may also happen with a loop that the starting condition may already exceed the finishing one. In this case, the loop body is not executed at all. In the statement

```
    for (int n = 0; n < finish; n++)
      System.out.print(n + "  ");
    System.out.println();
```

if `finish` is negative, the loop will be in this situation, and only a blank line will be printed.

3   **Nested.**   Loops within loops is a third option. Here, the body of a loop may itself contain a loop, as illustrated in Example 3.3. The rule here is that the loop variables of the loops must be different to avoid confusion.

4   **Endless.**   Sometimes we have other ways of stopping a loop than by counting up or down. As we shall see in the next chapter, working with a graphical user interface enables the user to stop a program by pressing a button on the screen. To make a for-loop perform without ever stopping, we leave out the check part as in

```
for (int i = 0; ; i++)
```

i will still increase with each iteration, and can be used as usual in the loop. If *i* is not needed, then we could say

```
for (; ;)
```

but this is not very good practice and a conditional loop, covered in Chapter 4, would be a better choice. However, in this chapter only we shall use an endless for-loop when needed.

5   **Unfinished.**   Later on in Chapter 4 we will find that there are circumstances when we want to stop a loop in the process of an iteration. There is a special statement called **break** which will immediately pass control to the end of the loop. It is used in conjunction with the if-statement, also covered in Chapter 4. An example of its use is shown in Quiz Question 4.7.

EXAMPLE 3.3   Table of square roots

Problem   We wish to print a table of square roots for numbers between 1 and 60, so that the whole table fits nicely on the screen.

Solution   We can use the Math.sqrt method inside a print statement to print out the square root of the number. We need to think about how to arrange the layout of the table. A standard computer screen has lines 80 characters long. Allowing for 4 decimal places for the square root, the minimum field widths for the number will be three and for the root six, and we need to add on a bit for space in between the numbers, as in

```
~~~~ 80 ~~~ 8.1234 ~~~~~ 81 ~~ 8.2345 ~~~~ 82 ~~ 8.3456 ...
```

Thus 15 characters will be ample for each pair, giving five pairs per line. For the 60 numbers, this gives 12 lines, which will fit nicely on a screen. We can then use nested loops to get the desired effect.

Program design   We can tackle the solution from the top. Assuming that we know how to print one line, we can set up a loop to print 12 lines. Printing one line can be put in a nested loop with its own loop and loop variable, say *col*. The expression for printing a number on a given line will be

```
col + line * 5
```

assuming that *line* starts at 0 and goes on to 11. (Check this out by hand.)

One issue is the exact field widths for the numbers and the size of the gaps in between. Instead of printing a gap, we can add the gap onto the field width for the numbers, giving :6 for the number and :8:4 for its root. This has the added advantage of giving a bit of space for larger numbers, should the program be adapted to print from 1 to 1000, say.

Program

```
import javagently.*;

class SquareRoots {

  /* The Square Roots Table Program        N T Bishop
   * ===============================        1990, 1999
   *
   * Prints a table of square roots over a fixed range
   * Illustrates nested for-loops
   */

  public static void main (String args []) {
    System.out.println("Table of square roots of " +
                      "numbers 1 to 60");
    System.out.println("==========================" +
                      "================");

  // Print the headings for 5 columns
    for (int col = 1; col <= 5; col++)
      System.out.print("   No.   Root ");
    System.out.println();

    int number;
    for (int line = 0; line < 12; line++) {
      for (int col = 1; col <= 5; col++) {
        number = col + line * 5;
        System.out.print(
            Text.format(number, 6)+
            Text.format(Math.sqrt(number),8,4));
      }
      System.out.println();
    }
  }
}
```

Testing   Running the program confirms that it does produce the required effect, and the right answers as follows:

```
Table of square roots of numbers 1 to 60
========================================
   No.   Root   No.   Root   No.   Root   No.   Root   No.   Root
     1  1.0000     2  1.4142     3  1.7320     4  2.0000     5  2.2361
     6  2.4495     7  2.6458     8  2.8284     9  3.0000    10  3.1623
    11  3.3166    12  3.4641    13  3.6056    14  3.7417    15  3.8730
    16  4.0000    17  4.1231    18  4.2426    19  4.3589    20  4.4721
```

21	4.5826	22	4.6904	23	4.7958	24	4.8990	25	5.0000
26	5.0990	27	5.1962	28	5.2915	29	5.3852	30	5.4772
31	5.5678	32	5.6569	33	5.7446	34	5.8310	35	5.9161
36	6.0000	37	6.0828	38	6.1644	39	6.2450	40	6.3246
41	6.4031	42	6.4807	43	6.5574	44	6.6332	45	6.7082
46	6.7823	47	6.8557	48	6.9282	49	7.0000	50	7.0711
51	7.1414	52	7.2111	53	7.2801	54	7.3485	55	7.4162
56	7.4833	57	7.5498	58	7.6158	59	7.6811	60	7.7460

3.3 Input and output on a display

The careful reader will have noticed that although we spent some time in the last chapter on output, we did not mention its counterpart, input. The reason is that input of numbers in Java is even more difficult to manage than output. The full details of Java's input facilities are discussed in Chapter 10 as an advanced topic. They *are* powerful, but Java itself does not present a simple alternative. Using raw Java input can distract one from the primary purpose of learning to program and more importantly from that of solving scientific problems. For this reason, we have devised two classes for use with this book:

1   Text, which is a simple means of input and outputting text-based data with a Java console, command line window or text file;

2   Display, which is a generalized graphical user interface, showing input and output at the same time, and easily integrated with graph drawing facilities.

Text was written in 1997 for the 1st edition of *Java Gently* and has been successfully integrated into programs by many thousands of users. Display was written especially for this book and represents a genuine advance in easy-to-use GUI control.

We have already seen the Text class method, format. The rest are discussed in the next chapter when input–output with files are covered. We shall not be offering any more text-based programs from now on, and shall use the GUI display exclusively.

The GUI Display Class

Let us first look at a display produced by a simple program to add two numbers repeatedly, as shown in Figure 3.1. The display is divided into two sections, the left hand side for input and the right hand side for output. Both sections are visible at the same time, and are **scrollable** and can have more boxes or lines than the screen can show at once. Thus one can go back and look at previous results from the program.

At the bottom of the screen are two control **buttons**: a large Ready bar which provides interaction between the user and the program being written; and a small Close button on the right hand side which will shut down the window and the program using it.

It would of course be possible to program such a display from scratch in Java for a particular program, and we shall certainly learn how to do so in Chapter 7. However, doing so involves quite a lot of tedious GUI programming, which can make simple programs into monsters. The look and feel of the `Display` class is just what we would want in such a program, but what we have done is apply the principle of reusability and program it once, for multiple use.

The output section

From the point of view of the output section of Figure 3.1, we see that the program would go through three steps:

1   Display an introductory message about the data required.
2   Tell the user what to do when the data is ready.
3   Get the values from the input section, do the computation and display the results.

This program is set up to repeat these steps until the Close button is pressed. Thus the output section presents the active flow of the program in the usual way.

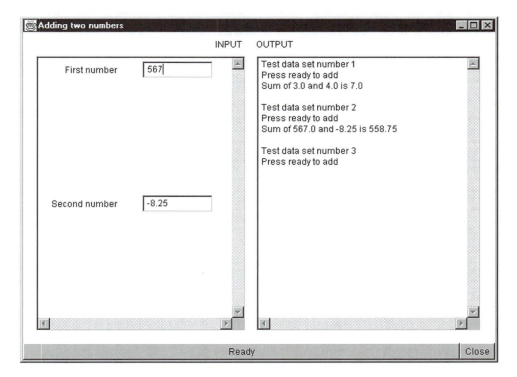

Figure 3.1 *The display produced for a simple program*

The input section

The input section presents the data values that the program may wish the user to change. The steps involved in using this section are:

1   The program initially tells the display what data values need to be altered. For each of these, a label alongside a standard-sized box is drawn. Initial values can be supplied for the boxes, which is a very useful facility for testing programs, as the user does not have to think of new data for every field.

2   The user makes changes to the values in the boxes as required. Not all need to be changed, and values can be repeatedly overwritten until correct.

3   The user presses the Ready bar. The Display class fetches all the values from the boxes, updates its internal table of values and passes control back to the program.

4   The program gets whatever values it needs (presumably all of them) and continues with its calculations and output.

For further runs of the program with different data, steps 2 to 4 are repeated.

The Display class' methods

Having looked at the Display class informally, we now examine the methods it provides, in the same way as we outlined the capabilities of the Math class in section 2.5. The difference here is that the working of the methods may need more explanation than did the Math ones, which exactly mirrored our scientific experience.

The Display class	
new Display (*String*)	– sets up a new Display object with a title
void println (*String*)	– prints a string in the output section
void prompt (*String, value*)	– makes a box in the input section with the given string label and an initial value which is int, double or string
void ready (message)	– prints a message then waits for ready bar to be pressed
double getDouble (*String*)	– reads the double value that was set with that string label
int getInt (*String*)	– gets the int value that was set with that string label
String getString (*String*)	– gets the string value that was set with that string label
reposition (*Graph*)	– takes a graph and places it on the bottom of the input section

An entire program can be written using just the first five methods. The next two – get Int and getString – are merely variations on getDouble. The final method is used for integration with plotted graphs, which we shall explain in Example 3.7.

Starting up the Display class

The first step in using the Display class is to create a Display object. The declaration is

```
Display display = new Display ("Add two numbers");
```

The object name is display, with a small d, whereas the class is Display, with a big D. This is the only time that we refer to the class name, so there will be no confusion later on. Of course, we could call our display object anything we like, e.g.

```
Display myWindow = new Display ("Add two numbers");
```

or even

```
Display d = new Display ("Add two numbers");
```

In any one program, there could be more than one display, but this is rather unlikely. Therefore, it is better to stick to a standard name, and to use it in all one's programs. We use display in this book. A similar convention is that of using i for loop variables; it is accepted usage, even though i is itself not a very expressive identifier.

The parameter supplied to the Display class when the object is created is the name of the window, and it is displayed in the top line, as we can see in Figure 3.1, and in the tab if we minimize the window while doing something else.

Next we have to write out the initial instructions in the output screen. Display reuses the well-known method name println, and all we learnt about output in section 2.3 applies. The println for the display in Figure 3.1 is

```
display.println("Test data set number " + i);
```

The only difference between this statement and a text-based one is that we sent the string to our display instead of to System.out (which has a very specific and somewhat old-fashioned connection to the console screen or command line window).

Inputting interactively

We now consider how input is done on a GUI display. Each data item is identified by the label shown next to it. To get a data item onto the input section, we use

```
display.prompt("First number", 0);
```

Zero will be the initial value, but there is no reason why we could not have said

```
display.prompt("First number", 14);
```

or even

```
display.prompt("First number", a);
```

where the inital value is stored in a. The program asks that the user indicates when the data is ready, by calling

```
display.ready("Press ready to add");
```

The message is displayed and the Ready bar (which may have been momentarily grey) becomes active.

To get the data out, we first press the Ready bar. Don't forget that part! Without the action of pressing the bar, there is no way for the program to know when the user has finished making alterations. We then call one of the three get methods, depending on the type of data we want, e.g.

```
a = display.getDouble("First number");
```

The string supplied here identifies which of the boxes in the input section is relevant. The Display class returns the current value and assigns it to the variable as shown.

Values can be picked off in any order, so that the following is perfectly valid (although a bit eccentric):

```
b = display.getDouble("Second number");
a = display.getDouble("First number");
```

EXAMPLE 3.4 Adding numbers on the display

Although we hardly need a computer to help us add two numbers, it is a useful little example with which to introduce the display. We want to be able to enter two numbers, print them out with their sum and then repeat the process with two new numbers.

We see that the program defines the two variables, a and b, and sets up the input boxes in the initialization phase. Thereafter it enters a loop which does not have a check part, making it into an endless loop. This is not a problem because the program will end when the Close button is pressed by the user, not when the program thinks it has performed enough iterations! The println-ready-get sequence follows and then the computations are done.

This program forms a model for many of the interactive input–output programs that follow.

```
import javagently.*;

class AddTwoNumbers {

    /* The add two numbers program     by  J M Bishop
     * ============================        July 1999
     *
     *   Repeatedly adds pairs of numbers on a GUI display
     *   Illustrates the simple use of the Display class
     */
```

```
public static void main (String args []) {

    Display display = new Display("Adding two numbers");

    double a, b;
    // Requesting input
    display.prompt("First number", 0);
    display.prompt("Second number", 0);

    for (int i = 1; ; i++) {
      // Performing input
      display.println("Test data set number " + i);
      display.ready("Press ready to add");
      a = display.getDouble("First number");
      b = display.getDouble("Second number");

      // Displaying the results
      display.println("Sum of " + a + " and " + b
              + " is " + (a+b)+"\n");
    }
  }
}
```

Testing   The output has already been shown in Figure 3.1.

EXAMPLE 3.5   Effective resistance with input

As a more realistic, but still simple, example, consider the program in Example 2.4 for calculating effective resistance of three resistors connected in parallel. Clearly, here we have a case for input, while keeping the design of the output the same.

Using the Display class, and including input of the resistances, the program is:

```
import javagently.*;

class ResistanceDisplay {

  /* The Resistance Program with the Display   N T and J M Bishop
   * -----------------------------------   July 1999
   *
   * Shows how the Display class can be used for input and output
   */

  public static void main (String args []) {

    Display display = new Display("Resistance");

    // Set up the boxes for entering the data
    // giving default values
    double r1 = 3.5;
    double r2 = 1.2;
    double r3 = 0.8;
    display.prompt("Resistor 1", r1);
    display.prompt("Resistor 2", r2);
    display.prompt("Resistor 3", r3);
```

```
    // Display initial instructions
    display.println("For resistors connected in parallel");

    for (; ;) {
    // Get the values as in the display (maybe changed)
      display.ready("Check the three values and press ready\n");
      r1 = display.getDouble("Resistor 1");
      r2 = display.getDouble("Resistor 2");
      r3 = display.getDouble("Resistor 3");

      // Display the results
      display.println
        ("              \t|----------\t"+ r1 +
         " kohms --------|");
      display.println
        ("------------\t|----------\t"+ r2 +
         " kohms --------|----");
      display.println
        ("              \t|----------\t"+ r3 +
         " kohms --------|");

      double effectiveResistance = 1 / (1/r1 + 1/r2 + 1/r3);
      display.println("\nThe effective resistance is " +
                      Text.format(effectiveResistance,5,2)
                      + " kohms");
    }
  }
}
```

The output from the program is given in Figure 3.2. The program sets default values for the resistors – the same ones as in Example 2.4. Thus in order to get the same answer as then, all the user has to do is press Ready. However, here we have altered the value of resistor 2 from 1.2 kΩ to three times that. The resulting effective resistance is 0.55 kΩ as compared to 0.42 kΩ.

3.4 Making methods

The concept of a method was introduced in section 2.2 and we have become familiar with using methods from other classes (such as `Math.pow`), and writing programs with a `main` method.

Methods are an essential structuring tool in programming. They are the means whereby we break larger parts into smaller ones, and they give us the ability to **abstract** away from the details that we do not need to know about. For example, the `prompt` and `getDouble` methods of the `Display` class are quite complex inside, but all we need to know is their effect. In other words, we separate the **what** from the **how**.

The issue of where to put the line of separation is one of design, and this book aims to teach good design practice. At the end of this section, therefore, we shall establish a certain model of program design in Java which is appropriate for scientific

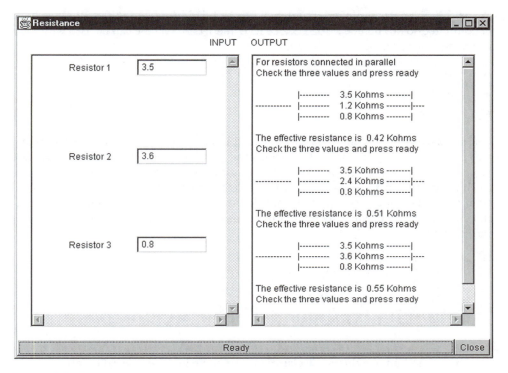

Figure 3.2 *Display for the effective resistance program*

computing. If one compares these programs to those in Java books for general programming, differences will be evident. As we go along, we shall explain by example why we have chosen this model.

Defining methods also enables us to cut down on **repetition**, as we have illustrated so well with the `Display` class. Finally, by choosing the name of a method carefully to reflect the action it performs, **readability** is also enhanced.

Declaring a method

A **method** is a group of fields and statements which is given a name and may be called upon by this name to perform a particular action. The form of a method declaration is

Method declaration

```
modifiers kind name (parameters) {
  fields and statements
  return expression;  // typed methods only
}
```

As before, the parts in italics are intended to be filled in. The modifiers that we have encountered so far include `public`, `static` and `final`. These can be used with their same meanings. The kind can be one of:

- void
- a type
- a class.

`void` indicates that the method can be called to perform an action in a self-standing way, e.g. `println`. In contrast, methods that have a type (e.g. `double`) or a class (e.g. `Planets`) will return a value and are called in a different way. These methods must have a return-statement somewhere which is executed to assign to the method a final value. The brackets after the identifier are compulsory and introduce the parameters (more about which below). An example of a simple `void` method without parameters is

```
static void box () {
   System.out.println ("-------------");
   System.out.println ("|           |");
   System.out.println ("|           |");
   System.out.println ("|           |");
   System.out.println ("-------------");
}
```

Creating a method like this is a **declaration**. The name `box` is declared to introduce the performing of the given statements.

As an example of a typed method, consider the conversion from degrees Celsius to Fahrenheit. If this operation is to be performed frequently, we could create a method for it as follows:

```
static double Fahrenheit (double Celsius) {
   return 9 * Celsius / 5 + 32;
}
```

Calling a method

If a method is declared as void, it is called by mentioning its name and parameters (if any). For example, to display a box, all we need to say is

```
box();
```

the effect of which will be to print

If it has a type or class (known generally as a **typed method**), then a call to it constitutes an expression and can be used wherever an expression of that type is permitted. Typically, typed methods would be called in assignments, as parts of expressions, or in output statements. Calling the conversion method defined above in a display print would be

```
display.println (28 + "C is " + Fahrenheit(28) + "F");
```

which would print out

```
28C is 82.4F
```

If we wanted the output to be a nice round integer, we could add another method around the Fahrenheit call, to display 8 F, as in

```
display.println (28 + "C is " +
                 Math.round(Fahrenheit(28)) + "F");
```

There are five method calls in this statement:

- Three we can see: `println`, `round` and `Fahrenheit`.
- Two hidden calls do the string conversions: `Integer.toString` for the constant 30 and `Long.toString` for the result of the `round` and `Fahrenheit` combination.

(The intervention of `toString` in `println` statements was discussed in section 2.3.) A nuance of method calls that we have already mentioned in section 2.2 is that the prefix depends on the method's modifiers and where it is defined relative to the call.

Method calls	
`object.method (parameters)`	– declared in another object
`classname.method (parameters)`	– declared static in another class
`method (parameters)`	– declared in this class

Specific examples of these different calls will arise as we get into the design of classes.

Passing parameters

Methods can be made more powerful by allowing their effect to differ each time the method is called. For example, if we have a method that prints a 5 by 5 box, it would be useful if it were able to print a 10 by 10 box, or a 12 by 16 box, or whatever. In other words, the action of printing a box by means of `println` methods should appear to be independent of the number of `println`s that are actually needed. This is called **generalizing** or **parameterizing** a method, and the values that are going to be different are known as **parameters**.

What we are aiming at is a means of being able to write

```
box (5, 5);
box (10, 10);
box (12, 16);
```

We achieve this goal by declaring the method with parameters that are given names and receive their values at the time the method is called. For the box, the declaration would become

```
static void box (int width, int depth)
```

Although we refer to the items in the declaration and the call as parameters, strictly speaking the declaration introduces **formal** parameters, and the call provides **actual** parameters. The form for a list of formal parameters is

Formal parameter declarations
(*type field*, *type field ...*)

whereas the form for actual parameters is

Actual parameters
(*expression*, *expression*, ...)

The number, types and order of the formal and actual parameters must match exactly. For example, the box method can be called with

```
int size = 60;
box (size, (int) size/2);
```

but not with any of

```
box (100);
box ("very wide");
box (12.5, 10);
```

Although we are concentrating on variables here, we note that objects can also be formal parameters, in which case the matching actual parameter must also be an object.

To understand how parameters work, study Figure 3.3 carefully.

EXAMPLE 3.6 Train travel

At this stage, we can show how a method can be used to structure a program with good effect. Consider the train travel program of Example 2.6. The structure of that program was:

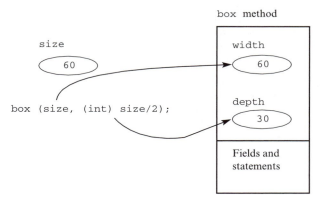

Figure 3.3 *An example of parameter passing*

1   Define constants.
2   Print introduction.
3   Perform calculations.
4   Print answer.

If we introduce the ability to read in the four values that govern the calculation, then there are more steps:

1   Declare **variables**.
2   Display introduction.
3   Get data values into the **variables**.
4   Perform calculations based on the **variables** returning a result.
5   Display the **variables** and the result.

By highlighting the role of the variables, we see that it is not going to be easy to disentangle these steps into methods unless they are all common to all methods. We shall see below that such a situation should be avoided.

It turns out that step 4, that of performing the calculations, can be isolated because it does not use the display, and returns one value, although it does need the four inputs. Thus we can compartmentalize this part of the program into a self-contained entity, whose only interface with the outside consists of its parameter list and its return value. The program follows.

```
import javagently.*;

class TrainTravelDisplay {

    /* The Train Travel Program with Display     J M and N T Bishop
     * ====================================      July 1999
     *
```

```
   * Calculates the distance travelled under acceleration,
   * constant speed and deceleration.
   * Illustrates a method created for structuring purposes
   * as well as further use of the Display class.
   */

  // method to perform all the calculations
  static double totalDistance
        (double ra, double t1, double t2, double rd) {

    double secs1 = t1*60;      // time1 in secs
    double secs2 = t2*60;      // time2 in secs
    double velocity = 0.5*ra*secs1;
    double distance1 = (ra*secs1*secs1) / 3;
    double distance2 = velocity*secs2;
    double distance3 = velocity*velocity / (2*rd);
    return (distance1+distance2+distance3) / 1000;
  }

  public static void main (String [] args) {

    Display display = new Display("Train travel");

    // The variables that can be read in
    double acceleration = 0.5;           //  m/s/s
    double deceleration = 1.0;           //  m/s/s
    double time1 = 2;                    //  min
    double time2 = 3;                    //  min

    // Start the display and request values
    // using the defaults as above
    display.println("******* Train travel *******");
    display.prompt("Initial acceleration in m/s/s", acceleration);
    display.prompt("Acceleration time in mins.", time1);
    display.prompt("Constant speed time in mins.", time2);
    display.prompt("Deceleration in m/s/s", deceleration);
    display.ready("Make changes and press ready\n");

    // Repeatedly get the values as displayed in the input section
    for (; ;) {
      acceleration = display.getDouble
                    ("Initial acceleration in m/s/s");
      time1 = display.getDouble("Acceleration time in mins.");
      time2 = display.getDouble("Constant speed time in mins.");
      deceleration = display.getDouble("Deceleration in m/s/s");

      // Call the method to calculate the final result
      double travelled = totalDistance
            (acceleration, time1, time2, deceleration);

      // Display the results
      display.println(acceleration +
                    " m/s/s decreasing to 0 in " +
                    time1 + " mins,");
```

```
        display.println("constant speed for " + time2 + " mins,");
        display.println("and " + deceleration + "m/s/s to rest");
        display.println("The journey covers " +
                       Text.format(travelled,5,2)+ " km");
        display.ready("\nPress ready for another set of values\n");
      }
    }
  }
```

The program is set up to perform the calculation repeatedly. Figure 3.4 shows a typical run with the first set of data matching that of Example 2.6, and the second being for a longer journey.

The implication of static

There is a complication with the last form for calling methods, which looks to be the simplest. If the method is called from a static one, then it must also be static. The same applies to all variables declared in the class: if they are used from a static method, they must be static. The problem is that our prime structuring method so far, `main`, has to be static. Therefore anything it calls or uses must also be static.

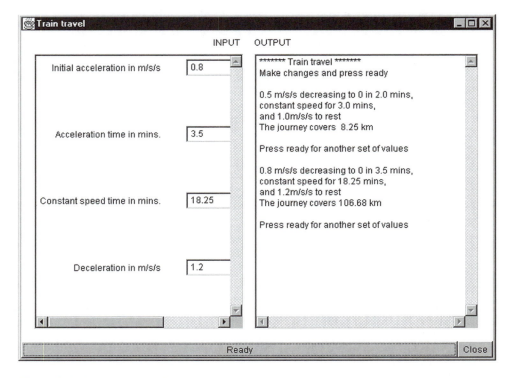

Figure 3.4 *Display from the train travel program*

If we were to divide our program into methods, and these methods were all sharing variables, then everything would be static. In programming terminology, such variables and methods would be considered to be **global**, and global is a bad idea. It is against the principle of declaring where needed, and it can genuinely lead to errors which are very hard to trace.

In this book, therefore, we do not use global variables and instead organize the program in an object-oriented way. The work is divided up between one or more classes. Each has its own methods and variables. The main program creates one or more objects from these classes, and then has access to the methods and fields via the object name. The class itself can place levels of protection on the use of its members, as discussed in sections 5.3 and 10.6.

Returning values from a method

Now we note a very subtle point. Although many other languages have in and out parameter-passing techniques, in Java parameter passing only goes in one direction. Values can be passed into methods via parameters, but not out of them. To get a value out of a method, we use the return process of typed methods, as described above. This is not a Java restriction; it is the essence of object-oriented programming. But what happens if we want more than one value to be returned? Typed methods are not adequate here. Instead, we fall back on objects again. Here are the design steps:

1   In a class with an appropriate name, we put the method together with the data fields that it needs. The class is going to be declared inside our program, and is therefore called a **nested** class. Other methods can also be added to the same class, such as one to get values for the variables from the display. Suppose we have

```
class Worker {
  double x, y;
  void solve (int q) {
    // calculations ending in
    x = // something
    y = // something else
  }
}
```

2   Then the main program creates an object of this class,

```
Worker work = new Worker ();
```

3   Thereafter the main program can refer to anything in the work object, e.g.

```
work.solve(5);
display.println ("Answers are " + work.x, " and " + work.y);
```

That's it. We have now set up a modern, extensible and object-oriented approach to multiple return values, which does not make use of global variables.

There are variations on the same theme, the most important of which is that sometimes a class will decide to protect all its variables, and only allow them to be accessed through methods. The Java convention is to use get and set methods, so we would refer to `work.getX()` instead of `work.x`. Java's packages are done in this way, and even in the `Display` class we use set methods such as `setColor`, rather than accessing the colour field which surely exists.

This form of program design is used in the examples in section 3.6 and thereafter.

3.5 The `Graph` class

It is now time to introduce the third member of the `javagently` package, the `Graph` class. Scientific insight relies heavily on visualizing what is going on. It is not as easy to read meaning into tables of numbers as it is to make deductions from a graph, no matter how roughly drawn. Errors can remain undetected in tables more easily than in their graphic equivalents.

Java has very good facilities for drawing at the dot and line level, but constructing a graph from such primitive components, complete with axes, is quite a lengthy process. In order to enable the insight we need at little programming cost, we have devised a very easy to use `Graph` class. As with the other two classes, `Display` and `Text`, `Graph` will be used as a Case study itself later on in the book.

Graph class methods

We have already seen the `Graph` class in action in Example 2.2. Here is a list of its ten methods and the four colour constants that `Graph` defines:

The Graph class

```
//Basic
new Graph ()          - Compulsory instantiation
add(x, y)             - Adds a point to a list.
                        Expects points to come in x-order.
showGraph()           - Compulsory call to get the axes and graph drawn
                        and the window made visible

//Advanced
new Graph (graphTitle, xAxisTitle, yAxisTitle)
                      - Version of instantiation with labelling options.
                        Use empty strings if not all titles applicable
nextGraph()           - Starts a new graph on the same axes.
                        One showGraph call applies to all the graphs.
setColor(int 0 to 3)  - Choice of black, magenta, blue, red
                        (constants are available instead of numbers)
```

```
setSymbol(boolean)    - Deduced from the colour
                        (Convenient if colours are being set)
setSymbol(int 0 to 3)- circle, upside down triangle, triangle,
                        square (Used if colours are not being set)
setLine(boolean)      - Normally on, can be turned off. Used when
                        lines between points don't make sense.
setTitle(String)      - Will appear on a key alongside the symbol
                        and/or in the chosen colour
black, magenta,       - constants for colours. Equivalent to 0-3
blue, red
```

To use `Graph`, we must declare a `Graph` object as in its simplest form:

```
Graph g = new Graph ();
```

or we can supply titles for the graph and axes as explained. Thereafter, all we have to do is add each new (x, y) point to the graph, and then show the graph. In other words, for a simple graph, we only need three methods. Consider the next example.

EXAMPLE 3.7   Liquid flow with a graph

In Example 3.2, we calculated the flow through a variety of pipes of different radii. We sampled the flow for radii increasing every 5 cm, but the formula used is continuous. Therefore, it would be nice to show the output in graphic form. Here is a revised program that uses the `Graph` class, and also switches to the `Display` class for input–output.

```
import javagently.*;

public class LiquidFlowGraph {

  /* Liquid flow in a pipe     N T Bishop
   * --------------------      1990, 1999
   *
   * Calculates the flow rate of pipes for
   * various radii.
   * Illustrates use of the Graph class
   */

  public static void main (String args []) {

    // All the initial data gathering
    Display display = new Display("Liquid Flow from a pipe");
    double    flow = 2;      // m/s
    double    increaseCm = 5; // radius increment (cm)
    double    radiusCm = 10;  // smallest radius (cm)
    display.println(
      "***** Volume of liquid flowing from pipes *****");
```

```
    display.prompt("Flow in m/s", flow);
    display.prompt("Radius increment (cm)", increaseCm);
    display.prompt("Smallest radius (cm)", radiusCm);
    for (; ;) {
      display.ready("\nMake changes and press ready\n");

      radiusCm = display.getDouble("Smallest radius (cm)");
      increaseCm = display.getDouble("Radius increment (cm)");
      flow = display.getDouble("Flow in m/s");
      display.println("For flow at " + flow + "m/s");
      display.println("Radius in cm\tVolume in cu m/s");

      double radiusM = radiusCm / 100;     // smallest radius (m)
      double increaseM = increaseCm / 100;  // radius increment (m)
      double volumeFlow;

      // Declare the graph window with title and axes labels
      Graph g = new Graph ("Liquid flow from pipes","Radius (cm)",
                   "Flow (cu m/s)");

      for (int i = 0; i < 9; i++) {
        volumeFlow = Math.PI *
                Math.pow((radiusM + increaseM * i), 2)*flow;
        display.println(Text.writeDouble(radiusCm +
                    increaseCm * i, 8, 2) + "\t" +
                    Text.writeDouble(volumeFlow, 16, 4) );

        // add the points to the graph
        g.add(radiusCm + increaseCm * i,volumeFlow);
      }
      // show the graph
      g.showGraph();

      // position it over the display window
      display.reposition(g);
    }
  }
}
```

The display is given in Figure 3.5 and the graph output is shown on top of the display in a small window. This feature is activated by the `display.reposition` method. If we don't call `reposition`, then the graph window is quite large and one must switch between it and the display. However, there is no disadvatage in using `reposition`, because the graph window is completely resizable and can be stretched to any size by dragging the bottom right corner.

How `Graph` works

The `Graph` class takes the point supplied to it, and adds it to a list of points. When `showGraph` is called, the minimum and maximum point values for both *x* and *y* are used to determine the scale for the axes. There is no set axes that the points fit onto,

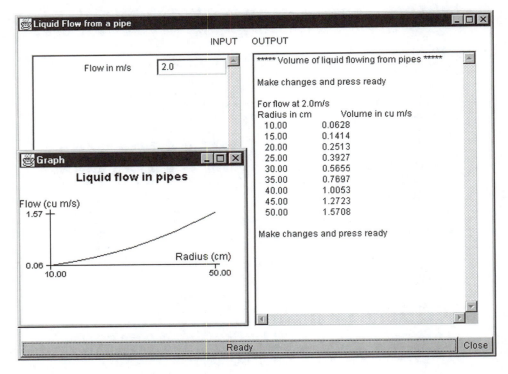

Figure 3.5 *Graph of liquid flow in a pipe*

and each graph window will therefore have a different set of axes. In the case of the above example, the minimum and maximum values as read off the display are

x	*y*
10.00	0.0628
50.00	1.5708

The origin and end of each axis are labelled accordingly. No attempt is made to place other labels along an axis, as there is no sure way of predicting what the user would like. The graph provides a rough impression of what is going on; for accurate values, the table printed on the display is used.

Advanced features

Before we get to the extra methods `Graph` provides, we discuss the issue of multiple graphs. Since `Graph` is a class, we can create multiple `Graph` objects, and each will have its own window. A program can therefore add points to different windows. This technique would be appropriate if we wanted the axes to differ.

If, however, we want to compare different graphs on the same axes, then we call `nextGraph`. This method starts up a new set of data points, `d`, for a new graph, and resets the parameters as follows:

```
d.plotType = black;
d.symbolRequired = false;
d.colorRequired = false;
d.titleRequired = false;
d.lineRequired = true;
```

Using the methods shown above, all of these can then be changed by the program. For example, a full set of changes would be

```
g.setColor(blue);
g.setSymbol(true);
g.setTitle("Rainfall");
g.setLine(false);
```

There is a relationship between the colour and the symbol: both map onto the integers 0 to 3, and in the absence of instructions to the contrary, the same integer is used for the symbol as that set for the colour. Thus black lines have circles, blue have triangles, and so on. If in the above set of instructions we want a blue line with circles, we would add

```
g.setSymbol(0);
```

Although colour is very effective on a screen, it cannot be shown easily in black and white, so graphs that are to be copied into reports should use symbols more often than those that won't. If there is no title, the symbol is still shown in the key at the bottom of the graph. If there is no symbol or title, then the colours are not explained in a key; it is assumed that the user can see them.

Further aspects of `Graph` are explored in the examples that conclude this chapter.

3.6 Numerical methods with for-loops

We now have enough knowledge of Java to turn our attention to our first numerical methods for solving scientific problems. The general area concerns simple circuits and the way to find approximate answers to problems in calculus that cannot be solved exactly. In the course of this book we shall be looking at several different types of such problems. The first we shall tackle is how to solve a differential equation.

Differential equations

Simple differential equations can be solved analytically, but as they become more complex, numerical techniques are necessary. An example of a first-order ordinary differential equation would be the formula for the velocity of an object falling under gravity through a fluid, e.g. water. This is

$$\frac{\mathrm{d}v}{\mathrm{d}t} = g - \frac{kv^a}{m}$$

The equation can be solved analytically if $a = 1$ or 2 but in general, e.g. for $a = 1.95$, this cannot be done.

Differential equations can be divided into **initial value problems** where information is given at only one value of x, and **boundary value problems**, where data is specified at both ends of a range of values for x. We shall consider here the theory for initial value problems and home in on a good method for solving one first-order equation. Solutions to boundary value problems are discussed in the case studies of Chapters 5 and 6. Consider the single first-order differential equation

$$\frac{\mathrm{d}y}{\mathrm{d}x} = f(x, y)$$

with y given at some initial value of x. Suppose that we want to solve for y in the interval $0 \le x \le L$ and with the initial value of y at $(x = 0)$ equal to y_0.

Euler's method

The simplest and probably best-known method for finding values of y for values of x is **Euler's method** (named after Leonhard Euler (1707–1783)). We split the interval $[0..L]$ up into n equal subintervals as shown in Figure 3.6 and let the length of each subinterval be $h = L/n$. Then we successively estimate a value for y_{i+1} in terms of x_i, y_i. For Euler's method the formula is

$$y_{i+1} = y_i + h f(x_i, y_i)$$

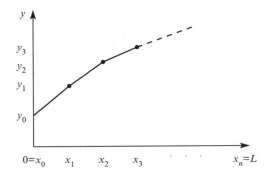

Figure 3.6 *Euler's method for solving a differential equation*

Most methods are set in the same framework but differ in the above formula. Although well known, Euler's method's poor accuracy means that it is rarely used in real life.

The predictor–corrector method

A more accurate method is the **predictor–corrector** method. Each step consists of two stages. First we use a **predictor** formula which gives a first estimate of the solution, i.e.

$$y_p = y + h f(x, y)$$

and then a **corrector** formula which uses y_p to obtain a better approximation, i.e.

$$y = y + \tfrac{1}{2}h[f(x, y) + f(x + h, y_p)]$$

This new value of y is fed back into the predictor, and the process repeated until the desired range of x values has been covered. Other methods that will be found in texts on numerical methods are Runge–Kutta methods (discussed in Problem 6.8), multi-step methods, and various improvements to the basic predictor–corrector method.

The algorithm for the predictor–corrector method is dominated by the loop over the interval of values for x. At each iteration, we need to compute the predictor value for y_{i+1}, compute the corrector value and then move on to the next subinterval, as in

> **Predictor–Corrector**
> Get a starting value for y at $x = 0$
> For n steps in the given interval of x
> Calculate y_p from y and the predictor formula
> Calculate y from y_p and the corrector formula

This algorithm can be translated into a Java method, with input and output added, but it will not be for general use, because the formula will be specific to the problem in hand. There is a way in Java of abstracting away from the formula, which is discussed in Chapter 6, where the method is taken up again. In the example that follows, we implement the algorithm for a specific case.

EXAMPLE 3.8   Current variation in an RL circuit

Problem   An electrical circuit consists of an inductance L, a resistance R and a constant power source E, as shown below. Initially the switch is open, and there is no current in the circuit. At time $t = 0$, the switch is closed and the current builds up. We want to know the variation in the current over the first 1 s after the switch is closed.

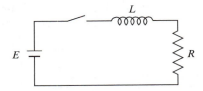

Solution   Once the switch is closed, the voltage changes around the circuit must add up to zero, by Kirchhoff's law. This gives

$$L\frac{\mathrm{d}I}{\mathrm{d}t} + RI - E = 0$$

which gives the differential equation

$$\frac{\mathrm{d}I}{\mathrm{d}t} = \frac{E}{L} - \frac{R}{L}I$$

Taking this as $f(t, I)$, we can use the predictor–corrector method to solve the differential equation for I at various intervals for t up to 1 s.

Program design   Obviously, we shall use the display for input–output, and shall also incorporate the Graph class, so that we can see what happens graphically. The question is how to divide the program into methods and classes. We adopt the model explained earlier at the end of section 3.4.

We define a class called CurrentPCSolver. The name indicates that it is a predictor–corrector solver, but that it is specific to the present problem. Inside the class we declare all the relevant data fields corresponding to the formula, e.g.

```
double E = 20;
double L = 5;
double R = 10;
double h = 0.01;
int    imax = 10;
double TS = 1;
```

Then we have an initialize method, which does the input and output, and a solve method, which does the predictor–corrector loop. To back up solve, we define the function for d*I*/d*t* as

```
double dbydt (double c) {
    return E/L - R*c/L;
}
```

The parameter, c, will be the current for the predictor formula and then the predicted current for the corrector formula. In other words, the two statements for predictor–corrector are

```
currentp = current + h * dbydt(current);
current += h * (dbydt(current) + dbydt(currentp)) / 2;
```

Going back to the data values, we see that, typically, *h* is taken as 0.01 and we may need to find the value of *I* for times up to *t* = 1 (seconds). That means that 100 intermediate values are calculated. We would probably like to know some of these intermediate values, but not all of them. We can use a nested loop, suppressing writing in the inner loop, and only printing values in the outer loop. Thus no writing gets done in solve, only in the loop that calls it.

Program   First let us consider the class we have described:

```
static class CurrentPCSolver {

  /* This predictor-corrector solver is customized for
   * an RL circuit. The data fields and formula are
   * specific to it.
   */

  double E = 20;
  double L = 5;
  double R = 10;
  double h = 0.01;
  int    imax = 10;
  double TS = 1;
  double current = 0;
  double t = 0;

  void initialize () {
    display.prompt("Emf source in volts", E);
    display.prompt("Inductance in henries", L);
    display.prompt("Resistance in ohms", R);
    display.prompt("Step length", h);
    display.prompt("Iterations before reporting", imax);
    display.prompt("Stopping time in seconds", TS);
    display.ready("Make changes and press ready");

    E = display.getDouble("Emf source in volts");
    L = display.getDouble("Inductance in henries");
    R = display.getDouble("Resistance in ohms");
    h = display.getDouble("Step length");
    imax = display.getInt("Iterations before reporting");
    TS = display.getDouble("Stopping time in seconds");
  }

  double dbydt (double c) {
    return E/L - R*c/L;
  }

  void solve () {
    double currentp;

    // The predictor-corrector loop
    for(int i = 1; i <= imax; i++) {
      currentp = current + h * dbydt(current);
      current += h * (dbydt(current) + dbydt(currentp)) / 2;
```

```
        t += h;
      }
    }
  }
```

The program will include this class and create its `CurrentPCSolver` object in order to be able to access both the variables and the methods. For example, if the object declaration is

```
CurrentPCSolver pc = new CurrentPCSolver();
```

then the number of reports, which is local to the `main` methods, is calculated from

```
int reports = (int) (pc.TS / pc.h / pc.imax);
```

`pc` is the object and `TS`, `h` and `imax` are all fields of the object. Here is the program itself.

```
import javagently.*;

class RLCurrent {

  /* Solving an RL Circuit
   * with a Predictor-Corrector        N T and J M Bishop
   * ===========================       1990, 1999
   *
   * An RL Circuit that obeys Kirchhoff's Law is solved
   * by a predictor-corrector method customized for
   * this problem
   *
   * Illustrates the Graph class and the structuring of
   * a numerical algorithm as methods in a member class.
   */

  static Display display = new Display("RL Current");

  static class CurrentPCSolver {

    /* This predictor-corrector solver is customized for
     * an RL circuit. The data fields and formula are
     * specific to it.
     *
     */
    double E = 20;
    double L = 5;
    double R = 10;
    double h = 0.01;
    int    imax = 10;
    double TS = 1;
    double current = 0;
    double t = 0;

    void initialize () {
      display.prompt("Emf source in volts", E);
      display.prompt("Inductance in henries", L);
```

```java
      display.prompt("Resistance in ohms", R);
      display.prompt("Step length", h);
      display.prompt("Iterations before reporting", imax);
      display.prompt("Stopping time in seconds", TS);
      display.ready("Make changes and press ready");

      E = display.getDouble("Emf source in volts");
      L = display.getDouble("Inductance in henries");
      R = display.getDouble("Resistance in ohms");
      h = display.getDouble("Step length");
      imax = display.getInt("Iterations before reporting");
      TS = display.getDouble("Stopping time in seconds");
    }

    double dbydt (double c) {
      return E/L - R*c/L;
    }

    void solve () {
      double currentp;

      // The predictor-corrector loop
      for(int i = 1; i <= imax; i++) {
        currentp = current + h * dbydt(current);
        current += h * (dbydt(current) + dbydt(currentp)) / 2;
        t += h;
      }
    }
  }

  public static void main (String [] args) {

    Graph g = new Graph("RL Circuit", "Time", "Current");
    display.println(
            "***** Electrical current in an RL circuit *****");
    display.println(
            "***** Using predictor-corrector algorithm *****");
    display.println("Solves: dl/dt = E/L - RI/L");
    display.println("The current, I, is given in amps\n");

    CurrentPCSolver pc = new CurrentPCSolver ();

    pc.initialize();
    display.println("  t \t I");
    int reports = (int) (pc.TS / pc.h / pc.imax);

    for(int j = 0; j <= reports; j++) {
      display.println(Text.format(pc.t,5,2)+
                      Text.format(pc.current,18,4));
      g.add(pc.t,pc.current);
      pc.solve();
    }

    g.showGraph();
  }
}
```

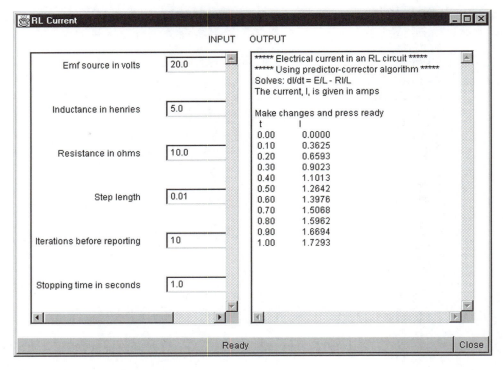

Figure 3.7 *Display for the* RL *current solver*

Testing The display for the program is given in Figure 3.7 A graph for this data is shown in Figure 3.8. We could vary the data by running the process over 5 seconds instead of 1 second, and would find that the current reaches the stable value of about 2 amps after about 3 seconds.

Fourier series

There are many problems in engineering which depend on periodic functions, such as the current in a circuit with an alternating voltage. For example, the waveform of a cathode-ray oscilloscope sweep generator is given by

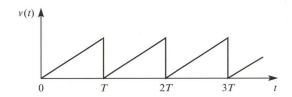

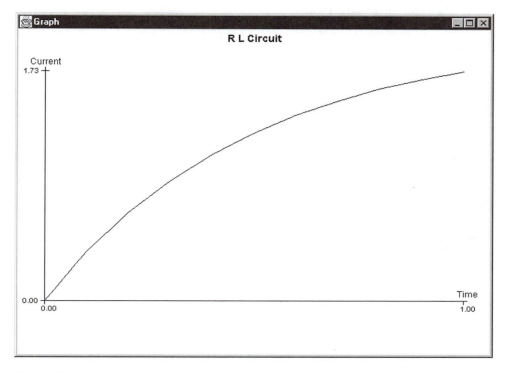

Figure 3.8 RL *circuit solved over 1 second*

where T is the fundamental period of the function. This sort of function can be approximated by a series of trigonometrical functions, known as a **Fourier series** (named after Jean Baptiste Joseph Fourier (1768–1830)). The value of the function at successive points can then be calculated by evaluating the series. Fourier showed that if $f(t)$ is periodic, then it can be expressed as

$$f(t) = a_v + \sum_{n=1}^{\infty} (a_n \cos n\omega t + b_n \sin n\omega t)$$

where a_v, a_n and b_n are Fourier coefficients and are calculated from $f(t)$, and ω is related by $\omega = T/2\pi$ to the fundamental period, T, of the function. For example, the simple square-periodic wave function given by

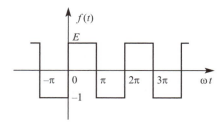

can be approximated by the Fourier series

$$f(t) = \frac{4E}{\pi}(\sin \omega t + \tfrac{1}{3}\sin 3\omega t + \tfrac{1}{5}\sin 5\omega t + \dots)$$

Given the symmetry in the terms, this kind of formula should be easy to convert into a program. One problem would be how to sum to infinity. Clearly, we shall have to cut off somewhere. There is a way of calculating how many terms are needed, which depends on the accuracy required, and this is covered in Example 6.7 on the temperature in a plate. We shall meanwhile choose some large number, such as 100, for the example that follows.

EXAMPLE 3.9 Circuit with a rectified sinusoidal voltage

Problem The circuit in Example 3.5 is to be supplied not with a constant power source, but one with a voltage that has the following waveform:

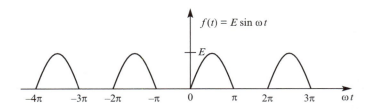

We want to examine the current in the circuit over the first two seconds this time.

Solution The voltage with the above waveform can be approximated with a Fourier series:

$$v(t) = \frac{E}{\pi} + \frac{E}{2}\sin \omega t - \frac{2E}{\pi}\left(\frac{\cos 2\omega t}{2^2 - 1} + \frac{\cos 4\omega t}{4^2 - 1} + \frac{\cos 6\omega t}{6^2 - 1} + \dots\right)$$

The current in the circuit is given by

$$I = \frac{V}{Z}$$

where

V	is the voltage computed at $\omega t - \alpha$
α	is the phase lag $= \arctan(L\omega / R)$
Z	is the impedance given by $\sqrt{R^2 + L^2\omega^2}$.

So we can write a program to calculate I for various values of t.

There are a lot of formulas! Nevertheless, it is possible to break the problem down. We want to evaluate *I* at various values of *t*. This reduces to evaluating *v*(*t*) and dividing by *Z*. Evaluating *v*(*t*) consists of taking the first two terms and the multiplier, and then doing the series, which we shall call *S*, i.e.

$$v(t) = \frac{E}{\pi} + \frac{E}{2}\sin\omega t - \frac{2E}{\pi}S$$

Evaluating *S* is done in a loop for *i* = 2, 4, 6 …, adding up the terms

$$\frac{\cos i\omega t}{i^2 - 1}$$

Program design   Once again, we adopt the model of taking all the data, its input–output and the solver process out into its own class, which we call `Fourier Approximation`. This class is completely self-contained, and we give it first:

```
static class FourierApproximation {

    //Input data fields
    double omega;      // rad/s
    double TS;         // seconds
    int    noterms;    // no. of terms
    double h;          // time between reports
    double E;          // volts
    double L;          // inductance in henries
    double R;          // resistance in ohms
    String name;       // characteristics of the data set

    // Calculation variables
    double v;          // volts
    double alpha;      // phase lag
    double Z;          // impedence

    void initialize() {

        // Display default values
        display.prompt ("Data set name", "Default");
        display.prompt ("Voltage amplitude in Volts, E", 20);
        display.prompt ("Periodic frequency in rad/s, w",10);
        display.prompt ("Inductance in henries, L", 5);
        display.prompt ("Resistance in ohms, R", 10);
        display.prompt ("Stopping time in secs, TS", 2);
        display.prompt ("Interval between reports", 0.1);
        display.prompt ("No. of Fourier terms", 100);
    }

    void getData () {
        // Open for changes
        display.ready("Press the button when values are ready");
```

```
                // Read current values off input display
                name = display.getString("Data set name");
                E = display.getDouble("Voltage amplitude in Volts, E");
                omega = display.getDouble("Periodic frequency in rad/s, w");
                L = display.getDouble("Inductance in henries, L");
                R = display.getDouble("Resistance in ohms, R");
                TS = display.getDouble("Stopping time in secs, TS");
                h = display.getDouble("Interval between reports");
                noterms = display.getInt("No. of Fourier terms");
                display.println("Graph for data with "+name);
            }

            double sumOfFourierTerms (double t) {
                double S = 0;   // sum of Fourier terms
                for(int i = 1; i<=noterms; i++)
                S += Math.cos(2*i*(omega*t - alpha)) / (Math.pow(2*i,2)-1);
                return S;
            }

            double solve (double t) {
                alpha = Math.atan(L * omega / R);
                Z = Math.sqrt(Math.pow(R,2) + Math.pow(L,2)
                    * Math.pow(omega,2));
                v = E / Math.PI +
                    E * Math.sin(omega*t - alpha) / 2 -
                    2 * E / Math.PI * sumOfFourierTerms(t);
                return v/Z;
            }
        }
```

Now the main program is quite small, and concerned mainly with driving the display and the graph in a loop, so that several options can be tried out. In the above nested class, we include one field, for the name of the data set. This name is passed on to the Graph class, and used to identify the graph being drawn. Thus we can test several different sets of data and get a feel for how they compared on the same set of axes. The program is

```
import javagently.*;

class RLCircuitSinusoidal {

    /* Solving an RL Circuit with sinusoidal voltage
     * using Fourier series              N T and J M Bishop
     * =====================             1990, 1999
     *
     * Illustrates summation of a Fourier series,
     * as well as the use of the Graph class to plot
     * several graphs for different values
     * of the parameters.
     */

    static Display display = new Display("Sinusoidal Voltage");

    insert member class here
```

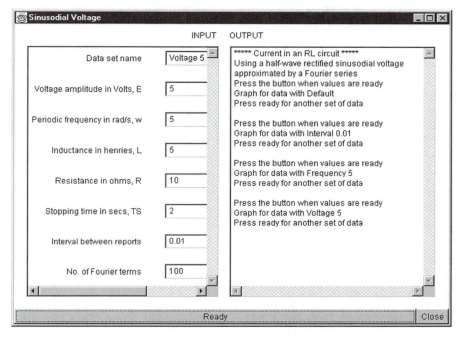

Figure 3.9 *Display for the* RL *circuit program*

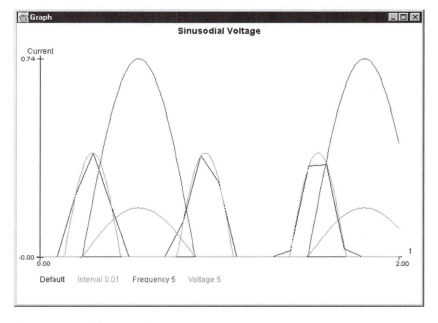

Figure 3.10 *Four half sinusoidal graphs using Fourier series*

```
public static void main (String [] args) {

    Graph g = new Graph ("Sinusoidal Voltage",
                "t", "Current");
    FourierApproximation fa = new FourierApproximation ();

    int reports;
    double current;    // amps
    double t;       // seconds

    display.println("***** Current in an RL circuit *****");
    display.println("Using a half-wave rectified " +
                "sinusodial voltage");
    display.println("approximated by a Fourier series");
    fa.initialize();
    fa.getData();

    for (int i=0; ;i++) {
      reports = (int) (fa.TS / fa.h);
      t = 0.0;
      g.setTitle(fa.name);
      g.setColor(i%4);

      for(int j=0; j<=reports; j++) {
        current = fa.solve(t);
        g.add(t, current);
        t += fa.h;
      }
      g.showGraph();
      display.ready("Press ready for another set of data\n");
      fa.getData();
      g.nextGraph();
    }
  }
}
```

Testing A display with the default data is given as Figure 3.9. After four data sets have been tried, the graph is shown in Figure 3.10. The default graph with an interval of 0.1 was too rough, so we decreased the interval to 0.01, giving a smoother graph. Changing the frequency from 10 to 5 produced fewer maxima but at a maximum current of 0.74 amps, compared to the original 0.39. For the final test, we brought the voltage right down to 5, giving the low curve.

QUIZ

3.1 How many stars (asterisks) would the following loop print out?

```
for (int star = 9; star<0; star--){
  System.out.print("**");
}
```

3.2 Write a loop to print out the decades of the twentieth century (e.g. 1900, 1910 ... 1990)

3.3   If the following prompt on the display had been made, give **two** methods that would be needed in order to retrieve the corresponding real value.

```
display.prompt("Starting value in Ohms", 3.5);
```

3.4   If we forget to call the `ready` method in the `Display` class, and go straight from prompts to gets, what will happen?

3.5   Give a typed method to convert dollars into euros, where one parameter is the amount to be converted and the other is the exchange rate.

3.6   What method do we call in the `Graph` class to start a new graph on the same axes?

3.7   We created two graphs, but there is no output. What do you think happened?

3.8   Give the `Graph` method calls to set the points we are drawing to be plotted as magenta circles, with no lines between them, on a graph called `Readings`.

3.9   In Examples 3.8, why did we call the class with the predictor–corrector solve methods `CurrentPCSolver` rather than just `PCSolver`?

3.10   If we had a similar class called `CurrentEulerSolver`, give a statement to create a Euler solving object.

PROBLEMS

3.1   **Multiple resistances.**   Extend Example 3.5 to cater for a variable number of resistances in parallel. The program should start off by asking for the number of resistors. The output should be simplified to exclude the diagram of the resistors (since we won't know how many to draw).

3.2   **Checksums.**   Savanna University gives each student a student number which consists of four digits and ends with a checksum digit which is computed by taking the sum of the preceding digits modulo 4. These checksums need to be verified. Write a program which uses the display and will repeatedly allow a student number to be entered, and will check it and display the result.

Some sample numbers might be

```
1234 2        1 + 2 + 3 + 4 = 10;      10 mod 4 = 2;      correct
5682 1        5 + 6 + 8 + 2 = 21;      21 mod 4 = 1;      correct
7007 1        7 + 0 + 0 + 7 = 14;      14 mod 4 = 2;      incorrect
```

Hint: The number will have to be decomposed, digit by digit. This can be done simply by repeatedly taking modulo 10. At the same time, the digits can be added and then the sum checked against the check digit.

3.3   **Variable shifts.**   Working from Problem 2.6, make a general shift calculator program using the display for entering the time and for showing the remaining hours and minutes.

3.4   **Inverted amplifier.**   Consider the following inverting amplifier circuit, representing an ideal operational amplifier operating within its linear range. The terminal voltage v_0 is given by

$$v_0 = \frac{-R_f}{R_s}v_s$$

and the amplifier saturates when

$$\left|\frac{V_{CC}}{v_s}\right| > \frac{R_f}{R_s}$$

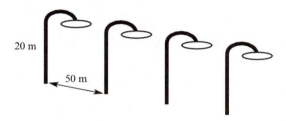

Write a program which reads in values for the two resistors R_f and R_s in kΩ, and the operational amplifier voltage V_{CC} in volts, and calculates the range of input voltages v_s such that the amplifier does not saturate. For this range of inputs, print the output voltage v_0.

3.5 **Street lamps.** A street is lit by four lamps of 1000 W each on lamp posts 20 m high and 50 m apart, i.e.

20 m

50 m

The intensity of illumination, in candelas, produced by a lamp of height h and power C at a point d from the post is given by

$$L = \frac{Ch}{(h^2 + d^2)^{1.5}}$$

The level of illumination at any one point can therefore be found by adding up the contributions of each of the four lamps. Write a program which calculates the intensity of illumination at 10 metre intervals under the lamps. Present your results in a graph.
Hint: Although specific values have been given for C, h and d, construct the program so that these values are read in, and test your program for various different sets of data.

3.6 **Trigonometric and hyperbolic functions.** Java provides `sin`, `cos`, `tan`, `asin`, `acos` and `atan` functions in the `Math` class. We would like to extend this repertoire to include the inverse and hyperbolic functions. The formulas for these functions, in terms of functions that are already known, are

cot(x) $\dfrac{\cos(x)}{\sin(x)}$

sec(x) $\dfrac{1}{\cos(x)}$

csc(x) $\dfrac{1}{\sin(x)}$

sinh(x) $\dfrac{e^x - e^{-x}}{2}$

| cosh(x) | $\dfrac{e^x + e^{-x}}{2}$ |
| tanh(x) | $\dfrac{e^x - e^{-x}}{e^x + e^{-x}}$ |

Write a class called `Trig` which supplies these as static methods. Test your class by plotting the functions on a graph for values from $-\pi$ to π.

3.7 **A number triangle.** Write a program which uses for-statements and `print/println` statements to produce the following triangle on the display. Read in the number of lines required (five are shown here).

```
1
2 2
3 3 3
4 4 4 4
5 5 5 5 5
```

Adapt the program to print the triangle so that the numbers are centred, as below. Adapt it again to print the triangle upside down. This is called Pascal's triangle.

```
    1
   2 2
  3 3 3
 4 4 4 4
5 5 5 5 5
```

3.8 **Approximating logs.** The natural logarithmic function ln(x) can be approximated by the series

$$\ln(1 + x) = x - \frac{x^2}{2} + \frac{x^3}{3} + \frac{x^4}{4} \ldots$$

for $-1 < x < 1$. Write a program which computes the first eight terms of the series and outputs the value of the function for values of x in a given interval and with a given step. In each case, print the corresponding value of Java's log function. Plot two graphs on the same axes, one showing the approximation and one the actual values.

3.9 **Sensitive drug.** A sensitive drug cannot sustain a change in temperature of more than 30°C in a 24 hour period. The temperatures are monitored and recorded at 05, 11, 17 and 23 hours. Write a program that runs in the lab and on which the lab technician on duty can enter the values at the four monitor times. At any time, the program can report a table and graph of the values for the past 24 hours, so the technician can decide whether or not to throw the drug away.

3.10 **The Fibonacci series** consists of a series of numbers in which each number is the sum of the two preceding ones, i.e.

```
1  1  2  3  5  8  13  21  34  55 ...
```

Write a program to display the first 50 terms of the series. Using a nested for-loop, adapt the program so that it displays only every third number. What do you notice about the numbers?

3.11 **RL circuit again.** The *RL* circuit discussed in Example 3.9 is to be supplied with a voltage having a simple square waveform which is approximated by the Fourier series

$$f(t) = \frac{4E}{\pi}(\sin\omega t + \tfrac{1}{3}\sin 3\omega t + \tfrac{1}{5}\sin 5\omega t + \dots)$$

Adapt the program in Example 3.9 to print out the current for this new waveform.

3.12 **Euler's method.** Write a method to implement Euler's method for solving a differential equation (section 3.6). Test the method by placing it in a class and program as described in Example 3.8, and test it on the same formulas and data. Compare the results to those obtained for the predictor–corrector method, showing both on a graph.

3.13 **Gravity.** The velocity of an object starting from rest and falling under gravity through a fluid is given by the differential equation

$$m\frac{dv}{dt} = mg - kv^2$$

where

m and v are the object's mass and velocity (take m = 2 kg),
t is time,
g is the gravitational acceleration, taken as 9.8 m/s^2,
k is a constant depending on the object's size and shape and on the fluid (take k = 100 N/m^{2}s^2).

Use the predictor–corrector method (Example 3.8) to find the terminal velocity v_T.

3.14 **Method comparison.** Use the `Euler` class developed in Problem 3.12 to solve the problem in 3.13, and compare the results obtained to those for the predictor–corrector method on a graph.

3.15 **More comparisons.** Use the Euler method and the predictor–corrector method to solve the following differential equations:

(a) Find q(π) if dq/du = q^2sin(u) with q(0) = 0.2.

(b) Find y(2) if dy/dt = $\sqrt{t(1 + y)}$ with y(1) = –0.88888.

3.16 **Birthdays.** The probability of two people in a group of n having the same birthday is

$$p(n) = 1 - \frac{365}{365} \times \frac{364}{365} \times \frac{363}{365} \times \dots \times \frac{365 - n + 1}{365}$$

Write a program to evaluate and print this probability for groups of 2 to 60 people. Plot n against $p(n)$ on a graph.

3.17 **Many currents.** Example 3.8 on the current variation in an RL circuit uses the `Display` and `Graph` classes, but does not allow for more than one set of data. Extend the program so that data can be re-entered.
Note: the initialize method will have to be split in two.

CHAPTER 4

Controlling

4.1 Files for input and output

The `Display` class introduced in Chapter 3 provides an easy interaction with a program. However, as we already saw when tables were being printed, it can become unwieldy. In scientific computing, there is often the need to read in large quantities of data, or to print out tables which may occupy several pages of paper. In these cases, the `Display` class is inadequate and we need to use the time-honoured method of **files**.

Java's approach to reading numbers

Java can easily read numeric values if they are already in binary form and stored in a file. To get them into binary form, they would have to be written out by some other program to the file. In the first instance, however, the data will most likely be created via a text editor, and consist of numbers (and strings perhaps) stored as text.

The Java approach is that we do the conversion from text to binary explicitly in the program. The conversion routines are supplied with classes associated with the primitive types, as well as through special classes available in the `java.text` package. The same classes can be used for output formatting.

Although powerful, these classes are not simple to use, which is a shame because reading a number is, after all, an operation that we may need to perform frequently. Here is what reading a real number would look like:

```
double d = Double.valueOf(in.readLine()).doubleValue();
```

Of course, such complexity can be easily hidden in a method and similar methods can be made for integer numbers and the other types. To collect the methods together, we created the `Text` class which provides the functionality required.

In fairness, it must be said that the `java.text` classes are well designed and make for very versatile programming in the international context, as they cover such input as dates and currencies, as well as numbers. This aspect is covered in Chapter 10.

Java Gently's `Text` class

The class defined for the *Java Gently* family of books is called `Text`[†] and it provides the methods shown in the following form:

The `Text` class

```
BufferedReader open    (String filename)
BufferedReader open    (InputStream in)
printWriter create     (String filename)

int     readInt        (BufferedReader in)
double  readDouble     (BufferedReader in)
String  readString     (BufferedReader in)
char    readChar       (BufferedReader in)

void    prompt         (String s)
String  format         (int number, int align)
String  format         (double number, int align, int frac)
```

The first three methods are concerned with getting files ready for use. The next four substitute for Java's difficult approach to input, and the last three give more control over output as we have already examined in section 2.5. All the methods in `Text` are declared static, and are therefore referred to via their class name, e.g. `Text.open`.

When using the `Text` class for input (as opposed to output) we actively make use of classes in `java.io`, e.g. `BufferedReader`. Therefore we must import the `java.io` package in which these classes are defined.

[†] There is fortunately no confusion with Java's `text` package because that has a small t. Moreover, `java.text` is a package, whereas our `Text` is a class. Our `Text` class pre-dates `java.text` package, which came out with version 1.1.

One side effect of reading is that something could go wrong, e.g. the data might end unexpectedly or have the wrong format. Such events are called **exceptions** and we shall see later in the chapter how to deal with them. However, Java requires that we indicate in every method those exceptions which can occur. Therefore if we are going to read, we also need to add the phrase `throws IOException` after the method declaration, e.g.:

```
static public void main (String args []) throws exception {
```

Opening a file for reading

To open a file for reading, we must have a valid file name as a string. If `numbers.data` is such a file name, then we can call

```
BufferedReader fin = Text.open ("numbers.data");
```

If `numbers.data` is not a valid file name, an exception condition will occur. How to handle exceptions is covered later on in this chapter. There is nothing special about the name `fin`. It is a common abbreviation for file input, but we can call files by any identifier that is meaningful. We can also perform several opens on different actual files, and access them simultaneously. Merging values from a group of files is an example where this facility would be useful.

Reading data

`BufferedReader` is a class in Java's input–output package and is the best one provided for accessing text data. The above statement creates `fin` as a `BufferedReader` object, which means that `fin` can then be passed to any of the `Text` methods which needs a `BufferedReader` parameter, e.g.:

```
int i = Text.readInt(fin);
```

`Text` allows multiple items on a line. It allows – and ignores – blank lines and spaces between data items. It does not allow them inside strings, however, for the simple reason that a space is taken to end a data item.

EXAMPLE 4.1   Summing numbers

Problem   We have 40 numbers to be read and totalled.

Solution   It is highly recommended to type the numbers into a file with a text editor, check them (by printing them out first), and then submit them to a program.

Program design   Let's call the file `numbers.data`. Without using the display this time, we can write a simple console-based program to print out the required sum.

```
import java.io.*;
import javagently.*;

class Summation {

  /* The Summation program        by J M Bishop Aug 1996
   * --------------------         Java 1.1 Oct 1997
   *                              adapted July 1999
   *
   * Reads in numbers from a file and displays their sum.
   *
   * Illustrates the use of input files.
   */

  public static void main(String args []) throws IOException {

    BufferedReader fin = Text.open("numbers.data");

    double total = 0;
    double number;
    System.out.println(
            "****** Summing from numbers.data file ******");
    for (int i = 1; i <= 40; i++) {
      number = Text.readDouble(fin);
      total += number;
    }
    System.out.println("The total is "+total);
  }
}
```

If the file contained all zeros, except for the first five numbers which were 23, –18, 45, 11 and 2, then the output would be

```
**** Summing from numbers.data file ****
The total is 63.0
```

Of course, the program is only really useful if the number of input items is indeterminate; we shall learn how to handle such a case in section 4.4.

Outputting to a file

It is very useful to be able to send output to a file. Not only does it make it easy to retain the results and print them out, but very often programs produce too much output to appear sensibly on the screen. Furthermore, we may produce data which is actually never seen by humans, but serves as input to some other program.

In the same way as we set up a file input stream, we can set up a file output stream, but this time we use the create method:

```
PrintWriter fout = Text.create("results.out");
```

PrintWriter corresponds to BufferedReader (although it doesn't sound like it). To write out numbers to a file where a neat format is not necessary, we just use `println`. But if there are more than one number on a line, then we ourselves must separate them by spaces, otherwise they will not be able to be read in again. For example, if *x* is 4.5 and *y* is 0.001, then

```
fout.print((x) + (y));
```

and what will appear on the file is

4.50.001

So the better course of action, even for a file, is to use formatted output via the `Text` class, as in

```
fout.print(Text.format(x,10,4)+ Text.format(y,10,4));
```

An important consideration for output files is that they must be closed before the program ends, otherwise all the writing done to them is lost. The method in `PrintWriter` is

```
fout.close();
```

Connecting to the keyboard

So far we have studiously avoided discussing how data is simply read from the keyboard. We have access to files and the display, but what about the Java console? We shall now complete the picture, but do note that several development environments on the market will not react correctly to what follows.

The Java equivalent of `System.out` is `System.in`. Although `System.in` is also a pre-declared field, its class is `InputStream`, which is an **abstract** class in Java terms. Abstract classes are covered fully in Chapter 6, but what we need to know here is that `System.in` is not automatically available for use like `System.out` is. The `System.in` object must be supplied as a constructor parameter to `Text.open` as follows:

```
BufferedReader in = Text.open(System.in);
```

which will declare `in` as the stream that is connected to the keyboard. Let us look first at how to read strings from the keyboard.

Reading strings

There are two ways to read strings:

Reading a string
string = Text.readString(*stream*); *string* = *stream*.readLine();

There is only one difference between the two: `readLine` gets a whole line of input, whereas `Text.readString` picks off the next piece of text ending with a space or end-of-line. Thus to read a single word, `readString` can be used to maintain compatibility with the other read methods, but if we know that the string is going to contain spaces, we use the second version.

There is a third way of reading strings, where the end of each string can be customized. Tokenizers are used here, as described in Chapter 10.

EXAMPLE 4.2 Greetings

The next example shows simple interaction through the keyboard and screen. We want to read in a name of someone (which might contain spaces) and print it out again. Therefore we choose the `readLine` method. Notice that we have to import `java.io` (because of `readLine` and the possibility of the request to open the file not working and throwing an exception) as well as `javagently` (to gain access to `Text.open`).

```
import java.io.*;
import javagently.*;

class Greetings {

  /*  A simple greetings program   by J M Bishop  Oct 1996
   *  -------------------------    Java 1.1  Dec 1997
   */

  public static void main (String args []) throws IOException {

    BufferedReader in = Text.open(System.in);

    System.out.print("Who is your hero? ");
    String name = in.readLine();
    System.out.println("I also like " + name);
  }
}
```

Testing   Here is a sample run, using plain type for the input and bold for output as before:

```
Who is your hero? Albert Einstein
I also like Albert Einstein
```

Reading numbers from the keyboard is made reasonable by using the methods in the `Text` class, as already explained. Example 4.3 uses the keyboard, the screen and two files.

More about reading

There are two interesting aspects about reading with the `Text` class. Firstly, the read methods are couched as typed, rather than void, methods. Therefore they return the value read in. That is why there are four of them: we must choose the correct one for the type of variable that we are assigning. Secondly, the Text class has a very forgiving nature. It is programmed so that if reading a number fails because the data is incorrect, then it will go round and try the next part of the data. This feature is only a blessing when reading from the keyboard; when reading from a file, it is not useful, because the data and the program will quickly get out of synchronization.

EXAMPLE 4.3   Part numbers

Problem   A technical laboratory has a file of some 200 parts used in its products. The technicians wish to assign serial numbers to the parts, starting from the code for the laboratory, which is 5000.

Solution   Regard the parts as lines of text and copy them to a destination stream, adding on the part numbers. To add flexibility, the starting number can be read off the keyboard in response to a query.

Example   Given a disk file called parts.data containing parts such as

```
Widgets, curly
Widgets, plain
Gadgets, purple
Thingies, bolted
Ghizmos, striped
```

the required table will be written to a file parts.out with numbers starting at 5000, as in

```
5000   Widgets, curly
5001   Widgets, plain
5002   Gadgets, purple
5003   Thingies, bolted
5004   Ghizmos, striped
```

Program   The program makes use of four streams: fin, fout, in and out. Only out is predefined by Java, so the other three are declared in the program. Because we have not yet learnt how to stop reading from a file, we have set the number of parts at five for now.

```java
import java.io.*;
import javagently.*;

class PartCodes {

    /* The Part Codes program    by J M Bishop 1990
     * ----------------------    Java July 1999
     *
     * Assigns numbers to parts read from a file.
     * Illustrates file input and output.
     */
```

```
public static void main(String args []) throws IOException {

    BufferedReader in  = Text.open(System.in);
    BufferedReader fin = Text.open("parts.data");
    PrintWriter    fout= Text.create("parts.out");

    int number = 0;
    String part;
    System.out.println(
            "****** Parts from parts.data file ******");
    Text.prompt("Part starting number? ");
    number = Text.readInt(in);
    Text.prompt("Writing to file parts.out");

    for (int i = number; i < number+5; i++) {
      part = fin.readLine();
      fout.println(i+"  "+part);
      Text.prompt(".");
    }
    fout.close();
  }
}
```

Once again we used readLine instead of readString because the parts consist of more than one word.

Testing   When the program is run, the following will appear on the screen:

```
****** Parts from parts.data file ******
Part starting number?  5000
Writing to file parts.out . . . . .
```

We have used a time-honoured technique here of showing what is happening while a file is being read. Each time round the loop, we print a dot on the screen to signify another line read. For very long files, this enables the user to see that the program is still running.

4.2 The types boolean and char

Before we go on to the main methods of controlling a program – if, switch and exception – we first introduce the remaining two primitive data types in Java, boolean and char.

Booleans

Conditions govern the decisions made in programs as to alternative paths to follow. A condition yields a value **true** or **false**. Another name for a condition is a **boolean**

expression.[†] Boolean expressions use the six comparison operators to compare the results of numeric expressions. The operators are

==	equal to
!=	not equal to
>	greater than
<	less than
>=	greater than or equal to
<=	less than or equal to

The result of such an expression can be stored in a **boolean variable**. For example, given the declarations

```
boolean isaMinor, isaPensioner;
int age;
```

we can store various facts about the age of someone as

```
isaMinor = age < 18;
isaPensioner = age >=65;
```

and display these later using

```
System.out.println ("Driver's licence denied: " + isaMinor);
```

If your age is 15, then `isaMinor` would be false so the statement would print

Driver's licence denied: true

As another example,

```
System.out.println ("It is " + isaPensioner +
            " that you can ride the bus for free.");
```

will display for a 15-year-old:

It is false that you can ride the bus for free.

Boolean expressions

There are also the boolean operators:

&	and
|	or
^	xor, the exclusive or
!	not

† Named after George Boole, the nineteenth-century mathematician.

and &	false	true		xor ^	false	true
false	false	false		false	false	true
true	false	true		true	true	false

or |	false	true		not !	
false	false	true		false	true
true	true	true		true	false

Figure 4.1 *Boolean operator tables*

For the expression (x & y) to be true, both x and y must be true; for the expression (x | y) to be true, either x or y or both can be true. There is also a precedence between the operators, so that in the absence of brackets, & will always be evaluated before |. The results of the operators are summarized in Figure 4.1.

    Referring back to the earlier example with the minor and pensioner conditions, suppose we make the declarations:[†]

```
boolean isEmployed, isaYoungWorker, isaVoter, isaTaxpayer;
```

Then further facts can be deduced as follows:

```
isaYoungWorker = isaMinor & isEmployed;
isaVoter = ! isaMinor;
isaTaxpayer = isaVoter | isEmployed;
```

Boolean operators can be combined to express more complex conditions. For example, if both minors and pensioners can go free on the buses provided they are not working, then we have

```
boolean freeBus = (isaPensioner | isaMinor) & !isEmployed;
```

The brackets are needed so that the | is evaluated first.

    Boolean operators are very useful in conjunction with the comparison operators in establishing detailed conditions. An example is an expression for deciding whether school should be cancelled because it is too cold or too hot, i.e.:

```
goHome = temperature > 40 | temperature < 0;
```

In Java, the precedence between the comparison operators and the boolean ones is such that the comparisons will always be executed first (i.e. they have higher precedence). In other languages, the reverse is true, and many programmers are used to putting brackets around conditions. You might often see an expression such as the go home test written as

```
goHome = (temperature > 40) | (temperature < 0);
```

---

† It is a useful habit to preface boolean variables with is or isa so that expressions that use them read more naturally.

On the other hand the concatenation operator does take precedence over & and |. To print out a&b and a|b, we cannot use

```
println(a&b + a|b);  // wrong
```

because + will try to operate on the central b + a, and will report an error. Instead, we introduce brackets:

```
println((a&b) + (a|b));
```

Java also has 'short-circuit' versions of *and* and *or* which are the && and || operators respectively. In the case of

```
c && d
```

d will only be evaluated if c is true. Similarly, for ||, once c has been established as true, d is ignored. A nice example of such operators is establishing whether one date (comprised of three integers) is earlier than another. The statement – quite long – would be

```
boolean earlier = y1 < y2 ||
                  (y1 == y2 && m1 < m2) ||
                  (y1 == y2 && m1 == m2 && d1 < d2);
```

To summarize, the precedence of the boolean operators and comparisons is

```
group 0:   ()
group 1:   !
group 2:   &
group 3:   |
group 4:   &&
group 5:   ||
```

Characters

We have already looked informally at strings in Java and they are covered formally in Chapter 10. A string in Java is an object, and a single character in quotes, e.g. "a", is also a string. Java provides a more simple type for single characters on a keyboard, typically

A to Z

a to z

! @ # $ % ^ & * ( ) _ + - = { } [ ] : " | ; ' ~ `? /

In addition, we can represent some other keyboard characters with the escape prefix:

\b	backspace
\t	tab
\n	new line
\f	new page (i.e. form feed)

Notice that these particular keyboard keys cannot otherwise appear on the screen: they cause special effects when pressed.

Characters in Java are written with a single quote, e.g. 'a', and the following operations are automatically valid for them:

- assignment
- comparison (all the six comparison operators described above)
- concatenation to strings.

The result of a comparison for less or greater than depends on the order of the characters as set up in Java. What we need to know is that the letters are in order so that 'g' < 'z', for example.

There are several useful class methods defined for characters via char's companion class Character. These are shown in the form

```
Character class methods

int     digit (char ch, int radix)
char    fordigit (int digit, int radix)
int     getNumericValue(char ch)
boolean isDigit(char ch)
boolean isLetter(char ch)
boolean isLowerCase(char ch)
boolean isUpperCase(char ch)
char    toLowerCase(char ch)
char    toUpperCase(char ch)
... and 13 others
```

At first glance, these methods make for some interesting examples in character processing. Unfortunately, the character reading facilities of Java are not well-developed and it is more likely that reading will be done into a string which is then processed as discussed in Chapter 10.

Finally, Java also provides, through the escape charater \u, space for an additional 10000 characters which are not available on the usual keyboards. These are called Unicode characters and enable Java to be truly international. There are Unicode sequences for letters in Greek, Cyrillic, Hebrew, Arabic, Tibetan and so on, conforming to international standards where they exist. However, we do not need to be concerned with these while we are working in what is called the Latin alphabet.

4.3 Selection with `if-else` and `switch`

Two methods for changing the values of variables have been covered so far: assignment and reading in. We now consider how to check the values in variables, and choose alternative actions based on the result of the check. Java has two **selection** statements known as the **if-statement** and the **switch-statement**. If-statements make extensive use of booleans, and switches often involve characters.

Form of the if-statement

The general form of the if-statement is

If-statement

`if (condition)`
  `statement;`
`else statement;`

The condition is a boolean expression:

```
speed > speedlimit
(age >= 16) & (age < 75)
isaMinor
year == 1066
day != 29
initial != 'J'
```

In the if-statement we refer to the statement following the brackets as the **then-part** and to the statement following the `else` as the **else-part**. The whole if-statement is executed as follows. Firstly, the condition is evaluated. If this result is true, the then-part is executed, and the else-part is skipped. If the result is false, the then-part is skipped and the else-part is executed. A simple example would be

```
if (number >= 0)
   System.out.println("Positive")
else
   System.out.println("Negative");
```

In the form of the if-statement, the `else` is given in italics. This means that it is optional and the statement can be used in an 'if–then' version. For example,

```
if (day == 25)
   System.out.println("Christmas, Hooray");
```

In either case, the then- and else-parts can be blocks, which would be surrounded by braces.

EXAMPLE 4.4 Assessing random numbers

Problem Java provides various random number generators. We would like to assess them in terms of seeing how many positive numbers are generated per hundred. In addition, we'd like to know the sum of the positive numbers and the minimum and maximum positive number.

Solution The available random number generators are

1   `Math.random();`
2   `nextInt` in the `Random` class of the `util` package; and
3   `nextGaussian`, also in the `Random` class of the `util` package.

Without knowing their properties in advance, let us write a program to look at what they generate.

Program Checking whether a number is positive can be done by comparing it to zero. A more interesting check is for the minimum and maximum. Here we must start off with the smallest maximum we could have, which for positive numbers would be zero, and the largest minimum. How do we know what the largest number is? Referring to section 2.5, we see that the largest double number is given by `Double.MAX_VALUE`. This is the initial setting for posMin. The program follows easily, and makes use of if-statements.

```
import javagently.*;

class AssessRandom {

  /* The Random number assessment program    by J M Bishop
   * ----------------------------------       July 1999
   *
   * Assesses a set of random numbers in
   * various ways.
   *
   * Illustrates the use of if-else and random.
   */

  public static void main(String args []) {

    double total = 0;
    double posTotal = 0;
    int    posCount = 0;
    double posMin = Double.MAX_VALUE;
    double posMax = 0;
    double number;

    System.out.println(
        "****** Assessing 100 random numbers ******");
    for (int i = 0; i < 100; i++) {
      number = Math.random();
```

```
      total += number;
      if (number > 0) {
        posTotal += number;
        posCount++;
        if (number > posMax) posMax = number;
        if (number < posMin) posMin = number;
      }
    }
    System.out.println("Positives " + posCount);
    System.out.println("Minimum   " + posMin);
    System.out.println("Maximum   " + posMax);
    System.out.println("Pos Total " + posTotal);
    System.out.println("Total     " + total);
  }
}
```

Testing   The result is quite interesting:

```
****** Assessing 100 random numbers ******
Positives 100
Minimum    0.020052848856120797
Maximum    0.9953375873292147
Pos Total 49.57903013096493
Total     49.57903013096493
```

From this we deduce that `Math.random` produces only positive real numbers evenly distributed between 0 and 1. Now let us try `nextGaussian`. Because `Random` is a class, we first have to create an object for generating the numbers, as in

```
Random generator = new Random ();
```

and the generation call is

```
number = generator.nextGaussian();
```

The rest of the program stays the same. The results are interesting, over three different runs:

```
****** Assessing 100 random numbers ******
Positives 52
Minimum    0.04782274851884717
Maximum    2.5889948020970004
Pos Total 45.29678012097319
Total     14.496145957922451

****** Assessing 100 random numbers ******
Positives 47
Minimum    0.004383902399470737
Maximum    2.6516615715446097
Pos Total 35.76045535082636
Total     -17.46472767556487
```

```
****** Assessing 100 random numbers ******
Positives 47
Minimum   1.9534854083804097E-4
Maximum   2.379956811257525
Pos Total 36.80780920978156
Total     -6.8659903671349385
```

Now we only have approximately half as many positive numbers, The minimum gets quite close to zero, but the maximum is around 2.5. It looks like we need to do more explorations. Two useful exercises follow.

Exercises

1   Plot the generated values on a graph. What you will see will be random points. In the next chaper we will investigate how to gather the frequency of random numbers and then plot a distribution curve.

2   Consult the documentation for the Java API for the `util` package on your computer and see what it says about `nextGaussian`.

Successive else–ifs

Sometimes, there are more than two possibilities that need to be considered. One way in which this is done is by **successive else–ifs**. The condition of the first if-statement eliminates one case, leaving the rest to the else-part. The else-part in its turn introduces another if-statement which selects out another condition and leaves the rest to its else-part, and so on. Else–ifs are illustrated nicely in an example that assigns a grade for various ranges of marks, thus:

```
int marks;
char grade;

if      (marks >= 80)  grade='A';
else if (marks >= 70)  grade='B';
else if (marks >= 60)  grade='C';
else if (marks >= 50)  grade='D';
else                   grade='E';
```

Notice that the conditions are carefully ordered, so that each eliminates a certain range of marks. Thus, the line that writes out a D for anything over 50 will be reached only when it has already been established that the mark is under 60.

The switch-statement

The if-statement is a two-way selection statement based on conditions. However, if there are several simple tests for given values, successive else–if-statements can become unwieldy. Java provides for so-called **keyed selection** with the switch-statement. The form of the switch-statement is:

> **Switch-statement**
>
> ```
> switch (switch-expression) {
>   case value : statement; break;
>   case value : statement; break;
>   . . .
>   default : statement; break;
> }
> ```

The switch-statement considers the value of the switch-expression and, starting at the first case value, endeavours to find a match. If a match is found, then the corresponding statement is executed and the **break** causes control to pass to the end of the whole switch. We already mentioned the break-statement's potential use in loops (section 3.2).

The **default** keyword is a catch-all for values that have not been mentioned. The break-statements and the default part are not strictly compulsory but it is considered good programming practice to have them. Without a break statement, control falls through to the next case. This could be useful if the statement part is empty, as shown in the examples that follow.

The switch-expression must produce a value which is an integer or a character. It may not be real. The case values are expressions of the same type as the switch-expression, and there may be one or more case value for a given statement. The case values do not have to be in any order and may occur only once.

A typical example of a switch-statement is to call different methods depending on a character. For example, the heart of a calculator program might be

```
char operator;
// Get in the operands x and y and the operator
switch (operator) {
  case '+' : add(x,y); break;
  case '-' : subtract(x,y); break;
  case '*' : multiply(x,y); break;
  case '/' : divide (x,y); break;
  default  : display.println("Invalid operator "+operator);
}
```

Case ranges

In the previous example, the switch-expression was a single variable, and it mapped directly onto the case values. Sometimes, there are many values for each statement, but there is a simple way of adjusting them so that there is only one per statement. For example, suppose that given an examination mark, it is required to set a symbol depending on the multiple of ten, with anything over 80 being A, over 70 being B, and so on down to anything under 40 being F. The switch to achieve such a mapping is

```
switch ((int) (mark / 10)) {
  case 10:
  case 9:
  case 8:  symbol = 'A'; break;
```

```
case 7:   symbol = 'B'; break;
case 6:   symbol = 'C'; break;
case 5:   symbol = 'D'; break;
case 4:   symbol = 'E'; break;
default: symbol = 'F'; break;
}
```

This is the clearest and most efficient way of solving this problem, but it is not the only way. The same effect could be achieved using successive if–else-statements as described above. However, it is usually easier to see what is going on in a table as opposed to a calculation, so switch-statements should be used in preference to if-statements where possible.

When not to use switches

The clarity of the switch makes it a natural choice for many types of selections. However, it cannot be used in situations where the selection is based on conditions. For example, the following is not valid Java:

```
/* NOT VALID JAVA */
switch (number) {
  case < 0   : Addtonegatives;
  case = 0   : Donothing;
  case > 0   : Addtopositives;
}
```

The cases must be actual values. A suitable approach here would employ successive if–else-statements.

Another place where switch-statements are inappropriate is for checking strings. A string is a more complex entity than a switch can handle. Later on we shall see how to match strings as keys to values (section 6.2).

4.4 Conditional loops with `while` and `do`

This book introduced loops early on in order to emphasize the power of programming in handling repetitive tasks in a simple way. Following on from counting loops, we have conditional loops, which enable statements to be repeated while conditions are true.

The form of a while-loop

Conditional loops are phrased in terms of while- or do-statements. A general form of a loop using the while-statement is:

While-statement

```
Initialize the conditions
while (conditions) {
  Statements to perform the loop
    and change the conditions
}
```

After statements to initialize variables involved in the conditions, the loop itself starts by checking the conditions. If they evaluate to true, the body of the while-statement is entered and executed. When the end of the loop is reached, control goes around again to the beginning and the conditions are checked again. This process is repeated until the test of the conditions evaluates to false, at which point the looping stops, and control is passed to the statement following the body of the loop.

EXAMPLE 4.5 Highest common factor

Problem We wish to find the highest common factor (HCF) of two numbers.[†]

Solution One possible solution would be to find all the factors of each number and then compare both lists for the highest one. Fortunately, there is a quicker way!

Suppose a and b are the numbers, a is larger than b and their HCF is f. Then $a - b$ and b will also have an HCF of f. If we use this fact, repeatedly replacing the larger of the two numbers by their difference, until the two numbers are the same, then this figure will be the HCF, even if it is 1.

Examples

a	b	$|a - b|$
65	39	26
26	39	13
26	13	13
13	13 HCF	

a	b	$|a - b|$
99	66	33
33	66	33
33	33 HCF	

Program Looking at the program, we see that there are two while-loops. Because we would like to do several runs, and use the `Display` class, we can set up the outer loop as `while (true)`, which is a more elegant construct than `for ( ; ; )` which we used in the past. We know that stopping the program is accomplished by pressing the Close button on the display.

† Some may know the HCF as the GCD – Greatest Common Divisor.

The second while-loop is then nested inside the first. It has two actions to perform: printing out the current values, and then changing a or b. The condition is easily expressed as (a!=b) i.e. a not equal to b.

```
import javagently.*;

class HCFRepeat {

  /* The HCF Program        by J M Bishop Aug 1996
     ===============        Display version July 1999
     Calculates the highest common factor of two integers.
     Illustrates a while loop.
  */

  public static void main (String args []) {
    Display display = new Display("HCF");
    display.println("***** Finding the HCF *****");
    display.prompt("Integer 1", 567);
    display.prompt("Integer 2", 123);
    int a, b;

    while (true) {
      display.ready("Press ready when data has been entered");
      a = display.getInt("Integer 1");
      b = display.getInt("Integer 2");
      display.println("a\tb");

      while (a != b) {
        display.println(Text.format(a,6)+"\t"+Text.format(b,6));
        if (a > b)
          a -=b;
        else
          b -=a;
      }
      display.println("The HCF is " + a);
      display.ready("Press ready for another data set");
    }
  }
}
```

Testing   After two runs, we have the display as in Figure 4.2.

The do-loop

The general form of the do-statement is similar, as shown below. The do-loop starts off by going through its body at least once before checking the conditions. This can sometimes be a desirable property, but in general the while-statement is favoured by programmers.

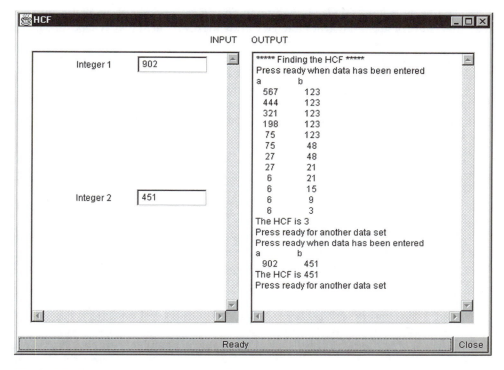

Figure 4.2 *Display output for finding the HCF*

> **Do-statement**
>
> ```
> Initialize the conditions
> do {
>   Statements to perform the loop
>     and change the conditions
> } while condition;
> ```

For example, if we know that a and b are definitely not the same, then we could rephrase the above while-loop as

```
do {
   if (a > b) a -=b;
   else       b -=a;
} while (a != b);
```

Developing conditional loops

The two very important points about conditional loops are that:

1   the condition must be initialized;

2   the condition must change during the loop.

If the condition is not initialized, then the loop will be working on incorrect or even undefined information. If it is not altered during the loop, then there will be no chance of it changing and causing the loop to end.

Before going on to a problem, consider a small illustrative example of conditional loops, bearing in mind the importance of formulating them correctly. In order to convey the sense of the looping process, the example makes use of booleans and methods, which have the effect suggested by their names.

Let us simulate trying to find a pair from a drawerful of mixed coloured socks. The Java program to do this would be

```
PickaSock();
PickAnotherSock();
while (!aPair()) {
  DiscardaSock ();
  PickAnotherSock ();
}
```

The loop is initialized by having two socks in hand; this is essential so that the check for a pair can be correctly performed. The loop is correctly formulated in that the condition will change each time round, as a new sock is selected. There are, however, two crucial flaws in the loop.

Suppose a pair is never found. The condition is not met so the loop continues, but the method to `PickAnotherSock` will eventually fail when the drawer is empty, and the whole operation will crash. The other problem is similar – suppose there were no socks in the drawer to start with. In this case, neither of the initializing statements can be performed, and the program as it stands will not be able to execute. These two situations can be summed up as:

1   guard against not being able to begin;

2   guard against never ending.

The remedy is to provide additional conditions as the guards. In this case, we need to know if sufficient socks (i.e. at least two) exist to be able to test for a pair, and then we need to know when the drawer becomes empty. Both conditions are based on the number of socks in the drawer, and we assume that this figure can be provided in some way. The corrected version of the loop then becomes

```
if (NumberofSocksinDrawer >= 2) {
  PickaSock ();
  PickAnotherSock ();

  while (NumberofSocksinDrawer > 0 && !aPair()) {
    DiscardaSock () ;
    PickAnotherSock () ;
  }
}

{At this point, a pair may or may not have been found}
```

There is one final consideration with any conditional loop. If there is more than one part to the condition governing the loop, it may be necessary to know at the end which part caused the loop to stop. In the example, it seems sensible to be able to decide whether the search was successful or not. This is called **a follow-up action**, and is performed by rechecking some of the conditions, as in

```
if (aPair()) System.out.println("Got a pair of socks.");
else System.out.println("Bad luck, no pair found.");
```

Note that when conditions are connected (as they often are), one must be careful as to which is tested. In this case, it would not have been correct to test for the drawer being empty as in

```
if (NumberofSocksinDrawer == 0)
  System.out.println("Bad luck, no pair found.");
else System.out.println("Got a pair of socks.");
```

since the pair could have been found on the very last time round the loop. The drawer would also be empty, but that is irrelevant for this purpose.

Exercise Write the necessary if-statements to report on whether a pair was found or not, whether the drawer was empty initially, or whether it became empty during the search.

4.5 Handling exceptions

If-statements provide a means of control over the state of the current method. We can check the values of data to which we have access and react accordingly. But what happens if a condition is set in another method and we, the caller of the method, have to react to it? The if-statement is not powerful enough to handle this. We need another construct.

Java's role in web programming puts it in the position of the old adage that 'if things can go wrong they will': a user could disconnect, a file could have been deleted, incorrect input could be entered, a host server might be unavailable. In order to operate within such a volatile environment, Java has a special concept known as an **exception**.

An exception is an object which signals that some unusual condition has occurred. Java has many predefined exception objects, and we can also create our own. The point about exceptions is that they are intended to be **detected** and **handled**, so that the program can continue in a sensible way if at all possible. Should an exception occur outside our immediate environment, we shall be informed as to what has happened. We then have the opportunity to handle the situation that has arisen. If we do not react, the method we are in is terminated and the exception is sent up to the method that called us. This process may repeat until eventually an unhandled exception will pass to the JVM which will terminate the program.

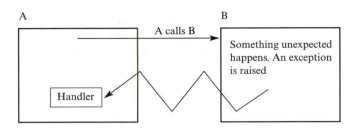

Figure 4.3 *The process of exception handling*

Figure 4.3 illustrates the process of one method calling another and having a handler ready for a possible exception. Depending on how the rest of A is structured, it may be able to continue operating after it handles the exception, or it may exit.

Now let us consider a concrete example related to the `PartCodes` program (Example 4.3). It is unlikely that a user of a program will wish to count precisely the number of parts that are stored on the data file before running the program. There could be hundreds, and even a one-off error would make a difference either by crashing the program because there is not enough input, or missing the last part and not assigning it a number. It would therefore be useful to be able to detect in some other way that the data is at an end.

In the fundamental reading methods supplied with Java, a check is made each time as to whether the input has been exhausted (either by the file ending or by the user indicating end-of-input on the keyboard). If the check turns up true, then the `read` method causes an `EOFException` (for end-of-file exception). The program can then react to the exception.[†]

Catching an exception

To react to a predefined exception such as `EOFException`, we have to do two steps, called **try** and **catch**:

1   **Try**.   Create a block around statements where the result of any method calls or other operations might cause an exception, and preface the block with the keyword `try`.

2   **Catch**.   Follow the try-block with one or more handlers prefaced by the keyword `catch`.

A handler is itself a block and contains statements related to reporting the exception or error, and getting the program back on track. The form for these statements is:

---

† In other languages, the end-of-input condition can be checked separately in advance using an if- or while-statement and the method can decide how to proceed based on the outcome. This is not the case in Java: in order to handle variable length input, we *must* use exceptions.

> **Try–catch-statement**
>
> ```
> try {
>   statements in which an exception
>   could be raised, including method calls in
>   which exceptions could be raised
> }
> catch (Exceptiontype e) {
>   statements to react and recover
> }
> ```

So the matter of reading till the end of a file would be handled by

```
try {
  number = Text.readInt(fin);
  Do something with number
}
catch (EOFException e) {
  display.println("All the data read");
}
```

The parameter e is of the type of the exception. There is a method defined for e, i.e. getMessage. This can be useful as we shall see later if we catch some more general exceptions, such as IOException, and then want to print out the specific details.

Note that on the keyboard, the user types in data and, when finished, presses the character which the system uses for ending the stream. This may be Ctrl-D, Ctrl-Z or Esc, for example. The presence of this special character is detected by the Text class and is relayed to the caller by throwing the EOFException.

Recovering from an exception

The previous discussion focused on how we could handle an exception in order to conclude a program gracefully. There may also be cases where we do not wish to end the method, but to go back and retry the operation that caused the exception. An example of such a situation is the opening of a file. If we have the file name incorrect, we may wish to give the user the chance to enter another name. The algorithm is shown in Figure 4.4.

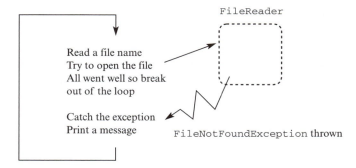

Figure 4.4 *An algorithm for opening a file securely*

If we go back to the `PartCodes` program where we open the file, we can protect that statement and put a loop around it as follows. We have switched to using the display now because it is more general (as we mentioned before, reading from a Java console does not work for all Java systems).

```
BufferedReader fin = Text.open(System.in);
String filename = "parts.data";

for (int i = 1; i <= 5; i++) {
  try {
    display.prompt("File name of parts");
    display.ready("Press ready");
    filename = display.getString("File name of parts");
    fin = Text.open(filename);
    display.println(filename +" opened successfully");
    break;
  }
  catch (FileNotFoundException e) {
    display.println(filename + " not found");
    if (i<5)
      display.println("Enter another name.");
    else
      display.println("Too many tries: ");
      display.println("Connected to keyboard by default");
  }
}
```

We notice several points about this sequence:

- Firstly, it is a rule that any value that is set inside a try-statement must be regarded as potentially unset because the exception could occur before it is assigned to. The compiler checks this rule. The implication is that these variables should be given default values first. In the case of the file name, that is easy enough. In the case of the file itself, we have to be careful. We cannot assign the file to any name at all because it might not exist. Therefore we use the only sure file object, which is `System.in`, the keyboard.

- Secondly, we use a for-loop around the try instead of a while because we wish to limit the number of tries. If the user cannot enter a valid file name within five tries, the program gives up and tries to limp along from the keyboard. Within the catch-statement, we detect whether this is the last try or not and display an appropriate message.

- If the file is opened successfully, then we want to get out of the loop before the five tries are up; hence the break-statement at the end of the try.

Number format exception

Another important exception is the `NumberFormatException` which is raised when an attempt is made to convert a string into a number, and the type is incorrect. For example, an integer cannot have a decimal point and numbers cannot have strange characters in them. Consider the input section of Example 3.8. There are five double numbers to read, and one integer. If the user enters an incorrect character into a box, the corresponding get method will fail. We can protect the whole section as follows:

```
while (true) {
  try {
    display.ready("Make changes and press read");
    E = display.getDouble("Emf source in volts");
    L = display.getDouble("Inductance in henries");
    R = display.getDouble("Resistance in ohms");
    h = display.getDouble("Step length");
    imax = display.getInt("Iterations before reporting");
    TS = display.getDouble("Stopping time in seconds");
    // successful so
    break; // from the loop
  }
  catch (NumberFormatException e) {
    display.println("Error in input: "+e.getMessage());
  }
  // go and try again
}
```

In this case we chose to force the user to enter valid data by using an endless loop.

User-defined exceptions

Apart from the exceptions already defined in the Java library packages, users can also set up their own exceptions, particular to the situation in hand. To define such an exception, the form is

---

Defining a new exception

```
class name extends Exception {
  public name () { }
  public name (String s) { }
}
```

We now have an exception class called `name` and we can throw exception objects of this class as in

---

Throwing and catching a new exception

```
throw new name ("message");

catch (name e) {
  do something with e.getMessage();
}
```

The message can be used by the exception handler (the catch-statement) to give information to the user by calling the `getMessage` method, or it can be empty (accounting for the two options in the declaration above). Opportunities for using user-defined exception arise later in the book. Remember, though, that exceptions are for communicating between methods and objects, and are not meant as a substitute for if-statements within a method.

4.6 Arithmetic accuracy

Since computer arithmetic is done in fixed-size storage called **words**, there has to be some way of handling calculations that go outside the range of numbers provided by the number of bits in a word. There are two possibilities:

1   an approximate value is used and calculation continues;
2   an error occurs and calculation is abandoned.

The first approach is used when there is a loss of precision in how the number is stored, and the second is used when the number actually goes outside the range. These two cases are now considered. The second will give us a chance to explore exceptions again.

Rounding error

Real numbers are stored in the computer in a form called floating point. This means that the point is positioned before the first non-zero digit, and an **exponent** is kept to indicate the point's real position. This representation allows for a range of very large numbers or very small ones within the given 17 digits for Java's double type.

The fraction of a floating point number (called the **mantissa**) holds all the digits of precision available. Sometimes an operation may produce a number which has more digits than can be accommodated. Some digits will be lost, and this may affect subsequent calculations and the end result. This effect is known as **rounding error**.

To illustrate this effect, assume that there is a little computer with reals stored with

●   four digits in the mantissa, and
●   one digit in the exponent.

First consider the problem of inexact division. The expression `10 / 3 * 3` should produce `10`, but in fact may work out as

```
10 / 3 * 3    =    3.333
                    * 3
             = 9.999
```

Precision was irretrievably lost in the division. This is quite a common result and you should see if it happens on your computer. If the answer is printed in floating point form, the inaccuracy should be apparent. If printed in fixed point with a field width for the fraction smaller than the digits provided by the mantissa, then the number may be rounded and appear to be correct. Thus on the little computer with four digits in the mantissa,

```
display.println (10 / 3 * 3,  Text.format(10 / 3 * 3, 8, 1));
```

gives

```
.999E0              10.0
```

This phenomenon is the same no matter how large the mantissa.

The second problem occurs in large multiplications. If two four-digit numbers are multiplied, the result will have seven or eight digits, but still, on our little computer, only four can be stored. For example,

$$60.08 * 4.134 = 248.37072$$

cannot be represented

$$= 248.4$$

Such effects become more noticeable with very large numbers. On this little computer with a four-digit mantissa, we have

largest number	0.9999 E 9 or	999 900 000
second-largest number	0.9998 E 9 or	999 800 000

In between these, there is nothing, so that any of the 100 000 missing values have to be represented by one of these. For example

999 934 628	is represented by	999 900 000
999 876 543	is represented by	999 900 000

When multiplying, see what happens:

$$73.56 * 1101 = 80 989.56$$

cannot be represented

$$= 80 990$$

EXAMPLE 4.6 Demonstration of rounding error

Problem Many formulas in calculus involve taking a limit as some quantity (say h) tends to zero. One would suppose that making h smaller and smaller would lead to better and better results. However, because of rounding error, this is not so. We wish to illustrate this effect.

Solution Let us consider the square root function. The first two derivitives of `sqrt(x)` can be estimated by the formulae

$$\frac{d}{dx}\sqrt{x} = \frac{\sqrt{x+h} - \sqrt{x-h}}{2h}$$

$$\frac{d^2}{dx^2}(\sqrt{x}) = \frac{\sqrt{x+h} - 2\sqrt{x} + \sqrt{x-h}}{h^2}$$

with *h* tending to zero. We shall calculate these expressions for *h* starting at 0.1 and being divided by 10 at successive times round the loop. If we choose a value for *x* such as 1, we know in advance that the correct answers are 0.5 and –0.25. We can then ascertain when the answers are closest to these results.

The program is straightforward except for one point. The formula $-\log_{10}(|x|)$ is used repeatedly in the program, and so we have put it in its own method, `f`. This simplifies the calculations in the loops. The program makes use of `Graph` and the display.

```
import javagently.*;

class RoundingError {

  /* Illustrating rounding error program  by N T Bishop
   * =================================== 1990, 1999
   *
   * Calculates a numerical approximation to the
   * first and second derivatives of sqrt(x) at x=1
   * for various step lengths, h.
   *
   * Illustrates how real numbers suffer from rounding
   * error by displaying the calculated values compared
   * to the known analytic values.
   *
   */

  static final double ln10 = Math.log(10);

  static double f (double x) {
    return -Math.log(Math.abs(x))/ln10;
  }

  public static void main ( String [] args ) {

    Display display = new Display ("Rounding Error");
    Graph g = new Graph("Rounding error",
                        "-log(10) h ","-log(10) error");
    double x = 1;
    double h;
    double deriv1, deriv2, deriv1Analytical, deriv2Analytical;
```

```
display.println
   ("******* Demonstration of rounding errors *******\n");
display.println
   ("Finite difference calculation of 1st and 2nd");
display.println("derivatives of sqrt(x) at x = 1");
deriv1Analytical = 0.5;
deriv2Analytical = -0.25;

display.println("Analytic answers are\nderiv1 ="
   +deriv1Analytical+
   "\nderiv2 = "+deriv2Analytical);
display.println("\n h \t\tderiv1 ");
g.setColor(g.blue);
g.setSymbol(true);
g.setTitle("1st Derivative");
h = 1;

for(int i = 1; i <= 8; i++) {
  h = h / 10;
  deriv1 = (Math.sqrt(x + h) - Math.sqrt(x - h)) / (2 * h);
  display.println("10e-" + i + "\t\t" + deriv1);
  g.add(f(h), f(deriv1 - deriv1Analytical));
}

g.nextGraph();
g.setColor(g.red);
g.setSymbol(true);
g.setTitle("2nd Derivative");
h = 1;

display.println("\n h \t\tderiv2");
for(int i = 1; i <= 8; i++) {
  h = h / 10;
  deriv2 = (Math.sqrt(x + h) + Math.sqrt(x - h)
                  - 2 * Math.sqrt(x)) / (h * h);
  display.println("10e-" + i + "\t\t" + deriv2);
  g.add(f(h), f(deriv2 - deriv2Analytical));
}
g.showGraph();
display.reposition(g);
  }
}
```

The output together with a graph are shown in Figure 4.5.

The vertical axis represents $-\log_{10}(\text{error})$, so that the error decreases as one moves up the axis; also, the horizontal axis plots $-\log_{10}(h)$, and h decreases towards the right. For $h \geq 10^{-5}$ for the first derivative and $h \geq 10^{-3}$ for the second derivative the graph is a straight line. It indicates that the error is proportional to h^2, as expected from calculus theory. For smaller values of h, the graph shows that the effect of rounding error is to increase the overall error.

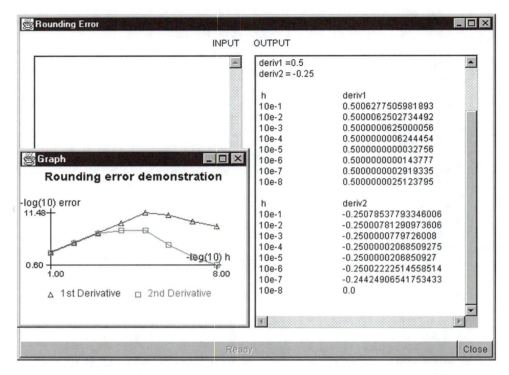

Figure 4.5 *Display from the rounding error program*

Overflow and underflow

These are error conditions where a number itself, rather than just its precision, is too large or too small. They apply to integers and reals.

The largest integer values are given by the constants `Integer.MAX_VALUE` and `Long.MAX_VALUE`. It is not possible to create or store values larger than these in correspondingly typed variables. The computer will catch such attempts and raise an `ArithmeticException`. More subtly, it is also not permissible to go out of range during a computation, even if the final result is within range. So, for example, the following expression cannot be evaluated

```
Long.MAX_VALUE * 2 / 3
```

because twice the value of `Long.MAX_VALUE` cannot be represented, even as a temporary value. However, if the expression is rewritten in the following way, the evaluation becomes possible:

```
Long.MAX_VALUE / 3 * 2
```

In the first version, one could switch to real arithmetic, by making one operand real, as in

```
Long.MAX_VALUE * 2.0 / 3
```

It is, however, always better to use integers if they are applicable, because rounding error problems are avoided. Moreover, real variables cannot be used in several places where integers are acceptable, e.g. as loop variables in for-statements or as switch-expressions in case-statements.

At the other end of the scale, for floating point numbers we have for our little four-digit computer

smallest number 0.1000E–9 or 0.0000000001

Any value less than half of this will be stored as zero. This fact must be remembered when performing computations with very small numbers. Multiplication is especially vulnerable, as shown in this expression:

$a/(b * c)$ where
$a = 0.0000004$ or 0.4E–6
$b = 0.00001$ or 0.1E–4
$c = 0.000004$ or 0.4E–5

$b*c$ produces 0.4E–10 which is smaller than the smallest real, and therefore is represented as 0. As a result, the division will fail. As often happens, reordering an expression enables it to be evaluated more accurately. In this case, the equivalent form of $a/b/c$ will work. a/b gives 0.04, and this divided by c gives the answer of 10 000.

EXAMPLE 4.7 Numeric exceptions

Problem   When will exceptions be raised in calculations, what are they and what can we do with them?

Approach   Let us start our investigation by running a small program:

```
class ArithmeticErrors {

/* Forcing errors to occur          by J M Bishop
 * ----------------------           August 1999
 *
 * Testing Java's reaction to invalid real calculations.
 */

  public static void main (String args []) {
    double x = 0;
    System.out.println("**** Arithmetic test ****");
```

```
    try {
      x = Math.acos(3);
      System.out.println(x);
      if (Double.isNaN(x))
        System.out.println("So computation failed");
      x = 1.0 / 0;
      System.out.println(x);
      x = 1/0;
      System.out.println(x);
    }
    catch (ArithmeticException e) {
          System.out.println("Error: "+e.getMessage());
    }
  }
}
```

which when run gives

```
**** Arithmetic test ****
NaN
So computation failed
Infinity
Error: / by zero
```

Java raised an exception for the incorrect integer calculation. We caught it, and printed out the message that was contained in the prameter e. However, it is not easy to see what recovery could accomplish. If a number is divided by 0 by mistake, then either the porgram or the data is at fault and they will need attention before the program can run successfully.

In Java, exceptions are not raised for calculations involving real numbers. Instead, calculations could result in one of the special values

```
Double.POSITIVE_INFINITY
Double.NEGATIVE_INFINITY
Double.NaN
```

NaN means 'Not a number' and in the program above, an invalid calculation such as acos(3) produces Nan. Dividing by 0 produces infinity. These constants can be checked for, using the boolean methods

```
Double.isNan()
Double.isInfinity()
```

as shown in the program.

When writing scientific programs, though, it is more likely that one will pick up errors resulting in Nan or infinity by seeing these words printed out in one's results. Then the program can be corrected and rerun.

4.7 **Numerical methods with while-loops**

A large number of engineering applications include the need to solve an algebraic equation for x. We call this finding the root of the equation. The equation may be a polynomial such as $x^2 - 2x + 1$ or include trigonometric and other functions.

Finding the real roots of a quadratic equation (polynomial of order 2) is usually covered in school mathematics, and ways of doing this are suggested in Problems 4.9 and 6.9. Here we want to concentrate on general polynomial and transcendental equations. The kinds of applications for root finding would include surface temperatures resulting from heat transfer, terminal velocity of particles, frequency of vibration and so on.

The bisection method

There are several methods for finding such roots. They all rely on making a guess at the root and then iterating in some way towards a better guess until a value for x is found for which $|f(x)| < \varepsilon$ for some small value ε.

The simplest method is to search for the place in which the curve of the function cuts the x axis. For example, in the graph in Figure 4.6, if we start off searching from $x = 0$ and move along in steps of h then we shall find that $f(x_i)$ is negative and $f(x_{i+1})$ is positive. Therefore there must be a root in the interval x_i to x_{i+1}. To find the root more precisely, we reduce the size of h by one-half and proceed to search from x_i again. This process, called the **bisection method**, could be repeated until the root is found to the required accuracy.

Although simple and effective, the bisection method is not very efficient because the number of function evaluations needed to achieve a reasonble accuracy, ε, is of the order of $-\log_2\varepsilon$. For example, for $\varepsilon = 10^{-6}$ there would be about 20 evaluations. We shall therefore leave its further development as a problem (see the end of the chapter) and proceed to the method most commonly used for root finding.

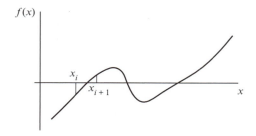

Figure 4.6 *Diagram illustrating the bisection method*

The Newton–Raphson method

Finding the roots of an equation is an essential task in engineering problems, and we would like to have a method which is reliable and quick. It should be applicable to a wide range of functions and produce real as well as complex roots.

The method we shall discuss here is the Newton–Raphson method (developed by Sir Isaac Newton (1642–1727)), one of the most popular as it is simple and produces a root relatively quickly. In Newton's day, of course, the computation was done with pen and paper, so the method *had* to be both simple and efficient. In comparison to the bisection method, Newton–Raphson typically takes five or six evaluations.

In Chapter 6 we shall look at another method, the so-called **secant method**. Other methods that one may find in a text on numerical methods would be the search method, *regula falsi* method and the method of successive substitution.

The Newton–Raphson method for finding a root of an equation $f(x) = 0$ relies on having a fairly good initial estimate of the root, and on knowing the derivative $f'(x) = df/dx$. If the derivative is not known, another method must be used (e.g. the secant method discussed in section 6.5). If x_0 is an estimate of the root, then a better estimate x_1 is

$$x_1 = x_0 - \frac{f(x_0)}{f'(x_0)}$$

This formula is obtained by modelling the curve by its tangent at the point x_0 as shown in the Figure 4.7.

x_1 can then be used to calculate the next and better approximation x_2 and so on, but until when? That is going to depend upon what tolerance can be accepted for the error in the solution. The stopping criterion is given by

|current estimate – previous estimate| < tolerance,

and a typical value for tolerance could be 10^{-6}. However, this is not the whole story for the stopping criterion. If the initial estimate of the root is too far out, the algorithm may never converge – for example, in the figure, if the initial estimate had been $2x_0$ rather than x_0. To prevent the possibility of the program being caught in a loop from which it cannot exit, we place a limit on the number of times the loop is executed.

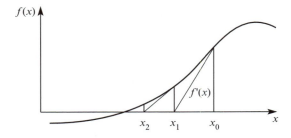

Figure 4.7 *The Newton–Raphson method for iterating towards the root of $f(x) = 0$.*

The method can also be used to find complex roots, as discussed in section 6.3, where a class for complex numbers is introduced.

EXAMPLE 4.8   Specific volume of a gas

Problem   We want to find the specific volume of a particular gas whose state equation at a specific temperature and pressure is given by

$$f(v) = 70v^3 - 3v^2 + 4v - 16$$

Solution   Use the Newton–Raphson method to find the root. To do this we need to:

- have an estimate of the root;
- know the derivative of the equation.

$v = 1$ is a reasonable starting value, and the derivative is

$$f'(v) = 210v^2 - 6v + 4$$

Program design   As before, we are keen to keep the numerical method part of the program separate from its use for this particular problem. Newton–Raphson lends itself to this separation, as the values that are required can be expressed in very general terms. Thus the input and output can be handled by a Newton–Raphson class without upsetting its generality. The class is

```
static class NewtonRaphson {

  // These declarations are independent of any
  // problem that NewtonRaphson will solve.
  double xnew = 1;
  double tolerance = 1E-6;
  int    imax = 10;
  int    iterations = 0;
  double xold = 0;

  void initialize ()  {
    display.prompt("Initial estimate for root", xnew);
    display.prompt("Required error limit", tolerance);
    display.prompt("Maximum iterations permitted", imax);
    display.ready("Change values and press ready");
    tolerance = display.getDouble("Required error limit");
    xnew = display.getDouble("Initial estimate for root");
    imax = display.getInt("Maximum iterations permitted");
    display.println("i\tRoot estimate");
  }

  // solve is almost self-contained except for the
  // need to call the two functions
```

```
     void solve () {
       do {
          iterations++;
          display.println(iterations+"\t"+xnew);
          xold = xnew;
          xnew = xold - f(xold) / df(xold);
       } while (Math.abs(xnew - xold) > tolerance
                  & iterations < imax);
          if (iterations == imax) {
            display.println("Failed to converge: xnew = "+xnew);
            display.println("  xold = "+xold+"  i = "
                      +iterations);
       } else {
          display.println("Root is: "+xnew);
       }
          display.println(iterations+" iterations required");
     }
   }
```

The only access that Newton–Raphson must make outside of itself is to the display, and to the two functions, f and df, which it calls to find the root. When we examine how to make the functions general in Chapter 6, we shall fix this problem.

Program   The main program then just introduces the problem, declares a solver object and calls its two methods. The output is given in Figure 4.8.

```
import javagently.*;

class SpecificVolume {

  /* Finding the specific volume of a gas    N T & J M Bishop
   * ====================================    1990, 1999
   * using the Newton-Raphson method
   *
   * The NewtonRaphson class is self-contained except for
   * the need to call the two functions related to the
   * problem in hand.
   *
   * The main program displays anything to do with the
   * problem itself. The NewtonRaphson class reports on
   * its result and the way in which it stopped.
   *
   * Illustrates separation of concerns.
   *
   */

.... Insert NewtonRaphson class here

  static Display display = new Display("Specific Volume");

  // These are the two functions relating to the
  // specific volume of the gas. They get called
  // directly from a NewtonRaphson object.
```

```java
static double f (double x) {
  return 70*x*x*x -3*x*x+4*x-16;
}

static double df (double x) {
  return 210*x*x -6*x+4;
}

// The main program merely sets the scene,
// creates the solver object, and then calls it.

public static void main (String args []) {
  display.println
    ("***** Finding the specific volume of a gas *****");
  display.println("using the Newton-Raphson root finder");
  display.println("Solves 70 v**3 - 3 v**2 +4 v - 16 = 0\n");

  NewtonRaphson nr = new NewtonRaphson();
  nr.initialise();
  nr.solve();
}

}
```

Testing   Figure 4.8 shows the result of a run of the program.

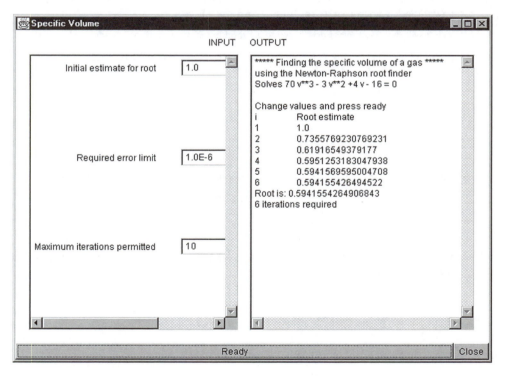

Figure 4.8 *Display for the specific volume program using the Newton–Raphson method*

To see the method in real action, we tried an initial guess of 100; the method eventually converged, but took 17 steps. The root can be verified as correct by substituting in the equation.

Input–output in methods

We notice that input–output for the values associated with the finding of the root are done in the Newton–Raphson class. Since the names of the values and the way in which the result is reported are fairly standard, there is no harm in doing so. The class is still fairly general. However, in Chapter 6 when we see how to make classes completely general, we shall endeavour to remove input and output from library methods, and communicate with them via their object fields or via parameters.

QUIZ

4.1   Countries can have spaces in their names. Write a statement to read a country name from a file called `fin`.

4.2   Write a statement to print out on one line the values of two boolean variables called `checked` and `thisMonth`.

4.3   Write a while-loop which will check ten characters read off a stream called `in` and stop if any of them is not a digit. (Use `Text.readchar`.)

4.4   What will the `Text` class do if a string is typed in where a number is required?

4.5   In the following try-statement, where could exceptions occur? What are their names?

```
try {
  for (int count = 0; ; count++) {
    x = Text.readDouble (in);
    y = 1/x;
    System.out.println (x, y);
  }
}
```

4.6   The following set of statements is inefficient. Why is this so? Rewrite it more efficiently.

```
if (pre == 'm') System.out.print("milli");
if (pre == 'c') System.out.print("centi");
if (pre == 'K') System.out.print("kilo");
System.out.println("metre");
```

4.7   Each of the following three loops is meant to read characters until a $ is found. Do they all have the same effect?

```
char ch;
for (;;) {
  ch = Text.readChar(in);
  if (ch == '$') break;
}
```

```
char ch;
do
   ch = Text.readChar(in);
while (ch != '$');

char ch;
while (ch != '$')
   ch = Text.readChar(in);
```

4.8   Write a switch-statement that will print out the name for each of the days of the week, given a number from 0 to 6.

4.9   On the four-digit computer used as an example in section 4.6, what would happen if we tried to print the value 999 555 444?

4.10   Why is the Newton–Raphson method favoured over the bisection method?

PROBLEMS

4.1   **Random numbers.**   Complete the investigation in Example 4.4 by checking the other random number generator in the `Random` class, namely `nextInt`.

4.2   **Splitting files.**   Suppose we have a file of numerical readings, some of which are negative and some of which are positive. We wish to create two new files, one with all the positive numbers and one with the negative numbers, and then go back and print out both from the program, with the positive numbers file first. Use a suitable random number generator to create the files in the first place, allowing for a total of 100 numbers.

4.3   **Voting.**   A board of directors consists of three members, each of which has a two-way switch marked yes/no. When votes are taken, a lamp comes on if the yes votes are in the majority. The circuit that implements the turning on of the lamp is represented by the boolean function

   $L = a \, \& \, (b \mid c) \mid b \, \& \, c$

Write a program which writes to a file a table of the alternate yes/no values for a, b and c, and the value of L. Implement L using a boolean method.

4.4   **Timetable.**   It is always useful to have a blank timetable to fill in for one's lectures. Write a program that will write out such a timetable to a file, with Monday to Friday across the top, and the hours 8 to 15 down the left. The timetable should have suitable borders.

4.5   **Conversion tables.**   Using Example 3.3 (square roots) as a model, devise a program which can write to a file a conversion table from degrees Celsius to Fahrenheit. Then make separate versions of the program for the folllowing conversions:

●   miles to kilometres

●   litres to gallons

●   dollars to your (or another) currency.

4.6   **Rabbits!**   Scientists need to determine when they will run out of space to house their rabbits. They start with two rabbits and it is known that a pair of adult rabbits (those more than three months old) produce on average two rabbits every three months. The scientists have space to house 500 rabbits. Write a program which will determine how many months it will be before the scientists run out of space. Adapt the program to print out a table of the rabbit populations (adult, non-adult and total) every three months for five years. Assume no rabbits die.

4.7 **Sine approximation.** The sine function can be approximated by the series

$$\sin(x) = x - \frac{x^3}{3!} + \frac{x^5}{5!} - \frac{x^7}{7!} \cdots$$

Write a program which will calculate the value of sine at an angle to be read in, using as many terms as necessary to achieve (a) an accuracy of 10E − 6. and then (b) the same accuracy as the built-in sine function.

Hint: Don't calculate the powers and factorials anew for each term − keep running totals which are updated. Plot the calculated version and the actual values on a graph.

4.8 **Bisection method.** The Newton–Raphson method requires a guess at the root of an equation. One way of finding such a guess is to employ the bisection method (section 4.7). Use this algorithm to find the rough positions of the other two roots in Example 4.8, and the Newton–Raphson method to evaluate them to a better accuracy.

Hint: They may not exist. Add the search algorithm as a second method to the Newton–Raphson class.

4.9 **Roots of a quadratic.** The formula for a root of a quadratic is well known, i.e.

$$x = \frac{-b \pm \sqrt{b^2 - 4ac}}{2a}$$

Write a program which uses the display to receive values for a, b and c and displays the roots in the output section. Report on the special root cases, e.g. one root, two equal roots, two real roots, two imaginary roots.

4.10 **Examinations.** An examination paper has four questions in Section A and four in Section B. Each question is valued at 20 marks. Students must answer five questions in total, with at least two from Section A and two from Section B. If more questions than required are answered, then the first ones are counted and the latter ones disregarded. Unanswered questions are indicated by a zero mark.

Write a program to read in from a file eight marks for each of several students and print out their final marks according to the rules. The output should be made to a file and should echo the input as shown here. If rules are broken, print appropriate messages. Sample data and results are

Sample Input								Sample Result	Output Comment
Section A				Section B					
10	15	0	0	20	8	17	0	70	
10	9	7	20	0	0	0	10	36	Too many from A.
5	6	10	0	19	5	3	14	45	More than 5. Too many from B.

4.11 **Bisection method.** Following on from the class developed for Problem 4.8, use the bisection method followed by the Newton–Raphson method to find all the roots of

$$x = 2 \sin(x)$$

4.12 **Rainfall figures.** The rainfall figures in mm are available for each day of the past four weeks. We want to know the total rainfall for each week, the most recent wettest day and the driest week.

Write a program that will read in several sets of 28 rainfall figures from a file and write out to another file the 3 bits of information required together with an echo of the data. Sample data and results would be

```
Sample data              Sample results
3 0  0  7 8 21  0        39 mm
0  1  1 0 0 0   4          6 mm
9 6 7 0 0 0     0         22 mm
0  0  0 0 0 0   1          1 mm
The wettest day was day 6.
The driest week was week 4.
```

4.13 **Golf scores.** Savanna Golf Course has nine holes. At each hole, a player is expected to be able to sink the ball in the hole in one to five shots. This gives a course average or par of 30. A player's score for the course is the sum of the numbers of shots for each hole. Depending on past performance, a player is granted a handicap which is subtracted from his or her score to give the actual result for a game. Players are also interested in knowing whether they have scored under par or not. When players play together, the winner is the one with the lowest score. If the scoring of a golf game were computerized, sample input and output might be

```
Player   Handicap    Shots per hole       Total   Result   Under Par?
1        6           1 3 6 2 1 4 3 2 4      26     20          yes
2        3           2 2 2 2 4 4 4 2 2      24     21          yes
3        2           4 5 4 3 4 1 3 5 4      33     31          no
The winner is player 1 with a handicapped result of 20
```

Write a program which

- reads in from a file the shots per hole for several players;
- calculates each total score, handicapped score and par decision;
- determines the winning player and the winning score;
- writes the results together with an echo of the data to another file.

4.14 **Parking meters.** The Savanna Traffic Department wants to decide whether or not to mount a campaign against illegal parking. A number of traffic inspectors are sent to different zones in the city where parking time is restricted. The different zones have different time restrictions. Each of the traffic officers has to monitor any ten cars in their zone and record the actual time the vehicle was parked in the time-restricted zone. If 50% or more of the cars were parked for a longer period than allowed, the Traffic Department will decide to launch a massive campaign. Write a program that

- reads in from a file the number of zones, the time limit and actual parking time for ten vehicles for each of the zones;
- determines the number of cars exceeding the time limit in each of the zones;
- decides whether a campaign should be mounted or not;
- identifies the zone where the situation is the worst;
- writes the results and an echo of the input to another file.

Sample combined output might be

```
Number of zones: 3
Area Limit    Parking times                      Over limit
1     60      20 40 70 35 45 78  34 56 73   5     3
2     45      62 47 68 40 53 62 120   8 15 72    7
3     30      66 32 41 89  7 25  29 33 54 17     6
A campaign must be mounted.
Concentrate on area 2
```

4.15   **Engineering apparatus.**   A certain engineering apparatus is controlled by the input of
successive numbers. If there is a run of the same number, the apparatus can optimize its performance. Hence we would like to arrange the data so as to indicate that a run is coming.
Write a program that reads a sequence of numbers and prints out each run of numbers in
the form (n*m) where m is the number to be repeated n times. These instructions are
printed in brackets on a new line, to indicate that they are going to the apparatus. Note that
a run could just consist of a single number. The numbers are terminated by a zero, which
halts the apparatus. Sample input and output would be

```
Sample input and output
20 20 20 20 20 20 20 20 20 20 50
(10*20)
50 50 50 50 60
(5*50)
60 60 60 60 20
(5*60)
30
(1*20)
30 30 30 90
(4*30)
0
(1*90)
(0)
```

CHAPTER 5

Arrays and matrices

5.1 Simple arrays

We are beginning to realize that there is a need to be able to store and manipulate multiple values in a program. If there are relatively few values, simple variables can possibly be used, but consider the following example.

Suppose we have several hundred scores between 0 and 19 which have to be analyzed for frequency of occurrence of each score. We could set up 20 counters, one for each score. As the scores are read in, the counter corresponding to the score could be incremented. It would be very unwieldy if we had to invent 20 different names for the counters and then use a big switch-statement every time one of them needed updating. What we need is the concept of the *ith variable* so that we can read a score value, say i, and then update the corresponding counter called $score_i$. Programming languages provide for this facility with the **array**. Figure 5.1 illustrates what we would like to set up.

Figure 5.1 *An array of score counters*

Declaring an array

An array is a bounded collection of elements of the same type, each of which can be selected by indexing with an integer from 0 upwards to a limit specified when the array is created. The relevant form is

---

Array declaration

```
type arrayname [ ] = new type [limit];
type arrayname [ ] = {value1, value2, ...};
```

The similarity to an object instantiation is striking: the difference is that the [ ] before the assignment designate the identifier as an array, and after the type we give the limit, again in square brackets, rather than the initial parameters, as given for an object.

Arrays can be declared to contain any type or class, but the index and hence the limit must always be an integer. The limit gives the number of elements in the array, with each element being indexed by a number in the range from 0 to *limit* − 1. Examples of array declarations of the first form shown above are:

```
int frequencies [] = new int [20];
String rainbow   [] = new String [7];
double results   [] = new double [101];
```

The `frequencies` array will have 20 integers, numbered 0 to 19. There will be seven strings stored in the `rainbow` array, numbered 0 to 6, and 101 double values in the x array, numbered 0 to 100. Notice that array names are frequently given as plurals.

The second form of array declaration creates an array with initial values. The size of the array is then deduced from the number of values given, for example

```
char vowels [ ] = {'a','e','i','o','u'};
```

The `vowels` array has five characters, numbered from 0 to 4.

To access an array element, we give the name of the array variable and an index expression enclosed in square brackets. The index is sometimes known as the **subscript**. For example, we could have

```
for (int i=0; i<20; i++)
  frequencies[i] = 0;
rainbow[3] = "Violet";
System.out.println(vowels[1]); // which prints 'e'
```

Arrays starting at 0 or 1

Remember that arrays are always indexed starting at 0, so that the last example here will print the second element, which is 'e', not 'a'. The fact that Java and other newer languages index arrays from 0 rather than 1 can be disconcerting for a scientific programmer, whose mathematics may be worked out with *i* going from 1 to *n*. Fortunately, we can adapt our programs to a 1 to *n* model, by declaring arrays from 1 to *n* + 1 and not using the zeroth value. This technique is intended to be used with the `results` array declared above. We could run *i* from 1 to 100 quite successfully, and just ignore the zeroth element.

In the programs that follow we do not adopt one technique or the other exclusively, but adapt arrays to the problem in hand. Most need arrays that start from 1, but some will start at 0.

EXAMPLE 5.1   Frequency count

Problem   Going back to the example where we assessed random numbers rather crudely (Example 4.4), let us now look at their distribution. The aim is to see how fair the generator would be for simulating scores between 0 and 19.

Approach   We shall generate numbers with the integer generator, converting each into a number between 0 and 19. We set up an array and as each score is calculated or read, the appropriate element of the array is incremented. The heart of the program would be

```
Random generator = new Random ();
int frequency [] = new int [20];
int score;

for (int i = 0; i < 1000; i++) {
  score = Math.abs(generator.nextInt());
  // reduces the number to between 0 and 19
  score %=  20;
  frequency [score] ++;
}
```

Notice that although the constant mentioned twice in this excerpt is 20, the actual scoring is done from 0 to 19. In the case of the array, the number given in square brackets is the number of elements in the array, but starting from 0, i.e. 0 to 19. In the case of the modulus operator, %, by giving it 20 as an operand we also create values from 0 to 19. Finally, nextInt creates numbers spread over the whole range of integers, including negative ones, so Maths.abs was needed.

Program   Before we put the above excerpt in a program, we decide to generalize it in three ways:

1   Make both the number of numbers generated and the maximum score variable.
2   Link the program to the Display class so that these values can easily be read in.
3   Add in a graph to show the spread of the numbers in the form of a histogram.

This is what emerges:

```
import javagently.*;
import java.util.*;

class ScoreFrequencies {

  /* The Score Frequencies program        by J M Bishop
   * ----------------------------         1997, 1999
   *
   * Assesses a set of random numbers for
   * use in the range 0 to 19.
   * Based on the AssessRandom program (Ex. 4.4).
   *
   * Illustrates the use of simple arrays.
   */

  public static void main(String[] args) {

    int frequency [] = new int [100];
    int score;
    int maxScore, limit;
```

```
Random generator = new Random ();
Display display = new Display ("Score Frequencies");
Graph g = new Graph("Score frequencies","Score","Frequency");

display.println(
     "****** Calculating Score Frequencies ******");
display.prompt("Scores to be generated",1000);
display.prompt("Maximum score",19);
display.println("Keep maximum score small (<30)");
display.ready("Press ready");
limit = display.getInt("Scores to be generated");
maxScore = display.getInt("Maximum score");
g.setLine(false);
g.setColor(g.blue);
g.setSymbol(true);

for (int i = 0; i < limit; i++) {
  score = Math.abs(generator.nextInt());
  // reduces the number to between 0 and maxScore
  score %=  maxScore+1;
  frequency[score] ++;
}

g.add(0,0);// force the y-axis to include 0.
for (int i = 0; i < maxScore+1; i++) {
  display.println(i+"\t"+frequency[i]);
  g.add(i,frequency[i]);
}

// show a straight line which is where the numbers per score
// should fall if evenly distributed
g.nextGraph();
g.setLine(true);
g.setSymbol(false);
g.add(0, limit/(maxScore+1));
g.add(maxScore,limit/(maxScore+1));
g.showGraph();
display.reposition(g);
  }
}
```

Testing   The program has the display shown in Figure 5.2, including the all-revealing graph. Although we postulated that we would show scores between 0 and 19, we have actually changed it in this run to 0 and 10. As can easily be seen from the graph, for 1000 numbers the spread is not very even. Try it with more numbers.

Properties of arrays

To formalize our treatment of arrays, here is a summary of their properties:

1   **Element type.**   Arrays can be formed of any type or class, from simple types to objects to arrays themselves. The last leads to multi-dimensional arrays, discussed in detail in section 5.2.

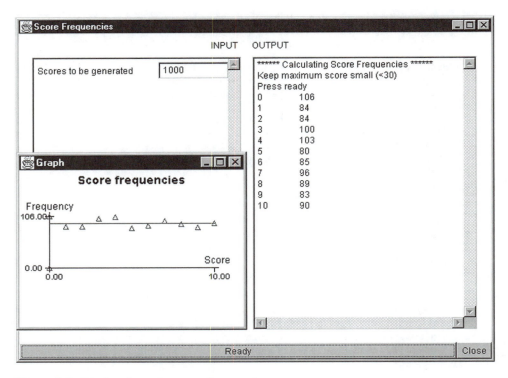

Figure 5.2 *Display from the score frequencies program*

2 **Size.** The size of an array is limited only by the computer's memory, which is usually adequate for most applications. The size is **fixed** at the time that the array is created, and cannot be changed thereafter.

3 **References.** When an array is declared, a **reference** is set up for it. This reference will point to the place where the array's elements are stored. The declaration

```
int A [] = new int [4];
```

therefore has the following effect:

When arrays are assigned or passed as parameters, it is their references that move around, not the array itself. This is efficient, and useful for scientific programming.

4   **Delayed sizing.** The declaration of an array can be done in two stages: one to declare the array name and create the reference, and then later another to set up the storage. This option is very useful when the size of the array is going to be read in as a data item. We can then say

```
int A [];
n = Text.readInt(in);
A = new int [n];
```

5   **Array operator.** The only operator that applies to a whole array is assignment. Assigning one array to another, though, does not create a copy of the whole array. Instead, it copies the references, so that both arrays will refer to the same storage, and changes made to one will affect the other. Copies of the actual values of arrays can be made in the same way as copies of objects, by a method called **cloning**, and this topic is taken up in section 6.1. Should we wish to copy an array at this point, we could do it simply by creating a new array and copying each element across in a loop.

6   **Element access.** Java is quite firm about allowing access only to array elements that actually exist. Every time an array is accessed, the index supplied is checked against the bounds given in the array declaration. If the index is out of bounds, an `ArrayIndexOutOfBoundsException` is raised. The exception can be caught and handled, and if it is not, the program halts. For example, with the above declarations, both `frequencies[100]` and `vowels[5]` would cause errors.

7   **Length.** The length of an array can be established by means of a special property associated with every array, called `length`. Thus

```
frequency.length
```

will yield 20. In other words, `length` returns the limit used in the declaration. Note that `length` is not a method, but a property, and therefore does not have brackets after it.

8   **Parameters.** Arrays can be passed as parameters to methods. A very convenient feature of Java is that the formal parameter in the method does not have to specify the length of the array it expects. The method can accept arrays of the correct type of any length, and processes them by using the `length` property described in point 7. A prime example is the `main` method which declares

```
main (String args [])
```

If there are any arguments, `main` could print them out using a for-loop as follows:

```
for (int i=0; i<args.length; i++)
  System.out.println(args[i]);
```

EXAMPLE 5.2   Scalar product of two vectors

Problem   Vectors are used a great deal in scientific processing, and one of the more common operations on vectors is finding the scalar product. We would like to develop a self-contained method to do this for vectors of various lengths.

Solution   The scalar product gives the sum of each element of one vector, a, multiplied by the corresponding element of another vector, b. Formally, it is defined as

$$\text{prod} = \sum_{i=1}^{n} a_i b_i$$

Obtaining the answer in Java will involve a straightforward looping algorithm. However, we need to consider how to accommodate vectors of different lengths in different runs of the program. That is, in run 1 we may want to find

$$(1, 2) . (0, 3)$$

and in run 2, n is 6 and the data is:

$$(1, 2, 2, 3, 4, 5) . (7.5, 2, 3.1, 4, 5, 5)$$

There are two options for handling different lengths:

1   Read in the size of the array first and use delayed sizing as in point 4 above.
2   Read pairs of points until the end-of-file is detected.

Option 1 is explored here and option 2 in the next example.

Algorithm   The declarations related to defining an array with the flexibility required are

```
BufferedReader fin = Text.open("scalar.data");
int n = Text.readInt(fin);

// Now declare the two arrays of the correct size
double a [] = new double [n+1];
double b [] = new double [n+1];

for (int i = 1; i<=n; i++)
  a[i] = Text.readDouble(fin);
for (int i = 1; i<=n; i++)
  b[i] = Text.readDouble(fin);
```

So the arrays a and b will run from 1 to n, though the arrays are declared from 0 to n, with a limit of $n + 1$. The data will consist of a value for n, then n real numbers for a_i, then another n real numbers for b_i ($i = 1$ to n). Many array programs involve large amounts of data, which are usually read from a file, as we do so from "scalar.data".

Program   The full program is

```
import javagently.*;
import java.io.*;

class ScalarProduct {

  /* Program illustrating the scalar product
   * -------------------------------------
   *                                      J M Bishop Dec 1998
   * of two vectors,                      from Feb 1990
   * as well as the declaration of arrays
   * based on a read-in length.
   */

  static double product (double a [], double b [], int n) {
    double p = 0.0;
    for (int i = 1; i <= n; i++)
      p += a[i] * b[i];
    return p;
  }

  public static void main (String args []) throws IOException {
    Display display = new Display ("Scalar product");

    display.println("******** Scalar Product *********\n");
    display.println("Scalar product of two vectors a and b ");
    display.println("Set the file name");
    display.println
      ("The first line of the file contains the vector length");
    display.prompt("File name","scalar.data");
    display.ready("Press ready");
    String filename = display.getString("File name");

    BufferedReader fin = Text.open(filename);
    int n = Text.readInt(fin);

    // Now declare the two arrays of the correct size
    double a [] = new double [n+1];
    double b [] = new double [n+1];

    for (int i = 1; i<=n; i++)
      a[i] = Text.readDouble(fin);
    for (int i = 1; i<=n; i++)
      b[i] = Text.readDouble(fin);

    display.println("The scalar product is: " +
      Text.format(product(a, b, n),10,4));
  }
}
```

Testing Given the data in the file

```
5
3.0 4.5 6.0 7.5 9.0
2.0 2.0 2.0 2.0 10.0
```

the program will produce output on the display, with the result of 74.7.

EXAMPLE 5.3 Statistical analysis

Problem Common statistical operations on vector data include calculating the mean and standard deviation. We would like to develop methods for these operations with a view to making them readily available for use from a library.

Approach If we have a set of measurements x_i we can analyze them to find the mean $\bar{x}$ which gives the average measurement, and the standard deviation s, which shows the amount by which measurements are likely to differ from the mean. In other words, the standard deviation indicates the spread of the measurements.

Theory The mean of a set of measurements $x_i (i = 1$ to $n)$ is defined to be

$$\bar{x} = \frac{1}{n} \sum_{i=1}^{n} x_i$$

and the formula for the standard deviation is

$$s = \sqrt{\frac{\sum_{i=1}^{n} (x_i - \bar{x})^2}{n - 1}}$$

We can allow for expected errors and intrinsic randomness by saying that the result of a set of measurements will be within a certain standard deviation. In many cases we can say that the true result is in the range $\bar{x} \pm 2s$, i.e. the mean plus or minus twice the standard deviation.

Method design It is straightforward to write a method to calculate the mean, just by using a for-loop. However, the formula for the standard deviation uses the mean, and so has to be calculated after the mean has been decided. The two methods are as follows:

```
public static double mean (double a [], int n) {
   double sum = 0.0;
   for (int i=1; i<=n; i++)
     sum += a[i];
   return sum / n;
}
```

```
public static double stddev (double a [], int n, double ave) {
  double sum = 0;
  for (int i = 1; i<=n; i++)
    sum += (ave - a[i]) * (ave - a[i]);
  return Math.sqrt(sum / (n-1));
}
```

Both methods have an array as a parameter, but notice that we also include n as the number of elements actually in the array. This is because a large array may be used for different numbers of elements. When it is passed to mean or stddev, a.length will give the actual large limit (say 1000) rather than the current usage of the array (say 256)

Now let's investigate how to get them into a library.

Expanding the library

Clearly, mean and stddev are two excellent candidates for inclusion in a library of useful routines that we would like to start developing. Within Java the structure of such a library is: methods in classes in a package. Packages that we have already encountered include java.io and java.util, and of course the very useful javagently done for this book. The javagently package has four classes: Text, Display, Graph and List. List is used by the Graph class but we shall see later how to use it ourselves to good effect.

Rather than add to javagently, we shall postulate a new package for more scientific-type classes, of which a statistics one encompassing the two methods above would be a prime candidate. The Java way to create the methods in a new class in a new package is

```
package jgeslib;

public class Stats {

  public static double mean (double a [], int n) {
    ... as before
  }

  public static double stddev (double a [], int n, double m) {
    ... as before
  }
}
```

The above class is placed in a file called Stats.java in the usual way, and this class must be in a directory called jgeslib. It is compiled in that directory, and the class-path is augmented to include the directory *in which* jgeslib resides. See Figure 1.8 for an example.

In other words, we do *not* put jgeslib in the classpath: we give the directory in which jgeslib is to be found. Once this has been done, any program that wishes to use the methods simply imports jgeslib.* and can call the methods as in

```
ave = Stats.mean (myreadings, number);
```

Notice that both the class and its methods are declared as public, so that they can be seen from other packages, notably the default package associated with ordinary programs.

EXAMPLE 5.4   The lifetime of light bulbs

Problem   A factory manufactures light bulbs, and from the production line, bulbs are chosen at random to see how long they last. For quality control purposes, there must be regular reports on the mean lifetime and standard deviation in hours.

Algorithm   In setting up the array, we use option 2, discussed above, and declare a large array, from which we use an unspecified number of elements, depending on how many data items come in. Of course, we also check that no more than the maximum number of elements is entered. The segment of Java to handle such input is

```
double hourreadings [] = new double[max];
BufferedReader in = Text.open(System.in);
int n = 0;

try {
  for (n=1; n<max; n++)
    hourreadings[n] = Text.readInt(in);
  System.out.println("Can only take "+(max-1)+" samples");
}
catch (EOFException e) { }

n--;
System.out.println("That's the data, thanks");
System.out.println("There were "+n+" samples");
```

The intention is that the Stats class methods will process values with $i = 1$ to n. Because the formula for the standard deviation includes division by $n - 1$, we check whether $n = 1$, to prevent a run-time error.

Program

```
import java.io.*;
import javagently.*;
import jgeslib.*;

class LightBulbAnalysis {

  /* The light bulb program          J M Bishop
   * ----------------------          1990, 1998
   *
   * Calculates the average light of light bulbs
   * Uses the mean and stddev methods created
   * in a Stats class in the jgeslib package.
   *
   * Illustrates array i/o again
   */
```

```
static final int max = 101;

public static void main (String args []) throws IOException {

  System.out.println
      ("***** Light Bulb Analysis *****\n");
  System.out.println
      ("Statistical analysis of the lifetime of "+
       "light bulbs");
  System.out.println("with no. of readings < "+max);
  System.out.println("Type in the readings followed by");
  System.out.println("Enter Ctrl-z Enter\n");

  double hourreadings [] = new double[max];
  BufferedReader in = Text.open(System.in);
  int n = 0;

  try {
    for (n=1; n<max; n++)
      hourreadings[n] = Text.readInt(in);
    System.out.println("Can only take "+(max-1)+" samples");
  }
  catch (EOFException e) {}
  n--;
  System.out.println("That's the data, thanks");
  System.out.println("There were "+n+" samples");

  if (n == 1)
    System.out.println("Mean = "+
        Text.writeDouble(Stats.mean(hourreadings,n),10,6)+
        " but standard deviation not defined for n=1");
  else {
    double ave = Stats.mean(hourreadings,n);
    System.out.println("Mean = "+Text.writeDouble(ave,6,2)+
        " hours");
    System.out.println("Standard deviation = " +
        Text.writeDouble(
        Stats.stddev(hourreadings,n,ave),6,2) + " hours");
  }
 }
}
```

Testing   Any number of values can be read in. Here we submit just five.

```
***** Light Bulb Analysis *****
Statistical analysis of the lifetime of light bulbs
with no. of readings < 101
Type in the readings followed by
Enter Ctrl-z Enter
 1105    909    1043    989    961
That's the data, thanks
There were 5 samples
Mean = 1001.40 hours
Standard deviation =   75.48 hours
```

We deliberately ran this program from the keyboard so that we could see the values being entered. The display is not appropriate for array-type input, and if we put the values in a file, few as they are, the program might lose impact.

5.2 Matrices

Data arranged in rows and columns is very common in scientific applications. Since Java permits array elements to be of any type, including arrays themselves, arrays of multiple dimensions can be built up. Most of the time, though, there will not be more than two dimensions, and the resulting structure is known as a matrix. For a typical matrix such as that shown in Figure 5.3, the declaration would be

```
double matrix [] [] = new double [4] [5];
```

Rows are always mentioned first in the declaration. This enables a single row of the matrix to be represented. For example,

```
matrix[3]
```

would give the shaded row in Figure 5.3. Each element of the row can be selected by indexing twice, as in

```
matrix [3] [1]
```

which would give the darker element. To swap two complete rows, i and j, of the matrix, we could say

```
double row [] = new double [5];
row = matrix[i];
matrix[i] = matrix[j];
matrix[j] = row;
```

As we have mentioned before, assigning arrays only assigns the references, so that the data in the rows doesn't physically move; only the row references change.

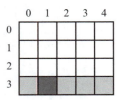

Figure 5.3 *A typical matrix*

EXAMPLE 5.5 Rainfall statistics

Problem The Savanna Weather Department has kept statistics on monthly rainfall figures for the past 20 years. Now it would like to calculate

● the average rainfall for each month;

● the standard deviation for each month.

Solution The table of rainfall figures that is provided by a clerk will look something like this:

Year	Jan	Feb	Mar	Apr	May	Jun	Jul	Aug	Sep	Oct	Nov	Dec
1989	20	22	17	14	5	0	0	0	7	12	30	20
1990	22	24	19	12	0	0	3	0	8	15	20	25
1991	17	17	17	15	0	0	0	0	6	17	8	20
1992	10	10	10	5	0	0	0	0	0	12	10	15
1993	10	10	10	5	0	0	0	0	0	12	10	15
1994	20	22	17	14	5	0	0	0	7	12	30	20
1995	22	24	19	12	0	0	3	0	8	15	20	25
1996	17	17	17	15	0	0	0	0	6	17	8	20
1997	25	30	25	15	7	0	0	0	20	15	20	30
1998	25	30	25	15	7	0	0	0	20	15	20	30

The data will be stored in this form in a file. As the values are read in, they are stored in a matrix which is indexed by both the years and the months. Since the rainfall for a month seems to be the crucial figure, the matrix should be str᠁ ᠁ured so that a whole column can be moved around at once. To do this, we make m᠁ ᠁ths the first subscript, and years the second. In other words, we would like to represent the matrix as in Figure 5.4.

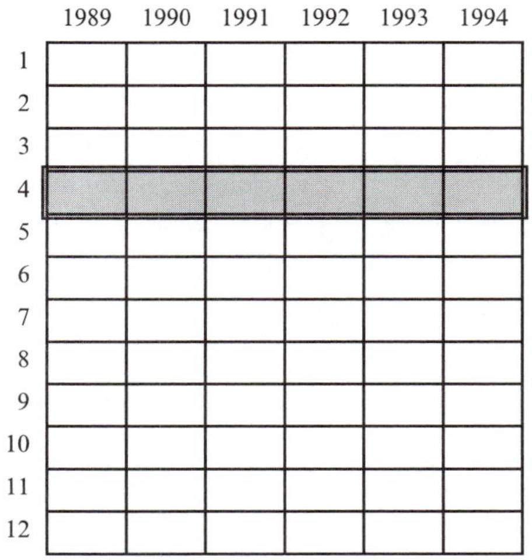

Figure 5.4 *Part of the matrix for storing rainfall data*

The appropriate Java declarations are

```
static final int maxyear = 70;
double rainTable [] [] = new double [13] [maxyear];
```

Because it is natural to do so, we run the month subscript from 1 to 12, which means we declare the array as length 13 (allowing for the zeroth element that we won't use). `rainTable[4]` then gives all rainfall for all the available years for April. April's row is the shaded area in Figure 5.4.

Program design   This program is a classic read–process–output program, where the input–ouput is based on files. Therefore we just create one class to handle everything, and call it from the main program. In additon to printing the data out and the results, we would like to draw a graph of the means for the various months and their respective standard deviations. Because the `Graph` class can only have points being added to one line at a time, we store the standard deviations in an array and then loop through them at the end, creating the second graph.

For the actual processing, we shall be able to make use of the mean and standard deviation methods safely stored in the `jgeslib` package's `Stats` class as described after Example 5.2.

Program   The program is set up to get data from the specific file `rain.data`. The name could be made a variable and be read in. Furthermore, because the results occupy a lot of space we have not used the display. The results will appear on the console output but we could send them to a file by running the program with redirections, as in

```
java Weather > weather.out
```

The program follows.

```
import java.io.*;
import javagently.*;
import jgeslib.*;

class Weather {

    /*  The Weather program      by J M Bishop    Jan 1997
     *  ====================     Graphics July 1999
     *
     *  Calculates mean and standard deviation of rainfall
     *  for each month over the number of years provided.
     *
     *  Illustrates handling of matrices and passing columns
     *  as parameters.
     *  The data must be in a file in the form:
     *  year followed by the 12 rainfall figures for
     *  the months of that year.
     */

    static class RainBase {
```

```
int    base = 1950;
int    startyear, endyear = 0; // range from 1950 upwards

// all arrays declared length 13 so months go from 1 to 12
double rainTable [] [] = new double [13] [70];
double averagetable [] = new double [13];
double stddevTable  [] = new double [13];

Graph g = new Graph("Rainfall", "month", "cm");

void readIn () throws IOException {
  BufferedReader fin = Text.open("Rain.data");
  int actualYear = 0; // e.g. 1989
  int yearIndex = 0;  // e.g. 0

  // The actual years are read in and might not be sorted
  // or contiguous. The yearIndex starts at 0 and is
  // to store the data in an orderly manner.

  try {
    while (true) {
      actualYear = Text.readInt(fin);
      System.out.print(actualYear+" ");
      if (yearIndex == 0) startyear = actualYear;
      for (int m = 1; m<=12; m++) {
        rainTable[m][yearIndex] = Text.readDouble(fin);
        System.out.print(
            Text.format(rainTable[m][yearIndex],6,1));
      }
      System.out.println();
      yearIndex++;
    }
  }
  catch (EOFException e) {
    // Pick up the last year of data read in.
    endyear = actualYear;
    System.out.println("Data read for "+startyear+" to "+
        endyear+"\n\n");
  }
}

void showResults () {
  System.out.println("Rainfall statistics for " +
      startyear + " to " + endyear);
  System.out.println("========================" +
      "===========\n");
  System.out.println("Month\tMean\tStd Deviation");
  int nyears = endyear-startyear+1;
  double a;
  g.setTitle("Mean");
  g.setSymbol(true);

  for (int m =1; m<=12; m++) {
    averagetable[m] = Stats.mean (rainTable[m], nyears);
    stddevTable[m] = Stats.stddev
        (rainTable[m], nyears, averagetable[m]);
```

```
            System.out.println(Text.format(m,2)+
                Text.format(averagetable[m],12,2)+
                Text.format(stddevTable[m],12,4));
            g.add(m,averagetable[m]);
        }

        g.nextGraph();
        g.setColor(g.blue);
        g.setSymbol(true);
        g.setTitle("Standard Deviation");
        for (int m = 1; m <= 12; m++)
            g.add (m, stddevTable[m]);
        g.showGraph();
        System.out.println("Type Ctrl-C to end");
    }
}

public static void main (String args [])throws IOException {

RainBase rain = new RainBase();

    rain.readIn ();
    rain.showResults ();
}
}
```

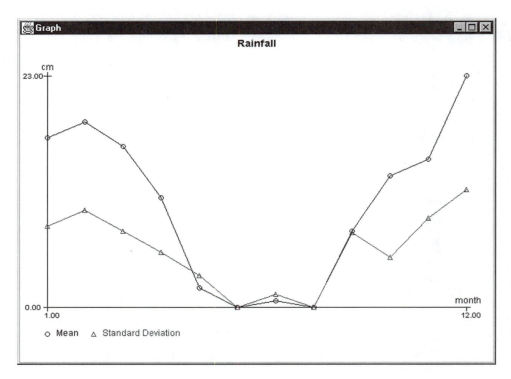

Figure 5.5 *Graphs from the weather program*

Testing For the data shown above, the output to the file would be as follows, and the graph is shown in Figure 5.5.

```
1989   20.0  22.0  17.0  14.0   5.0   0.0   0.0   0.0   7.0  12.0  30.0  20.0
1990   22.0  24.0  19.0  12.0   0.0   0.0   3.0   0.0   8.0  15.0  20.0  25.0
1991   17.0  17.0  17.0  15.0   0.0   0.0   0.0   0.0   6.0  17.0   8.0  20.0
1992   10.0  10.0  10.0   5.0   0.0   0.0   0.0   0.0   0.0  12.0  10.0  15.0
1993   20.0  22.0  17.0  14.0   5.0   0.0   0.0   0.0   7.0  12.0  30.0  20.0
1994   22.0  24.0  19.0  12.0   0.0   0.0   3.0   0.0   8.0  15.0  20.0  25.0
1995   17.0  17.0  17.0  15.0   0.0   0.0   0.0   0.0   6.0  17.0   8.0  20.0
1996   25.0  30.0  25.0  15.0   7.0   0.0   0.0   0.0  20.0  15.0  20.0  30.0
1997   25.0  30.0  25.0  15.0   7.0   0.0   0.0   0.0  20.0  15.0  20.0  30.0
1998   10.0  10.0  10.0   5.0   0.0   0.0   0.0   0.0   0.0  12.0  10.0  45.0
Data read for 1989 to 1998

Rainfall statistics for 1989 to 1998
====================================
Month   Mean    Std Deviation
  1     16.80     7.9833
  2     18.40     9.5940
  3     15.90     7.5344
  4     10.80     5.4528
  5      1.90     3.1073
  6      0.00     0.0000
  7      0.60     1.2649
  8      0.00     0.0000
  9      7.50     7.3522
 10     13.00     4.9441
 11     14.60     8.7965
 12     23.00    11.5950
```

5.3 Numerical methods – linear curve fitting

The two methods that follow are classics in the numerical methods repertoire and make good use of arrays and matrices in their algorithms.

Least squares fit

Suppose that we measure a value of y for various different values of x, and that we know from theory that the relationship between y and x is a straight line: $y = a + bx$. A simple example of this would be the extension of a spring for various different loads. Because of experimental error, the measured points do not lie exactly on a straight line, as shown in the figure overleaf.

Of course, knowing that there is a straight line in the data, we could move a ruler around until we get a good fit to the eye, but we would like to do this in a precise way.

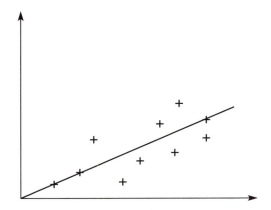

Fitting lines – or, in general, curves – to data is an important area of numerical methods. We shall look at the simplest form of linear curve fitting, known as linear regression. From this, the reader can move on to interpolating, i.e. finding approximate fits, and will encounter methods such as Lagrange interpolation, Newton's divided difference interpolation, and interpolating with cubic splines.

The notion of 'best fit' is open to interpretation, but the one usually used is the sense of minimizing the sum of the squares of the errors. That is, we want to find a, b so as to minimize

$$s = \sum_{i=1}^{n} [y_i - (a + bx_i)]^2$$

where the data points are (x_i, y_i) ($i = 1$ to n). Following this through we find that the solution reduces to two simultaneous equations in a and b, which are solved to give

$$a = \left(\sum x_i^2 \sum y_i - \sum x_i y_i \sum x_i \right) / D$$

$$b = \left(n \sum x_i y_i - \sum x_i \sum y_i \right) / D$$

where

$$D = n \left(\sum x_i^2 \right) - \left(\sum x_i \right)^2$$

Although we shall not discuss it here, note that the above ideas can easily be extended to fitting data to curves other than straight lines.

Public and private members

Before going on to look at how a least squares solver could be put in a public place for use by everyone (like the statistical methods of Example 5.3), we consider the aspect of privacy. In Java, classes and their members are by default visible to every other class *in the same directory*. If we put a class in another directory, such as `jgeslib`, then we must declare the class and the members – fields and methods – that are to be accessed as **public**.

By the same token, if the class contains members which are only used by the class, for partial calculations and so on, then it is considered good practice to emphasize this fact by declaring them **private**. There are other accessibility levels which are described in Chapter 10. Meanwhile, from now on we shall adopt a policy of designating everything in library routines as either private or public. In the programs we write, we shall remain in default mode.

EXAMPLE 5.6   A Least squares class for `jgeslib`

Problem   We would like to add the least squares method to our library of useful routines.

Program design   `LeastSquares` will be the name of the class. There is one method: `solve`. It takes in the two vectors and their length. It puts its answers in the variables a and b, which are publicly available to users of the class. `sumOne` and `sumTwo` are completely private to the class, and used to avoid repetition, because the above formulas use single and double summations repeatedly.

Library method

```
package jgeslib;

public class LeastSquares {

  /* The self-contained Least Squares class   by J M and N T Bishop
   * ====================================   July 1999
   *
   * provides a means for fitting a least squares
   * line to a set of data points. The results are
   * available in the variables a and b
   */

  public double a,b;

  public void solve (double x [], double y [], int n) {
    double D = (n*sumtwo(x,x,n)-Math.pow(sumone(x,n),2));
    a = (sumtwo(x,x,n)*sumone(y,n) -
        sumtwo(x,y,n)*sumone(x,n))/D;
    b = (n*sumtwo(x,y,n)-sumone(x,n)*sumone(y,n))/D;
  }

  private double sumone (double u [], int n) {
    double sofar = 0;
    for (int i=0; i<n; i++)
      sofar += u[i];
    return sofar;
  }
```

```
private double sumtwo (double u [], double v [], int n) {
  double sofar = 0;
  for (int i=0; i<n; i++)
    sofar += u[i]*v[i];
  return sofar;
}
}
```

Now we can consider an example application which uses our class.

EXAMPLE 5.7 Hooke's law

Problem Hooke's law (named after Robert Hooke (1635–1703)) states that $F = k(x - L)$, where L is the natural length of a spring and k is the spring coefficient, as in

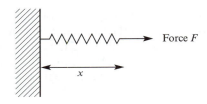

The length x is measured for various different applied forces F, and we wish to calculate the best fit to the data for L and k.

Furthermore, we would like to plot the points (x, F) and the resulting line that is obtained.

Solution To obtain L and k, we read in the data points x_i and F_i for $i = 1$ to n, and use the least squares function developed above. Plotting is done by making use of our handy Graph class in javagently, as described earlier. To use the LeastSquares solve method, y, a and b become F, $-kL$ and k.

Program design The program has data to read in from a file and results to print. The results should also be shown graphically, plotting x against F. It seems sensible to use the Display class, as we can also specify the file name there. In order to keep all the data together with its input–output routines, we set up a nested class in the program, which both defines and manipulates the variables, which are

```
double x [] = new double [100];
double F [] = new double [100];
int n;
```

The full program follows.

```
import java.io.*;
import javagently.*;
import jgeslib.*;
```

```
class LeastSquaresTest {

  /* Testing the Least Squares method     N T and J M Bishop
   * =================================     1990, 1999
   *
   * Joins with a HookesLaw object to
   * read in two vectors and pass them to
   * the LeastSquares object
   * for processing.
   *
   * Illustrates packages, arrays, and clear
   * class design.
   */

  public static void main (String args []) throws IOException {

    LeastSquares ls = new LeastSquares();
    HookesLaw hooke = new HookesLaw();

    hooke.preamble();

    // allow several datasets until the user presses close.
    while(true) {
      hooke.openFile();
      hooke.readAndPlot();

      // now switch to the least squares object
      ls.solve(hooke.x,hooke.F,hooke.n+1);

      // the results are found in a and b
      double L = -ls.a/ls.b;
      double k = ls.b;

      // end off
      hooke.plotTheFit(L, k);
    }
  }

  static class HookesLaw {
    double x [] = new double [100];
    double F [] = new double [100];
    int n;

    Display display = new Display("Hooke's Law");
    Graph g;
    BufferedReader fin;

    void preamble () throws IOException {
      display.println(
        "****** Least Squares Data Fitting ******");
      display.println(
        "******           Hooke's Law         ******");
      display.println
        ("Given a set of data xi and Fi we find L and k");
```

```
        display.println
            ("to give the best straight line fit in F = k(x-L)");
        display.println("The data is read from a file.");
        // Set a default file name
        display.prompt("Data file name","HookesLaw.data");
    }

    void openFile () throws FileNotFoundException{

        display.ready("Set the name and press Ready");
        String fileName = display.getString("Data file name");
        display.println("Reading from "+fileName);
        fin = Text.open(fileName);
        g = new Graph("Hooke's Law: best straight line", "x", "F");
        g.setColor(g.blue);
        g.setSymbol(true);
        g.setLine(false);
        g.setTitle(fileName);
    }

    void readAndPlot() throws IOException {
        n = 0;
        int i = 0; // initialize here too because of the try
        try {
            for (i = 0; ; i++) {
                x[i] = Text.readDouble(fin);
                F[i] = Text.readDouble(fin);
                display.println(i + Text.format(x[i],8,2) +
                            Text.format(F[i],12,2));
                g.add(x[i],F[i]);
            }
        }
        catch (EOFException e) {
            n = i-1;
            display.println("Points read = "+ i);
        }
        g.showGraph();
    }

    void plotTheFit (double L, double k) {
        // On the same axes
        g.nextGraph();
        g.setColor(g.red);
        g.setLine(true);
        g.add(x[0],k*(x[0]-L));
        g.add(x[n],k*(x[n]-L));
        g.showGraph();
        display.reposition(g);
        display.ready("To read another set of data, press Ready");
        g.dispose();
    }
  }

}
```

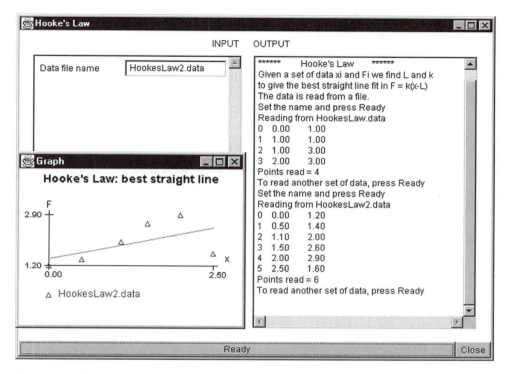

Figure 5.6 *The display for the Hooke's law program*

Testing   For a simple test, we choose a straight line, $F = 1 + x$, and then construct data for which the line would be the best fit. We try

$$(0, 1), (1, 1), (1, 3), (2, 3)$$

and as expected the program returns $L = -1$ and $k = 1$, as shown at the start of the display in Figure 5.6. The figure shows the graph for the second set of data listed on the output section.

5.4 Numerical methods – solving linear equations

Matrix calculations are very common in science and engineering applications. Usually we want to solve for x in

$$Ax = b$$

where A is an $n \times n$ matrix, and b and x are vectors of dimension n. This problem is the same as that of solving a system of n linear equations. For example, if $n = 3$, we have

$$A_{11} x_1 + A_{12} x_2 + A_{13} x_3 = b_1$$
$$A_{21} x_1 + A_{22} x_2 + A_{23} x_3 = b_2$$
$$A_{31} x_1 + A_{32} x_2 + A_{33} x_3 = b_3$$

There are two classes of methods for solving this problem: **iterative** methods and **direct** methods. Iterative methods are covered in this section, but direct methods – of which Gaussian elimination is the most well known – are beyond the scope of the book.

We have already looked at iterative methods in the solution of one equation – Newton's method (section 4.7) – and will discuss the secant method in section 6.5. These methods work by making an estimate of the solution and then successively providing a better estimate of the solution. We continue the process until the difference between two successive solution estimates is less than some tolerance.

What tolerance means

This raises a question: what does 'less than some tolerance' mean when the solution is an n-dimensional vector? Of course there is not a unique answer, but for the purposes of this book we will use what is known as the L_∞ norm, written as $\| \|_\infty$. For an n-dimensional vector x this norm is defined as

$$\|x\|_\infty = \max|x_i| \quad \text{where } i = 1 \text{ to } n$$

i.e. it is the value of the largest component in the vector. For example, if a convergence criterion $\|\text{error}\|_\infty \leq 10^{-6}$ is satisfied then for every component of the vector $|xnew_i - xold_i| \leq 10^{-6}$.

There are many different iterative matrix-solving algorithms. We give here a program for one of the more popular methods: SOR, which stands for Successive Over-Relaxation.

Successive Over-Relaxation

If we have an estimate $xold_i$ for the solution, then a better estimate is given by

$$x_i = (1 - \omega)xold_i + \omega \frac{\left[-\left(\sum_{j=1}^{i-1} a_{ij}x_j \right) - \left(\sum_{j=i+1}^{n} a_{ij}xold_j \right) + b_j \right]}{a_{ii}}$$

where ω is a parameter which depends on the matrix A. Unfortunately the relationship is not simple, and one can write down a value only in certain special cases. As a general guide, $1 < \omega < 2$, and it is usually in the middle of this range.

The right hand side involves x_i, but provided we calculate the components of x_i in order $x_1, x_2, ..., x_n$, we need only those components which have already been calculated. Then we set $xold_i = x_i$, and repeat the process.

As with all iterative methods, we have to decide when to stop. This will be when the norm of the difference between x and $xold$ is less than some tolerance. Here, we use the L_∞ norm and the tolerance required will depend very much on the physical properties that the equations represent. In many cases a tolerance of 10^{-6} would be usual, but if the values are expected to be whole numbers then a tolerance of 0.01 would be used.

EXAMPLE 5.8   SOR in the library

Our first consideration is to endeavour to get the SOR method into our library as a self-contained class. The variables that store results, and therefore need to be public are:

```
public double  xnew [] ;
public boolean convergence;
public int     iterations;
```

The method we call is called `solve`, as for the other numerical processes, and it uses a private method called `normLinfinity`.

```
package jgeslib;

public class SORSolver {

  /* Successive over relaxation solver     N T Bishop 1990, 1999
   * ==================================
   *
   * The solve routine needs seven parameters. The
   * results are available in 3 public variables.
   */

  public double  xnew [];
  public boolean convergence;
  public int     iterations;

  public void solve (double a [] [], double b [], double x [],
                     int n, double omega, double tolerance,
                     int kmax) {

    xnew = new double [n];
    convergence = false;
    iterations = 0;
    double xold [] = x;
    do {
      for (int i=0; i<n; i++) {
        double sumax = 0;
        double sumaxold = 0;
        for (int j=0; j<i; j++)
          sumax += a[i][j]*xnew[j];
        for (int j=i+1; j<n; j++)
          sumaxold += a[i][j]*xold[j];
        xnew[i] = (1-omega) * xold[i] -
        omega*(sumax + sumaxold - b[i]) / a[i][i];
      }
```

```
            iterations++;
            if (normLinfinity(xold, xnew, n) < tolerance)
               convergence = true;
            for (int j=0; j<n; j++)
               xold[j] = xnew[j];
         } while ((!convergence) & !(iterations==kmax));
      }

   private double normLinfinity(double x [], double y [], int n) {
      double highest = Math.abs(x[1]-y[1]);
      for (int i=0; i<n; i++)
         if (Math.abs(x[i]-y[i]) > highest)
            highest = Math.abs(x[i]-y[i]);
      return highest;
      }
   }
```

As before, we place this file in the `jgeslib` directory and compile it there.

EXAMPLE 5.9   Balancing manufacturing output

Problem   A factory manufactures six basic components and uses some of them in the manufacture of other items. The balance between the output and the production rate is given by the equations

$$4x_1 + x_3 + x_6 = 41$$
$$12x_2 + 4x_4 + 5x_5 = 109$$
$$x_1 + 10x_3 = 38$$
$$x_1 + 3x_4 + x_6 = 17$$
$$2x_2 + 5x_5 + 2x_6 = 67$$
$$2x_2 + 2x_3 + 8x_6 = 64$$

Solve this set of equations to establish the amount of each basic component that needs to be produced.

Solution   We shall use the SOR method. We set up the coefficients of the equations, including the zeros, in a 6×6 matrix. We also need an initial estimate for each x and a value for ω. Since the answers will be integers, the tolerance can be set low.

Program design   The design of such a large program requires careful thought. In fact, we soon see that it follows the same model as the least squares fit. There is a `solve` method, put in a class and stored in the publicly available `jgeslib`. Then we have a great deal of data to read in, echo, send to SOR for processing, and report back on. In this case, we keep the main program small and self-contained, as in

```
import jgeslib.*;
import java.io.*;
import javagently.*;

class SimultaneousEquations {

  /* Program to solve a system of simultaneous equations
   * ---------------------------------------------------
   * N T Bishop & A Moolman  1990 & 1999
   *
   * Uses the SOR method
   */

  public static void main (String args []) throws IOException {

    SORSolver SOR = new SORSolver();
    DataHandler data = new DataHandler();
    data.initialize();
    while(true){
      data.input();
      data.echo();
      SOR.solve(data.a, data.b, data.x, data.n,
                data.omega, data.tolerance, data.kmax);
      data.output(SOR.iterations, SOR.xnew);
    }
  }

}
```

What we have here is also self-contained. It instantiates another class, `DataHandler`, where all the input–output is handled. The main program communicates with its `DataHandler` object via the seven variables that it accesses directly and sends as parameters through to `SOR.solve`. The results from `SOR` are then available to `data` for outputting.

DataHandler is the only class which interfaces with the outside world. As such, it is rather longer than the other two. The data is read from a file and the results go to a file. The display is used for control purposes, and for inputting parameters, the most important of which are the file names.

```
static class DataHandler{
  Display display = new Display("Simultaneous equations");
  double a [][];
  double b [];
  double x [];
  double omega, tolerance;
  int    n;
  int    kmax;
  PrintWriter fout;

void initialize() throws IOException {

  display.println(
      "***** Solution of simultaneous equations *****");
```

```
        display.println(" using the SOR matrix solver\n");
        display.println(
            "Solution of n by n matrix equation A x = b \n");
        display.println("The data n, A, b, x (initial estimate)");
        display.println("are read from a file\n");
        display.prompt("SOR value, omega", 1.1);
        display.prompt("Max. iterations, kmax", 100);
        display.prompt("Tolerance", 1e-3);
        display.prompt("Input file name","Manufacture.data");
        display.prompt("Output file name","Manufacture.out");
    }

    void input() throws IOException {

        display.ready("Press the button when values are ready");
        omega = display.getDouble("SOR value, omega");
        kmax = display.getInt("Max. iterations, kmax");
        tolerance = display.getDouble("Tolerance");
        String inFile = display.getString("Input file name");
        String outFile = display.getString("Output file name");

        BufferedReader fin = Text.open(inFile);
        fout = Text.create(outFile);

        n = Text.readInt(fin);
        a = new double [n][n];
        b = new double [n];
        x = new double [n];
        for (int i=0; i<n; i++) {
          for (int j=0; j<n; j++)
            a[i][j] = Text.readDouble(fin);
          b[i] = Text.readDouble(fin);
          x[i] = Text.readDouble(fin);
        }
    }

    void echo () {

      fout.println("omega is "+omega+"; tolerance is "+tolerance+
                  "; the equations are:");
      for (int i=0; i<n; i++) {
        for (int j=0; j<n; j++)  {
          fout.print(a[i][j]+" x"+(j));
          if (j<n-1) fout.print(" + ");
        }
        fout.println("\t= "+b[i]);
      }
    }

    void output (int iterations, double x []) {

        if (iterations < kmax) {
          display.println("Solution found in "+iterations
                        +" iterations\n");
          fout.println("\nSolution, after "+iterations+" iterations, is");
```

```
            for (int i=0; i < n; i++)
              fout.println("x["+i+"]="+
                        Text.format(x[i],10,6));
      } else
        display.println(
           "Algorithm did not converge in iterations specified");
      fout.close();
    }
}
```

Testing   Testing involves setting up the data file as described above, giving

```
6
4   0   1   0   0   1   41    0
0  12   0   4   5   0  109    0
1   0  10   0   0   0   38    0
1   0   0   3   0   1   17    0
0   2   0   0   5   2   67    0
0   2   2   0   0   8   64    0
```

The display is given in Figure 5.7 and the output that went to a file follows.

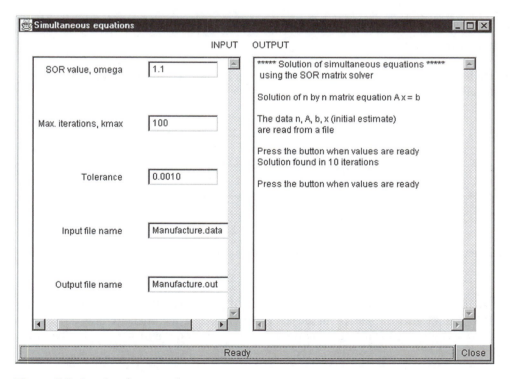

Figure 5.7 *Display for manufacturing output*

```
omega is 1.1; tolerance is 0.0010; the equations are:
4.0 x0 +  0.0 x1 +  1.0 x2 + 0.0 x3 + 0.0 x4 + 1.0 x5 =  41.0
0.0 x0 + 12.0 x1 +  0.0 x2 + 4.0 x3 + 5.0 x4 + 0.0 x5 = 109.0
1.0 x0 +  0.0 x1 + 10.0 x2 + 0.0 x3 + 0.0 x4 + 0.0 x5 =  38.0
1.0 x0 +  0.0 x1 +  0.0 x2 + 3.0 x3 + 0.0 x4 + 1.0 x5 =  17.0
0.0 x0 +  2.0 x1 +  0.0 x2 + 0.0 x3 + 5.0 x4 + 2.0 x5 =  67.0
0.0 x0 +  2.0 x1 +  2.0 x2 + 0.0 x3 + 0.0 x4 + 8.0 x5 =  64.0

Solution, after 10 iterations, is
x[0]=  7.999975
x[1]=  4.999883
x[2]=  3.000003
x[3]=  0.999977
x[4]=  9.000000
x[5]=  6.000025
```

Discussion   If we look at the equation for calculating the x_i, we see that it involves a_{ii} as a denominator. In order to avoid division by zero, a_{ii} must be non-zero for all $i = 1$ to n. If any $a_{ii} = 0$, we can often reorder the equations so as to make all the a_{ii} non-zero. If reordering is not possible then the matrix is singular and there is in any case no unique solution for x. There is some discussion of reordering in the next example. The SOR method has another restriction, which is discussed in Problem 5.7 at the end of the chapter.

EXAMPLE 5.10   Kirchhoff's laws

Problem   Given the electrical network shown below, we want to find the six currents labelled i_1 to i_6.

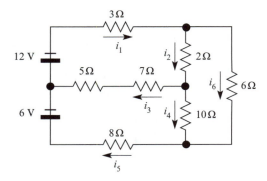

Solution   Kirchhoff's current law (named after Gustav Robert Kirchhoff (1824–1887)) states that the sum of all the currents at a node in a closed circuit is zero . From this we can write down three equations for the three nodes indicated by a •. These are

$$-i_1 + i_2 + i_6 = 0 \qquad (1)$$

$$i_1 - i_3 - i_5 = 0 \qquad (2)$$

$$-i_2 + i_3 + i_4 = 0 \qquad (3)$$

Then Kirchhoff's voltage law states that the sum of all the voltages around a closed path is zero. From this we get equations from each of the three meshes:

$$3i_1 + 2i_2 + 12i_3 = 12 \qquad (4)$$
$$-12i_3 + 10i_4 + 8i_5 = 6 \qquad (5)$$
$$2i_2 - 10i_4 + 6i_6 = 0 \qquad (6)$$

From these equations, we can set up a 6×7 matrix of values which can be fed into the SOR program developed in the previous example. However, we immediately encounter a problem: inputting the equations in the order above leads to a system with several values of a_{ii} being zero and the SOR method fails. The problem is overcome by ordering the equations as (2), (1), (4), (3), (5), (6), as in the data file below:

```
6
 1    0   -1    0  -1   0    0    0
-1    1    0    0   0   1    0    0
 3    2   12    0   0   0   12    0
 0   -1    1    1   0   0    0    0
 0    0  -12   10   8   0    6    0
 0    2    0  -10   0   6    0    0
```

The output is

```
omega is 0.7; tolerance is 0.0010; the equations are:
 1.0 x0 +   0.0 x1 +   -1.0 x2 +   0.0 x3 + -1.0 x4 + 0.0 x5  =   0.0
-1.0 x0 +   1.0 x1 +    0.0 x2 +   0.0 x3 +  0.0 x4 + 1.0 x5  =   0.0
 3.0 x0 +   2.0 x1 +   12.0 x2 +   0.0 x3 +  0.0 x4 + 0.0 x5  = 12.0
 0.0 x0 +  -1.0 x1 +    1.0 x2 +   1.0 x3 +  0.0 x4 + 0.0 x5  =   0.0
 0.0 x0 +   0.0 x1 +  -12.0 x2 +  10.0 x3 +  8.0 x4 + 0.0 x5  =   6.0
 0.0 x0 +   2.0 x1 +    0.0 x2 + -10.0 x3 +  0.0 x4 + 6.0 x5  =   0.0

Solution, after 19 iterations, is
x[0]=   1.401545
x[1]=   0.950970
x[2]=   0.491097
x[3]=   0.460038
x[4]=   0.911320
x[5]=   0.449989
```

Note that in this case we get better performance with a low value of ω (0.7). Here, for the first time, we have been able to apply a complete program to a different problem and use it by only entering new data. It shows that we designed the program well, and took care of all circumstances.

5.5 Case study 1: Linear boundary value problem

Consider the second-order differential equation

$$\frac{\mathrm{d}^2 y}{\mathrm{d}x^2} = e(x)\frac{\mathrm{d}y}{\mathrm{d}x} + f(x)y + g(x) \qquad (5.1)$$

We would like to solve it with y given at the end-points a, b:

$$y(a) = y_a, \quad y(b) = y_b$$

The predictor–corrector method discussed in section 3.6 can be used to solve an initial value problem in one or more differential equations. **Initial value** means that conditions are specified at one value of the independent variable x. Here we have a **boundary value** problem with conditions given at two values of x. Such problems arise in heat conduction, vibration of strings or membranes, deflection of beams under loading, fluid flow over a surface and diffusion through a porous medium.

There are two methods available for this type of problem:

1   Shooting method
2   Finite difference method.

The shooting method will be discussed in section 6.6. It can be used for linear problems as well as non-linear problems (those involving, for example, y^2 or $\sqrt{dy/dx}$, etc.). The finite difference method can only be used for linear problems. However, it is more stable than the shooting method, and is usually preferred for linear problems.

LBVP algorithm

We split the interval (a, b) into $n + 1$ subintervals:

$$a = x_0$$
$$b = x_{n+1}$$
$$x_i = a + hi$$

with $h = (b - a)/(n + 1)$ giving

$$a = x_0 \quad x_1 \quad x_2 \qquad\qquad\qquad x_{n-1} \quad x_n \quad x_{n+1} = b$$
$$y_a = y_0 \quad y_1 \quad y_2 \qquad\qquad\qquad y_{n-1} \quad y_n \quad y_{n+1} = y_b$$

We use standard formulas to represent the derivatives at the point x_i:

$$\frac{dy}{dx} = \frac{y_{i+1} - y_{i-1}}{2h}$$

$$\frac{d^2y}{dx^2} = \frac{y_{i+1} - 2y_i + y_{i-1}}{h^2}$$

where $y_i = y(x_i)$. Then at the points x_i, for $i = 1$ to n, equation (5.1) becomes

$$\frac{y_{i+1} - 2y_i + y_{i-1}}{h^2} = e(x_i)\frac{y_{i+1} - y_{i-1}}{2h} + f(x_i)y_i + g(x_i) \tag{5.2}$$

Since y_0 $(= y_a)$ and y_{n+1} $(= y_b)$ are known, equation (5.2) is a set of n linear equations in the n unknowns $y_1, y_2, ..., y_n$, and can be solved by the SOR method discussed earlier in section 5.4. Specifically the matrix equation is $AY = v$ where

$$A = \begin{bmatrix} p_1 & q_1 & 0 & \cdot\cdot\cdot & & 0 \\ r_2 & p_2 & q_2 & 0 & & \cdot \\ 0 & & & & & \cdot \\ \cdot & & & & & \cdot \\ & & & & & 0 \\ \cdot & & & & r_{n-1} & p_{n-1} & q_{n-1} \\ 0 & \cdot\cdot\cdot & & 0 & r_n & p_n \end{bmatrix}$$

with $p_i = 2 + h^2 f(x_i)$, $q_i = -1 + \frac{1}{2}he(x_i)$, $r_i = -1 - \frac{1}{2}he(x_i)$ and

$$v = \begin{bmatrix} -h^2 g(x_1) + (1 + \frac{1}{2}he(x_1))y_a \\ -h^2 g(x_2) \\ \vdots \\ -h^2 g(x_{n-1}) \\ (-h^2)g(x_n) + (1 - \frac{1}{2}he(x_n))y_b \end{bmatrix}$$

To test the above theory, let us solve the problem

$$\frac{d^2 y}{dx^2} = -\frac{2}{x}\frac{dy}{dx} + \frac{2}{x^2}y + \frac{\sin(\ln x)}{x^2}$$

which has the exact solution

$$y = \frac{3}{10}\sin(\ln x) - \frac{1}{10}\cos(\ln x) + Cx + \frac{D}{x^2}$$

Program design

Once again, we have the familiar steps of

Input	Number of subintervals in (a, b), y_a, y_b
Calculate	matrix A, vector v
Solve	$Ay = v$
Output	y (or message if matrix solver fails)

We use the SOR matrix solver as in section 5.4 (but see the problems below for a tri-diagonal solver) so that an initial estimate of y is required. For the estimate, we use the straight line between the points (in the (x, y) plane) (a, y_a) and (b, y_b). We take the SOR parameter ω to be 1.8, and the tolerance 10^{-6}.

Consider first the main program and its class alone:

```
import jgeslib.*;
import javagently.*;

class LinearBVP {

  /* Linear boundary value problem
   * ---------------------------
   * N T Bishop & A Moolman  1990 & 1999
   *
   * Uses the SOR method
   */

.... insert the DataHandler class here

  public static void main (String args []) {

    SORSolver SOR = new SORSolver();
    DataHandler data = new DataHandler();
    data.initialize();
    while(true) {
      data.input();
      data.CalculateMatrix();
      SOR.solve(data.m, data.v, data.solution, data.n,
                data.omega, data.tolerance, data.kmax);
      data.output(SOR.xnew,SOR.iterations);
    }
  }

}
```

We can see that `LinearBVP`'s structure is the same as that for the simultaneous equation solver in Example 5.8. Here is its `DataHandler`:

```
static class DataHandler{

  /* For the LBVP method
   * ------------------ */

  Display display = new Display("Linear Boundary Value Problem");
  double omega, tolerance, xa, xb, h, ya, yb;
  int kmax, n;
  double    m [] [];
  double    v [], solution [];

  void initialize () {
    display.println("***** Linear Boundary Value Problem *****");
    display.println("Solves y''(x) = e(x)y'(x) + f(x)y(x) + g(x)");
    display.println("with y given at the endpoints xa, xb");
    display.println("e(x)=-2/x   f(x)=2/(x*x), g(x)=sin(ln(x))/(x*x)");
    display.println("The equations are solved by the SOR method,");
    display.prompt("Value of y(a)", 1.9);
    display.prompt("Value of y(b)", 1.981388);
    display.prompt("Value of xa", 1);
```

```
    display.prompt("Value of xb", 2);
    display.prompt("Subintervals in (xa,xb)", 19);
    display.prompt("SOR parameter, omega", 1.8);
    display.prompt("Maximum iterations, kmax", 100);
    display.prompt("Tolerance", 1e-6);
}

void input () {
  display.ready("Press the button when values are ready");
  ya = display.getDouble("Value of y(a)");
  yb = display.getDouble("Value of y(b)");
  xa = display.getDouble("Value of xa");
  xb = display.getDouble("Value of xb");
  n = display.getInt("Subintervals in (xa,xb)");
  omega = display.getDouble("SOR parameter, omega");
  kmax = display.getInt("Maximum iterations, kmax");
  tolerance = display.getDouble("Tolerance");
  m = new double [n][n];
  v = new double [n];
  solution = new double [n];
  h = (xb-xa)/(n+1);
}

void CalculateMatrix() {
  for(int i=0; i<n; i++)
    for(int j=0; j<n; j++)
      m[i][j] = 0;
  v[0] = (1+h*e(xa+h)/2) * ya-g(xa+h)*Math.pow(h,2);
  v[n-1] = (1-h*e(xb-h)/2) * yb-g(xb-h)*Math.pow(h,2);
  for(int i=1; i<n-1; i++)
    v[i] = -Math.pow(h,2)*g(xa+(i+1)*h);
  for(int i=0; i<n; i++)
    m[i][i] = 2+Math.pow(h,2)*f(xa+(i+1)*h);
  for(int i=0; i<n-1; i++)
    m[i][i+1] = -1 + h*e(xa+(i+1)*h)/2;
  for(int i=1; i<n; i++)
    m[i][i-1] = -1 - h*e(xa+(i+1)*h)/2;
  for(int i=0; i<n; i++)
    solution[i] = ya + (yb-ya)*(i+1)*h/(xb-xa);
}

double e(double x) {
  return -2/x;
}

double f(double x) {
  return 2/Math.pow(x,2);
}

double g(double x) {
  return Math.sin(Math.log(x))/Math.pow(x,2);
}

void output(double x [], int iterations) {
  Graph g = new Graph
        ("Linear boundary value problem","x","y");
```

```
        if (iterations < kmax) {
          display.println("Solution obtained after "
              +iterations+" iterations:");
          display.println("x = "+ Text.format(xa,4,2)+
              "\ty = "+Text.format(ya,10,6));
          g.add(xa,ya);
          for (int i=0; i<n; i++){
            display.println("x = "+ Text.format((xa+(i+1)*h),4,2)+
                "\ty = "+Text.format(x[i],10,6));
            g.add((xa+(i+1)*h),x[i]);
          }
          display.println("x = "+Text.format(xb,4,2)+
              "\ty = "+Text.format(yb,10,6));
          g.add(xb,yb);
          g.showGraph();
          display.reposition(g);
        }
        else
          display.println("Algorithm did not converge "+
            "in iterations specified");
      }
    }
```

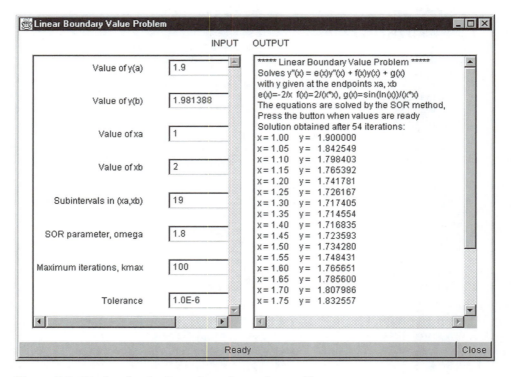

Figure 5.8 *Display for the linear boundary value problem*

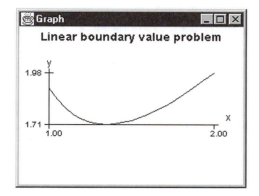

Figure 5.9 *Graph for the linear boundary value problem*

Testing Let us put $C = 1$, $D = 1$; then

$$y_a = y(1) = 1.9$$
$$y_b = y(2) = 1.981388$$

Using these boundary conditions in the program with 19 subintervals we find

$$y(1.5) = 1.734280$$

whereas the correct result is 1.734219, so the error is 6×10^{-5}. With 49 subintervals the error is 3×10^{-5}. The display is given in Figure 5.8 and the graph in Figure 5.9.

There is a sequence of extensions to this Case study in Problems 5.10 and 5.11 at the end of the chapter.

QUIZ

5.1 Write an array declaration for the days of the week, at the same time initializing it to the relevant strings.

5.2 What is wrong with the following statements?

```
int A [] = new int A[10];
System.out.println (A[A.length()]);
```

5.3 We have declared an array:

```
double B [] = new double [100];
```

Would it be possible to send it to the mean method defined in Example 5.3 and, if so, what would the call look like?

5.4 In the multi-dimensional array shown in Figure 5.4, which will be the first index, the rows or the columns?

5.5 What error message is printed by Java if you try to access an array with an invalid index?

5.6   Can subscripts be negative integers?

5.7   Can part of a matrix be passed as a parameter? If so, what part?

5.8   Can a method return an array as a result?

5.9   An array has to be declared to handle a number of real numbers, but we don't know how many. Explain how we set up the declaration of the array in this case.

5.10   Write a method to return the highest number in an array of any length, where the whole array is not necessarily used up.

PROBLEMS

5.1   **Pass rate.**   The Senate at Savanna University has decreed that at least 75% of students in each class must pass. As a result, the pass mark for each class will differ. Write a program which will read in a file of marks and determine the highest pass such that the Senate's rule applies.

5.2   **Mains voltage.**   The mains voltage supplied by a substation is measured at hourly intervals over a 72 hour period, and a report made. Write a program to read in the 72 readings from a file and determine:

- the mean voltage measured;
- the hours at which the recorded voltage varies from the mean by more than 10%;
- any adjacent hours when the change from one reading to the next was greater than 15% of the mean value.

The program should also display a graph of the voltage over the 72 hours.

5.3   **Scalar product in the library.**   Although small, the scalar product method could also be a useful addition to `jgeslib`. Enclose it in a suitable class and add it to the package. Then redo the program in Example 5.2, checking that everything works smoothly as before.

5.4   **Many light bulbs.**   Taking the program in Example 5.4, adapt it so that it reads many values from a file, and uses the display. Then adapt it again so that it can accept data from ten different light bulb manufacturers and plot the mean and standard deviations for each. Draw the graphs without lines, as there is no connection between the manufacturers. Use a random number generator with a Gaussian distribution to create the data if you like.

5.5   **Diving competition.**   The judging of international diving competitions relies on judges from several countries. In order to avoid bias, such as judges rewarding competitors from their home country with higher scores, the result for a single dive is calculated as the average of all the scores, less the highest and lowest score. We would like to computerize these calculations. Write a program which will read in from a file the scores for eight judges for four different dives (32 scores) and for each dive calculate the average (excluding highest and lowest) and then the overall average for the competitor. Output the results of the dives with an echo of the input to a file.

5.6   **Gold exploration.**   Savanna Exploration Inc. has obtained data of infrared readings of a portion of desert where gold is believed to be present. The data should show up the boundaries of a gold reef, based on readings which are greater than the average of those around them. Can you help find the gold? The map of the readings can be considered a point at a time, and a corresponding map plotted on a graph showing those with higher than average infrared levels. Sample data to work on is

```
21 21 22 30 40 21 34 45
21 22 23 30 45 21 37 40
22 23 24 45 46 47 38 39
22 23 24 35 46 47 38 38
23 24 25 36 46 49 37 36
23 24 25 37 39 48 36 35
23 24 25 25 26 25 26 25
23 25 26 27 28 29 30 31
```

5.7 **SOR primer.** The SOR method requires that the elements on the diagonal are non-zero. It is also only guaranteed to work if the matrix is diagonally dominant, in other words if

$$|a_{ii}| > \sum_{i \neq j} a_{ij}$$

Write a method which looks at a matrix and establishes whether it is suitable for the SOR method, and, if not, endeavours to reorder the rows such that it will be suitable. Insert the method into Example 5.9 and run the program with the data from Example 5.10.

5.8 **Linear regression.** Data has been collected which should fit the curve Ae^{kx}. Use linear regression to find A and k to give the best fit. The data is

x	y
1.00	5.10
1.25	5.79
1.50	6.53
1.75	7.45
2.00	8.46

Illustrate your results on a graph.
Hint: If $y = Ae^{kx}$, $\ln(y) = \ln(A) + kx$.

5.9 **SOR testers.** Using the SOR method, solve the following matrix problems:

(a)
$$\begin{bmatrix} 4 & 2 & 0 & 1 \\ 1 & -6 & 1 & 2 \\ 2 & 1 & -5 & 0 \\ -3 & 0 & 0 & 4 \end{bmatrix} x = \begin{bmatrix} 9 \\ -9 \\ 4 \\ 1 \end{bmatrix}$$

(b)
$$\begin{bmatrix} 2 & 3 & 1 & 2 \\ -2 & 4 & -1 & 5 \\ 3 & 7 & 1.5 & 1 \\ 6 & 9 & 3 & 7 \end{bmatrix} x = \begin{bmatrix} 2 \\ 3 \\ 4 \\ 5 \end{bmatrix}$$

(c)
$$\begin{bmatrix} 4 & 2 & 1 & 0 \\ 1 & 6 & 2 & 1 \\ 3 & 0 & 0 & -4 \\ -2 & 1 & 5 & 0 \end{bmatrix} x = \begin{bmatrix} 14 \\ 19 \\ 2 \\ 8 \end{bmatrix}$$

5.10   **LBVP accuracy.**   Test the accuracy of the program in Case study 1 (section 5.5). Instead of outputting the value of y, output the difference between the calculated value of y and the exact solution; and the L_∞ norm of this difference. Examine how the accuracy depends on the number of subintervals, and the value of tolerance. Test the program with some other differential equations.

5.11   **Better LBVP.**   There is a much better way to solve $Ay = v$ than the SOR method. We can use a special method for a tridiagonal matrix – one, like A, which is non-zero only on the main diagonal and the two diagonals on either side of it. We write the matrix in terms of the diagonals, using the three vectors introduced earlier:

$$p_i = a_{ii} \qquad (i = 1 \text{ to } n),$$
$$q_i = a_{i, i+1} \qquad (i = 1 \text{ to } n - 1),$$
$$r_i = a_{i, i-1} \qquad (i = 2 \text{ to } n)$$

The solution of $Ay = v$ is calculated by the following algorithm:

1.   Introduce intermediate vectors u_i, w_i, z_i.

2.   Let $u_i = p_i$.

3.   For $i = 2$ to n
     (a)   let $w_{i-1} = q_{i-1}/u_{i-1}$
     (b)   let $u_i = p_i - r_i w_{i-1}$

4.   Let $z_1 = v_1/u_1$.

5.   For $i = 2$ to n let $z_i = (v_i - r_i z_{i-1})/u_i$.

6. $y_n = z_n$.

7.   For $i = (n - 1)$ down to 1, $y_i = z_i - w_i y_{i+1}$.

Introduce a new class `Tridagonal` that contains a method called `solve` that implements this algorithm, and then revise the LVBP program so that it calls this method instead of `SOR.solve`. Test the accuracy of the program.

5.12   **Gaussian frequencies.**   Using Example 5.1 as a guide, plot the frequency of the Gaussian distribution as provided by Java's random number generator `nextGaussian`.

CHAPTER 6

Abstraction

6.1 Class power

Object-oriented programming has several ways in which the use of classes is made more powerful. We have already been using classes extensively for what is known as **composition**, in other words, creating an object in a class based on another class. The graph, display and data handler objects are also examples of this use of classes. We shall now examine the real power of object orientation, which will enable us to generalize our programs in many more ways. In the process, we shall define formally some of the concepts that we have been using informally up until now.

Constructors

The general form of an object declaration is

> **Object declaration**
>
> ```
> modifier classname objectname = new classname ( );
> modifier classname objectname = new classname (parameters);
> modifier classname objectname;
> ```

The first form introduces a new object and creates space for it according to that required by the class. The second form does the same, but also supplies parameters to the construction process. Usually these values are stored in local fields of the new object. The final version does not create space: it merely introduces the name of the object, so that it can be referred to later in the program. However, when the program runs, the object must have been created before it is used.

Whenever we instantiate a class to make a new object, as in the now very familiar

```
Display display = new Display ("Trig Graphs");
```

we are calling a constructor, which is a special method in the class which gets the object ready for use by initializing local data and calling any preparatory routines. For example, the constructor for `Display` looks like this:

```
public Display (String t) {
  title = t;
  initializeDisplay();
}
```

which does not say much, because all the real work is done by a local method, `initializeDisplay`. But it does make a copy of the title passed as a parameter.

In some of the classes we wrote, e.g. the data handlers, there were no constructors. In this case, a default constructor is assumed which creates space for the object, but does not get involved in any initialization.

Special object names and values

There are three special objects in Java's object world:

```
Object              this              null
```

Central to the theory of objects in Java is the `Object` class. Java achieves generality by using objects of different classes in the same parts of the program, while just calling them all `Objects`. This principle is important in cloning, which we discuss below.

Every object can access all of its members by name. The full name for a member is `this.member`, where `this` is an identifier signifying the current object. When there is no ambiguity over member names, the use of `this` is unnecessary. We would employ it in a case where a method has a local field or parameter with the same name as that defined in the class; then we can refer to the class field by its full name, prefixing it with `this`.

Objects that have not been through a construction process are given the special value `null` by the JVM. We can test if an object is `null`, e.g.

```
if (s == null)
```

If we try to access members of a null object, then Java will raise an exception, called a `nullPointerException`.[†]

---

† It should of course be a `NullObjectException`, but Java shows its C++ influences here.

Multiple object instantiations

The examples up till now have had the common property that each class is instantiated only once. Within a given program, a class could be instantiated many times, leading to many objects of the same type being operative at any one time. As a simple example, we could have had two graph windows in Example 2.2, e.g.

```
Graph g1 = new Graph ("Sin graph");
Graph g2 = new Graph ("Cos graph");
```

and then the add methods would refer to g1.add or g2.add as appropriate.

We can also have arrays of objects. For example, suppose we have a simple Dates class with three fields for the day, month and year. We could declare an array of 14 dates as follows:

```
Dates holidays [] = new Dates [14];
```

Now we have to be careful. The above statement creates a new array, but it does not create the objects in it. Each of these must separately go through an instantiation process, as in something like

```
holidays [2] = new Dates(d, m, y);
holidays [5] = {16,6,2000};
holidays [1] = Dates.Millennium;
holidays [6] = holidays [5];
```

The first assignment is the most usual, and goes through the constructor process with variables containing defined values. The second uses constants for the construction. The third takes a date from within the class (presumably a constant) and assigns it to holidays[1]. The last uses assignment from another member of the array.

Until objects are given instantiations through new or some other means, their values are null, with the consequences described above.

Object equality and cloning

Like arrays, objects are stored as references. There are two implications of storing objects as references. The first concerns **equality**. A straight comparison such as

```
holiday[i] == holiday[j]
```

will compare the *references* of the two dates: that is, do they refer to the same storage? It will not compare the values, which is probably what we intended. To compare the values themselves (all together as a group) we use an equals method which we must define for each new class of objects. For example, in the Dates class we could define

```
boolean equals (Dates d) {
  return (this.day == d.day &&
          this.month == d.month && this.year == d.year);
}
```

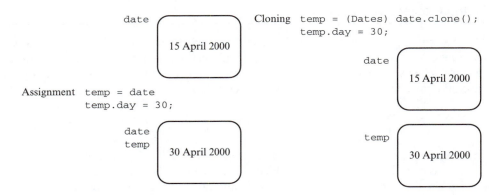

Figure 6.1 *The difference between assignment and cloning*

Because `equals` is user defined, the user (us) must decide on what basis to establish equality. Here we have said that two dates are equal if the three fields are equivalent in both dates.

The second implication is for **assignment**. Assigning two objects, e.g.

```
tempDate = holidays[i];
```

will copy the *references*. To copy the values, we need to **clone**[†] the object using a method that once again must be defined for each new class. Figure 6.1 illustrates the difference between the assignment and cloning of objects.

For assignment, `temp`'s reference becomes the same as `date`'s. Any changes made to `date` are reflected in `temp`. With cloning, a copy of the object is made, and `temp` refers to the copy. Now `temp` and `date` can change independently.

As mentioned, the class is responsible for defining what is meant by `equals` and `clone`. For our example, a clone for `Dates` could be

```
public Object clone () {
   return new Dates (day, month, year);
}
```

Copying the date means making a new date object and supplying the fields of the existing one to its constructor. Cloning is a special operation in Java, and therefore any class that wants to clone must implement the `Clonable` interface. Interfaces are discussed fully in Chapter 10. Meanwhile, we can give the general form for a clone declaration:

Clone declaration

```
modifier class classname implements Clonable {

  public Object clone ( ) {
    classname obj = new classname (parameters);
    statements to copy the fields to obj
    return obj;
```

---

† For clone, read copy if you like – a much easier word.

Class conversions

We saw that variables of primitive types can be converted into each other if this is meaningful. The same applies to objects. In particular, there are methods defined for the Java superclass, `Object`, which can be used by other objects. However, before the results are assigned, an explicit type cast must be made. `clone` is one of these methods. Thus to clone a date and print it out would require

```
Dates temp = (Dates) date.clone();
System.out.println(temp);
```

Calling the `clone` method on `date` will return an object of the superclass `Object` because that is what the `Clonable` interface requires. But we can convert it to a date by mentioning the class name.

Envelopes

One of the strict rules in Java is that values of primitive types and objects cannot be mixed. For most of the time, this causes little inconvenience, but there are times when a standard package, like the `Hashtable` class we'll see in section 6.2, requires an object, and we wish to send it, say, a value of type `int`. In order to do so, we first place the value in what is known as an **envelope** class, thus making it an object. The envelope class provides access to the value and also has various conversion methods available.

The Java `lang` package has envelope classes associated with each of the primitive types, which classes are called `Boolean`, `Charact` `r`, `Double`, `Float`, `Integer` and `Long` (notice the capital letters). As their name, suggest, they provide class-level versions of their respective primitive data types.

As an example, the important methods of the `Integer` class are given in the following form:

Integer and int conversions
| ```
Integer (int value);          // constructor
Integer valueOf (String s);   // class methods
String  toString (int i);
int     parseInt (String s);
int     intValue ();          // instance method
``` |

The constructor and the instance method provide for moving back and forth between types and classes. Thus if `i` is an `int`,

```
Integer Iobj = new Integer (i);
```

makes an object out of it. To get the `int` back in order, say, to print it, we use

```
System.out.println(Iobj.intValue());
```

The other selected methods convert from strings and back. The other envelope classes have corresponding methods. Those for `Character` were shown in section 4.2.
```

6.2 Class-independent tables

Having examined much of the theory of classes, we bring it together in an example which uses objects in an extension of the array concept, a **dictionary**. A dictionary, as the name suggests, has the following properties:

- keys are mapped to values;
- keys and values can be anything;
- there is a fast way of finding a key.

In a real dictionary, words are mapped to explanations, and the speed of searching is obtained because the keys are sorted. Knowing this, we can arrive very rapidly at the right place for a word. Dictionaries overcome many of the restrictions of arrays, specifically that the size must be fixed when the array is created, and that the index is always an integer.

Hash tables

What we really want is a dynamically sized structure, which also has the property that the indices can be, well, anything. Java's hash tables fit this bill completely. A hash table is a collection of pairs of items (key, value). The key is the index (in array terms) and the value is what is associated with the key. We can therefore see that an array is a special case of a hash table, with the key being of type int. With hash tables, though, the key can be of any type of object, including Double, String, Dates or whatever. The proviso is that the key cannot be a primitive type, which is where envelopes come in handy.

A prime example of a hash table is that kept by the Display class, as illustrated in Figure 6.2. When we send the input section information about a data field to

Key	Value
Initial accelerations in m/s/s	0.8
Constant speed time in min	18.25
Deceleration in m/s/s	1.2
Acceleration time in m/s/s	3.5

Figure 6.2 *An example of a dictionary or hash table*

be shown with a label and an initial value, these are put in a hash table, with the label as the key. Later on, when the program asks for the value, it supplies the label as the key, and gets the value in return.

If we compare Figure 6.2 to the example shown in Figure 5.1, we notice that the essential difference is that with an array (or matrix) the indices are external to the table, whereas here they are part of it – the key part. Also, values are not inserted contiguously from the beginning; there may be gaps. This does not affect the access of the data, as we shall see. In fact, it makes it faster!

A word about the term 'hash' table: hash refers to the fact that the items are not stored sequentially in the table, but in a manner which makes them efficient to retrieve. In fact, in a fairly empty table, the efficiency can approach that of an array. As a result, hash tables are not ordered by key, and if we print out what is in one, the items will appear in some seemingly random order. It is a pity that we cannot continue to use the word dictionary, rather than hash table, as that term better decribes what we are after, but it is better to be specific.

Declaring and accessing a hash table

Some of the ways of declaring and manipulating a hash table are summarized in the form

Hash table declaration and access

```
Hashtable name = new Hashtable ( );
void      put (Object key, Object value);
Object    get (Object key);
boolean   containsKey (Object key);
boolean   contains (Object value);
void      remove (Object key);
```

Hashtable is defined based on Object so that it can be used with any class. For example, suppose we wish to associate names with dates. We could do the following:

```
Hashtable holidays = new Hashtable ();
Dates d;

holidays.put ("Millennium", new Dates (2000,1,1));
holidays.put ("Christmas", new Dates (2000,12,25));
d = (Dates) holidays.get ("Millennium");
```

The last statement will successfully get the date 1 January 2000 out of the table. But why does the cast to (Dates) appear in the assignment? The reason is that hash tables are potentially available for any kinds of objects. The result type of a get is Object. In order to ensure that we have obtained an object of type Dates, Java requires that we **cast** the Object, as described in section 6.1.

Enumerations

Another class that is closely associated with hash tables is `Enumeration`. In fact, `Enumeration` is not a real class: it is a special kind of class called an **interface**, described at the beginning of the next section. In this context, the difference is not important. To declare an `Enumeration` we simply state

```
Enumeration e;
```

Interfaces are fully discussed in Chapter 10.

Enumerations provide a means for iterating over a collection of objects. There are only two methods:

Enumerations
`Object   nextElement ();` `boolean hasMoreElements ();`

Once we declare an enumeration, `nextElement` will repeatedly provide the next element, and we can ask it to do so until `hasMoreElements` becomes false. For example, if `table` is a `Hashtable` and has been filled with keys that are `Strings` (the type of the values does not matter at this point), then the loop for printing out the keys will be

```
System.out.println("In the table");
for (Enumeration e = table.keys(); e.hasMoreElements();) {
  String s = (String) e.nextElement();
  System.out.println(s);
}
```

Notice that because of the casting required (as explained just above), the update part of the loop is done as a separate assignment in the body, rather than along with the initialize and check parts, as is usual. Putting this all together, we can tackle the following example.

EXAMPLE 6.1   Currency converter

Problem   We would like to be able to look up the exchange rate for any country for a currency called ZAR, and do a conversion for a given amount.

Approach   There is an Internet site called www.xe.net which has daily updates of worldwide exchange rates. From it, one can obtain a table in text form, a fragment of which looks like this:

Currency unit	ZAR/Unit	Units/ZAR
====================	===================	================
DZD Algerian Dinars	0.777	12.9
USD American Dollar	4.556	0.2195
ARP Argentinian Pesos	4.556	0.2195
AUD Australian Dollars	3.356	0.2980
ATS Austrian Schillings	0.3614	2.767
BSD Bahamian Dollars	4.556	0.2195
BBD Barbados Dollars	2.265	0.4415
DEF Belgian Francs	0.1231	8.121

Omitting the headings, what we have here is a table of five values per country: a code, the country name, its currency and two reciprocal exchange rates. According to the problem statement, the index to the table should be the second field, namely the country. Because country is a string, we cannot store the data in an array, but can use a hash table.

We shall read all the values into a hash table, row by row, and then interrogate the table by the key, which is the country name. If that is a valid name, we can go ahead, get the exchange rate and output how much exchanged currency would be provided.

Class design Together, the fields that appear on one line above form an object, so what we need to do is create a class for it. This class is unlike those we have set up before in that its primary purpose is not to provide any methods, but to be a receptacle for data. In addition, the class can provide a method for reading the fields in from a file. Let us call this class Rates.

Once we have the Rates class we can set up a hash table of these objects and interrogate it in the manner explained.

Program Firstly, here is the Rates class:

```
import java.io.*;
import javagently.*;

class Rates {
  /* The Rates class    by J M Bishop  Dec 1998
   * ---------------
   * Stores a country name, currency, code and rate
   */

  String country;
  String code;
  String currency;
  double conversion;

  void setRate (BufferedReader in) throws IOException {
    code = Text.readString(in);
    country = Text.readString(in);
    currency = Text.readString(in);
```

```
        // we don't want the first rate,
        // ignore it by reading over it
        conversion = Text.readDouble(in);
        conversion = Text.readDouble(in);
    }

    }
```

The `Converter` program follows the lines set out above. Of interest are the lines in the transactions method of `DataHandler` where the objects are retrieved from the hash table, and a type cast is done.

```
c = display.getString("Country");
if (table.containsKey(c)) {
  amount = display.getDouble("Amount");
  r = (Rates) table.get(c);
```

As usual, the program makes use of the display, and the results are shown in Figure 6.3.

```
import java.io.*;
import java.util.*;
import javagently.*;

class Converter {

    /* The Converter Program      by J M Bishop  Dec 1998
     * --------------------
     * Keeps the exchange rates from one currency into
     * many others and enables currency exchanges to be
     * estimated.
     *
     * Illustrates the use of hash tables.
     */

    public static void main(String[] args) throws IOException {
        DataHandler data = new DataHandler ();
        data.initialize();
        data.readIn();
        data.echo();
        data.transactions();
    }

    static class DataHandler {
      Hashtable table = new Hashtable();

      // read in each line of data and store in
      // the hash table with country as key

      Rates rate;
      Display display = new Display ("Currency Converter");

      void initialize () {
        display.println("Currency Converter\n"+
                        "==================");
```

```
          display.prompt("Rates file", "rates.data");
          display.ready("Press ready when the file is ok");
      }

      void readIn() throws IOException {
          String filename = display.getString("Rates file");
          BufferedReader fin = Text.open(filename);
          try {
              for (int i = 0; ; i++) {
                  rate = new Rates();
                  rate.setRate(fin);
                  table.put(rate.country, rate);
              }
          }
          catch (EOFException e) {
              display.println("Data read in and stored\n");
          }
      }

      void echo() {
          display.println("In the table");
          int i = 1;
          for (Enumeration e = table.keys(); e.hasMoreElements(); i++) {
              String country = (String)e.nextElement();
              display.println(country);
          }
      }

      void transactions () {
          display.prompt("Country", "American");
          display.prompt("Amount", 1000);
          String country;
          double amount;
          String c;
          Rates r;

          while (true) {
              display.println("Scroll up to see countries");
              display.ready("Enter country and amount and press ready");
              c = display.getString("Country");
              if (table.containsKey(c)) {
                  amount = display.getDouble("Amount");
                  r = (Rates) table.get(c);
                  display.println(amount+" in "+c+" "
                      +r.currency+" is "+
                      Text.format(amount * r.conversion,6,2)+"\n");
              } else
                  display.println("Sorry, country "+c+" not in table\n");
          }
      }
  }

}
```

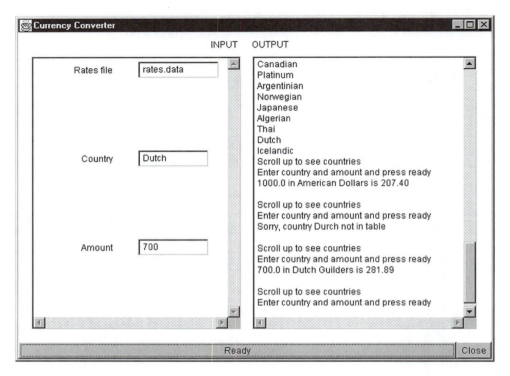

Figure 6.3 *Display from the* `Converter` *class*

6.3 Abstract methods and classes

Abstraction enables a class or method to concentrate on the essentials of what it is doing – its behaviour and interface to the world – and to rely on the details being filled in at a later stage. In a way, we can think of it as a more elaborate form of parameter passing, but this time at the class level. Java has three ways of providing abstraction: **inheritance**, **abstract classes** and **interfaces**. We introduce them all here. Inhertitance is discussed further in section 6.4 and interfaces in Chapter 10.

   So far, all our classes have related to concrete descriptions of natural items, such as graphs, displays, data handlers, and so on. If we wanted to perform an operation on more than one of these classes, such as writing out the titles of graphs and displays, then up until now we would need to have three different write methods. Abstraction aims to cut down on repetition and aids reuse – two of our goals right from the start.

Inheritance

With **inheritance**, we concentrate on defining a class that we know about, and leave open an option to define additional versions of it later. These versions will inherit the properties and characteristics of the original class, and therefore can be smaller in themselves and neater. In this way we build up hierarchies of classes and can focus changes and additions at the right level. Because all the classes in the hierarchy belong to the family, they have the same type in Java's typing mechanism, and one can be used where the other might be required.

Put more formally, each new level of class is said to **extend** the class above it. The term conveys the impression that the new class can have more fields and methods than the original. The terms for the different class are **superclass** or **parent** (the original) and **subclass** or **child** class.

Inheritance is also transitive: that means that if *a* is a class and *b* extends it, with *c* extending *b*, then *c* is also related by inheritance to *a*. The same would be true in a family, in this case *a* being the grandparent, *b* the parent and *c* the child. We shall see several examples of inheritance in what follows, but in scientific programming it seldom goes beyond one level.

The form for inheriting is

Inheriting

```
class Subclass extends OriginalClass {
```

In Java, unlike some other languages, a class may only inherit from one other class.

Abstract methods

Abstract methods provide 'place holders' for methods that can sensibly be mentioned in one class, but which are going to be implemented in a variety of ways in other classes. Take for example the methods f and df in the Newton–Raphson example (section 4.7). We should not define them with Newton–Raphson itself, because the precise functions will change each time we want to employ the method to solve a problem. What we are looking for is the concept of an abstract method. Thus we declare

```
abstract double f (double x);
```

and in the place where the actual calculation for the method is known, we shall declare, for example,

```
double f (double r); {
  return Math.sin(r);
}
```

Notice that while the names of the methods themselves must match in both cases, the names of the parameters are immaterial as long as their types match. A method name and a list of parameter types is called a **signature**.

Abstract classes

Abstract methods reside in classes, and any class with at least one abstract method becomes abstract. An abstract class can no longer be used to declare objects: the presence of the abstract method means that it is incomplete. It must first be subclassed and the abstract method(s) filled in. The form is

---

Abstract class

```
class abstract Original {
  abstract type name (parameters) {
     statements
  }
  more of the class
}

class Subclass extends Original {
  type name (parameters) {
     statements
  }
  Any other additions
}

Subclass MyClass = new Subclass();
```

This process is best illustrated by means of a real example (Example 6.2). Meanwhile, just note that inheritance is used as the mechanism for moving from abstract to actual classes, and is also used as a composition technique in its own right, as discussed in section 6.4.

Interfaces

An interface is a specification of methods that form a useful group. Any class can then declare that it implements this interface and thus achieves a certain amount of inter-operability with other classes which do the same. In implementing an interface, a class must provide a version for each of the methods listed in the interface. In that sense, an interface is similar to an abstract class, but there are two differences:

1   Interfaces only declare methods.
2   A class may implement several interfaces, but extend only one parent class.

The form for implementing an interface is

Interface implementation

```
class classname implements interfacename {
   .... rest of class
}
```

We have already used an interface in section 6.2, and there will be many opportunities to use some of Java's APIs when we discuss customizing in Chapter 7. Designing our own interfaces is left to Chapter 10.

EXAMPLE 6.2   Generalized Newton–Raphson

Problem   We would like to generalize the NewtonRaphson class of Example 4.8 so that it makes no reference to global methods.

Approach   The first step is to remove all the input–output into a DataHandler class. This is easily done. Then because what remains is a generally useful root finder, we shall take the additional step of preparing it for the jgeslib library. In so doing, we must decide what to do with the remaining interface via variables and functions. There are three categories:

1   Input variables, such as tolerance and imax, become parameters to the solve method.

2   The two abstract methods already mentioned, f and df, and the solve method are made visible by declaring them as public.

3   The solve method creates the number of iterations required, and the values calculated at each point which are of interest to the user. Since we may not always wish to have these printed out, we arrange things so that solve puts each value in an array called estimate. From there they can be collected and handled as necessary. There is no panic about the size of the array, since we only need to create it once we have the value of imax in hand, i.e. the maximum number of iterations the user wishes to allow.

Library class   The library version of NewtonRaphson now is

```
package jgeslib;

public abstract class NewtonRaphson {

    /* Newton-Raphson solver        J M and N T Bishop
     * --------------------         July 1999
     *
     * To extend the class, supply versions of f and df
     * To make use of it, call solve.
     * The root is available in estimate[iteration]
     * The earlier values of the estimation can also be
     * examined, as can iteration
     */

    public abstract double f (double x);
    public abstract double df (double x);

    public int iteration;
    public double estimate [];
```

```
public void solve (double xnew, double tolerance, int imax) {

    estimate = new double[imax+1];
    double xold;
    estimate[0] = xnew;
    iteration = 0;
     do {
        iteration++;
        xold = xnew;
        xnew = xold - f(xold) / df(xold);
        estimate[iteration]=xnew;
     } while (Math.abs(xnew - xold) > tolerance & iteration < imax);
  }
}
```

Using the class   To complete the picture, we see how the same program would now use the Newton–Raphson solver method from the class in the library:

```
import javagently.*;
import jgeslib.*;

class SpecificVolumeA {

  /* Finding the specific volume of a gas      J M and N T Bishop
   * ====================================      July 1999
   *
   * using Newton-Raphson in a library
   *
   * Illustrates abstract classes and array handling.
   */

// This small class inherits NewtonRaphson from the library and
// supplies actual values for the two functions.
// The functions are public because the abstract ones had to be.

  static class MyNewtonRaphson extends NewtonRaphson {

    public double f (double v) {
      return 70*v*v*v -3*v*v+4*v-16;
    }

    public double df (double v) {
      return 210*v*v -6*v+4;
    }
  }

  public static void main (String [] args) {

    NewtonRaphson newton = new MyNewtonRaphson ();
    DataHandlerNR data = new DataHandlerNR ();
    data.initialize();
    while(true) {
      data.getData();
      newton.solve(data.v, data.tolerance, data.imax);
```

```
          data.output(newton.iteration,
                    newton.estimate[newton.iteration]);
      }
  }

  static class DataHandlerNR {
    Display display = new Display("Heat Exchange Unit");
    double v, tolerance;
    int imax;

    void initialize () {
      display.println
          ("***** Finding the specific volume of a gas *****");
      display.println("using the Newton-Raphson root finder");
      display.println("Solves 70 v**3 - 3 v**2 +4 v - 16 = 0\n");
      display.prompt("Estimate for v", 0.5);
      display.prompt("tolerance", 1e-6);
      display.prompt("Maximum iterations, imax", 10);
    }

    void getData () {
      display.ready("Press ready button when the data is right");
      v=display.getDouble("Estimate for v");
      tolerance=display.getDouble("tolerance");
      imax=display.getInt("Maximum iterations, imax");
    }

    void output (int i, double v) {
      if (i < imax) {
        display.println ("\nConverged after "+i+" iterations");
        display.println ("v = "+Text.format(v,8,6));
      }
      else display.println("The method did not converge");
    }
  }
}
```

Testing   There is no difference in the output: see Example 4.8.

A class for complex numbers

To follow on from Example 6.2, we are going to see how to find roots for complex
numbers. The real numbers we have used up until now have belonged to the primitive
type double. We are now going to define our own number type with its own operations expressed as methods.

```
package jgeslib;

public class Complex {

  /* Complex numbers class        J M Bishop 1990
   *  --------------------        Java A Moolman 1999
   */
```

```
    public double re;
    public double im;

    public Complex(double r, double i) {
      re = r;
      im = i;
    }

    public Complex(double r) {
      re = r;
      im = 0;
    }

    public Complex() {
      re = 0;
      im = 0;
    }

    public static Complex add(Complex a, Complex b) {
      Complex c = new Complex();
      c.re = a.re + b.re;
      c.im = a.im + b.im;
      return c;
    }

    public static Complex mult(Complex a, Complex b) {
      Complex c = new Complex();
      c.re = a.re*b.re - a.im*b.im;
      c.im = a.re*b.im + a.im*b.re;
      return c;
    }

    public static Complex div(Complex a, Complex b) {
      Complex c = new Complex();
      c.re = (a.re*b.re + a.im*b.im)/(b.re*b.re + b.im*b.im);
      c.im = (b.re*a.im - b.im*a.re)/(b.re*b.re + b.im*b.im);
      return c;
    }

    public static Complex sub(Complex a, Complex b) {
      Complex c = new Complex();
      c.re = a.re - b.re;
      c.im = a.im - b.im;
      return c;
    }

    public double abs () {
      return Math.sqrt(re*re + im*im);
    }
  }
```

There are two fields for a complex number: `re` and `im`. We give three constructors, for ease of use, so that the user does not have to specify imaginary parts if they are zero. The methods themselves show an interesting design. They are all declared as static, but with two parameters and a return value. This means that they are called like this:

```
Complex a, b, c;
a = new Complex(1,0);
b = new Complex (3,1);

c = Complex.add(a,b);
```

If we had not declared `add` as static, then it would have had one parameter and referred to the substantive object for its other parameter, as in

```
public Complex add(Complex b) {
   Complex c = new Complex();
   c.re = this.re + b.re;
   c.im = this.im + b.im;
   return c;
}
```

The call would be

```
c = a.add(b);
```

just as we had `d1.equals(d2)` for the dates above. This second form is the more correct object-oriented one. However, it seemed more informative to retain the phrase `Complex.add` in the call, and so we kept the first approach.

EXAMPLE 6.3   Finding complex roots

To show how complex numbers can be put to use, we are going to transform the Newton–Raphson root solver to work with complex numbers, and then make it run in a test program. The library class is

```
package jgeslib;

public abstract class ComplexNewtonRaphson {

   /* A Newton-Raphson solver for complex numbers      N T and J M Bishop
    * ---------------------------------------------     July 1999
    * Uses methods from class complex.
    */

   public abstract Complex f (Complex x);
   public abstract Complex df (Complex x);
   public int iteration;
   public Complex estimate [];

   public void solve (Complex xnew, double tolerance, int imax) {
```

```
      estimate = new Complex[imax+1];
      Complex xold;
      Complex temp;
      estimate[0] = xnew;
      iteration = 0;
       do {
          iteration++;
          xold = xnew;
          temp = Complex.div (f(xold), df(xold));
          xnew = Complex.sub(xold, temp);
          estimate[iteration]=xnew;
          temp = Complex.sub(xnew,xold);
        } while (temp.abs() > tolerance & iteration < imax);
  }
}
```

Because we are calling methods instead of using symbols to perform operations, the expressions become a little more long-winded. Compare for example the previous version of the calculation for xnew:

```
xnew = xold - f(xold) / df(xold);
```

with the complex one:

```
xnew = Complex.sub(xold, Complex.div (f(xold), df(xold)));
```

Finally, a program to test the new class for the case $x^2 + 2x + 2 = 0$ is

```
import javagently.*;
import jgeslib.*;

class ComplexEquation {

  static class MyCNewtonRaphson extends ComplexNewtonRaphson {
    Complex two = new Complex(2,0);

    public Complex f (Complex v) {
      // calculate f = x*x + 2x + 2
      Complex temp =
      Complex.add(Complex.mult(v,v), Complex.mult(two,v));
      return Complex.add(temp,two);
    }

    public Complex df (Complex v) {
      // calculate df = 2*x + 2
      return  Complex.add(Complex.mult(two,v),two);
    }
  }

  public static void main (String [] args) {
```

```
        ComplexNewtonRaphson newton = new MyCNewtonRaphson ();
        DataHandlerCE data = new DataHandlerCE ();
        data.initialize();
        while(true) {
          data.getData();
          newton.solve(data.v, data.tolerance, data.imax);
          data.output(newton.iteration,
                      newton.estimate[newton.iteration]);
        }
      }

      static class DataHandlerCE {
        Display display = new Display("Complex root finder");
        Complex v;
        double tolerance;
        int imax;

        void initialize () {
          display.println("***** Newton-Raphson program*****");
          display.println("*****   for a COMPLEX root   *****\n");
          display.println("Solves: x*x + 2x +2 = 0\n");
          display.prompt("Estimate for v (real)", 2);
          display.prompt("Estimate for v (imaginary)", 3);
          display.prompt("tolerance", 1e-6);
          display.prompt("Maximum iterations, imax", 10);
        }

        void getData () {
          display.ready("Press ready button when the data is right");
          double vr=display.getDouble("Estimate for v (real)");
          double vi=display.getDouble("Estimate for v (imaginary)");
          v = new Complex (vr, vi);
          tolerance=display.getDouble("tolerance");
          imax=display.getInt("Maximum iterations, imax");
        }

        void output (int i, Complex v) {
          if (i < imax) {
            display.println ("\nConverged after "+i+" iterations");
            display.println ("v = "+Text.format(v.re,8,6)+
                             " + "+Text.format(v.im,8,6)+" i");
          }
          else display.println("The method did not converge");
        }
      }
    }
```

Testing   The analytical solutions are $x = -1 \pm i$, and the results of the program are shown in the display in Figure 6.4.

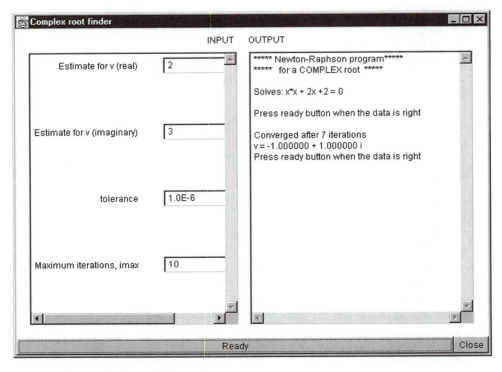

Figure 6.4 *Display from the complex roots program*

6.4 Working within a hierarchy

The purpose of setting up a hierarchy of classes is to enable us to deal with objects at different levels.

An example hierarchy

Consider the diagram in Figure 6.5. We postulate a `Nature` class consisting of birds, trees and animals. Animals can be herbivores or carnivores. Possible herbivores are elephants and rhinos. Now the field holding the name of the animal could be right in the top class, in `Nature` itself, since all birds, trees and animals will need a name. Similarly a method to write the name would also be placed here. If we had an elephant object and wanted to write the name, the method that would be called would be the one up in `Nature`. However, peculiar to an elephant would be its tusk length. This field and a method to display it would be kept in `Elephant` itself. Along the way in the hierarchy, there could be a tally of how much grass a herbivore eats in a day. Since this applies to all herbivores, we store the information in the `Herbivores` class. All of these design decisions are illustrated in Figure 6.5.

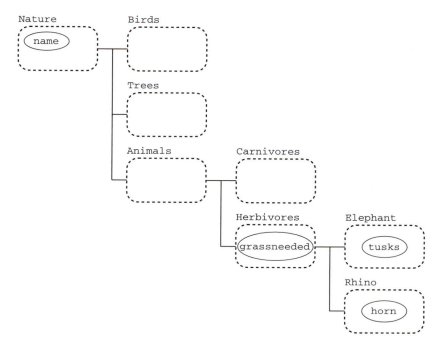

Figure 6.5 *A hierarchy in nature*

Figure 6.6 shows the effect of two object declarations on the classes at the lowest level of the hierarchy, Elephant and Rhino. jumbo and mafuta each have three variables, but the last one is different in each case. The other two were inherited from classes higher up.

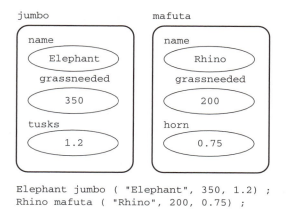

```
Elephant jumbo ( "Elephant", 350, 1.2) ;
Rhino mafuta ( "Rhino", 200, 0.75) ;
```

Figure 6.6 *Object declarations in the nature hierarchy*

Assigning objects within a hierarchy

In Figure 6.5, at the top level, we just need to know about names of natural things. At each level below that, we have more information and can perform in appropriate ways. The key to this multi-level operation is being able to assign objects freely within a hierarchy. Put formally:

- any object of a subclass can be assigned to an object of its superclass;
- any object of a superclass can be assigned to a subclass with an appropriate **cast**.

When these assignments are done, the object does not change at all: only the compiler's view of it, for typing purposes, is changed. As an example, if we have

```
Animals a;

a = jumbo;          // okay
mafuta = a;         // not okay: compiler error
mafuta = jumbo;     // not okay: compiler error
mafuta = (Rhino) a; // okay
```

The example shows that we cannot assign variables across levels. `jumbo` and `mafuta` are of quite different classes and it would never make sense to assign them. But, of course, we can work with them together under the `Herbivores`' banner, or one of the higher ones. The following example shows this:

```
Herbivores greedier;

if (jumbo.grassneeded > mafuta.grassneeded)
  greedier = jumbo;
else
  greedier = mafuta;
```

Note that a restriction in Java is that a class may only extend one other class; there is no provision for multiple inheritance. However, classes can implement several interfaces, thereby getting much the same effect.

Shadowing variables

In addition to adding to any inherited data, a subclass can decide to replace data with its own version. It does this by declaring a variable with the same name as one higher up. Mostly we do this to change the type to something more suitable. When the object is created, all the variables still exist, but the higher one is masked out. This is called **shadowing**. For example, if the zoologists working with elephants want to be more precise about what they eat, they could decide to record the grass as a real number. Therefore we would add to `Elephant`

```
double grassneeded;
```

When dealing with elephants, we shall get this version of the variable. Other classes will get the original integer version from the `Herbivores` class.

It is also possible to get at a shadowed variable by using the **super** prefix. Thus, from `Elephant`,

```
super.grassneeded;
```

would refer to the original variable in `Herbivores`.

Overriding methods

Similar to shadowing (but not exactly the same) is **overriding**. A subclass can decide to supply its own version of a method already supplied by a superclass. We would use this facility when we start off defining a general or default method in a superclass, and as we get down the hierarchy we can provide more specialized versions.

For example, all animals sleep, so in the `Animals` class we could add a `sleep` method:

```
class Animals extends Nature {
  // All sorts of things here

  void sleep () {
    // describes the sleeping habits of animals in general
  }

  void makeNoise (String audioclip) {
    // see Section 8.3 on how to do this
  }
}
```

Then once we have researched how elephants sleep, we would add in the specialized method as follows:

```
class Elephant extends Herbivores {

  Elephant (String n, int w, double l) {
    name = n;
    grassneeded = w;
    tusks = l;
  }

  void sleep () {
    // how elephants sleep
  }
}
```

Dynamic binding

Overriding uses **dynamic binding** to find the correct method. Each object has a table of its methods and Java searches for the correct versions of any overridden methods at run time. The default is that methods will need dynamic binding, and this can incur a performance overhead. If we know that a method will not be overridden, we can declare it with the modifier `final`, and save on speed. Dynamic binding is illustrated very well in Example 6.4.

Overridden methods are more powerful than shadowed variables in the following way. When there are several instances of a method in a hierarchy, the one in the closest subclass is always used. This is true even if an object of the subclass is assigned to an object of the superclass and called from there. Consider the following, using `jumbo` as an example:

```
Animals a;

a.sleep();         // calls Animals version of sleep
jumbo.sleep();      // calls Elephant version of sleep
a = jumbo;
a.sleep();         // still calls Elephant version of sleep
```

Another example of overriding is that employed to replace abstract classes with actual ones, as we saw in Example 6.2.

Overloading methods

Note that overriding is not the same as **overloading**. Overloading involves providing several methods with the same name, but with different parameter lists or signatures, so that Java sees them as distinct entities. In overriding, the parameter lists are the same. An example of overloading that we have already used extensively is the format methods of the `Text` class, where there are two with different parameter lists (see section 2.5):

```
String format (int n, int align);
String format (double n, int align, int width);
```

In Example 6.4 we shall look at an example of inheritance in a small system. There will be many more examples in the next chapter as inheritance is used extensively in Java's own packages.

Designing an object really means designing a class and its members. One of the cardinal principles in such design is **separation of concerns**. What this means is that a class should endeavour to be as self-contained as possible, and only reveal to other classes that which is necessary. Going further, it is even considered good practice to protect a field by not allowing direct access to it, but by providing get and set methods which give controlled access. Protection of this sort is indicated by **modifiers**, and a short study of Java's available modifiers is given in Chapter 10.

Example 6.4 brings together some of what we have done so far, showing very clearly how inheritance can be used for data objects kept in a table.

EXAMPLE 6.4   Veterinary tags

Problem   The Savanna Veterinary Association developed several years ago a system of tagging pets so that if they were found straying, they could be traced back to their owners. The tags were small and simple and had the animal's name and owner's phone number on them. If a pet was found by a member of the public, he or she could try to phone the owner in order to return it. However, the SVA found that when owners moved, they did not always update their tags, and so tracing owners was more difficult.

It then started to keep a central register of all tags, so that people could phone in and check whether a pet was recorded missing or not. In addition, it wants to introduce an improved XTag which has the vet's name on it as well. Obviously, the old system must continue to run, and the new system along with it. The register is being built up over several months, and will consist of old and new tags together.

Solution 1   The solution is to use inheritance. The old program already exists and runs with the old tags. What we do is define a new tags class, called XTags, which extends the old tag and has the new data item in it. But both can be stored as Tags – the 'family' name – in the register.

Class design   The program can be done in one class, with the Tags and XTags classes for the creation of the objects. main calls three methods that do the processing as required. makeTags will be the method that actually creates the Tags objects and puts them in the array, declared as

```
static Tags register [] = new Tags [100];
```

showTags will display the current register, and checkTags is the facility offered to the public for finding the phone numbers of pets, given the name of their tags. The original Tags class looks like this:

```
class Tags {

  /* The Tags class        by J M Bishop January 1997
   * for keeping data on a pet.
   */

  String name, phone;

    public Tags(String n, String p) {
      name = n;
      phone = p;
    }

    public String toString() {
      return name+" tel: "+phone;
    }

}
```

It has a constructor and one method – the standard toString method – which enables tags to be concatenated with other strings and used in println and other statements where strings are required. The part of makeTags which adds a tag to the register is

```
Tags tag = new Tags (petsName, ownersPhone);
register[index] = tag;
```

In showTags it is printed out with

```
display.println(i+"\t"+ register[i]);
```

Data for the program is in the form of pet's names and phone numbers, and is stored on a file. The full original veterinary program is on the web site, but here we press on immediately to the extension to illustrate inheritance.

Solution 2   Now we want to add the XTags to the system. Their class is given by

```
public class XTags extends Tags {

  /* The XTags class      by J M Bishop  January 1997
   * for extended vet tags with vet numbers.
   * Uses inheritance */

  String vet;

  public XTags(String n, String p, String v) {
    super(n, p);
    vet = v;
  }

  public String toString() {
    return name+" tel: "+phone+" Vet's tel: "+vet;
  }

}
```

Notice several points here. XTags has access to the name and phone variables in Tags. It overrides the toString method in Tags. It declares its own new field, vet.

Program   Before we consider the full Veterinary program, let us look at the important section related to inheritance.

```
1.   char kind = Text.readChar(fin);
2.   petsName = Text.readString(fin);
3.   ownersPhone = Text.readString(fin);
4.   Tags tag;
5.   switch (kind) {
6.     case 'p':
7.     case 'P':
8.       tag = new Tags(petsName, ownersPhone);
9.       break;
10.   default:
11.   case 'x':
12.   case 'X':
13.       String vetsPhone = Text.readString(fin);
14.       tag = new XTags(petsName, ownersPhone, vetsPhone);
15. }
16. register[index] = tag;
```

The very first line obtains information about whether the pet is to have a tag or Xtag; this is indicated by means of a 'P' (for plain) or 'X' for Xtag. Lines 2–3 are concerned with getting the common information of pet's name and owner's phone number. Now we use a switch-statement to deal with creating the two types of tags. The XTag option is also the default because we would like to move the public towards the new version. By using multiple case labels, we can easily accommodate both capital and lower-case letters.

The statement under case 'P' comes from the old program and creates a new Tags object. However, if one of the new tags is requested, then we read in more information and create an XTag object, *but in the same tag field.* Whichever tag is created gets assigned into the register, which is still declared of the superclass, Tag. Because XTag inherits from Tag, in other words comes from the same family, it is accepted wherever a Tag would be welcome. In this way inheritance aids significantly in keeping programs reusable and maintainable.

Now here is the full updated program. As usual, the main program instantiates a data handler, which is where most of the work gets done.

```java
import java.io.*;
import javagently.*;

class VeterinaryTags {

    /* The updated Vet tagging program    by J M Bishop Jan 1997
     * -----------------------------       Java 1.1 Oct 1997
     *                                     Display class July 1999
     * Keeps a register of pets' tags and enables it to be
     * checked if a stray pet is found.
     * Uses two types of tags.
     * Illustrates inheritance.
     */

    public static void main (String args []) throws IOException {
        TagDataHandler vetAssoc = new TagDataHandler ();
        vetAssoc.initialize();
        vetAssoc.makeTags();
        vetAssoc.showTags();
        while (true)
            // ends when close button is pressed on display
            vetAssoc.checkTags();
    }

    static class TagDataHandler {

        int index;
        Tags[] register = new Tags[100];
        Display display = new Display ("Veterinary tag system");
        BufferedReader fin = Text.open(System.in);

        void initialize () {
            // fin defaults to the keyboard in case there is no file
```

```
      display.println("Savanna Pet Tag System");
      display.prompt ("Pet file name", "tags.data");
      while (true) {
        display.ready("Set file name and press ready");
        String filename = display.getString("Pet file name");
        try {
          fin = Text.open(filename);
          break;
        } catch (FileNotFoundException e) {
          display.println("No such file, try again");
        }
      }
    }

    void makeTags( ) throws IOException {
      String petsName, ownersPhone;
      while (true) {
        try {
          char kind = Text.readChar(fin);
          petsName = Text.readString(fin);
          ownersPhone = Text.readString(fin);
          Tags tag;
          switch (kind) {
            case 'p':
            case 'P':
              tag = new Tags(petsName, ownersPhone);
              break;
            default:
            case 'x':
            case 'X':
              String vetsPhone = Text.readString(fin);
              tag = new XTags(petsName, ownersPhone, vetsPhone);
          }
          register[index] = tag;
          index++;
        }
        catch (EOFException e) {
          break;
        }
      }
      display.println("All "+index+" pets read in.\n");
    }

    void showTags() {
      display.println("The Pet Register\n");
      display.println("Pet No.  Name and phone no.");
      for (int i = 0; i < index; i++)
        display.println(i+"   "+register[i]);
      display.prompt("Found pet's tag name","Buster");
    }

    void checkTags() {
      display.ready("\nEnter pet's name as on tag and press ready");
      String info = display.getString("Found pet's tag name");
      boolean found = false;
```

```
            for (int i = 0; i < index; i++)
              if (register[i].name.equals(info)) {
                display.println("The pet called "+
                  info+" is registered no. "+i);
                display.println("Full info: "+register[i]);
                found = true;
                break;
              }
              if (!found)
                display.println("The pet called "+
                  info+" is not registered.");
          }
        }
      }
```

Testing   Figure 6.7 gives a sample run of the program.

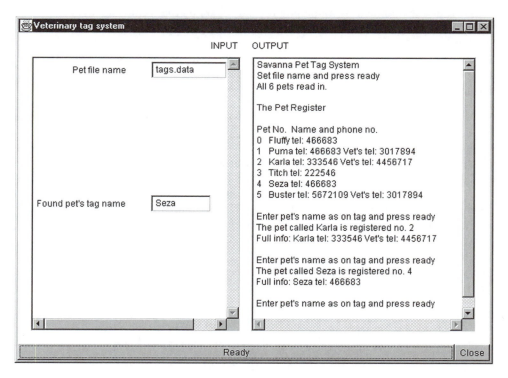

Figure 6.7 *Display for the veterinary tags program*

6.5 **Numerical methods with abstraction**

In Chapter 4, we discussed how to find the roots of an equation $f(x) = 0$ using the Newton–Raphson method. This method depended on a guess of the root, and on knowing the derivative of the function. Now suppose that the derivative df/dx is unknown, so we cannot use the Newton–Raphson method, and use instead the **secant** method.

The secant method

If x_1, x_2 ($x_1 \neq x_2$) are estimates of the root, then a better estimate is

$$x_3 = \frac{x_1 f(x_2) - x_2 f(x_1)}{f(x_2) - f(x_1)}$$

The formula is obtained by modelling the curve $f(x)$ by the secant through the points x_1, x_2 and taking the geometric relationship between the two triangles thus formed as in Figure 6.8.

The algorithm is very similar to the Newton–Raphson method. What we need to do now is to package the algorithm in a self-contained class, as already described in Example 6.2. We start by defining the interface required:

Uses : two initial estimates, tolerance, maximum iterations

Returns : two final estimates, iterations taken

From this, we can devise a list of parameters and class fields, and proceed to write the `solve` method in the usual way.

An important consideration when writing methods to implement iterative (i.e. looping) numerical algorithms is whether they should print out temporary results or not. In some cases, a program is working and only the result of the method is required, but in many cases, it may be useful or necessary to have the intermediate results printed out. As we did with Newton–Raphson, we store these values in the `estimate` array, from where the user can collect and print them if wanted. The complete class, ready to go into `jgeslib`, is

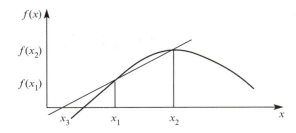

Figure 6.8 *The secant method*

```
package jgeslib;

public abstract class Secant {

  /* Root finding by the secant method     by N T Bishop, 1990, 1999
   * --------------------------------
   *
   * To extend the class, supply the function, f
   * Then call solve.
   * The root will be in estimate[iteration]
   * Earlier estimates are also available
   */

  public abstract double f (double x);

  public int iteration;
  public double estimate [];

  public void solve (double x1,
             double x2,
             double tolerance,
             int imax) {

    estimate = new double[imax+1];
    double f1, f2;
    double x;

    f1 = f(x1);
    estimate[0] = x1;
    estimate[1] = x2;
    x = x2;
    iteration = 1;
    do {
      x2 = x1;
      x1 = x;
      f2 = f1;
      f1 = f(x1);
      x = (x1*f2 - x2*f1) / (f2-f1);
      iteration ++;
      estimate[iteration] = x;
    } while ( (Math.abs(x-x1) > tolerance) & (iteration < imax));
  }
}
```

The next example shows how we would use the secant method to good effect.

EXAMPLE 6.5 Heat exchange unit

Problem In a heat exchange unit, energy is transferred from condensing steam to water. The mass flow rate of the water, w, in kg/s, is to be found from the energy balance equation. The desired rate of transfer of energy is 200 kW. For a particular heat exchange unit, the conservation equation is

$$276w\left[1 - \exp\left(\frac{-942}{101 + 371w}\right)\right] - 200 = 0$$

Solution   We need to solve the above equation for *w*. The secant method is ideal, since we do not have to differentiate the equation first.

Program design   The program consists of the now familiar three parts: the worker class (MySecant) which is based on the library and supplies the function f, the main method which drives everything, and the DataHandler class.

```java
import javagently.*;
import jgeslib.*;

class HeatExchangeUnit {

  /* The Heat Exchange Unit program      N T Bishop 1990, 1999
   * ----------------------------        Java, A Moolman Aug 1997
   * Calculates the water flow rate
   * Illustrates the use of the secant algorithm in the library
   */

  static class MySecant extends Secant {
    public double f (double w) {
      return (200 - 276*w * (1-Math.exp(-942/(101+371*w))));
    }
  }

  public static void main (String [] args) {

    Secant secant = new MySecant ();
    DataHandlerHE data = new DataHandlerHE ();
    data.initialize();
    while(true) {
      data.getData();
      secant.solve(data.w1, data.w2, data.tolerance, data.imax);
      data.output(secant.iteration,
                  secant.estimate[secant.iteration]);
    }
  }

  static class DataHandlerHE {
    Display display = new Display("Heat Exchange Unit");
    double w1, w2, tolerance;
    int imax;

    void initialize () {
      display.println("***** Flow Rate in a Heat Exchange Unit *****");
      display.println("Solves f(w)=0, with");
      display.println("f(w)=200 - 276w(1-exp(-942/(101+371w)))\n");
      display.prompt("1st estimate for w, w1", 0.5);
      display.prompt("2nd estimate for w, w2", 1);
      display.prompt("tolerance", 1e-6);
      display.prompt("Maximum iterations, imax", 10);
    }
```

```
    void getData () {
      display.ready("Press ready button when the data is right");
      w1=display.getDouble("1st estimate for w, w1");
      w2=display.getDouble("2nd estimate for w, w2");
      tolerance=display.getDouble("tolerance");
      imax=display.getInt("Maximum iterations, imax");
    }

    void output (int i, double w) {
      if (i < imax) {
        display.println ("\nConverged after "+i+" iterations");
        display.println ("w = "+Text.format(w,8,6));
      }
      else display.println("The method did not converge");
    }
  }
}
```

Testing   Sample output is shown in Figure 6.9.

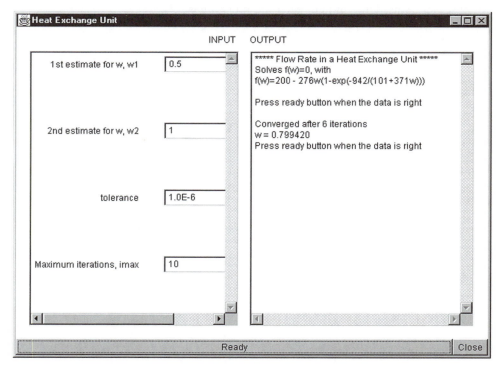

Figure 6.9 *Display from the heat exchange unit program*

Integration using Simpson's rule

Having looked at differential equations and finding roots of ordinary equations, we now consider how to integrate a function between two limits, i.e. to find

$$\int_a^b f(x)\,\mathrm{d}x$$

The basic technique is to divide the area under the curve into strips and to calculate the area of each of these, summing them to obtain the integral. There are various methods for doing this. Simple ones are the mid-point rule and the trapezoidal rule. These are examined in the problems at the end of the chapter. Here we shall look at a method which gives a better accuracy and is in daily use by engineers.

Simpson's rule is a numerical method which computes the integral as the sum of an even number of strips underneath the curve. The area of each pair of strips is approximated by fitting a parabola through the three points at the top of each strip. This is shown in Figure 6.10.

We start by dividing the interval of integration a, b into an even number, n, of equal subintervals. The length of each subinterval h is

$$h = \frac{b-a}{n}$$

Simpson's rule estimates the integral s as

$$s = \frac{h}{3}\left(f(a) + 4 \times \sum_{(i=1,3,5\ldots)}^{n_1} f(a+ih) + 2 \times \sum_{(i=2,4,6\ldots)}^{n_2} f(a+ih) + f(b)\right)$$

In other words, we compute the value of $f(x)$ at the start of the interval and at the end, then add in four times the value of $f(x)$ at the odd subintervals and twice the values at the even subintervals, and then multiply the whole thing by $h/3$.

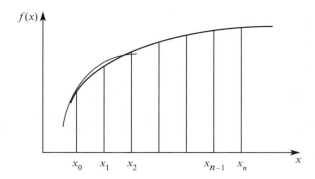

Figure 6.10 *Simpson's rule*

The evaluation of the formula given by Simpson's rule involves summing two series. Since they are independent, we can do them together. Two subtotals will be needed into which we add the values of the odd-numbered and the even-numbered strips. Simpson's rule returns a single value, so we can envisage it as a typed method. The method needs as parameters the values of *a* and *b*, the number of subintervals, *n*, and the function to be integrated. As in the previous method, we shall assume that the function to be integrated is called *f* and that it is declared elsewhere.

Simpson's rule is only one of several ways of integrating functions; two others are discussed in the problems. Therefore, we shall call the class `Integrate`, and the method `simpson`, with an eye to adding more methods such as for the mid-point and trapezoidal rule (see Problem 6.3).

```
package jgeslib;

public abstract class Integrate {

   /* Integrating a function class        by N T Bishop  1990, 1999
    * ------------------------
    *
    * Extend the method and supply the function f.
    * Integrate by Simpson's rule from a to b with
    * n strips (n must be EVEN).
    * Result is the value of the method.
    */


   public abstract double f (double x);

   public double simpson (double a, double b, int n) {
      double h = (b-a)/n;
      double s1 = 0;
      double s2 = 0;
      double x = a;

      for (int i=1; i<n; i++) {
        x+=h;
        if(i%2==1)
          s1 += f(x);
        else
          s2 += f(x);
      }
      return (h/3*(f(a) + 4*s1 + 2*s2 + f(b)));
   }
}
```

In the `simpson` method, there is an example of an **optimization**. In scientific programs, there are often many calculations to be done, and although computers are fast, the cumulative effect can sometimes make a program run unacceptably slowly. Good programmers, therefore, try to reduce the calculations, provided this does not make the program obscure. Instead of calling the function *f(x)* with $a + i * h$, which is what the formula said, we keep a variable, x, initialized to a and add h to it at each iteration. Thus we eliminate the multiplication, which is a slow operation.

Notice, too, the use of i%2 to decide whether to add the term to s1 or s2.

EXAMPLE 6.6   Charge and voltage across a capacitor

Problem   A capacitor in an electrical circuit is initially at zero charge. At time $t = 1$ s, a switch is closed and a time-dependent electric current $I(t)$ charges up the capacitor according to the formula

$$I(t) = 4(1 - e^{-0.5})\, e^{-0.5(t-1)}\, (1 - e^{-t})$$

We want to compute the charge Q and voltage V across the capacitor as functions of time up to 10 s.

Solution   The charge stored by the capacitor is given by the integral

$$Q(t) = \int I(t)\mathrm{d}t$$

and the voltage computed by simply dividing this by C:

$$V(t) = \frac{Q(t)}{C}$$

We can use Simpson's rule to compute the integral at each second from 0 to 10 s, and print out the values of Q and C.

Program design   The structure is by now quite familiar: the worker class which extends a library class and supplies the function, the main method which drives everything, and the DataHandler class. The computation involves a loop which runs through the seconds over the specified range, say 0 to 10 s. For each such t, the integral is calculated using Simpson's rule, and this involves looping over the n steps. Note that n must be an even number, and we check this in the initialization phase.

```
import javagently.*;
import jgeslib.*;

class CapacitanceCharge {

    /* Finding the charge across a capacitor     N T Bishop 1990
     * ------------------------------------
     *             A Moolman Aug 1997, N T Bishop July 1999
     *
     * Illustrates the use of a library routine
     * Integrate.simpson
     */
```

```java
static class MyIntegrate extends Integrate {
  public double f (double t) {
    return (4*(1-Math.exp(-0.5)) * Math.exp(-0.5*(t-1)) *
    (1-Math.exp(-t)));
  }
}

public static void main (String [] args) {

  MyIntegrate worker = new MyIntegrate ();
  DataHandlerCC data = new DataHandlerCC ();
  data.initialize();
  data.getData();

  double Q;
  for (int t = data.start; t <= data.end; t++) {
    Q = worker.simpson(data.start, t, data.intervals);
    data.output(t, Q);
  }
  data.finalize();
}

static class DataHandlerCC {

  Graph g = new Graph ("Voltage across a capacitor",
                    "t", "Voltage");
  Display display = new Display ("Capacitance Charge");
  double C;
  int start, end;        // in seconds
  int intervals;

  void initialize () {

  display.println("***** The voltage across a capacitor *****");
  display.println
      ("Integrates the formula for I(t) using Simpson's rule");
  display.println("finding the charge and voltage over time");

  display.prompt("Capacitance in farads, C: ",0.05);
  display.prompt("Start time in seconds", 0);
  display.prompt("End time in seconds", 10);
  display.prompt("Sub-intervals per second", 20);
  }

void getData () {
  display.ready("Press ready when the data is right");
  C =          display.getDouble("Capacitance in farads, C: ");
  start =      display.getInt("Start time in seconds");
  end =        display.getInt("End time in seconds");
  intervals = display.getInt("Sub-intervals per second");

  // Ensure no. of intervals is even
  if (intervals%2==1) intervals++;
  display.println("Integrating from "+start+" to "+end+" seconds");
```

```
        display.println("Over "+intervals+" intervals");
        display.println("t\t\t Q\t\t  V");
    }

    void output (int t, double Q) {
        display.println(t+"\t"+Text.writeDouble(Q,14,6)+"\t"
                    +Text.writeDouble(Q/C,14,6));
        g.add(t, Q/C);
    }

    void finalize () {
        g.showGraph();
        display.reposition(g);
    }
    }


}
```

Testing   A sample ouput is given in Figure 6.11. We should run the program for different values of *a*, *b* and *n* and compare the results. Obviously, with more intervals, the answer will become more accurate.

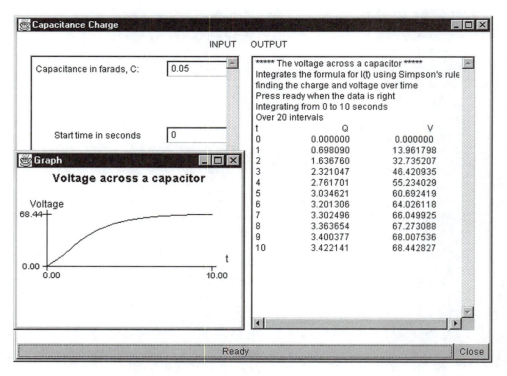

Figure 6.11 *Display for the capacitance charge program*

Laplace's equation with an infinite series

A steady-state temperature distribution satisfies Laplace's equation (named after Pierre-Simon Laplace (1749–1827)), i.e.

$$\frac{\partial^2 T}{\partial x^2} + \frac{\partial^2 T}{\partial y^2} = 0$$

Usually Laplace's equation is solved by finite difference methods that are beyond the scope of this book. We shall look at the case where it is possible to express a solution of Laplace's equation as the sum of an infinite series. Then we will give a graphical representation of the results.

EXAMPLE 6.7   Temperature in a plate

Problem   The case we would like to solve is that of a semi-infinite strip, with the temperature on the boundary as in

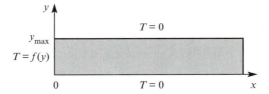

Solution   The temperature as a function of x and y is

$$T = \sum_{n=1}^{\infty} a_n \sin\left(\frac{n\pi y}{y_{max}}\right) \exp\left(\frac{-n\pi x}{y_{max}}\right) \tag{6.1}$$

where the constants a_n are found by Fourier analysis and are

$$a_n = \frac{2}{y_{max}} \int_0^{y_{max}} f(y) \sin\left(\frac{n\pi y}{y_{max}}\right) dy \tag{6.2}$$

The specific problem that we will deal with in the program has $f(y)$ as shown in

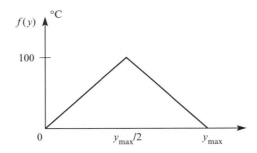

For this case the coefficients a_n work out to be

$$a_n = 0 \qquad \text{if } n \text{ is even}$$

$$a_n = \frac{800}{(n^2\pi^2)} \qquad \text{if } n = 1, 5, 9, \dots \text{ (i.e. if } n \bmod 4 = 1) \qquad (6.3)$$

$$a_n = -\frac{800}{(n^2\pi^2)} \qquad \text{if } n = 3, 7, 11, \dots \text{ (i.e. if } n \bmod 4 = 3)$$

On a computer we cannot work out $\sum_1^\infty b_n$ but only $\sum_1^N b_n$, and we must decide, for a given tolerance requirement, what value to use for N. We cannot just take N such that $|b_N| <$ tolerance. For example, if $b_n = 1/n$, the true value of $\sum_1^\infty b_n$ is infinite! There are two techniques that can be used here to estimate N. Let

$$\text{error}(N) = \left| \sum_1^\infty b_n - \sum_1^N b_n \right|$$

Then if $b_n = k/n^p$, with k and p constant and $p > 1$,

$$\text{error}(N) = \frac{k}{(p-1)N^{p-1}}$$

For a geometric progression $b_n = kr^n$, with k and r constant and $r < 1$,

$$\text{error}(N) = \frac{kr^N}{(1-r)}$$

In the present problem we wish to find equation (6.1) with a_n given by (6.3). At $x = 0$, the series is of the type $800/(n^2\pi^2)$, so the error in summing to N is $800/(\pi^2 N)$. To obtain an accuracy of better than 1°C we should therefore take $N = 200$. For $x > 0$ we can regard the series as a geometric progression with

$$r = \exp(-\pi x / y_{\max})$$

Then we can estimate N as

$$N = \frac{y_{\max}}{\pi x \ln \{ \textit{tolerance } \pi^2 [1 - \exp(-\pi x / y_{\max})]/800 \}}$$

We do this because in general this value of N will be much lower than 200, and by using it we save computer time.

We calculate the temperature at every point on an x–y grid, and then find the temperature range and divide it into a number of equal subintervals. We are now ready to plot the contours. For each y grid value, we find the x grid values at which the temperature is just below and just above that of the contour. We then use linear interpolation to estimate the x value of the contour. The program also allows for the case where the given y value is not found on the contour, and also finds the contour's y value at $x = 0$.

Program design   There are no library routines, and the program consists of a
`DataHandler` class that is driven by method `main`. In the present version of the
program only three contours are plotted, but that could be changed.

Program

```
import javagently.*;

class Contour {

  /* The contour program        N T Bishop 1990
   * -------------------         Java: A Moolman August 1997
   *                             N T Bishop July 1999
   * Draws the constant temperature
   * contours in a plate.
   */

  public static void main (String arg []) {
    DataHandler data = new DataHandler();

    data.initialize();
    while(true) {
      data.getData();
      data.makea();
      data.makeTemperature();
      data.makeDiscrete();
      data.printContour();
    }
  }

  // -------------------------------------------------
  static class DataHandler {
    int      nmax;
    double   tolerance;
    int      imax;
    int      jmax;
    int      kmax;
    double   ymax;
    double   xmax;

    double   a[], contourtemp[];
    double   temperature[][];
    double   size;
    Graph    g;
    Display display = new Display("Contour map");

    void initialize () {
      display.println("***** Temperature contour "+
            " plotting program *****\n");
      display.prompt("Maximum series length, nmax", 200);
      display.prompt("Series convergence: tolerance", 0.5);
      display.prompt("Grid points in x-direction, imax", 40);
      display.prompt("Grid points in y-direction, jmax", 20);
      display.prompt("Number of contours, kmax", 9);
```

```java
    display.prompt("Domain size: xmax", 1);
    display.prompt("Domain size: ymax", 1);
}

void getData () {
  display.ready("Press the button when values are ready\n");
  nmax = display.getInt("Maximum series length, nmax");
  tolerance = display.getDouble("Series convergence: tolerance");
  imax = display.getInt("Grid points in x-direction, imax");
  jmax = display.getInt("Grid points in y-direction, jmax");
  kmax = display.getInt("Number of contours, kmax");
  xmax = display.getDouble("Domain size: xmax");
  ymax = display.getDouble("Domain size: ymax");
  a = new double[nmax];
  contourtemp=new double[kmax+1];
  temperature = new double[imax+1][jmax+1];
}

void makea() {
  // Calculate the coefficients in the Fourier series
  for (int n=0; n<nmax; n++)
    if (n%2==0) a[n] = 0;
    else
      if (n%4==1) a[n] = 800/Math.pow(n*Math.PI,2);
      else a[n] = -800/Math.pow(n*Math.PI,2);
    size = 800/Math.pow(Math.PI,2);
}

void makeTemperature() {
  // Sums the Fourier series to find the temperature
  // at each point of the grid
  int nlimit;
  for (int i=0; i<=imax; i++) {
    double x = i*xmax/imax;
    if (i==0) nlimit = nmax;
    else {
      nlimit = (int) (-ymax / (Math.PI*x) * Math.log(tolerance/size
                  * (1- Math.exp(-Math.PI*x/ymax))));
      if (nlimit > nmax) nlimit = nmax;
    }
    for (int j=0; j<jmax; j++) {
      double y = j*ymax/jmax;
      double sum = 0;
      for (int n=0; n<nlimit; n++)
        sum += a[n]*Math.sin(n*Math.PI*y/ymax)
              *Math.exp(-n*Math.PI*x/ymax);
      temperature[i][j] = sum;
    }
  }
}

void makeDiscrete() {
  // Calculates the minimum and maximum temperatures in the plate,
  // and divides this range into equal intervals for contour
  // plotting
```

```
      double tempmin = temperature[0][0];
      double tempmax = tempmin;
      for (int i=0; i<=imax; i++)
        for (int j=0; j<=jmax; j++) {
          if (tempmin > temperature[i][j]) tempmin = temperature[i][j];
          if (tempmax < temperature[i][j]) tempmax = temperature[i][j];
        }
      double factor = kmax/(tempmax-tempmin);
      display.println("\nMinimum temperature is: "+tempmin);
      display.println("Maximum temperature is: "+tempmax+"\n");
      for (int k=0; k<=kmax; k++) {
        contourtemp[k]=(tempmin+k/factor);
        display.println("Contour "+k+" is at temperature: "+
                        contourtemp[k]);
      }
    }

    void drawContour(int k) {
      // Called as many times as required from printContour
      g.setSymbol(true);
      g.add(contourtemp[k]*ymax/200,0);
      for (int j=0; j<=jmax; j++) {
        double y=j*ymax/jmax;
        if (temperature[0][j] > contourtemp[k]) {
          int i=1;
          while(temperature[i][j] > contourtemp[k])
            i++;
          double x=(i-(contourtemp[k]-temperature[i][j])/
                  (temperature[i-1][j]-temperature[i][j]))*xmax/imax;
          g.add(y,x);
        }
      }
      g.add(ymax*(1-contourtemp[k]/200),0);
      display.println("Contour "+k+" plotted");
    }

    void printContour() {
      g = new Graph ("Temperature contour map","y", "x");
      drawContour(1);
      g.nextGraph();
      g.setColor(g.red);
      drawContour(3);
      g.nextGraph();
      g.setColor(g.blue);
      drawContour(5);
      g.showGraph();
      display.reposition(g);
    }
  }// DataHandler
}//Contour
```

Testing   The output is shown in Figure 6.12, with the graph in Figure 6.13 so that the input values can be clearly seen.

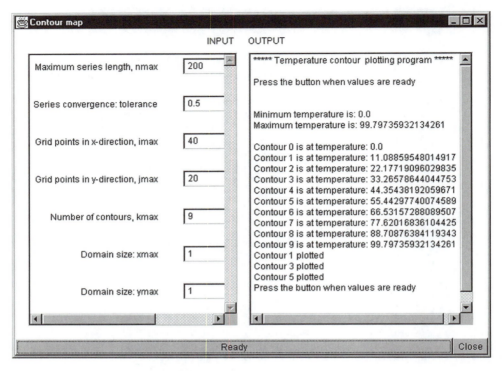

Figure 6.12 *Output from the contour program*

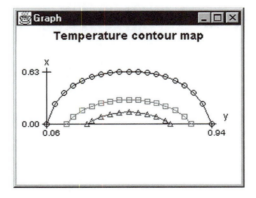

Figure 6.13 *Graph from the contour program*

6.6 Case study 2: Process control

The purpose of this Case study is to take a real engineering problem and work through the methods, algorithms and programming required to solve it. In the process, we shall make use of several of the techniques – both programming and numerical – that have gone before. The reader thus has a chance to consolidate earlier knowledge and gain an appreciation of how and where it can be effectively applied.

Background

Many industrial processes can be viewed as a process with two inputs and an output, as shown in

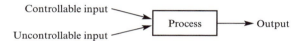

Some of the input can be controlled in that we can freely choose the values (within limits). This could apply to the flow rates of the input materials, the rate of heat input, the pressure, temperature, etc. However, some of the input cannot be controlled, e.g. the composition of the raw materials may change significantly from one batch to another. We probably want the output to remain constant. In a simple control problem we monitor the uncontrolled input, and then calculate an adjustment to the controllable input so as to achieve the desired output.

Problem: liquid in a catalytic unit

We consider the case of a liquid being passed through a catalytic unit of length L. The liquid contains in solution an uncontrolled concentration of chemical A; a controlled concentration of chemical B is added on input. On output, we want the concentration of chemical A to have a fixed value. The chemicals A and B react together in the catalytic unit, and their concentrations are described by the equations shown:

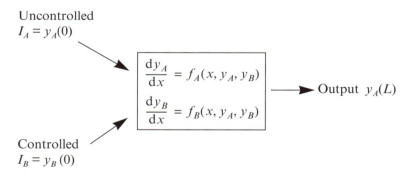

The variables, input and output values can be summarized as follows:

Concentrations of A, B in catalytic unit:	$y_A(x)$, $y_B(x)$
Input concentration of control B:	$I_B (= y_B(0))$
Output concentrations:	$y_A(L)$, $y_B(L)$
Desired output concentration of A:	A_{wanted}
Measured input concentration of A:	$I_A (= y_A(0))$

Objective   To find I_B such that $y_A(L) = A_{\text{wanted}}$

The following diagram shows how different values of the control input concentration I_B lead to different output concentrations $y_A(L)$.

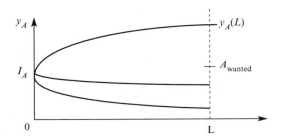

We wish to find the root of the equation

$$y_A(L)(I_B) - A_{\text{wanted}} = 0$$

where we regard $y_A(L)$ as depending on I_B. Because it is difficult to work out the derivative we cannot use the Newton–Raphson method, but we can use the secant method (as in Example 6.5). Thus at the top level our algorithm is the same as the secant method root-finding algorithm, with each function evaluation being the solution of a pair of differential equations.

The shooting method

How are we to solve such a pair of equations? We saw in section 3.6 that one differential equation can be solved by the predictor–corrector method. We use a method known as the 'shooting method'. We solve (numerically) the ordinary differential equations for y_A, y_B with initial conditions

$$y_A(0) = I_A$$
$$y_B(0) = \text{various estimates of } I_B$$

and then adjust the estimate of I_B until we hit the target, i.e. until $y_A(L) = A_{\text{wanted}}$. We will then have found the correct control I_B.

We already have a secant method program, and one to solve an ordinary differential equation by the predictor–corrector method (Example 3.8). We need to make the (straightforward) extension from one to two differential equations in the predictor–corrector algorithm. Consider several such equations, e.g.

$$\frac{dy}{dx} = p(x, y, z)$$

$$\frac{dz}{dx} = q(x, y, z)$$

with $y(0) = y_0$ and $z(0) = z_0$. This case is a straightforward generalization of that for one equation. For the Euler method the formulas become

$$y_{i+1} = y_i + hp(x_i, y_i, z_i)$$
$$z_{i+1} = z_i + hq(x_i, y_i, z_i)$$

and for the predictor–corrector method the formulas are

$$y_p = y_i + hp(x_i, y_i, z_i)$$
$$z_p = z_i + hq(x_i, y_i, z_i)$$
$$y_{i+1} = y_i + \tfrac{1}{2}h[p(x_i, y_i, z_i) + p(x_{i+1}, y_p, z_p)]$$
$$z_{i+1} = z_i + \tfrac{1}{2}h[q(x_i, y_i, z_i) + q(x_{i+1}, y_p, z_p)]$$

Program design

First we write a `PredictorCorrector` class and put it in `jgeslib`. As before, we construct estimate arrays which contain the values of $y_A(L)$, $y_B(L)$ as well as intermediate values. The method `solve` performs the computation and requires as input data: the initial values of y_A, y_B and x, as well as the step length h, the number of iterations between reports (`imax`), and the number of reports.

```
package jgeslib;

public abstract class PredictorCorrector {

    /* Predictor-Corrector method        N T Bishop 1990
     * -------------------------        J M Bishop, N T Bishop 1999
     *
     * Integrates up to two first-order
     * differential equations
     * Extend by supplying the two equations in fA and fB
     * The result is in estimateB[reports]
     * Intermediate results can also be examined
     */

    public abstract double fA (double x, double yA, double yB);
    public abstract double fB (double x, double yA, double yB);

    public double estimateA [];
    public double estimateB [];
    public double estimatex [];
```

```
public void solve (double x,
                   double yA,
                   double yB,
                   double h,
                   int imax,
                   int reports) {
    double yAp, yBp;
    estimateA = new double[reports+1];
    estimateB = new double[reports+1];
    estimatex = new double[reports+1];

    estimateA[0] = yA; estimateB[0] = yB; estimatex[0] = x;
    for(int i=1; i<=reports; i++) {
      for(int j=1; j<=imax; j++) {
        yAp = yA + h*fA(x,yA,yB);
        yBp = yB + h*fB(x,yA,yB);
        yA = yA + 0.5*h*(fA(x,yA,yB) + fA(x+h,yAp,yBp));
        yB = yB + 0.5*h*(fB(x,yA,yB) + fB(x+h,yAp,yBp));
        x += h;
      }
      estimateA[i] = yA;
      estimateB[i] = yB;
      estimatex[i] = x;
    }
  }
}
```

The above class is abstract, and next we define an extension that supplies the specific equations needed in the process control problem. The extension is self-contained and is kept in its own file. The functions f_A and f_B that we use are

$$f_A = -\frac{y_B}{\exp(y_A)} \quad f_B = 1$$

The system has an analytic solution, against which the computed results can be tested. It is

$$y_A = \ln[-I_B x - \tfrac{1}{2}x^2 + \exp(I_A)] \quad y_B = I_B + x$$

The extension of `PredictorCorrector` is

```
import jgeslib.*;

class ProcessControlPC extends PredictorCorrector {

  public double fA (double x, double yA, double yB) {
    return (-yB / Math.exp(yA));
  }

  public double fB (double x, double yA, double yB) {
    return 1;
  }
}
```

Now we can start to write the `ProcessControl` class. As usual, the `main` method is just a driver, and there is a nested class `DataHandler` that handles input–output and the production of a graph. The class starts with the definition of `MySecant`, which is an extension of `Secant`. We include in `MySecant` a constructor so that `DataHandler` and `PredictorCorrector` can be passed to it as parameters by `main`. The function to be solved by `Secant` is the difference between the value of y_A wanted at $x = L$ and that calculated by `PredictorCorrector`.

```java
import javagently.*;
import jgeslib.*;

class ProcessControl {

  /* A process control problem     N T Bishop 1990
   * -----------------------       A Moolman and N T Bishop
   *
   * Calculates the liquid in a catalytic unit.
   * Illustrates the combined use of the library routines
   * secant and predictor corrector.
   */

  static class MySecant extends Secant {
    DataHandlerPC data;
    PredictorCorrector pc;

    MySecant (DataHandlerPC d, PredictorCorrector p) {
      data = d;
      pc = p;
    }

    public double f (double x) {
      pc.solve( data.x0,
                data.IA,
                x,
                data.h,
                data.n,
                data.reports);
      return (pc.estimateA[data.reports]-data.Awanted);
    }
  }

  public static void main (String [] args) {
    DataHandlerPC data = new DataHandlerPC ();
    PredictorCorrector pc = new ProcessControlPC ();
    Secant secant = new MySecant (data, pc);
    data.initialize();
    while(true) {
      data.getdata();
      secant.solve(data.IB,data.IB1,data.Tolerance,data.imax);
      data.output(pc,secant);
    }
  }
}
```

```
static class DataHandlerPC {
  Display display = new Display("Process control");
  double L;
  double Tolerance;
  double   Awanted;
  double   IB2;
  double IA;
  double IB;
  double IB1;
  double h;
  double x0;
  int   imax;
  int   reports;
  int   n;

void initialize () {
    display.println("***** Process Control program *****");
    display.println("Solves yA'(x) = fA(x,yA,yB), " +
                    "with fA = -yB/exp(yA)");
    display.println("        yB'(x) = fB(x,yA,yB), with fB = 1");
    display.prompt("Error limit, tolerance", 1e-6);
    display.prompt("Maximum iterations, imax", 20);
    display.prompt("Desired output of A, Awanted", 1);
    display.prompt("Input value of A, IA", 2);
    display.prompt("1st estimate of control B, IB", 3);
    display.prompt("2nd estimate of control B, IB1", 4);
    display.prompt("Value of x at input, x0", 0);
    display.prompt("Value of x at output, L", 1);
    display.prompt("Number of reports", 10);
    display.prompt("Iterations between reports, n", 50);
  }

  void getdata() {
    display.ready("\nPress the button when values are ready\n");
    Tolerance=display.getDouble("Error limit, tolerance");
    imax=display.getInt("Maximum iterations, imax");
    Awanted=display.getDouble("Desired output of A, Awanted");
    IA=display.getDouble("Input value of A, IA");
    IB=display.getDouble("1st estimate of control B, IB");
    IB1=display.getDouble("2nd estimate of control B, IB1");
    x0=display.getDouble("Value of x at input, x0");
    L=display.getDouble("Value of x at output, L");
    reports=display.getInt("Number of reports");
    n=display.getInt("Iterations between reports, n");
    h=L/(n*reports);
  }

  void output (PredictorCorrector pc, Secant secant) {
    if(secant.iteration==imax)
      display.println("No convergence after "+imax+" iterations");
    else {
      display.println("Finished after "+secant.iteration+" iterations");
      display.println("The value of the control IB is "
                  +Text.format(secant.estimate[secant.iteration],6,3));
```

```
    Graph g = new Graph("Process Control: concentration of "
              + "A, B", "x",            "yA, yB");
    g.setTitle("yA");
    for(int i=0; i<=reports; i++)
      g.add(pc.estimatex[i],pc.estimateA[i]);
    g.nextGraph();
    g.setColor(g.red);
    g.setTitle("yB");
    for(int i=0; i<=reports; i++)
      g.add(pc.estimatex[i],pc.estimateB[i]);
    g.showGraph();
    display.reposition(g);
  }
 }
 }
 }
```

Considering the analytic solution stated above, we test the program with the following data. The x domain is the interval $(0, 1)$, the input value of y_A is 2, and the desired output value of y_A is 1. Then the analytic value for the control, i.e. the input value of y_B, is 4.170774. The output is given in Figure 6.14 and the graph in Figure 6.15 and we see that the error is quite acceptable.

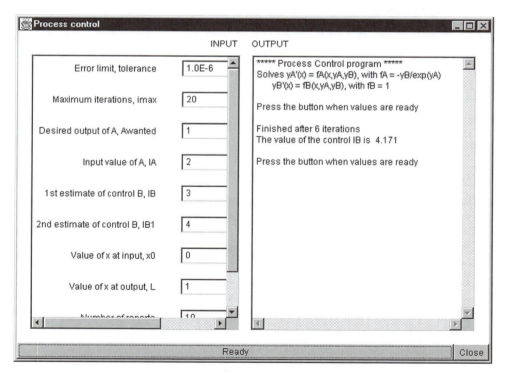

Figure 6.14 *Output from the catalytic unit program*

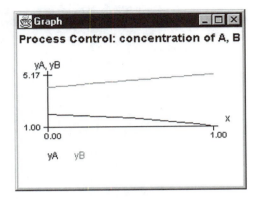

Figure 6.15 *Graph from the catalytic unit program*

6.1   A giraffe is also a herbivore. Give the class definition, including a constructor, for a giraffe which records the length of its neck.

6.2   Why will the following statement not give the result expected (i.e. true)?

```
System.out.println("s is an empty string is " + (s == null));
```

6.3   The following statements will not compile. What is wrong? Can you fix them?

```
Hashtable holidays = new Hashtable ();
holidays.put ("Foundation Day", new Dates (12, 6, 2001));
Dates d = holiday.get ("Foundation Day");
```

6.4   Why is the Display class sometimes instantianted as a static object (as in Example 3.9) and sometimes not (Example 5.8)?

6.5   Would the following be a valid declaration for a companion elephant to jumbo?

```
Elephant dumbo = new Elephant (1);
```

6.6   There is a temporary Elephant object called patient. Write a statement to make jumbo the patient, copying all his details.

6.7   In Example 6.4 (veterinary tags) give an example of a method declaration which illustrates overriding.

6.8   In Example 6.4 the statement

```
System.out.println("Full info should be "+register[i]);
```

sometimes prints out two values (name and phone) and sometimes three (name, phone and vet's phone). Explain carefully how this happens.

6.9   How does the VeterinaryTags program shut down?

6.10   Based on Figure 6.4 (the hierarchy of `Nature`) which of the following statements are incorrect, and why?

```
Nature n;
Animals a;
Herbivores h;
Elephant e;
Rhino r;
a = n;
e = r;
h = e;
a = h;
```

PROBLEMS

6.1   **Judges' countries.**   In Problem 5.5, instead of printing out the judges' numbers, we would like to print out the country from which they come. Use a hash table to set up a list of country names for the judges on duty, and adapt the program to make the output more explanatory.

6.2   **Bilingual calendars.**   Design a program to print out a calendar, one month underneath each other. Then, using hash tables, set up versions for the months and days of the week in another language (say, French, Spanish or German), and let the user select which language the calendar should be printed in.

6.3   Other approximations for integrals are given by the

Mid-point rule

$$\int_a^b f(x)\,dx \ = \ \sum_{i=1}^n hf\left(\frac{x_i + x_{i-1}}{2}\right)$$

Trapezoidal rule

$$\int_a^b f(x)\,dx \ = \ \frac{h}{2}\left(f(x_0) + 2\sum_{i=1}^n f(x_i) + f(x_n)\right)$$

Implement these as functions and incorporate them in Example 6.6. Calculate the charge across the capacitor using all three methods and compare their accuracy graphically.

6.4   **More accurate integration.**   By reducing the size of the subinterval, h, Simpson's rule will give a more accurate result. Alter the program in Example 5.6 so that it repeatedly reduces h until a result within a required tolerance is found.
Hint: Will rounding error (as described in Example 4.6) have an effect?

6.5   **Double integrals** can also be computed numerically. We simply apply the rule (Simpson's or whatever) in a nested loop. The work W done by a force $F(x, y)$ in a two-dimensional dynamics problem is given by the integral

$$W \ = \ \int_0^1\int_0^1 x^2 - 2xy + 3xy^2 + y^3 \, dy\,dx$$

Adapt the program in Example 5.6 to handle double integrals, and compute W.

6.6   **Secant example.**   Use the secant method to find the strictly positive root of $x = 2\sin(x)$.

6.7 **Temperature in rods.** The temperature $T(x)$ in a moving rod, which loses energy to the environment at temperature T_∞, is given by the equation

$$\frac{d^2 T}{dx^2} - \frac{1}{10}\frac{dT}{dx} - 20(T - T_\infty) = 0$$

where x is the distance from a die out of which the material emerges at temperature T_0. The boundary conditions are as follows:

At $x = 0$: $T = T_0$
At $x = \infty$: $T = T_\infty$

Taking $T_0 = 600$ K and $T_\infty = 300$ K adapt the program for the shooting method (section 6.6) to find $T(x)$. For the second boundary condition, start with a large value of x, say, 1 m, to represent ∞, and then vary this value until the results are not significantly affected by the increase.

6.8 **Runge–Kutta method.** A popular method for solving an ordinary differential equation $dy/dx = f(x, y)$ is the classic fourth-order Runge–Kutta method. The algorithm for getting y_{i+1} and x_{i+1} from y_i and x_i is

$q_1 = f(x_i, y_i)$
$q_2 = f(x_i + h/2, y_i + h\,q_1/2)$
$q_3 = f(x_i + h/2, y_i + h\,q_2/2)$
$q_4 = f(x_i + h, y_i + h\,q_3)$

$y_{i+1} = y_i + h/6\,(q_1 + 2q_2 + 2q_3 + q_4)$
$x_{i+1} = x_i + h$

Using the same approach as described with the predictor–corrector method, write a method which can be put in a library class `RungeKutta` for solving a differential equation. Apply it to the problems that have already been solved by the predictor–corrector method (Example 3.8, Problem 3.13, Problem 3.15). How do the two methods compare?

6.9 **Quadratics again.** Following on from Problem 4.9, create a class which holds the roots of a quadratic, including information about the kinds of roots that there are. Place a `solver` method in the class. Compile this class into `jgeslib` and test it with a small test program which uses the display so that several different values of a, b and c can be tested.

6.10 **Block of wood.** A block of wood, resting on a horizontal surface, is attached to a wall through a spring, as follows:

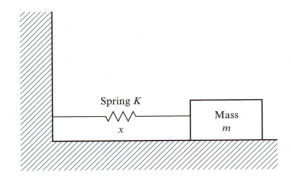

Spring K
Mass m
x

The displacement x of the block from its equilibrium position is governed by

$$\frac{d^2x}{dt^2} = -\frac{k}{m}x - \mu g \operatorname{sign}\frac{dx}{dt}$$

where

$\operatorname{sign}(x) = +1$ if $x > 0$, or -1 if $x < 0$, and 0 if $x = 0$
t is time in s
k is the spring constant in newtons/metre, say 300 N/m
m is the mass of the block in kg, say 5 kg
μ is the coefficient of friction, say 0.5, and
g is the gravitational acceleration, 9.8 m/s^2

Using the predictor–corrector method described in section 3.6 and Example 3.8, extended for second-order equations as in section 6.6, compute x as a function of time up to 3 s, with x starting at 0.2 m and at rest. Illustrate the results on a graph.

CHAPTER 7

Customizing

7.1 Introduction to the awt

The real world has been converted to wysiwyg[†] and GUI[‡] interfaces, and Java is fully equipped to provide these options. The GUI part is provided inside a package called awt – abstract windowing toolkit – that is, Java's platform-independent approach to user interfacing. A complete tour of all the facilities available through awt is beyond the scope of this book. What we aim to do is to reveal the overall structure of the package and then to introduce several of the most used features through examples. Of course, we have already been making extensive use of the awt through the Display and Graph classes, but we have not called awt methods directly yet.

Overall structure of the awt

The classes in the awt package can be classified as:

- graphics;
- components, including windows and menus;

† What you see is what you get, pronounced 'wizzywig'.
‡ Graphical user interface, pronounced 'gooey'.

- layout managers;
- event handlers;
- image manipulation.

Graphics permits the drawing of shapes, lines and images, and the selecting of fonts, colours and so on. **Components** are items such as buttons, text fields, menus and scroll bars. We can put them in **containers** and then choose one of a selection of **layout managers** to arrange them suitably on the screen. The subpackage `java.awt.event` handles external **events** (such as pushing buttons and moving the mouse) by means of a suite of event **handlers**, **listeners** and **adapters**. Finally, `java.awt.image` is another subpackage which is used by `awt` to incorporate **images** in a variety of formats. Figure 7.1 gives an overall picture of the main `awt`.

There are four main abstract classes: `Component`, `Container`, `Menu Component` and `Graphics`. Other abstract classes are `FontMetrics`, `Image`, `PrintJob` and `Toolkit`. `LayoutManager` is an interface (along with five other specialized ones not shown), and all the rest are classes, inheriting from the classes drawn above them. Thus `Frame` is a `Window`, which is a `Container`, which is a `Component`.

With all these different parts to the graphical user interfacing, it is actually hard to know where to start. We shall start with a very simple example – the one in Chapter 2 for drawing a virus warning box on the screen – and introduce the various parts of `awt` as they are needed. In particular, we shall see that there are several ways of achieving similar effects, and that the `awt` has a rich selection of features from which to choose.

Frame – the basic window

Graphical interfaces are presented to the user in **windows**. Java has a `Window` class, but in practice we usually use one of its subclasses, `Frame`. So we start off with `Frame` as the basic presenter of GUI items. Each application can have several windows and, for each, we declare a class that inherits `Frame` and includes the methods necessary to display information in the window and perform other actions.

In the main program a frame object is declared, created as a new instance of our class that is to occupy the frame. Then we perform three essential functions: setting the title of the window and its size, and activating the drawing of the frame itself. The methods are delared in `Frame` and `Component` (which `Frame` inherits). The form, including the enclosing class, is

---

Creating a frame

```
modifier class classname extends Frame {
  public static void main (String args []) {
    Frame f = new classname ();
    f.setTitle ("title");
    f.setSize (width, height);
    f.setVisible (true);
  }
}
```

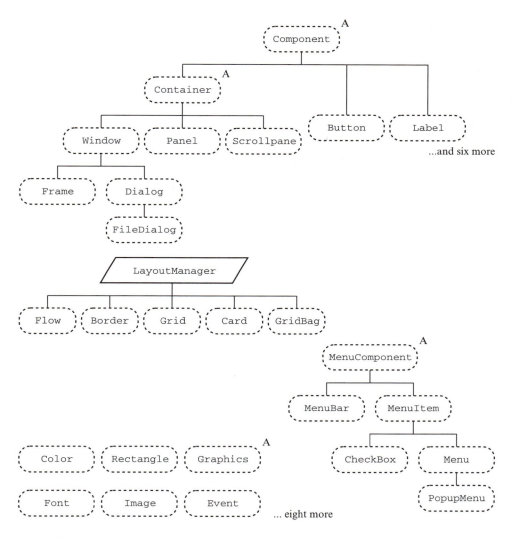

Figure 7.1 *The awt class structure (A indicates an abstract class)*

Adding graphics to a window

At this point, the awt will look for a paint method to add any further graphics to the contents of the window. The form for a paint method, which overrides that defined in Component, is

---

Redefining the paint method

```
public void paint (Graphics g) {
    Calls to methods in Graphics, prefixed by g.
}
```

The paint method is supplied with a Graphics object customized for the particular platform the program is running on. In this way, Java can take advantage of the good points of any particular platform, and make the awt present a familiar look and feel to the users of different platforms.

The Graphics class is quite extensive, but a summary of it is given in the form below. All the methods listed, except getColor, are **static void**.

Graphics class specification

```
clearRect  (int x, int y, int width, int height);
clipRect   (int x, int y, int width, int height);
copyArea   (int x, int y, int height, int width, int dx, int dy);
draw3DRect (int x, int y, int width, int height, boolean raised);
drawChars  (char data [], int offset, int length, int x, int y);
drawLine   (int x1, int y1, int x2, int y2);
drawOval   (int x, int y, int width, int height);
drawRect   (int x, int y, int width, int height);
drawString (String str, int x, int y);
fill3DRect (int x, int y, int width, int height, boolean raised);
fillOval   (int x, int y, int width, int height);
fillRect   (int x, int y, int width, int height);
setColor   (Color c);
Color getColor ();
// plus 33 others
```

Graphics includes methods for drawing rectangles, arcs, polygons and so on. For example, to draw a rectangle (as the only output), we would say

```
public void paint (Graphics g) {
  g.drawRect (10, 10, 200, 100);
}
```

which starts at a point 10 pixels in from the top left corner of the screen, and draws a rectangle 200 wide by 100 deep as in Figure 7.2.

Displaying text in a window

Working with the Graphics package, the equivalent of println in awt is drawString. For example, we could say

```
g.drawString ("Temperature in a plate",30,15);
```

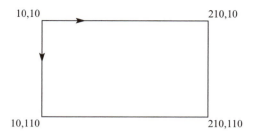

10,10   210,10

10,110   210,110

Figure 7.2 *Drawing a rectangle in the* awt *package's* Graphics *class*

which would write the string 30 pixels in from the left and 15 pixels down from the top of the screen. The size and number of pixels varies from screen to screen, but typically a screen will have 640 × 480 or more.

The difference between println and drawString is that drawString gives a choice of fonts, font styles and font sizes, and these affect the dimension of each letter. Consequently the positioning of the start of a string can be difficult. Font Metrics is an awt abstract class which has methods for finding out the size of letters, which is helpful. We are now ready for our first example, a very simple one indeed.

EXAMPLE 7.1   Virus warning using graphics

Problem The virus warning of Example 2.3 should appear in its own window and be more striking.

Solution Use an awt window and the drawString and rectangle facilities as described above. To make the rectangle striking, we need colour. Colour is provided by the setForeground and setBackground methods in the Component class, using the colour constants defined in the Color class. We will use a cyan background, Color.cyan.

Program We set up letter and line constants and base the text writing on multiples of these. The drawRect and setSize methods also use suitable multiples of letter and line.

```
import java.awt.*;
import java.awt.event.*;

public class GraphicWarning extends Frame {

  /* The Graphic Warning Program  by J M Bishop Oct 1996
   * ------------------------------  Java 1.1 by T Abbott Oct 1997
   * produces a warning message on the screen in cyan
   * and black.
   * Illustrates setting up a window, painting in it
   * and enabling the close box.
   */
```

```
static final int line = 15;
static final int letter = 5;

public GraphicWarning( ) {
  setBackground(Color.cyan);
}

public void paint(Graphics g) {
  g.drawRect(2*letter, 2*line, 33*letter, 6*line);
  g.drawString("W A R N I N G", 9*letter, 4*line);
  g.drawString("Possible virus detected", 4*letter, 5*line);
  g.drawString("Reboot and run virus", 5*letter, 6*line);
  g.drawString("remover software", 7*letter, 7*line);
}

public static void main(String[] args) {
  Frame f = new GraphicWarning();
  f.setTitle("Graphic Warning");
  f.setSize(50*letter,10*line);
  f.setVisible(true);
  f.addWindowListener(new WindowAdapter () {
  public void windowClosing(WindowEvent e) {
    System.exit(0);
  }
  });
}

}
```

Testing Figure 7.3 shows the output of the program (reduced to black and white, unfortunately). To stop the program, we click on the close button on the right.[†] The window closes, and the final statement is a call to `System.exit(0)`. How the program is enabled to close in this way is discussed next.

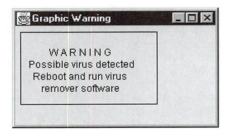

Figure 7.3 *Graphic output for the virus warning program*

---

† The picture shows Windows output which is similar to Unix; on a Macintosh, the close box will be on the left.

Closing a window

A program that runs in a window needs some way of stopping. One of the accepted methods is for the user to click on the window close box in a top corner. Clicking is an **event** and can be detected by one of the **listeners** in the event package in the awt. In the main method, we establish a link to such a window listener from the frame being built, by calling the method addWindowListener and instantiating a new version of a window adapter. In the implementation of the adapter that follows we override the WindowAdapter method called windowClosing and perform the appropriate action, which is to call System.exit(0).

The sequence of definitions and actions for closing a window is summarized in the following form:

Closing a window

```
f.addWindowListener(new WindowAdapter () {
   public void windowClosing(WindowEvent e) {
     System.exit(0);
   }
});
```

Everything in this form is a keyword (in bold) or an identifier already defined in the awt package (in plain) – except for the event parameter e which is not used, so it can always remain as e anyway. The form becomes a mantra that can be put in the main method of all GUI programs. It uses an **anonymous class**, defined formally in Chapter 10. However, the syntax is novel and illustrates interesting features of object orientation, so let us go through it carefully here.

WindowAdapter is a simple abstract class which implements the Window Listener interface and provides dummy bodies for various methods contained therein. We can decide which to override, and in this case the only interesting method is windowClosing (there are six others). The instantiation of a new Window Adapter object and the overriding of windowClosing are done inline, as part of the parameter to addWindowListener.

The alternative to an anonymous class would have been to supply (new x()) as the parameter and then define x as a local class, with a heading that extends WindowAdapter and a body just the same as that shown here, i.e. an implementation of windowClosing. All in all, the anonymous class is neater.

EXAMPLE 7.2   A weather chart

Problem   Draw a histogram of rainfall figures for Savanna, based on the data of Example 5.5.

Solution   We already saw how to draw a graph of means and standard deviations (Figure 5.5) using the Graph class. But the Graph class does not do histograms, so we can investigate how to accomplish this from first principles using the awt Graphics class instead. By using Example 5.5, we can get in the data for several years, calculate the mean for each month (as before) and then use these figures in drawing each histogram bar in graphics.

Program design   The program will follow the pattern described above. The class will inherit Frame. Its main program will contain exactly the same instructions as in our previous example to set up the window properly.

The constructor is rather novel. We shall use it to read in all the data, a task previously performed by a readIn method. The contents, however, do not change. The most important part of the program is how to draw a satisfactory graph. We would like output such as Figure 7.4.

Let us take each of the parts of the chart in turn.

1   **The axes.**   Firstly, drawing the lines for the axes establishes a basis for the other parts. 'Zero' on the graph will be at about $x = 50$, $y = 300$, where the values are pixels, and the orientation is given as in Figure 7.2.

2   **The bars.**   Next, to draw the bars, we use fillRect and must supply parameters as shown in the graphics form above. In other words, we need a bottom point, a width and a height. The width is some constant, such as 20. The height is the actual value of the month's mean rainfall, which we shall multiply by 10 so that it is decently represented on the screen (i.e. a rainfall of 10 mm will use 100 pixels). The y starting point of the rectangle is then y height, where y is our zero point (300, as defined above). Lastly, the x starting point is a bit complicated, because it will vary for each month. The formula is based on the width and on a gap between bars as follows:

```
g.fillRect(month*(width+gap)+gap+x, y-a, width, a);
```

3   **The labels.**   Labelling the axes involves two loops which are fairly easy to understand, though admittedly take some time to develop correctly from scratch! The x axis makes use of an array of string names for the months.

4   **The title.**   Finally, writing out the title shows how we can change fonts in Java. There is a Font class which can be instantiated with three parameters: font name, style and size. The available font names are: Serif, SansSerif, Monospaced, Dialog and DialogInput. The styles are PLAIN, BOLD and ITALIC and the sizes the usual point measurements, e.g. 12 is normal, 24 is large, and you should not go below 8. Changing the font is done for the last drawString, so we do not need to change it back again.

Program   For what it does, the program is short, compared to Example 5.5 which did very little. This shows that graphics, like all programming, can be very powerful when repetition is involved. But if every little thing has to be custom-made and mentioned individually, then the programming can get long and tedious, which is why we developed the Graph class.

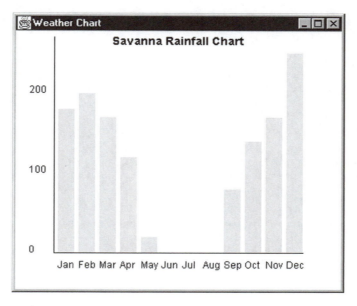

Figure 7.4 *Weather chart drawn with graphics*

```
import java.io.*;
import javagently.*;
import jgeslib.*
import java.awt.*;
import java.awt.event.*;

class WeatherChart extends Frame {

    /* The Weather Charting program    by J M Bishop Dec 1997
     *                                 Java 1.1
     * Draws a histogram of monthly rainfall
     * from data taken over a few years.
     * The data must be in the form:
     * year followed by the 12 rainfall figures for
     * the months of that year.
     * Illustrates simple graphics.
     */

    static final int base = 1950;
    static int startYear, endYear, nYears = 0;
    static double[][] rainTable = new double[12][70];

    public void paint (Graphics g) {
      int x = 50;
      int y = 300;
      int width = 20;
      int gap = 5;
```

```
// the axes
    g.drawLine (x,y,x+12*(width+gap),y);
    g.drawLine (x,y,x,30);

// labelling the axes
    for (int m = 0; m < 12; m++)
        g.drawString(Months[m],m*(width+gap)+gap+x,y+20);
    for (int i = 0; i <y; i+=100)
        g.drawString(String.valueOf(i),20,y-i);

// the title
    Font heading = new Font("SansSerif",Font.BOLD,14);
    g.setFont(heading);
    g.drawString("Savanna Rainfall Chart",120,40);
    g.setColor(Color.cyan);

// the bars
    for (int month = 0; month < 12; month++) {
        int a = (int) Stats.mean
                (rainTable[month], nYears)*10;
        g.fillRect(month*(width+gap)+gap+x, y-a,width,a);
    }
}

public WeatherChart () throws IOException {
    BufferedReader fin = Text.open("rain.data");

    int actualYear = 0;        /* e.g. 1985 */
    int yearIndex = 0;         /* e.g. 0 */
    try {
        while (true) {
            actualYear = Text.readInt(fin);
            if (yearIndex == 0)
                startYear = actualYear;
            for (int m = 0; m < 12; m++)
                rainTable[m][yearIndex] = Text.readDouble(fin);
            yearIndex++;
        }
    } catch (EOFException e) {
        /* Pick up the last year of data read in. */
        endYear = actualYear;
        nYears = endYear-startYear+1;
    }
}

public static void main(String[] args) throws IOException {
    Frame f = new WeatherChart ();
    f.setTitle("Weather Chart");
    f.setSize(400,350);
    f.setVisible(true);
    f.addWindowListener(new WindowAdapter() {
        public void windowClosing(WindowEvent e) {
            System.exit(0);
        }
    });

}
```

```
private static String Months [] = {"Jan","Feb","Mar","Apr",
    "May","Jun","Jul","Aug","Sep","Oct","Nov","Dec"};

}
```

7.2 Laying out a GUI

Although versatile, the Graphics class is not all that convenient for handling text. Java's awt provides a different range of classes for this purpose. These are the components shown under Component in Figure 7.1. The two simplest are Label and Button which provide for limited text. There are more such components, some of which are studied in later sections. There is a summary of all of them at the end of this section.

The Label class provides for the output of simple text via a parameter to its constructor, as in:

Creating a Label
add(**new** Label ("*Text*"));

Thus we could say

```
add(new ("School:");
```

to get the label School: displayed on the screen. Button is similar, but has the additional facility of being reactive; that is, we can press the labelled button on the screen and the program can make something happen.

Creating a Button

// as a name
private Button *buttonname*;
 	
// as a component
buttonname = **new** Button ("*Text*");
  add(*buttonname*);

The add method is defined in the Container class, so what we are doing here is adding the button to the default container of the frame we are working in. We shall see soon how to declare other containers.

The difference between declaring labels and buttons is that labels are passive: you can't react to them, so it is seldom necessary to give their objects names. Buttons on the other hand will certainly be referred to later in the program, so they need permanent names. It is also the case that the name will be used outside of the constructor, which is why we declared it before creating the button.

For example, to set up a Submit button and put it in the window, we could say

```
// as a name
private Button submitButton;

// as a component
submitButton = new Button ("Submit");
  add(submitbutton)
```

Why are there no parameters indicating *x*, *y* positions on the screen when we add the components to the frame? The reason is that these components (unlike graphics drawings) work with **layout managers**.

Layout managers

Layout managers take over control of the positioning of components that are added to a window, and arrange them sensibly. If the window is resized by the user, the layout manager endeavours to adjust the components in the new area so that they are all still visible.

Java has five such managers, but we shall look at only the first three: flow, border and grid. They all implement the interface `LayoutManager`, as shown in Figure 7.1. The form for incorporating a layout manager is

Incorporating a layout manager
setLayout (**new** *Manager*(*parameters*));

where `setLayout` is a call to a method in `Container`, the abstract class from which `Window` and hence `Frame` inherit. The default layout manager is `BorderLayout`, but `FlowLayout` is actually more useful for our purposes. It also has the desirable property that it is the default manager for applets (see section 8.1). An example layout set-up is

```
setLayout (new FlowLayout(FlowLayout.CENTER,horigap,vertigap));
```

The first parameter indicates that the items added to the frame should be centred; they could also have been left or right justified. The `horigap` and `vertigap` parameters are constants that indicate the minimum distance (in pixels once again) between items in the frame. All three parameters are optional. Examples of flow layout are given in the sample programs later on.

Reacting to buttons

In addition to closing the window, we now also need to react to buttons being pressed. Like the `windowListener`, there is an `actionListener` defined in `awt.event`. This listener interface has only one method to be implemented: `actionPerformed`.

So the strategy for buttons is to link them to the `actionListener`, and to provide a version of `actionPerformed`. The linking is done in the constructor immediately after the button is declared and added to the container. The three statements for a Submit button would be

```
submitButton = new Button ("Submit");
   add(submitButton)
   submitButton.addActionListener (this);
```

The reference to `this` indicates that the current frame will be responsible for defining the `actionPerformed` method. `ActionPerformed` has one parameter, which is an `ActionEvent`, and it can be successively interrogated to see whether it matches any of the buttons that could be pressed. The following form spells this sequence out:

Reacting to a button

```
public void actionPerformed (ActionEvent e) {
  if (e.getSource () == buttonname1) {
    statements
  } else
  if (e.getSource () == buttonname2) {
    statements
  }  // etc
}
```

If there are several buttons, all with different string labels, then the only way to distinguish between them is to have a sequence of if–else-statements, checking for each possibility. How to handle others will be discussed in section 7.3.

Extended indentation guidelines

Up until now, indentation in our programs has followed the traditional approach inherited from older languages such as Pascal and C: that is, that we indent whenever there is a new method or statement block. Statements within the same block remain at the same level of indentation.

With GUI programming, one finds that there are often very long sequences of statements involved with setting up a number of components on the screen. Each component can have three or more statements associated with it. There is no prescribed order in which the statements have to be executed, but normally, we deal with each component in turn and follow a create–link–add pattern. For Java programs, therefore, we have decided to introduce a new indenting scheme which regards the creation of a component as introducing a new level. Then all statements referring to that component can easily be seen. This effect has already been used in the `submitButton` example above, and is evident in the examples that follow.

EXAMPLE 7.3   Warning with two responses

Problem   Improve the warning notice by including two buttons. One should enable the user to acknowledge the message, but wait. In this case, the whole window should turn red. The other button should pretend to force a reboot.

Program design   Use the flow layout manager, labels and buttons to achieve the necessary effect. Select background and foreground colours from the `Color` class. For the actions, the Reboot button being pressed causes a simulated reboot in a similar way to closing the window. Pressing the Wait button changes colours as specified. The constructor performs associations between components and listeners. A listener activates `actionPerformed` so that it can react to events.

Program   The program is quite simple, and illustrates the essential sequential nature of GUI programming. The message to be displayed is passed to the new extension of the `Frame` as an array of strings. Each line is displayed through adding it as a label.

```
import java.awt.*;
import java.awt.event.*;

public class ButtonTest extends Frame implements ActionListener {

  /* The Button Test Program      J M Bishop Sept 1996
   * ----------------------       Java 1.1 T Abbott, J M Bishop Oct 1997
   *
   * Prints a warning message, but when a Wait
   * button is pressed, it turns the window red.
   *
   * Illustrates buttons, listeners and the
   * handling of events.
   */

  static final int horigap = 15;
  static final int vertigap = 10;
  Button waitButton;
  Button rebootButton;

  public ButtonTest(String message[], int n) {
    /* The constructor is responsible for setting
     * up the initial buttons and colour background.
     */
    setBackground(Color.cyan);
    setForeground(Color.black);
    setLayout(new FlowLayout(FlowLayout.CENTER, horigap, vertigap));
    for (int i = 0; i < n; i++)
      add(new Label(message[i]));
    waitButton = new Button("Wait");
      add(waitButton);
      waitButton.addActionListener(this);
    rebootButton = new Button("Reboot");
      add(rebootButton);
      rebootButton.addActionListener(this);
  }
```

```
public void actionPerformed(ActionEvent e) {
  if (e.getSource() == rebootButton) {
    setVisible(false);
    dispose();
    System.exit (0);
  } else if (e.getSource() == waitButton) {
    setForeground(Color.white);
    setBackground(Color.red);
  }
}

public static void main(String[] args) {
  String[] message = {
    "W A R N I N G",
    "Possible virus detected.",
    "Reboot and run virus",
    "remover software" };

  Frame f = new ButtonTest(message, 4);
  f.setTitle("Button Test");
  f.setSize(180,200);
  f.setVisible(true);
  f.addWindowListener(new WindowAdapter () {
    public void windowClosing(WindowEvent e) {
      System.exit(0);
    }
  });
}

}
```

Testing   The first display from this program will be as shown in Figure 7.5.

Figure 7.5 *Output from the button test program*

Other layout managers

In addition to `Flow`, the other four layout managers and their features are:

1   **Border**.   Allows positioning of items (scroll bars, menus, buttons, etc.) in fixed-size borders indicated by a parameter which can nominate the `North`, `South`, `East` or `West` of the window, with the remainder of the space being the `Center`.[†]

2   **Card**.   Overlapping panels of information can be selected by clicking on tabs on the top of each panel.

3   **Grid**.   The frame is divided into a specified number of rows and columns which can be selected by number.

4   **GridBag**.   Fine-grained layout where each component is given exact pixel constraints. Although complex to use, it is the most versatile and portable.

Since `LayoutManager` is an interface, it is possible to define your own layout manager, with customized (and sometimes very pleasing) results.

Other component options

Labels and buttons are components, and we indicated that there were other similar classes. To round things off, we name them and indicate their main functions here.

1   **TextComponent**, together with its two subclasses `TextArea` and `TextField`, handles multiple-lined text, text selecting and editing.

2   **Scrollbar** is useful with text and enables the contents of the container to move in the window.

3   **ScrollPane** is a container which enables a component with a larger area to be moved underneath it with scroll bars so that a portion is visible at any one time.

4   **Canvas** is an additional window area which can be used for drawing in, so as not to interfere with buttons.

5   **CheckBox** provides for yes/no or on/off selection. An example would be selecting bold on a toolbar in a text processor.

6   **Choice** provides dropdown lists from which choices can be made. One choice can be made.

7   **List** is similar to `Choice` except that the items are always on screen, and multiple selections can be made.

8   **Menus** can be created on the menu bar of the window, with pull-down items. One can be selected at a time. Some options can be made unselectable when necessary.

9   **PopupMenus** can be created anywhere in a window, and can have side submenus. Items can also be unselected.

† Note the American spelling of `Center`, not `Centre`.

10   **Print** is a command which can cause all or some of a window to be printed, in hardcopy, to a printer – a most useful feature, as it saves having to go through a screen dump process outside of Java.

Some of these options are used in other examples in this and later chapters.

Interaction with text fields

Clearly, responding to events is an important part of GUI programming. The Java's `awt.event` package provides the means for listenening for events, recording information about events as they occur, and linking up to user-defined event handlers. We need to consider:

- How are events classified and corresponding listeners and handlers set up?
- How can sequences of events be managed?

In preparation, we start off by completing our look at components, with special attention to text fields, an essential part of user interaction.

To get text into a GUI program, Java provides a component `TextComponent` with two subclasses, `TextField` and `TextArea`. `TextArea` is for multi-line text and works in conjunction with scroll bars. Text areas are used in the `Display` class, and will be discussed in section 9.2 when we look inside the `Display` class. For now, we shall just consider the single-line text fields. To declare a component as a `Text Field`, we use the form

---

Creating a text field

```
private TextField t;

t = new TextField("initial value",n);
  add(t);
```

---

n is the number of characters one expects in the field, but will not fully define its width, since the width is also influenced by the font chosen and the layout manager used. However, the field will scroll sideways if the user enters more than *n* characters, so there is no problem in guessing *n* incorrectly. Some of the methods available on a `TextField` are

---

Text field methods

```
String   getText ()
void     setText (String str)
void     setEditable (boolean booleanvalue)
boolean  isEditable ()
void     select (int start, int end)
void     selectAll()
```

---

getText and setText are the read and write equivalents for a TextField. Each field can also be open for input – that is, editable (the default) – or it can be locked. In the first state, it will be white, and the user must move the mouse there, click and start typing, ending with a return. If it is not editable, the field might be grey and data cannot be entered – this option depends on the computer being used. The need for these two states is illustrated in the next section. Finally, selectText allows a given part of the field to be highlighted, usually in blue, and selectAll encompasses the whole field.

Text fields usually have labels associated with them. To set up text fields to collect a person's name and age together in a Panel we would use

```
Panel p = new Panel ();
  p.add (new Label ("Name"));
    TextField name = new TextField("",40);
    p.add (name);
  p.add (new Label ("Age"));
    TextField age = new TextField("",5);
    p.add (age);
```

which would give

Notice that the flow layout manager would have taken care of setting the boxes out neatly in a frame of the right size. If the frame is bigger, the 'Age' label might land on the top row, whereupon some adjustment might be necessary to achieve the desired effect.

Inputting numbers

You may have noticed that there is only one get method for TextField, and it returns a String. Thus we are faced once again with translating the contents of the string to a number, if that is what we want. We discussed this process in section 4.1, showing a translation for reals. The corresponding key statement for integers would be

Translating a string to integer
i = Integer.parseInt(s);

Exactly the same technique can be used in GUI programming. However, a simple statement like this assumes that nothing will go wrong in the conversion, such as a non-numeric character in the string. The Text class took care of these problems, and one could envisage a similar class being written, called, say, `GUIText`, which would perform exactly the same function, but with input from a `TextField` instead of a `BufferedReader`. For now we shall live dangerously, and leave the development of `GUIText` as a worthwhile exercise for the reader.

Avoiding input

We mentioned at the end of section 7.1 that there were several other components in the `awt`, some of which provide for selections from lists or choices. Essentially, these save the user from typing in a lot of data, and also create a more secure environment because there is no opportunity for unexpected input. Take a simple example. If we want the user to give us a day of the week, we do not ask for text to be typed into a text field, with all its accompanying checking. Instead we provide a `Choice` list, which gives the seven choices, and the user simply selects one with the mouse. `CheckBox`, `List`, `Menu` and `Popup` have similar uses.

7.3 Events, listeners and handlers

The classification of events is tied to the types of components that generate the events, but there is not one event type for each component type. Rather there are 11 **event** types and they are shared by the many **component** types. Each event type has a **listener** associated with it (though `MouseEvent` has two), and each listener requires that a corresponding **handler** must implement one or more of its methods.

For example, we have already seen that a button component is associated with an `ActionEvent` and an `ActionListener` and that the `actionPerformed` method must be implemented. Table 7.1 gives the full list of Java events, listeners and methods with the components they handle. All the listeners are interfaces, so those that are referred to in a program must be listed in the class header.

We now consider a real GUI example, and come back to understanding the table once we have some concrete statements to examine.

EXAMPLE 7.4   Currency converter with a GUI

Problem   We think that the program for currency conversion developed in Example 6.1 has probably outgrown the `Display` class. We would like to create a better GUI design, and also expand the program so that it can convert from any one currency to another.

Screen design   With all GUI programs, we start by looking at screen design. To speed things up, Figure 7.7 below shows the result of our vision: this is the design we would like to achieve. It retains the ouput text area in the centre of the screen, and then puts two choice boxes on either side. Above and below the text area is the Amount text field and a Convert button which activates a conversion and the output.

Table 7.1 *Classification of events, listeners, methods and components*

Event	Listener	Methods	Components
ActionEvent	ActionListener	actionPerformed	Button List MenuItem TextField
AdjustmentEvent	AdjustmentListener	adjustmentValueChanged	ScrollBar
ComponentEvent	ComponentListener	componentHidden componentMoved componentResized componentShown	Component
ContainerEvent	ContainerListener	componentAdded componentRemoved	Container
FocusEvent	FocusListener	focusGained focusLost	Component
ItemEvent	ItemListener	itemStateChanged	CheckBox Choice List
KeyEvent	KeyListener	keyPressed keyReleased keyTyped	Component
MouseEvent	MouseListener	mouseClicked mouseEntered mouseExited mousePressed mouseReleased	Component
	MouseMotionListener	mouseDragged mouseMoved	
TextEvent	TextListener	textValueChanged	TextComponent
WindowEvent	WindowListener	windowActivated windowClosed windowClosing	Window

Given this goal, we need to break the interface down into panels, and decide on the layout for each panel. The overall layout is border layout, so we can put the three main panels in west, centre and east. South and north of the main panel are unused, but could contain a heading or instructions.

The west and east panels are also based on border layout, and have the label in the north and the choice box in the centre. The center panel is similar, but the north is itself a panel with a label and the text field for amount. The resulting layout is shown in Figure 7.6.

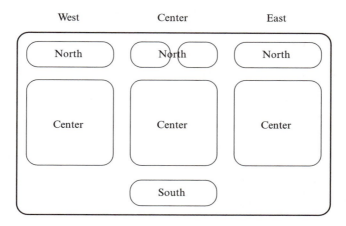

Figure 7.6 *Screen layout for the converter GUI*

Program design   In moving from the `Display` class, the structure of the program takes a different form. With the display, we are still bound to input, then ready, then output. Once we are in complete control of our own GUI, we have to be prepared to react to events at any time. Moreover, having two countries selected does not mean that a transaction will take place. So the main program basically initializes the GUI, reads in the rates file, and that's it. There is no endless loop calling the transactions method. Instead, the transactions method is called by `actionPerformed` when the Convert button is pressed.

```
import java.awt.*;
import java.awt.event.*;
import java.util.*;
import java.io.*;
import javagently.*;

class ConverterGUI extends Frame {

  /* The Converter Program      by J M Bishop  Dec 1998
   * --------------------        Display version July 1999
   *                             GUI version July 1999
   * Keeps the exchange rates from one currency into
   * many others and enables currency exchanges to be
   * estimated.
   *
   * Illustrates the use of a customized GUI.
   */

  public static void main(String[] args) throws IOException {
    DataHandler data = new DataHandler ();
    data.initialize();
    data.readIn();
  }

  static class DataHandler extends Frame
            implements ActionListener, ItemListener {
    Hashtable table = new Hashtable();
```

```
// read in each line of data and store in
// the hash table with country as key

Rates rate;
Choice fromChoice, toChoice;
boolean fromSelected, toSelected;
TextField amountField;
TextArea resultField;
int amount = 1000;
String toCountry, fromCountry;
Button goButton;

void initialize () {
  Panel p = new Panel (new BorderLayout());

    // left hand side panel
    Panel q = new Panel();
      q.add ("North",new Label ("From"));
      fromChoice = new Choice();
        fromChoice.addItemListener (this);
        q.add("Center",fromChoice);
      p.add ("West", q);
    // right hand side panel
    q = new Panel();
      q.add ("North",new Label ("To"));
      toChoice = new Choice();
        toChoice.addItemListener (this);
        q.add("Center",toChoice);
      p.add ("East",q);
    // Centre panel
    q = new Panel(new BorderLayout());
      Panel r = new Panel();
        r.add(new Label("Amount"));
        amountField = new TextField("1000  ");
        amount = 1000;
          amountField.addActionListener(this);
          r.add(amountField);
          q.add("North",r);
        resultField = new TextArea(8,20);
          q.add ("Center",resultField);
          resultField.append("First select the countries\n");
        goButton = new Button ("Convert");
          goButton.addActionListener(this);
          q.add("South",goButton);
      p.add("Center",q);
  add(p);
  setTitle("Currency Converter");
  setSize(610,300);
  addWindowListener(new WindowAdapter() {
    public void WindowClosing(WindowEvent e) {
      System.exit(0);
    }
  });
}
```

```
    public void actionPerformed (ActionEvent e) {
      amount = (int) Integer.parseInt(amountField.getText().trim());
      if (e.getSource() == goButton) {
        if (fromSelected && to Selected)
          transaction();
        else
          resultField.append("First select the countries\n");
      }
    }

    public void itemStateChanged(ItemEvent e) {
      String s = (String) e.getItem();
      if (e.getItemSelectable() == fromChoice) {
        fromSelected = true;
        fromCountry = s;
      }
      else {
        toSelected = true;
        toCountry = s;
      }
    }

    void transaction () {
      Rates fromRate = (Rates) table.get(fromCountry);
      Rates toRate = (Rates) table.get(toCountry);
      resultField.append(amount+" "+fromRate.country+" "+
          fromRate.currency+
          "\n in "+toRate.country+" "+toRate.currency+"\n was "+
          Text.format(amount/fromRate.conversion*
                      toRate.conversion,10,3)+"\n\n");
    }

  void readIn() throws IOException {
    BufferedReader fin = Text.open("Rates.data");
    try {
      for (int i = 0; ; i++) {
        rate = new Rates();
        rate.setRate(fin);
        table.put(rate.country, rate);
        toChoice.addItem(rate.country);
        fromChoice.addItem(rate.country);
      }
    }
    catch (EOFException e) {}
    setVisible(true);
    fromSelected = false;
    toSelected = false;
  }
 }
}
```

Testing   The GUI for the converter after a few runs is shown in Figure 7.7.

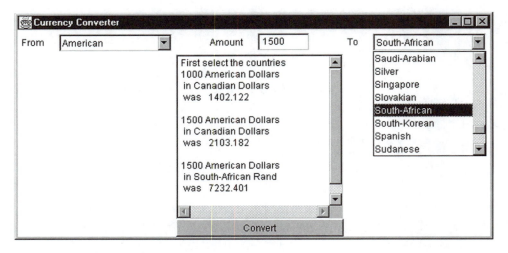

Figure 7.7 *GUI for the converter program*

Selecting different handlers

To understand Table 7.1, let's take an example from the previous program. In it, we defined two choice boxes, and we obviously will need to react to them. `Choice` is a component which is related to an `ItemEvent`, and needs an `ItemListener`. The method `itemStateChanged` must be implemented. What does such an implementation look like? Well, let us consider a handler we have seen already, namely `action Performed`. The `ConverterGUI` program has buttons and text fields and so also has a handler for them, which looks like this:

```
public void actionPerformed (ActionEvent e) {
   if (e.getSource() == amountField)
      amount = (int) Integer.parseInt(amountField.getText().trim());
   else
   if (e.getSource() == goButton)
      transaction();
}
```

`ActionEvent` uses the `getSource` method to return the object that caused the event. This object reference can be successively interrogated to establish which event occurred, and then the appropriate action can be taken. `getSource` is a method defined in a class called `EventObject` which is actually so high up in the hierarchy, it is in `java.util`, not `java.awt`! In every one of the event classes, there is a corresponding and more specific method which can be used instead of `getSource`. The problem is one of remembering all the names and return values, as they do not follow a pattern in the same way as the listeners and other methods do, as shown in Table 7.1. For example, for an `ActionEvent`, the alternative method to `getSource` is `getActionCommand` and it returns a string. Thus

```
    if (e.getSource() == rebootButton) {
```

would become

```
    if (e.getActionCommand() .equals( "Reboot")) {
```

However, for an `ItemEvent` (as generated by a `Choice`) the method is `getItem Selectable` and it returns a value based on an interface called `ItemSelectable`.
Returning to the original handler for a choice box, we see that it looks like this:

```
public void itemStateChanged(ItemEvent e) {
  String s = (String) e.getItem();
  if (e.getItemSelectable() == fromChoice)
    fromCountry = s;
  else toCountry = s;
}
```

We first get the item and then we decide from which choice box the event came, and copy the string into the appropriate variable.

Managing sequences of events

In terms of the `awt`'s interaction with the user, events are single happenings, but together they can form a chain of events. In other words, a certain event need not always elicit the same response. There may be two or three responses, depending on the events that have gone before. Alternatively, we may wish to restrict or ignore certain events if others have not already taken place.

How do we record what has gone before? In most cases, we use suitably named boolean variables which indicate whether or not a previous event happened. An example would be ensuring that an item had been selected from each choice box in Example 7.4, before allowing the Convert button to be used. If a boolean variable called `chosen` is set true by the `itemStateChanged` handler, then `choice` can be called over and over, with new selections being made until the user is satisfied. We can decide whether to reset this variable after a conversion, or just leave it on, so that following conversions will use existing choices unless new ones are selected (see Problem 7.4). There is a wide range of options that the programmer can build into the event logic of a program.

7.4 Inside the Graph class

The `Graph` class has been a great help in all our programs to date, enabling us to visualize the results that we get from our numerical calculations with the minimum of effort. Having now learnt about the `awt`, we can look inside the `Graph` class and see how it works. We shall examine the overall structure of the class, and then look at a few of the more interesting techniques used.

Structure of the `Graph` class

The class itself is some 360 lines long, with 10 public methods, 12 private ones and 2 inner classes. Figure 7.8 shows a simple calling structure of the class, so that all the methods are revealed. Those in bold are the public ones available to users of the class.

As can be seen from the diagram, the main activity takes place either in the `Graph-nextGraph` calls or in `showGraph`, which has to do all the drawing. `initializeGraph` does some initialization which is common to all graphs that might be drawn on the window, and then calls `nextGraph` to complete the set-up. The user can also call `nextGraph` directly to create a new line, so the split between it and `initializeGraph` saves on repetition.

The main activity takes place when `showGraph` is called. `showGraph` calls `repaint`, which activates `paint` from within a program. `paint` then takes over, and after calculating the length of the axes and the value spreads based on the minimum and maximum *x*–*y* values, it calls `drawAxes` and `plotGraphs`. `drawAxes` separately calls `drawTitles`, in case there are titles to be printed below the *x* axis for the key.

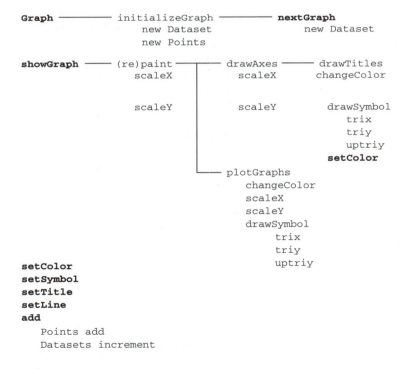

Figure 7.8 *Calling structure of the* Graph *class*

Graph's data structures

The two inner classes used by `Graph` complement each other in the following way. `Points` is a class from which a list of point objects is created by `initializeGraph`. Lists are a very versatile data structure which we cover fully in Chapter 10. At this stage, all we need to know is that one can add to a list, and iterate through it, referring to the current element when needed. Each point has an (x, y) coordinate, and that's all. `Graph` also keeps a record of the maximum and minium values received for x and y through all additions to the graphs, so that the axes can be correctly drawn at the end.

In order to accommodate several graphs on one set of axes, we use the notion of a data set. The data set records the number of points belonging to each graph, and also keeps track of the cosmetic details, i.e. symbols and colours and titles. The two data structures, as they may be set up for the `TrigGraphs` program (Example 2.2), are

```
Points     1 2 3 4 .......98 99 100 101 102 103 .........198 199 200

Dataset                 1                 2
    count               100               100
    plotType            2                 3
    title               Sine              Cosine
    colorRequired       true              true
    symbolRequired      true              false
    titleRequired       true              true
    lineRequired        true (default)    true (default)
```

From this we see that points 1–100 belong to data set 1 and the rest to data set 2. When `plotGraphs` comes to draw the graphs, it starts at the first point, then enters a loop over each of the data sets and an inner loop over the points for that set.

The `trix`, `triy` and `uptriy` methods are there to draw the triangular symbols, which unlike circle and square are not provided by the Java `Graphics` class.

Scaling for a graph

Scaling points to an axis is one of the more intricate activities that `Graph` takes care of. We have already seen scaling in action in the weather example (Example 7.2). Here we do much the same thing, but in a very general way. The section that calculates the scaling factors is at the start of `paint`, and consists of the following:

```
xBorder = 40;
yBorder = 80;

xAxisLength = (int) getWidth() - 2*xBorder;
yAxisLength = (int) getHeight() - 2*yBorder;

// calculate value spreads from mins and maxs which have
// been recorded as we go
xSpread = xMax - xMin;
ySpread = yMax - yMin;
if (xMin > 0) xOrigin = scaleX(xMin); else xOrigin = scaleX(0);
if (yMin > 0) yOrigin = scaleY(yMin); else yOrigin = scaleY(0);
```

getWidth and getHeight provide the size of the window currently, so we can base all our calculations on these figures. Firstly, we calculate the axis lengths by subtracting a border in pixels on each side. The *y* borders are slightly larger, to allow for the title and the key. Then we get the spread of actual numbers involved. Finally we calculate the origins. If all the values on an axis are positive, then the origin of that axis can be in the bottom left corner. This policy maximizes the size of the axis, even though (0,0) will not always appear on the graph. Note that we can force it to appear by separately creating a graph with only one point, adding (0,0). However, if any values are negative, then the origin will be at 0. Figure 7.9 shows a graph where the origin is not on the bottom left corner. The physical size of the axes are the same, but Graph has scaled the curves to accommodate the *x* range of –5 to 10 radians, compared to 0 to 10 as on Figure 2.1.

Colours and symbols

The approach of the Graph class to colours and symbols is deliberately simple. The idea was to make it as easy as possible to use. Graph has its own colour constants that the calling program can refer to. Otherwise the user would have to give a number, or import the awt in order to gain access to its colour constants. We really wanted to

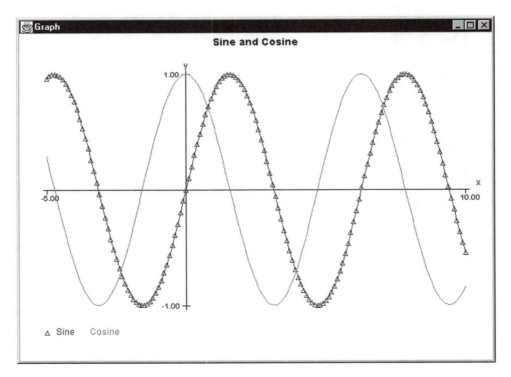

Figure 7.9 *A graph with negative axes*

avoid this option. Of course, more colours than four could be defined in an expanded version of the Graph class.

There are no constants for symbols. In the absence of any other instructions, the symbol is picked up for the colour: in other words, black always has a circle, blue a triangle and so on. However, setSymbol can take a number, in which case one could get a black graph with a triangle. In this way eight different sorts of lines could be drawn.

Program

Here follows the Graph class in its entirety, just as it is used in this book. Notice that the first line assigns it to the package javagently, so it must reside as a file in a directory of the same name.

```
package javagently;

import java.awt.*;
import java.awt.event.*;

public class Graph extends Frame {

   /*  Graph       by J M Bishop    June 1999
      *********
    is a simple class that provides facilities for
        - storing points
        - printing them as a dot or line graph
        - printing the graph.
       Several graphs can be printed in one window.
        The axes labels are worked out from the points themselves.
     Assistance given by J Lo, I de Villiers and B Worrall

   Interface:

   Basic
   -----
   new Graph () Compulsory constructor call
   add(x, y)    Adds a point to a list. Expects points to come in x-order.
   showGraph()  Compulsory call to get the axes and graph drawn

   Advanced
   --------
   new Graph (graphTitle, xAxisTitle, yAxisTitle)
                        Constructor with labelling options.
                        Use empty strings if not all titles applicable
   nextGraph()          Starts a new graph on the same axes.
                        One showGraph draws all the graphs.
   setColor(int 0 to 3) Choice of black, magenta, blue, red
                        (constants are available instead of numbers)
   setSymbol(boolean)   Deduced from the colour
                        (Convenient if colours are being set)
   setSymbol(int 0 to 3) circle, upside down triangle, triangle, square
                        (Used if colours are not being set)
```

```
    setLine(boolean)         Normally on, can be turned off
                             (Remember to turn it on again for the next line)
    setTitle(String)         Will appear on a key alongside the symbol and/or
                             in the chosen colour
    */

    private String xAxisTitle, yAxisTitle, graphTitle;
    private boolean keys;

    public Graph () {
//-------------
        /* the simple constructor -
           leaves the window and axes titles blank */
        initializeGraph();
        xAxisTitle = "";
        yAxisTitle = "";
        graphTitle = "";
    }

    public Graph (String g, String x, String y) {
//------------
        /* the alternative constructor -
           has window and axes titles */
        initializeGraph();
        graphTitle = g;
        xAxisTitle = x;
        yAxisTitle = y;
    }

    private class Dataset {
//---------------------
        /* Simple class for recording basic info
           about a set of points.  Allows more than one
           graph to be drawn on an axis.
           All initialization done in nextGraph. */
        int count;
        int plotType;
        String title;
        boolean colorRequired, symbolRequired, titleRequired, lineRequired;
    }

    private List points;
    private List datasets;

    private void initializeGraph () {
        datasets = new List ();
        nextGraph();
        points = new List ();
        xMax = yMax = Double.MIN_VALUE;
        xMin = yMin = Double.MAX_VALUE;
        keys = false;
        setSize (640,480);
        super.setTitle ("Graph");
```

```
    addWindowListener (new WindowAdapter () {
      public void windowClosing(WindowEvent e) {
        dispose();
      }
    });
  }

  public void nextGraph () {
//---------------------
    Dataset d = new Dataset ();
    d.count = 0;
    d.plotType = black;
    d.title = "";
    d.symbolRequired = false;
    d.colorRequired = false;
    d.titleRequired = false;
    d.lineRequired = true;
    datasets.add (d);
  }

  public void setColor (int c) {
//---------------------
    ((Dataset) datasets.current()).colorRequired = true;
    ((Dataset) datasets.current()).plotType = c;
  }

  public void setSymbol (boolean b) {
//---------------------
    ((Dataset) datasets.current()).symbolRequired = b;
  }

  public void setSymbol (int c) {
//---------------------
    ((Dataset) datasets.current()).symbolRequired = true;
    ((Dataset) datasets.current()).plotType = c;
  }

  public void setTitle (String s) {
//---------------------
    ((Dataset) datasets.current()).titleRequired = true;
    ((Dataset) datasets.current()).title = s;
    keys = true;
  }

  public void setLine (boolean b) {
//--------------------
    ((Dataset) datasets.current()).lineRequired = b;
    if (b==false)
      ((Dataset) datasets.current()).symbolRequired = true;
  }

  public void add (double x, double y) {
//----------------
    points.add (new Point (x,y));
```

```
      ((Dataset)datasets.current()).count++;
      if (x > xMax) xMax = x;
      if (x < xMin) xMin = x;
      if (y > yMax) yMax = y;
      if (y < yMin) yMin = y;
    }

  public void showGraph () {
//--------------------
      repaint();
      setVisible(true);
    }

 private class Point {
//------------------
      /* simple class for an x,y coordinate */
      double xCoord, yCoord;
      Point (double x, double y) {
        xCoord = x;
        yCoord = y;
      }
    }

  private void drawTitles (Graphics g) {
//-----------------------
      Dataset d;
      int x = xBorder;
      int y = getHeight()-yBorder/2;
      datasets.reset();
      boolean lastset = datasets.eol();
      while (!lastset) {
        d = (Dataset) datasets.current();
        if (d.colorRequired)
          changeColor(g, d.plotType);
        if (d.symbolRequired) {
          drawSymbol(g, d.plotType, x, y-cs);
          x += 4*cs;
        }
        g.drawString(d.title, x, y);
          x += g.getFontMetrics().stringWidth(d.title)+20;
        lastset = datasets.eol();
        if (!lastset) datasets.succ();
      }
      g.setColor(Color.black);
    }

  private void drawAxes (Graphics g) {
//---------------------
      Font plain = g.getFont();
      Font small = new Font(plain.getFamily(),Font.PLAIN,10);
      Font bold = new Font(plain.getFamily(),Font.BOLD,14);

      g.drawLine(xBorder-5,yOrigin,xAxisLength+xBorder+5,yOrigin);
      g.drawLine(xOrigin,yBorder-5,xOrigin,yAxisLength+yBorder+5);
```

```
    g.drawString(xAxisTitle,
                getWidth()
                -g.getFontMetrics().stringWidth(xAxisTitle)-xBorder/2,
                yOrigin-5);
    g.drawString(yAxisTitle,
                xOrigin-g.getFontMetrics().stringWidth(yAxisTitle)/2,
                yBorder-8);

    g.setFont(bold);
    g.drawString(graphTitle,
                (getWidth()
                 -g.getFontMetrics().stringWidth(graphTitle))/2,
                yBorder/2);
    g.setFont(plain);
    if (keys) drawTitles(g);

    // Tick and Label the four min/max points only
    int scaleXMin = scaleX(xMin);
    int scaleXMax = scaleX(xMax);
    int scaleYMin = scaleY(yMin);
    int scaleYMax = scaleY(yMax);
    g.drawLine(xOrigin-5,scaleYMax,xOrigin+5,scaleYMax);
    g.drawLine(xOrigin-5,scaleYMin,xOrigin+5,scaleYMin);
    g.drawLine(scaleXMax,yOrigin+5,scaleXMax,yOrigin);
    g.drawLine(scaleXMin,yOrigin+5,scaleXMin,yOrigin);

    g.setFont(small);
    g.drawString(Text.writeDouble(xMin,6,2),scaleXMin-10,yOrigin+15);
    g.drawString(Text.writeDouble(xMax,6,2),scaleXMax-10,yOrigin+15);
    g.drawString(Text.writeDouble(yMin,6,2),xOrigin-35,scaleYMin+4);
    g.drawString(Text.writeDouble(yMax,6,2),xOrigin-35,scaleYMax+4);
    g.setFont(plain);
  }

  private double xSpread, ySpread, xMin, xMax, yMin, yMax;
  private int xAxisLength, yAxisLength, xOrigin, yOrigin;
  private int xBorder, yBorder;

  public void paint (Graphics g) {
//-----------------
    // calculate length of axes from window size minus a border of 20
    xBorder = 40;
    yBorder = 80;

    xAxisLength = (int) getWidth() - 2*xBorder;
    yAxisLength = (int) getHeight() - 2*yBorder;

    // calculate value spreads from mins and maxs which have
    // been recorded as we go
    xSpread = xMax - xMin;
    ySpread = yMax - yMin;
    if (xMin > 0) xOrigin = scaleX(xMin); else xOrigin = scaleX(0);
    if (yMin > 0) yOrigin = scaleY(yMin); else yOrigin = scaleY(0);
```

```
    drawAxes(g);
    plotGraphs(g);
  }

  private int scaleX(double x) {
//------------------
    return (int) ((x-xMin) / xSpread*xAxisLength)  + xBorder ;
  }

  private int scaleY(double y) {
//------------------
    return (int) (yAxisLength - ((y-yMin) /
                  ySpread*yAxisLength)) + yBorder;
  }

  private void changeColor(Graphics g, int c) {
//------------------------
    switch (c) {
      case black : {g.setColor(Color.black); break;}
      case magenta : {g.setColor(Color.magenta); break;}
      case blue : {g.setColor(Color.blue); break;}
      case red :   {g.setColor(Color.red); break;}
    }
  }
 private static final int cs = 3; // pixel size of a symbol

  private void drawSymbol (Graphics g, int sy, int x, int y) {
//-----------------------
    switch (sy) {
      case black : {g.drawOval (x-cs, y-cs, 2*cs, 2*cs); break;}
      case magenta : {g.drawPolygon (trix(x),uptriy(y), 3); break;}
      case blue :  {g.drawPolygon (trix(x),triy(y), 3); break;}
      case red :   {g.drawRect (x-cs, y-cs, 2*cs, 2*cs); break;}
    }
  }

  private void plotGraphs (Graphics g) {
//----------------------
    Point p, q;
    int x1, y1, x2, y2;
    Dataset d;
    boolean lastset;
    Color c;

    // Loop through each dataset
    datasets.reset();
    /* The points are in one big list, split by the
    counts recorded in each dataset */
    points.reset();
    lastset = datasets.eol();

    do {
      d = (Dataset) datasets.current();
      if (d.colorRequired) changeColor(g, d.plotType);
```

```
      // Start with the first point in the list
      // for this graph
      p = (Point) points.current();
      x1 = scaleX(p.xCoord);
      y1 = scaleY(p.yCoord);
      if (d.symbolRequired)
        drawSymbol(g, d.plotType, x1, y1);

      // Loop through the points as stored in the list
      for (int i=1; i<d.count; i++) {
        points.succ();
        q = (Point) points.current();
        x2 = scaleX(q.xCoord);
        y2 = scaleY(q.yCoord);

        // plot the line and/or point
        if (d.lineRequired)
          g.drawLine(x1, y1, x2, y2);
        if (d.symbolRequired)
          drawSymbol(g, d.plotType, x2, y2);
        x1 = x2; y1 = y2;              '
      }
      lastset = datasets.eol();
      if (!lastset) {
        datasets.succ();
        points.succ();
      }
    } while (!lastset);
  }

  private int [] trix (int p) {
//--------------------
    int [] a = new int [3];
    a[0] = p-cs;
    a[1] = p+cs;
    a[2] = p;
    return a;
  }

  private int [] triy (int p) {
//--------------------
    int [] a = new int [3];
    a[0] = p+cs;
    a[1] = p+cs;
    a[2] = p-cs;
    return a;
  }

  private int [] uptriy (int p) {
//---------------------
    int [] a = new int [3];
    a[0] = p-cs;
    a[1] = p-cs;
    a[2] = p+cs;
    return a;
  }
```

```
public final int red = 3;
public final int blue = 2;
public final int magenta = 1;
public final int black = 0;


}
```

QUIZ

7.1   Create a method to read a double value from a `TextField`.

7.2   Given a panel p, write `awt` calls to create a text field with SCHOOL as a label to its left and add it to p.

7.3   What special facilities do `TextArea` and `ScrollPane` offer, over and above `TextField`? (Consult the Java API help for information.)

7.4   What event is caused by typing into a text field? Is this the same event as pressing a button?

7.5   What is the method call used in `ActionPerformed` to decide what kind of event has occurred?

7.6   Declare a choice box for the days of the week and write `awt` calls to set up the required strings in it.

7.7   The following declaration is not valid. Why not?

```
Component area = new Component ();
```

7.8   How does the `paint` method in a program such as Example 10.2 actually get called?

7.9   What is the default layout manager for a `Frame`?

7.10   Give a `Font` declaration to enable `drawString` to write your name in the centre of the screen in large italics in the font that looks like Times Roman (but isn't called that anymore).

PROBLEMS

7.1   **Shape selector.**   A teacher wishes to let toddlers draw shapes (circle, square, triangle) in three colours (red, blue, yellow). The children cannot read. Provide a suitable GUI interface for selecting a shape and colour and drawing the object at a position given by a mouse click.

7.2   **GUI text.**   Implement a companion class to `Text` (sections 4.1 and 10.2) for input from `TextFields`.

7.3   **Histograms for `Graph`.**   Without altering the file that `Graph` is in, inherit from `Graph` and make a new class which includes a facility for drawing histograms. The idea is that instead of plotting a symbol, a bar is plotted. By studying the `Graph` class, decide which methods have to be overridden. Test your new class by using it with the weather program (Example 7.2).

7.4   **Converter GUI.**   The `ConverterGUI` program in Example 7.4 does not check whether countries have been selected before a conversion is attempted, and could generate a `nullPointerException`. As discussed at the end of section 7.3, adapt the program so that it can keep track of which events have been activated and protect the transaction method accordingly.

7.5   **Digital watch.**   Design the display and knobs of a digital watch to appear in a window. (Later on in Problem 9.1 you will be asked to make it work.)

7.6   **Mobile phone.**   Design and program a screen version of a mobile phone.

CHAPTER 8

Networking

8.1 From applications to applets

A great deal of the excitement surrounding Java has had to do with its integration into the World Wide Web. As we shall see, once the mechanics of accessing Java through the web have been sorted out, and we have looked at the facilities available in the standard Java packages, it will be very easy for you to branch off on your own and create applets bounded only by your imagination.

So what is an applet? An applet is a Java program that operates within a browser, and hence can appear in a web page. The applet runs on the user's computer, even though it may have been fetched from far away.

The combination of factors which make this particular (and unique to Java) operation possible is **interpretation** rather than full compilation of programs, and the **enabling** of the JVM in all web browsers. Interpretation means that Java applications (which we have studied so far) can move around the web and be executed on a variety of machines. Java browser enabling extends this facility to create the concept of applets. As the name suggests, applets are normally small programs, each devoted to a single task on a single browser page. At this point, the reader might like to refer to the diagrams and screen shots in Figures 1.1 to 1.4, when applets were first introduced in the book.

The advantages of having applets in a web page are that:

- The work is done on the machine where the results are needed, rather than having the results sent there, so there is **less traffic** on the network.

- The user's machine can be **dedicated** to the applet and can run it much faster than could a share of a server machine from where the applet originates.

- The **full facilities** of the Java programming language are available,[†] unlike some specially designed web languages which have restricted calculation and structuring powers.

To get an idea of how an applet differs from an application, let us first look at the steps involved in the conversion, and then consider how Example 7.4 would have to change.

Converting an application to an applet

The steps to achieve the conversion are as follows:

1   Check that all **input–output** relevant to the user goes through the `awt` interface. For example, replace calls to `System.out.println` by calls to `g.drawstring`. Note that using the `Display` class qualifies for applet conversion straightaway, so that calls to `display.println` are fine, and can be left as is. This is one of the added advantages of the `Display` class.

2   Remove any means for **stopping** the program (e.g. Close buttons). Applets end when their viewer or surrounding browser pages end. They are not allowed to call `System.exit()`.

3   `Applet`'s **default layout** is flow, so if the frame was relying on border layout by default, add a call to make it specific, thereby overriding flow layout.

4   Import the `applet` package and in the main **window** extend `Applet`[‡] instead of `Frame`. For example, replace

```
class ConverterGUI extends Frame {
```

with

```
class ConverterGUIApplet extends Applet {
```

5   Ensure that the class you are writing is declared **public**.

6   Catch any **exceptions** that may be thrown by the class. In particular, look for `IOExceptions` thrown by the `main` method. The compiler will complain about any residual throws, and you can deal with them as requested.

---

† Barring some security restrictions discussed below.
‡ `applet` with a small a is the name of the package that is imported; `Applet` with a capital A is the name of the class that is extended.

7   Replace the class's constructor, `main` method, or some other driving method by an overriding of the **init** method, which will be called by `Applet` to make any initializations, and could also have the program's main loop. In the case of the converter program, we do not have a constructor, but the work of the constructor, i.e. setting up the GUI, is done in `DataHandler.initialize`. This method therefore gets renamed to

```
public void init ()
```

8   If the **main** method has not already been replaced by `init`, remove it from the program, as the `applet` package will take over its functions such as creating a window and setting its size and visibility. Anything else that is left in the `main` method should be redistributed to other methods. The `main` method will not get called once we are in applet mode. In the case of the converter program, all we have to do is take the call to `readIn` and put it at the end of `init`.

9   Create an **HTML** file which refers to the applet's class file, or include the appropriate applet HTML instructions (called **tags**) in a existing web page (see form below).

10   **Run** the HTML file through an applet viewer (by typing, in a command window, appletviewer *name*.html) or through a web browser such as HotJava, Netscape, Mosaic or Explorer.

Simple HTML

HTML stands for Hypertext Markup Language. We need to know only the bare basics of it to run applets. In fact, the form for activating an applet consists of one tag as follows:

HTML tags for an applet
`<APPLET code="name" width=n height=m>` `</APPLET>`

An HTML page created via the editor of a browser may generate additional tags indicating the start and end of the HTML and the BODY, but the above is sufficient. This is illustrated in Example 8.1 below.

EXAMPLE 8.1   Virus warning applet

Opportunity   The warning program in Example 7.1 has become popular, and others would like to use it.

Response   If the program is changed into an applet, it can be downloaded onto any other machine and run there. (Of course, this is a very simple program which would not draw much on the resources on either side, but we are using it for illustrative purposes.)

Design Following the steps above, we can convert the application of Example 7.1 into an applet. The HTML file that must be created contains the following:

```
<APPLET code="warningApplet.class" width=200 height=200>
</APPLET>
```

Program The program was pretty simple to start with, so it does not require much conversion. Notice that as an applet, it is shorter than the original because the main program has gone: its function has been taken over by the Java Runtime System in the browser or viewer.

```
import java.awt.*;
import java.applet.*;

public class warningApplet extends Applet {

    /* A Warning box in an applet    by J M Bishop  Oct 1996
     * =========================      Java 1.1
     * Must be run via its corresponding html file
     * in a browser or the appletviewer
     */

    static final int line = 15;
    static final int letter = 5;

    public void paint(Graphics g) {
      g.drawRect(2*letter, 2*line, 33*letter, 6*line);
      g.drawString("W A R N I N G", 9*letter, 4*line);
      g.drawString("Possible virus detected", 4*letter, 5*line);
      g.drawString("Reboot and run virus", 5*letter, 6*line);
      g.drawString("remover software", 7*letter, 7*line);
    }
}
```

Figure 8.1 *Applet output for the warning program*

Testing   The output from the applet looks exactly the same as that from an application, except that the title bar of the window is set up by the applet viewer as the file's name and there is a clear indication that the window is created by an applet. Figure 8.1 shows the window.

How applets work

If an applet does not have a main program, how does it get started, and how does it stop? An applet is started up by the Java Runtime System, which then looks to call one of the following four methods – which the applet has provided – at the appropriate time:

Applet methods

`init()`
`destroy()`
`start()`
`stop()`

Figure 8.2 shows the relationship between an applet called `myApplet` and the `Applet` class running in a web browser.

The `init` method is called in place of a constructor, to provide the initial setting up of the applet. Here the programmer would put the drawing of the user interface, its buttons and menus, and any other passive initialization. The `start` method, on the other hand, is called if there are dynamics to set up in an applet, such as animation and extra threads of control. There is an introduction to threads in the next section, which is completed in Chapter 9.

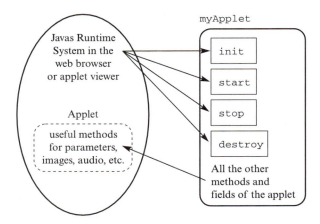

Figure 8.2 *The relationship between an applet and the* `Applet` *class*

At this point, the system calls any other methods which the program (in either its application or applet form) has overridden, such as `paint`. In Example 8.1, only the `paint` method is present, as the applet had no reason to define any of the others. The applet then returns to a passive state and waits for something to happen. There are two possibilities: the applet can become invisible, by means of the user scrolling it off the page in the browser, or there can be a normal GUI event such as a mouse click or a button press. If an applet becomes invisible, its `stop` method is called, which has the responsibility of halting any animation and so on. When it becomes visible again, `start` is called. Any of the other events are handled in the normal way via the `awt` methods redefined in the original program (such as `actionPerformed`).

Finally, a `destroy` method can be provided so that the applet can release any resources it may have before the viewer ends or the browser moves on to a different page. If we return to the page with our applet on it, the applet will start up from scratch again, going through its `init` sequence.

The above four methods are defined by the `Applet` class, but are overridden by the user, who provides the functionality. There is also a group of methods defined in the `Applet` class which we can use directly. These include methods to load images, audio and HTML parameters, and to establish where the applet is and where it came from. These methods are introduced in later sections and chapters.

Applets in browsers

Before Java, web browsers were mainly static, presenting information to the viewer exactly as it was stored at the original site. There were facilities for returning data to the host via form collecting and mailing, but Java's idea of having calculations at the host site is novel. With applets being able to be included in web pages, what comes down the link can now present a dynamic interface to the user (refer back to Figures 1.1 and 1.2).

Work can be done and results can be returned back to the host machine. Without Java, the same sequence of events as in Figure 1.2 occurs when web browsing, except that the display includes only text and images.

If an applet is stored on a host machine, then it is accessible to any other machine on the internet via its World Wide Web protocol and name or URL.[†] The `warningApplet`'s URL would be something like

```
http://www.cs.up.ac.za/jges/warningApplet.html
```

where the HTML file is stored on a web-accessible directory. The class file it refers to must be in the same directory, if it has the simple name as given in the tag:

```
<APPLET code="warningApplet.class" width=200 height=200>
```

If the applet is in another directory, then the tag must specify its full URL.

---

† URL stands for Uniform Resource Locator.

JAR files

A further consideration for applets is their access to user-defined packages, such as our `javagently` and `jgeslib`. In the normal course of events, the applet class loader will not be able to find the classes we need if they are in other directories. On the other hand, we cannot just copy all the class files we need into our working directory because then we shall disturb the package and import structure of our program and it will no longer compile.

Fortunately, Java has a solution. We can create a Java ARchive (JAR) of a package, and then refer to this in the HTML file that sets up the applet. To create a JAR, go to the directory above a package, and activate the JAR tool as in the form

---
JAR tool command

```
jar cf packagename.jar packagename\*.class
```

This will create an archive (compressed) of all the class files in the package. For example,

```
jar cf javagently.jar javagently\*.class
```

Then in the HTML file for the applet, add the additional tag

```
archive = javagently.jar
```

Apart from enabling the package structure to be retained on the distant computer, the compression factor of JAR means that the applet code is smaller and can be loaded much faster.

`Display` and `Graph` in applets

The good news is that the `Display` and `Graph` classes can be used as they are in applets. We can convert any of our existing programs into applets, and they will run correctly, at least from the point of view of `Display` and `Graph`.

What will happen is that a new window will pop up on top of the browser for `Display`, and another one for `Graph`. If `reposition` had been called in a display object, then the graph window will be correctly placed on the input section as before. If the user had created some explanatory text in HTML to run in the browser, then these windows would of course overlay the browser page, but they can always be minimized and viewed again.

The compatibility of `Display` and `Graph` with applets is significant in our desire to be effective scientific programmers. By essentially programming with graphics from Chapter 3, although we did not really know it, we have created a library of software which is truly web oriented.

EXAMPLE 8.2 *RL* current as an applet

We would like to show that programs built with the `Display` and `Graph` classes as their base can be very easily converted into applets. Let's start with the `RLCurrent` program (Example 3.8) which uses both `Display` and `Graph`. The changes are really minimal. We make the class public, import `java.applet.*`, rename the `main` method `init` and remove the string `args[]` from the brackets.

That is it! The inner class `CurrentPCSolver` does not change at all. To confirm the changes, here is the program minus the inner class:

```
import java.applet.*;
import javagently.*;

public class RLCurrentApplet extends Applet {

  /* Solving an RL Circuit
   * with a Predictor Corrector              N T and J M Bishop
   * ===========================             1990, 1999
   *
   * An RL Circuit that obeys Kirchhoff's Law is solved
   * by a predictor-corrector method customized for
   * this problem
   *
   * Illustrates the conversion of a class to an applet
   *
   */

static Display display = new Display("RL Current");

  static class CurrentPCSolver {
    ... exactly as before
  }

  public void init () {
    display.println("***** Electrical current in an RL circuit *****");
       ... and the rest of what was the main method exactly as before
    g.showGraph();
    display.reposition(g);
  }
}
```

The HTML file that must be called looks like this

```
<APPLET code = "RLCurrentApplet.class" width=200 height=200
   archive=javagently.jar>
</APPLET>
```

The output would be exactly the same, except for warning messages that we are working in an applet window (Figure 8.3). The reason for the warnings is described in the next section.

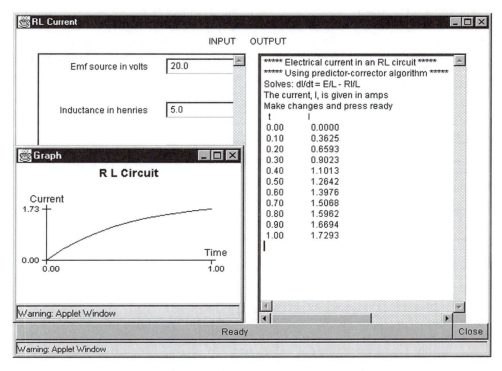

Figure 8.3 *The* RL *current display and graph windows from an applet*

Applet security

A potential concern when using applets on the web is that a downloaded program could be corrupt, and cause damage to your system. In every possible way, Java guards against this happening. These safeguards are:

1   There is a validity check on the bytecode that arrives at your computer. If it has been tampered with en route, your JVM will not run it.

2   The JVM itself will not perform any operation that could potentially harm your machine. For example, an applet from far away cannot find out your password, nor can it delete your files.

3   An applet cannot impersonate an application, thus leading a user into typing in information which can be transmitted back to the host. Hence the warning, as shown in Figure 8.3.

The full set of rules is summarized in Table 8.1. Let us consider the implications of this table. A Java application is a full program and as such can do anything that is required on your computer. An applet is quite different, and is subject to scrutiny and the rules above. Applets running in the applet viewer can do everything that an application can,

Table 8.1 *Applet security*

Operation	Java application	Applet in an applet viewer	Local applet in a browser	Remote applet in a browser
Access local files	✓	✓		
Delete a local file	✓			
Run another program	✓	✓		
Find out your name	✓	✓	✓	
Connect back to the host	✓	✓	✓	✓
Connect to another host	✓	✓	✓	
Load the Java library	✓	✓	✓	
Call exit	✓	✓		
Create a popup window	✓	✓	✓	✓

except for deleting files. However, once they run within a browser, their activities are curtailed somewhat.

Within a browser, an applet does not end; it ends when the page it is in is replaced by another page. Thus it does not call System.exit, nor is there any close box. The fact that applets cannot read or write to the local file system can be a distinct disadvantage. There are three ways around this restriction:

1 Define a security manager.
2 Use applet parameters.
3 Connect to the file via the Internet.

The first is a technique which is beyond the scope of this book, but is covered in the Java API documentation. We shall investigate the third possibility in the next section, as being the most general and consider applet parameters in Case study 5.

8.2 Connecting via the Internet

Java was built to access the network. It has extensive features for network programming at various levels from connecting via URLs or sockets to accessing remote methods (RMI). Because Java makes such connectivity so easy, we can justify including it in an introductory text such as this one, especially since we shall examine these new ideas by using examples in the usual *Java Gently* way.

All three methods for connecting are part of the Java core APIs and are available in the standard JDK and any browser that supports Java 1.1 or Java 1.2 in the `java.net` package. More advanced features are in the `java.rmi` and `java.jdbc` packages.

URL connections

Java has a class called `URL` which enables the data referred to by a URL on the Internet to be downloaded, and some interaction with the resource to be achieved. Given a string, Java will create an appropriate URL which can then be used to establish a `URLConnection`. The connection enables interaction as defined by the resource's protocol, perhaps via input–output streams.

The form for creating a URL is

```
URL creation

URL name = new URL (String);
getDocumentBase ();
getCodeBase ();
```

For example,

```
URL info = new info
        ("file:///C|/books/jges/chap8/rates.data");
```

will find the resource indicated and set up a reference to it from the Java program. Because we are accessing the C drive, it is clear that we are actually using a local file, but via the Internet technology. In this way, we get round the restriction that applets cannot read local files.

In order to maintain independence for the applets and their files, we can have relative URLs, which is the way we would normally do things. Firstly, we would get the URL from where the applet came, and then get the file relative to it, e.g.

```
URL info = new URL (getCodeBase(),"rates.data");
```

URLs can also be relative to the page that loaded the applet, using `getDocument Base`. The constructor makes sure that you have the correct syntax for forming a URL. If not, a `malformedURLException` is thrown. It is therefore usual to put the declaration in a try-statement and catch the exception.

To access the resource at the URL, we shall have to set up a connection. If the resource is a text file, then we can create an input stream to it. The relevant form for achieving this is

```
Creating a URL connection

URLConnection connection = URLname.openConnection ();
BufferedReader streamname = new InputStreamReader
    (connection.getInputStream());
```

The stream now acts as any normal input source. Its use is illustrated in the following example. Note that the opening of the stream can also be done using the Text class, as follows:

```
BufferedReader conin = Text.open(con.getInputStream());
```

Summarizing the above, we can postulate a method which will handle all the connecting, given a file name and returning a BufferedReader. It would be

```
BufferedReader connectTo (String fileName) {

/* A method to connect a filename to a BufferedReader
 * via the Internet. Uses the display for error messages
 */
   BufferedReader fin = null;
   try {
     URL dataFileURL = new URL(getCodeBase()+fileName);
     display.println("Connecting to "+dataFileURL);
     URLConnection con = dataFileURL.openConnection();
     try {
       fin = new BufferedReader(new InputStreamReader
              (con.getInputStream()));
     }
     catch (IOException e) {
       display.println("File "+fileName+" could not be opened");
     }
   }
   catch (Exception e) {
     display.println("Unexpected error when connecting");
   }
   return fin;
}
```

ConnectTo sends messages to the display, but could easily be changed to send them to the console via System.out.

EXAMPLE 8.3   Converter applet

Opportunity   The directors of Savanna Travel see the opportunity of offering the currency converter program on the Internet, so that prospective travellers can see what foreign exchange they will get for their trip.

Response   Convert the program into an applet as per the instructions. Create an HTML file and access it via a browser from anywhere on the Internet. The applet will be loaded into the HTML page.

Program design   The initial changes to the program in Example 7.4 follow the steps outlined in the previous section and Example 8.2. However, once the main program is removed, there is no need to keep the rest of the program in a separate class, so we may as well consolidate it into a single class.

There is only one further alteration. Since the applet may be running on a computer in one city and the travel agent is in another city, we will have a problem with the `rates.data` file. It will be on the travel agent's computer and cannot be opened in the usual way. The good news is that the file can be read in the ordinary way, provided we first connect to it via the Internet, as we described above.

The `Rates` class does not change for the applet version, which looks like this (with the unchanged method bodies not given in full):

```java
import java.awt.*;
import java.awt.event.*;
import java.util.*;
import java.io.*;
import java.applet.*;
import java.net.*;

public class ConverterGUIApplet extends Applet
           implements ActionListener, ItemListener{

  /* The Converter Program      by J M Bishop  Dec 1998
   * --------------------        Display version July 1999
   *                             GUI version July 1999
   *                             Applet version July 1999
   *
   * Converts the exchange rates from one currency into
   * many others and enables currency exchanges to be
   * estimated.
   *
   * Illustrates the conversion of a customized GUI
   * program to an applet
   */


  Hashtable table = new Hashtable();

  RatesApplet rate;
  Choice fromChoice, toChoice;
  boolean fromSelected, toSelected;
  TextField amountField;
  TextArea resultField;
  int amount = 1000;
  String toCountry, fromCountry;
  Button goButton;

  public void init () {
    Panel p = new Panel (new BorderLayout());
  ... exactly as before
    add(p);
   // This call moved from the main method
    readIn();
  }

  public void actionPerformed (ActionEvent e) {
   ... exactly as before
  }
```

```
public void itemStateChanged(ItemEvent e) {
  ... exactly as before
}

void transaction () {
  ... exactly as before
}

void readIn() {

  try {
    // Setting up access to the rates file via the Internet
    URL ratesFileURL = new URL(getCodeBase()+"rates.data");
    URLConnection con = ratesFileURL.openConnection();
    BufferedReader fin = null;

    try {
      fin = new BufferedReader(new InputStreamReader
             (con.getInputStream()));
    }
    catch (IOException e) {
      resultField.append("rates.data file not found\n");
    }

    try {
      for (int i = 0; ; i++) {
        rate = new Rates();
        rate.setRate(fin);
        table.put(rate.country, rate);
        toChoice.addItem(rate.country);
        fromChoice.addItem(rate.country);
      }
    }
    catch (EOFException e) {}
  }
  catch (Exception e) {
    resultField.append("Could not read the data\n");
  }

  fromSelected = false;
  toSelected = false;
}


}
```

Testing   We have added a little bit of text around the applet to illustrate how it is embedded in HTML. The creation of the HTML was done in the editor of Netscape in a wysiwig fashion, and the resulting file stored as `Converter.html`. This file is the one we open when we want to access the applet. If it was stored on a web server, we could access it via a web address. The output, running in Microsoft Internet Explorer browser, is shown in Figure 8.4.

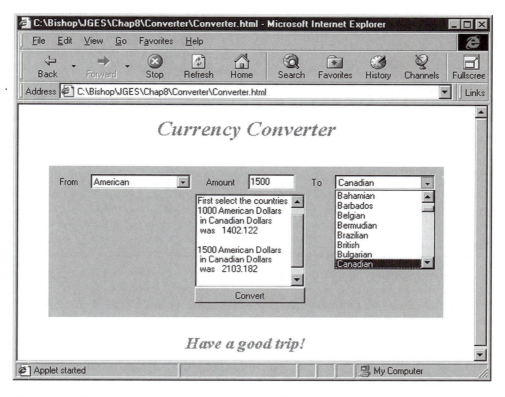

Figure 8.4 *The converter applet running under Microsoft Internet Explorer*

8.3 Sound and images

One of the joys of Java is being able to import sound and images easily and effectively into a program.

Sound

The `Applet` package has an interface called `AudioClip` which has three methods: `play`, `stop` and `loop`. The `Applet` method `getAudioClip` will return an object which implements this interface, and then we can play that object. The form is

---

Audio clip declaration and play

```
AudioClip name;
name = getAudioClip (getCodeBase (), filename);
name.play();
```

The `getCodeBase` method in `Applet` finds out where the applet is running, so that the sound can be played there. The file, at the moment, must be an `.au` file, not a `.wav` file. Suppose we have a file called 'ouch.au' and want to play it. The following statements will set this up:

```
AudioClip ouch;
ouch = getAudioClip (getCodeBase (), "ouch.au");
ouch.play();
```

There is also a shorthand version of the above which uses anonymous clips as follows:

```
play(getCodeBase (), "ouch.au");
```

The first form is preferable if you are going to use the clip more than once in a program. Sound is used in Example 8.4.

Images

Images are pixel data that is stored in a file, brought over the network or created in real time by a graphics engine or video camera. Java has extensive facilities for handling all these, and in particular for addressing the problems of working in a distributed, networked environment.

Like audio clips, Java has a class for images, and the form for getting one in an applet is exactly the same as above, with `AudioClip` replaced by `Image`. To display the image, we access the `drawImage` method within the `Graphics` class of the awt. Thus the form is

Fetch and display an image in an applet

`Image imagename;`
`imagename = getImage (getCodeBase (), filename);`
`graphic.drawImage (imagename, x, y, this);`

The *x* and *y* coordinates specify the top left corner of the spot where the image should be drawn on the screen. The fourth parameter is what is known as an observer – an active part of the program which watches the loading of the image. An example of fetching and drawing a simple image from the same directory as the applet is

```
Image pet;
pet = getImage (getCodeBase(), "Fluffy");
g.drawImage (pet, 0, 0, this);
```

The image formats that Java accepts are GIF and JPEG. Images in BMP, for instance, must first be converted to one of these before being fetched.

If we are working in an application rather than an applet, then `getCodeBase` no longer applies, and we also do not have the assistance of the browser or viewer in image loading. Intead we use a toolkit provided with each particular computer's operating system, and which Java can link into. In this case the fetch and load sequence is

---

Fetch and display an image in an application

```
Image imagename;
imagename = (Toolkit.getDefaultToolkit()).getImage (filename);
graphic.drawImage (imagename, x, y, this);
```

Media tracking

You will have already experienced the varying speeds at which images are downloaded within a browser. One of the more useful options in a browser is to set autoloading of images, meaning that the text will continue to come in while the image is also being displayed. Thus we are not held up just for a picture we may have already seen and do not particularly want.

Java can perform the same kind of control through objects called observers. While observers let us carry on with what we are doing while images are being loaded, we may wish to do the opposite, i.e. ensure that an image is loaded before continuing. It is important to do so when an applet is loading images in its `init` method. If each image is set to load, and the applet asks how big it is, it may get a spurious answer. So we set a media tracker on it. The form is

---

Media tracker

```
MediaTracker tracker = new MediaTracker(graphic);
... get the image in one or other form
tracker.addImage(imagename, 0);
try {tracker.waitForID(0);}
catch (InterruptedException e) {}
graphic.drawImage(imagename, x, y, this);
```

The tracker will watch the image and when a signal such as the zero (selected by us) is returned, we catch it and deduce that the image has been loaded. The Case study below uses this method successfully.

Moving images

The technique for moving an image around on the screen is a well-known one. Java just makes it easier. In many other systems, when you take an image and draw it somewhere else, you also have to take care to wipe out the old one. In Java, the use of the `paint` method means that the screen is written correctly as we want it each time. What we have to do is make sure that we specify the coordinates for moving objects in a relative way: that is, using variables rather than constants for their coordinates. Example 8.4 shows how this is done in a simple way.

Reacting to mouse events

In section 7.3, we described the different events, listeners and handlers that Java provides. Thereafter, we used mainly the `ActionEvent`, with its associated `ActionListener` and `ActionPerformed` handler method. `ActionListener` is actually special, because it has only one handler method. If you refer to Table 7.1, you will see that most other events have several methods.

The point is that the listeners are abstract interfaces, and when you use an interface, you have to provide real versions of **all** its abstract methods, even if you don't use them. Thus to detect a mouse press, we would have to define a `mousePressed` method (which is fine) and also dummy versions of all the other four mouse-related methods in the `MouseListener` class. To save on such wasted coding, the `java.awt.event` package includes for each of the abstract listener interfaces an implementation of it called an **adapter**. The abstract adapter class supplies dummy versions of all the methods in the listener. Then instead of implementing the listener, we inherit the adapter, and only override those methods that we really need.

So if an applet wants to listen to the mouse, it includes the following in its `init` method:

```
addMouseListener(new MouseHandler());
```

and an inner class called `MouseHandler` where the code for the `mousePressed` event is given. The next example illustrates the use of both the mouse listener and the mouse motion listener.

EXAMPLE 8.4   Catching the duke

Problem   We would like to have a little game where an image moves around the screen, and we move the mouse to try to catch it. The game should have sound as well.

Solution   Firstly we need to get hold of a `gif` file and two `au` files – one for a hit and one for a miss. In our experience, the `gif` files should not be larger than 10K and the `au` files should be at least 6K to be playable. These are guidelines; your computer could possibly handle different sizes. Then we shall draw the image and let the user track it with the mouse. Hits will be rewarded by one sound, and misses by another. In order to reinforce the sounds, we shall also print out corresponding messages.

Algorithm   The applet method for moving the image works like this. Once the image has been fetched and drawn, we can obtain its width and height. When the user clicks the mouse, a `mouseDown` event occurs and we can then check if the current mouse coordinates are within those of the image. After reacting with a win or lose sound and message, we repaint the screen, having moved the image. Moving the image is done by adding a random amount onto the coordinates that we pass to `drawImage`. The message is displayed in a special browser area called the status bar with the `showStatus` method. As a result, the message does not appear if the program is run with a viewer.

Now consider carefully the dynamics of the system. When do things actually move? Well nothing happens in the applet, unless we activate an event. So the image will remain stationary until we start to move the mouse. Every time the applet detects a `mouseMove` event (as opposed to a `mouseDown` event) it can repaint the screen. Repainting includes changing the x, y coordinates, so the image will seem to move randomly as we move the mouse, and we shall have to 'chase' it. In order to make the game realistic, we move the image only if a current position coordinate is a multiple of 3. Thus the x coordinate can change without the y coordinate changing.

Program   The program follows the algorithm and forms described above.

```java
import java.awt.*;
import java.applet.*;
import java.awt.event.*;

public class CatchM extends Applet {

  /* Catching the Duke program by J M Bishop Dec 1996
   * =========================    Java 1.1 Jan 1998
   *
   * Try to catch the duke and hit it by pressing the left
   * mouse button.
   * Illustrates sound, images and movement
   * and mouse handling events. */

   int mx, my, limitx, limity ;
   int wins;
   int boardSize;
   Image duke;

   public void init() {
     wins = 0;
     boardSize = getSize().width - 1;
     duke = getImage(getCodeBase(),"duke.gif");
     this.addMouseListener (new mousePressHandler());
     this.addMouseMotionListener (new mouseMotionHandler());
   }

   class mousePressHandler extends MouseAdapter {

     public void mousePressed (MouseEvent e) {
       int x = e.getX();
       int y = e.getY();
       requestFocus();
       if (mx < x && x < mx+limitx &&
           my < y && y < my+limity) {
         wins++;
         getAppletContext().showStatus("Caught it!  Total " + wins);
         play(getCodeBase(), "ouch.au");
       }
```

```
        else {
          getAppletContext().showStatus("Missed again.");
          play(getCodeBase(), "haha.au");
        }
        repaint();
    }
}

public class mouseMotionHandler extends MouseMotionAdapter {
  public void mouseMoved(MouseEvent e) {
    if (e.getX() % 3 == 0 && e.getY() % 3 == 0)
      repaint();
  }
}

public void paint(Graphics g) {
    // wait until the image is in before getting the
    // size. Can't put these statements in init
    limitx = duke.getWidth(this);
    limity = duke.getHeight(this);
    int change = boardSize-limitx;

    // draw a boundary
    g.drawRect(0, 0, boardSize, boardSize);

     // calculate a new place for the duke
     // and draw it.
     mx = (int)(Math.random()*1000) % change;
     my = (int)(Math.random()*1000) % change;
     g.drawImage(duke, mx, my, this);
  }
}
```

The HTML file that drives the program is

```
<title>Catch the Duke!</title>
<hr>
<applet code="CatchM.class" width=300 height=300>
</applet>
```

Testing   For obvious reasons, it is very difficult to show a test of the program in the book. Figure 8.5 shows a snapshot of the duke and a message, running in the Microsoft Internet Explorer browser, but this is one case where you are going to have to get onto the web to see and hear it! The program can be found on the *JGES* web site.

8.4 Animation through threads

The previous example showed movement by continually redrawing an image on the screen. It seemed as if the duke was animated, but in fact it only moved if the mouse moved. There is no independent movement: the screen is only repainted as a result of

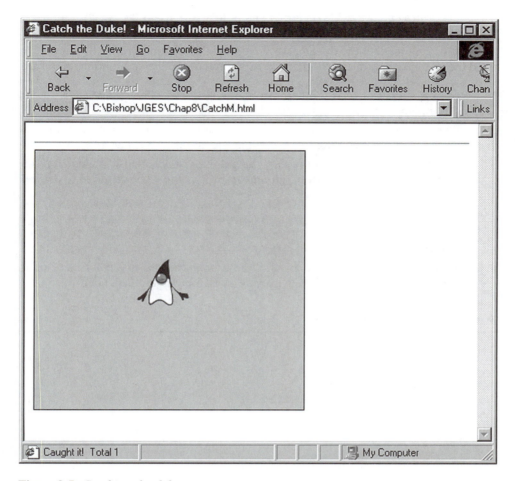

Figure 8.5 *Catching the duke*

mouse events. If we want movement to continue independently, and in addition to be able to have user interaction at the same time, then we need a new Java concept called threads. We shall deal with threads formally in the next chapter, and in this section introduce them solely for the purpose of achieving independent animation.

Simple threads

A program usually runs on one computer, which has one processor. The program follows a sequence of instructions which the programmer sets out. This sequence is called a 'thread of control'. If we want a program to do more than one thing at a time – such as animate a picture and watch buttons for user interaction – then we can create additional threads of control. Because the computer has only one processor, in reality only one thing is happening at a time, but the underlying system rotates the processor between the threads in such a way that the user of the program imagines that the threads are operating simultaneously.

If we assume that the thread associated with the main program will continue to mind the user interface, then the steps for creating and using a new animation thread are:

1   In the animation class, inherit from the `Thread` class. `Thread` is in the `java.lang` package, so no special importing is needed.

2   Override the `run` method of the `Thread` class so that it describes what this new thread of control is going to do. A typical form for `run` is given below.

3   Pass to the constructor of the class the graphics canvas that was created in the original window set-up. Store the canvas locally, and when required to draw in it use

```
Graphics g = area.getGraphics();
```

to establish a value for g.

4   In the main class, create an object of the animation class, and call `start` on it. The animation thread will then execute its `run` method independently.

A `run` method for animation

The form of a typical `run` method used for animation is

Run method for animation

```
public void run () {
  while (true) {
    try {
      sleep(500);
      change some values
      draw();
    }
    catch (InterruptedException e) {}
  }
}
```

The `run` method usually contains an endless loop, but it could refer to some valid stopping condition, such as a request from the user to stop. The try–sleep–catch sequence is used by the thread to alternate with other threads. The value 500 is milli-seconds and is a reasonable amount. Changing values (such as x, y coordinates) would be done before a `draw` method is called. The `draw` method replaces the `paint` method of single thread programs. Whereas `paint` is called automatically, `draw` is called by our `run` method. `draw` is not a Java method: it is a conventional name for this kind of routine.

Inside `draw`, we first get the `Graphics` area that we are meant to use, as in step 3 above, and then we can proceed to perform any `awt` calls at will. The next example shows animation rather nicely, as does the Case study that follows.

EXAMPLE 8.5   Martian lander simulator

Problem   At some time in the future it is intended that scientists all over the world will be able to interact with spacecraft flying to Mars and other distant planets via Java applets. For the purpose of training them, we want a program that simulates landing a spacecraft under manual control. We need only consider the vertical motion. Consider Figure 8.6.

Solution   The mass of the spacecraft consists of a fixed part, *mlander*, and a variable part, *mfuel*, the mass of the fuel. Standard Newtonian mechanics leads to a system of differential equations

$$(mlander + mfuel)\frac{\mathrm{d}v}{\mathrm{d}t} = -\frac{g_m(mlander + mfuel)}{(1 + s/r_m)^2} + fuelrate \times fuelfactor$$

$$\frac{\mathrm{d}s}{\mathrm{d}t} = v$$

$$\frac{\mathrm{d}mfuel}{\mathrm{d}t} = -fuelrate$$

where g_m is the gravitational acceleration on the surface of the Mars; r_m is the radius of the planet; *fuelrate* can be adjusted by the scientist to between 0 and an upper limit; and the *fuelfactor* converts *fuelrate* into units of force. As before, we will integrate the equations by the predictor–corrector method.

Program design   We have designed a screen output as in Figure 8.7. The bottom panel allows the user to regulate the fuel rate by 1 or 10 kilograms per second, up or down. The panel above that shows the current state of the lander in terms of its velocity in metres per second (negative for downwards), height in metres, time since the simulation began in seconds and the fuel reserves in kg. There is quite a lot of GUI programming here, and there is also the mathematics, so we split the program into three classes:

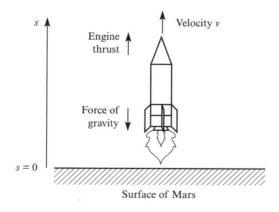

Figure 8.6 *Diagram of a Martian landing*

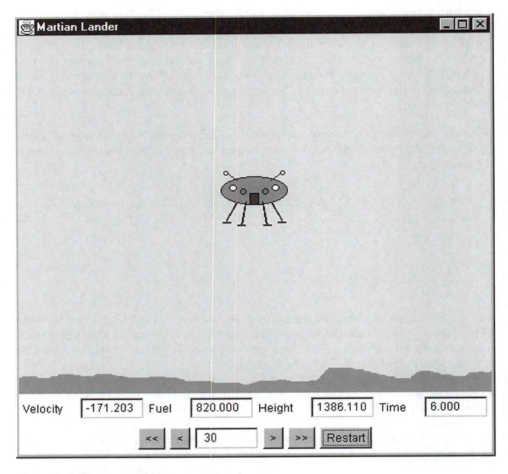

Figure 8.7 *The* MartianLander *simulator*

1 The MartianLander class which draws the initial window and handles the control panel events.

2 The LanderCalculations which keeps all the data and integrates it on request from the animator.

3 The LanderAnimation which has a separate thread for constantly redrawing the lander.

Programs First we look at the MartianLander. It is quite a long class. Notice that in fact the window has two forms: it starts out with some instructions as given in the instr panel. When the user presses the Start button, this panel is removed and the one as shown in Figure 8.7 replaces it. The Restart button is always active, and we can restart even before we land if things are not going well.

```
import java.io.*;
import javagently.*;
import java.awt.*;
import java.awt.event.*;

public class MartianLander extends Frame implements ActionListener {

  /* The Martian Lander programmer      N T Bishop  July 1999
   * =============================       based on Lunar Lander 1990
   *                                     assisted by A Moolman and
   * Simulates the landing of a craft    B Worrall
   * on Mars under user control of the
   * fuel thrusters
   *
   * Illustrates animation with threads
   * and incorporation of images
   */

  public MartianLander () {

    setTitle("Martian Lander");
    area = new Canvas();
    area.setBackground(Color.cyan);
    controlPanel = new Panel(new BorderLayout());
      Panel readingsPanel = new Panel();
        readingsPanel.add(new Label("Velocity"));
        velocity = new TextField(6);
          velocity.setEditable(false);
          readingsPanel.add(velocity);
        readingsPanel.add(new Label("Fuel"));
        fuel = new TextField(6);
          fuel.setEditable(false);
          readingsPanel.add(fuel);
        readingsPanel.add(new Label("Height"));
        height = new TextField(6);
          height.setEditable(false);
          readingsPanel.add(height);
        readingsPanel.add(new Label("Time"));
        time = new TextField(6);
          time.setEditable(false);
          readingsPanel.add(time);
      controlPanel.add("North", readingsPanel);
    Panel buttonsPanel = new Panel();
        decel10 = new Button("<<");
          buttonsPanel.add(decel10);
          decel10.addActionListener(this);
        decel1 = new Button("<");
          buttonsPanel.add(decel1);
          decel1.addActionListener(this);
        fuelRate = new TextField(6);
          fuelRate.setEditable(false);
          buttonsPanel.add(fuelRate);
        accel1 = new Button(">");
          buttonsPanel.add(accel1);
          accel1.addActionListener(this);
```

```java
        accel10 = new Button(">>");
          buttonsPanel.add(accel10);
          accel10.addActionListener(this);
        restart = new Button("Restart");
          buttonsPanel.add(restart);
          restart.addActionListener(this);
        controlPanel.add("Center", buttonsPanel);
    instr = new TextArea("", 0, 0, TextArea.SCROLLBARS_NONE);
    instr.setText("****Welcome to the Martian Lander simulation****\n" +
                    "Control the landing by altering the fuel" +
                    " rate.  Use the <<, <, > and >> buttons to" +
                    " do so.  The double arrows change the rate" +
                    " by ten units, the single arrows by one." +
                    " The restart button resets the simulation.\n\n" +
                    "Press Start to continue...");
      instr.setEditable(false);
      add("Center", instr);
    startButton = new Button("Start");
      startButton.addActionListener(this);
      add("South", startButton);
  }

  public static void main (String arg []) {
    MartianLander f = new MartianLander ();
    f.setSize(500,480);
    f.setVisible(true);
    f.addWindowListener(new WindowAdapter () {
      public void windowClosing(WindowEvent e) {
        System.exit(0);
      }
    });
  }

  public void resetLander(){
      setForeground(Color.black);
      if (done) {
        this.add("South", controlPanel);
        done = false;
      }
      this.validate();
      repaint();
      calc = new LanderCalculations();
      calc.fuelrate = 30;
      fuelRate.setText(Text.format((int) calc.fuelrate, 3));
      animator = new LanderAnimation(area, calc, velocity,
                      fuel, height, time);
      animator.start();
  }

  void startLander() {
    // Get rid of the instructions and replace
    // with the control panel and animation
    remove(instr);
    remove(startButton);
```

```
      add("Center", area);
      add("South", controlPanel);
    }

    public void actionPerformed(ActionEvent evt) {
      if (evt.getSource() == startButton) {
        startLander();
        resetLander();
      } else
      if (evt.getSource() == restart) {
        animator.endthread = true;
        animator = null;
        resetLander();
      } else {
        if (evt.getSource() == decel10)
          calc.changeRate(-10);
        else if (evt.getSource() == accel10)
          calc.changeRate(10);
        else if (evt.getSource() == decel1)
          calc.changeRate(-1);
        else if (evt.getSource() == accel1)
          calc.changeRate(1);
        fuelRate.setText(Text.format((int) calc.fuelrate,3));
      }
    }

    LanderCalculations calc;
    LanderAnimation animator;

    TextField velocity, height, time, fuel, fuelRate;
    TextArea instr;
    Panel controlPanel;
    Button restart, startButton,
          accel1, accel10, decel1, decel10;
    Canvas area;
    boolean done = false;

}
```

The next class is the LanderCalculations. It is the repository for the data
connected with the simulation and is called by both the other classes. The Martian
Lander submits changes in the fuel rate (as supplied by the user) and the animator
asks it to integrate the equations to get new x, y values for drawing the lander. The
integration is done around a predictor–corrector, but we cannot use the library
version because there are three equations to integrate (for velocity, height and fuel)
rather than two equations. Also, we want to be able to exit the loop if the height
becomes negative.

```
class LanderCalculations {

    /* This class keeps the data values for the
     * main application and the animator.
```

```
 * Integrate is called by the animator
 * and changeRate by the main application
 * in response to button presses by the
 * user.
 */

public double dt, fuel, fuelrate, v, s, t;
public double max;

LanderCalculations(){
  // initialization
  dt = timeinterval/imax;
  fuel = initialfuel;
  warning = false;
  v = -200;
  t = 0;
  s = 2500;
  max = 2500;
}

public void integrate () {
  // Predictor-corrector method
  double dfuel, vp, vc, sp;
  int i = 0;
  do {
    dfuel = -dt*fuelrate;
    i++;
    vp = v + dt*fv(fuel, s, t);
    sp = s + dt*v;
    vc = v + 0.5*dt*(fv(fuel,s,t) + fv(fuel+dfuel,sp,t + dt));
    s = s + 0.5*dt*(v+vp);
    v = vc;
    t = t + dt;
    fuel = fuel + dfuel;
    if (fuel <= 0)
      fuelrate = 0;
  } while (s>0 & i<imax);
}

public double fv(double fuel, double s, double t) {
  // fv is used only by integrate
  return -mg/Math.pow(1 + s/rmars,2) +
         fuelrate*forcefactor/(mlander+fuel);
}

public void changeRate(double mass) {
  // Called from Martian Lander in response to a user
  // change to the fuel rate, and ensures that the new
  // fuel rate is valid
  if (fuel > 0)
    fuelrate += mass;
  if (fuelrate > maxfuelrate)
    fuelrate = maxfuelrate;
  if ((fuel < 0) | (fuelrate < 0))
    fuelrate = 0;
}
```

```
private boolean warning;
static final int      imax = 100;
static final double mlander = 15000;
static final double maxfuelrate = 60;
static final double rmars = 3397000;
static final double mg = 3.69;
static final double forcefactor = 4500;
static final double timeinterval = 1;
static final double initialfuel = 1000;


}
```

The third class performs the animation. It starts off by getting the images, and then sets up its own thread to redraw the lander at regular intervals based on the new values supplied on demand from the LanderCalculations. Study the run method to see how it all fits together.

```
import java.awt.*;
import javagently.*;

class LanderAnimation extends Thread {

  /* This class handles the animation of the Martian lander.
   * It adds the three images to a media tracker
   * then has a simple run method to draw the lander at
   * each new coordinate. The coordinate values are fetched
   * dynamically from the calc class, where they are being
   * updated in response to user button pushes.
   */

  LanderAnimation (Canvas c, LanderCalculations LCalc, TextField v,
                   TextField f, TextField h, TextField t) {
    area = c;
    velocity = v;
    height = h;
    time = t;
    fuel = f;
    calc = LCalc;

    MediaTracker tracker = new MediaTracker(area);
    lander = (Toolkit.getDefaultToolkit()).getImage("Lander.gif");
    tracker.addImage(lander,0);
    chrasher = (Toolkit.getDefaultToolkit()).getImage("Chrash.gif");
    tracker.addImage(chrasher,0);
    marsscape = (Toolkit.getDefaultToolkit()).getImage("Landscape.gif");
    tracker.addImage(marsscape, 0);

    try {
      tracker.waitForID(0);
    } catch (InterruptedException e) {
      return;
    }
  }
```

```
public boolean endthread;

public void run () {
  while (calc.s > 0 && !endthread) {
    try {sleep (500);
        calc.integrate ();
        draw();
    }
    catch (InterruptedException e) {}
  }
  if (!endthread)
    if (calc.v < -10)
      drawEnd(chrasher,"You have crash-landed on Mars");
    else
      drawEnd(lander, "Congratulations: you have landed safely on Mars");
}

void draw () {
  Graphics g = area.getGraphics();
  area.paint(g);
  g.drawImage(marsscape,
        (area.getSize().width / 2) - (marsscape.getWidth(area) / 2),
        area.getSize().height - marsscape.getHeight(area), area);
  Dimension cv = area.getSize();
  x = (int) (cv.width-lander.getWidth(area))/2;
  y = (int) (cv.height - (calc.s/calc.max) *
        (cv.height-lander.getHeight(area))) - lander.getHeight(area);
  g.drawImage(lander, x, y, area);
  velocity.setText(Text.format(calc.v, 4, 3));
  fuel.setText(Text.format(calc.fuel, 4, 3));
  height.setText(Text.format(calc.s, 4, 3));
  time.setText(Text.format(calc.t, 4, 3));
}

void drawEnd (Image endImage, String message) {
  Graphics g = area.getGraphics();
  area.paint(g);

  g.drawImage(marsscape, (area.getSize().width / 2) -
            (marsscape.getWidth(area) / 2),
            area.getSize().height -
            marsscape.getHeight(area), area);
  Dimension cv = area.getSize();
  x = (int) (cv.width-endImage.getWidth(area))/2;
  y = cv.height-endImage.getHeight(area);
  if (calc.s > 0)
    y = (int) (cv.height -
        (calc.s/calc.max)*(cv.height-endImage.getHeight(area))) -
        endImage.getHeight(area);
  g.drawImage(endImage, x, y, area);
  g.setColor(Color.blue);
  g.drawString(message, 10,y-20);
}
```

```
    private LanderCalculations calc;
    private Canvas area;
    private TextField velocity, height, time, fuel;
    private int x,y;
    private Image lander;
    private Image chrasher;
    private Image marsscape;
}
```

Run the program with the fuel rate at 0 throughout, and you will find that the impact velocity is 241.739 m/s after 11.320 s. In this case the problem can be solved analytically

$$v \frac{dv}{ds} = \frac{-g_m}{(1 + s/r_m)^2}$$

so that

$$\frac{1}{2}v^2 = \frac{g_m r_m}{(1 + s/r_m)} + \text{constant}$$

The correct value for the impact velocity is calculated to be 241.736 m/s after 11.319 s.

The simulation starts with an initial fuel rate of 30 kg/s, but unless this is increased the lander will crash, as shown in Figure 8.8. The program can be extended by considering further options. These are covered in problems at the end of the chapter.

8.5 Case study 3: The Planets Project

In Chapter 1, we proposed a Java based system to show details about the planets, and to illustrate their orbits around the sun. We have now learnt enough Java to understand how such a system would be put together. It incorporates aspects of all the examples in this chapter, as well as introducing one new feature, the PARAM tag for communicating between Java and HTML.

Planetary orbits

Let us first consider the theory behind what we want to do. All planetary orbits are ellipses, and the **eccentricity** of an ellipse is a measurement of how much it is flattened. The eccentricity can vary between 0 and 1, with the value 0 representing a circle. Apart from Mercury and Pluto, the other planetary orbits have low eccentricity and are very nearly circular. If the orbit is highly eccentric, one can see that the planet speeds up when it is near the Sun (at perihelion), and slows down when it is far from the Sun (at aphelion).

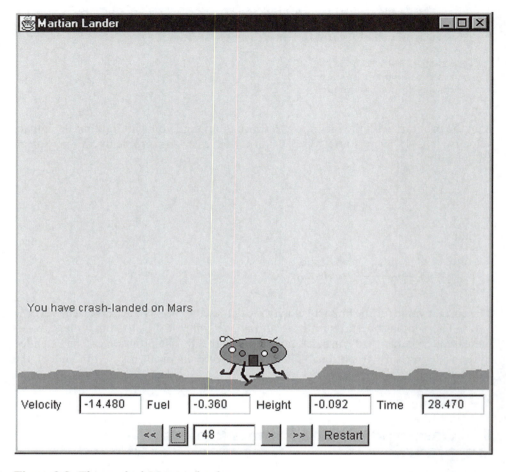

Figure 8.8 *The crashed Martian lander*

The unit of distance used in solar system astronomy is the AU, or Astronomical Unit, which is the radius of the Earth's orbit and is about 150 million km. More precisely 1AU is the **semi-major axis** of the Earth's orbit, but since the Earth's orbit is almost circular it can be regarded as the **radius** of the orbit. Planetary dimensions are usually given in terms of those of the Earth, which has a radius of about 6400 km and a mass of about 6×10^{24} kg.

The equations that we shall develop relate the radius, r, the eccentricity ε, orbit's semi-major axis a and the period of the orbit, p. We start with:

$$r = \frac{a(1 - \varepsilon^2)}{1 + \varepsilon \cos(\theta)} \tag{8.1}$$

$$r^2 \frac{d\theta}{dt} = \text{constant} \tag{8.2}$$

Combining the equations we get

$$\int \frac{d\theta}{(1 + \varepsilon \cos\theta)^2} = \int \text{constant } dt$$

Then integration yields

$$t = \frac{p}{2\pi}\left[2\tan^{-1}\left(\frac{\tan(\theta/2)(1-\varepsilon)}{d}\right) - \frac{\varepsilon d \sin\theta}{1 + \varepsilon \cos\theta}\right]$$

where $d = \sqrt{1 - \varepsilon^2}$.

We need to invert the above equation, so that when given t we can find θ. In the programs we construct a table of t-values for given θ, then use linear interpolation to find the inverse. In this way, given t, we can find θ and then use equation (8.1) to find r.

Overall structure

The system is driven though HTML, with a home page (shown in Figure 1.1) with links to any of the nine other pages for the planets (as for example, Mars in Figure 1.2). We discuss here the construction of the page for Mars, and give the data below for the construction of the others.

Each planet page consists of four parts as shown in Figure 8.9. The HTML is developed under a browser's composer system, such as Netscape. The necessary text is entered, and then tags are set up to insert the image, applet and table.

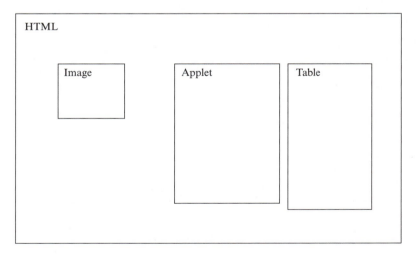

Figure 8.9 *Schematic view of the Planet webpage*

The HTML for Mars web page is given in full:

```
<HTML>
<BODY>
<FONT COLOR="#FF0000"><FONT SIZE=+4>Mars</FONT></FONT>
<TABLE BORDER WIDTH="100%" >
<TR>
<TD><IMG SRC="marssm97.jpg" HSPACE=6 VSPACE=6 HEIGHT=211
            WIDTH=200 ALIGN=LEFT> 
<PR>The red planet, Mars, is the planet most similar to Earth, but it is
much colder, has a very thin atmosphere, and contains very little water.
However, there is evidence that it had much more water in the past, and
in liquid form, prompting speculation that there may have been some form
of life on Mars.  
<P><FONT FACE="Arial,Helvetica"><FONT SIZE=-2>Picture: Hubble Space
Telescope, March 7, 1997</FONT></FONT>
 <BR> </TD>
<TD><APPLET CODE="OrbitApplet.class" WIDTH=290 HEIGHT=300>
<PARAM NAME="name" VALUE="Mars">
<PARAM NAME="axis" VALUE="1.52">
<PARAM NAME="eccentricity" VALUE="0.09">
<PARAM NAME="period" VALUE="1.88"></APPLET></TD>
<TD>
<CENTER><FONT COLOR="#FF0000">FACTS AND FIGURES
 </FONT></CENTER>
<CENTER> </CENTER>
<TABLE BGCOLOR="#66FFFF" >
<TR>
<FONT SIZE=-1>
<TD>Semi-major axis </TD><TD>1.52AU </TD>
</TR>
<TR>
<TD>Eccentricity </TD><TD>0.09 </TD>
</TR>
<TR>
<TD>Orbital period </TD><TD>1,88 year </TD>
</TR>
<TR>
<TD>Orbital speed </TD><TD>24 km/s </TD>
</TR>
<TR>
<TD>Inclination to ecliptic </TD><TD>2^o </TD>
</TR>
<TR>
<TD>Mass (times mass of Earth) </TD><TD>0.11 </TD>
</TR>
<TR>
<TD>Radius (times radius of Earth) </TD><TD>0.53 </TD>
</TR>
<TR>
<TD>Density </TD><TD>3.9 x 10^3 kg/m^3 </TD>
</TR>
<TR>
<TD>Length of day </TD><TD>24.6 days </TD>
</TR>
```

```
</TABLE>
 </TD>
</TR>
</TABLE>
 
<BR> 
<BR> 
</BODY>
</HTML>
```

The image

Images for this project were obtained from NASA's space telescope web site at www.stsci.edu. The copyright is such that the pictures may be reproduced provided due acknowledgement is given. To speed up the running of the applet, we have included the picture in JPEG format with the system. The HTML tag is:

```
<IMG SRC="marssm97.jpg" HSPACE=6 VSPACE=6
HEIGHT=211 WIDTH=200 ALIGN=LEFT>
```

The picture in the file marssm97.jpg is actually quite large, as can be seen if you open it from a browser. However, the height and width parameters are used to bring it to the desired size on the page.

It is obviously also possible to fetch the picture directly from NASA. The full web address for the image we used is:

```
http://oposite.stsci.edu/pubinfo/jpeg/marssm97.jpg
```

The applet

The purpose of the applet is to draw the orbit of a given planet around the sun. It does this by calculating a new x, y position, and then drawing a line from the current position to the new position, using the equations as described above. The class to draw the orbit is actually much simpler than the LanderAnimation in Example 8.5, because the calculations are simpler.

The class consists of an animator thread as follows:

```
class OrbitCanvas extends Thread {

    private Canvas area;

    OrbitCanvas (Canvas can) {
      area = can;
    }

    public void run () {
      Graphics g = area.getGraphics();
      g.setColor(Color.yellow);
      g.fillOval(scalex(0)-8,scaley(0)-8,16,16);
```

```
while (true) {
  t=t+dt;
  tyear=(int) t;
  tfrac=t - tyear;
  torbit=torbit+dt;
  if (torbit > p) {
    torbit=torbit-p;
    norbit=norbit+1;
    ith=0;
  }

  while (torbit > tref[ith+1])
    ith=ith+1;

  th=ith*pi/n + (torbit-tref[ith])*pi/n/(tref[ith+1]-
    tref[ith]);
  r=(1-ep*ep)/(1+Math.cos(th)*ep);
  newx=scalex(r*Math.cos(th));
  newy=scaley(r*Math.sin(th));
  g.setColor(Color.black);
  g.drawLine (x,y,newx,newy);
  g.setColor(Color.white);
  g.fillOval(x-1,y-1,3,3);
  g.setColor(Color.red);
  g.fillOval(newx-1,newy-1,3,3);
  x = newx;
  y = newy;
  orbitBox.setText(String.valueOf(norbit));
  yearBox.setText(String.valueOf(t));

  try { sleep(500);}
  catch(InterruptedException e) { }
  }
}
```

The first part of the `run` method performs calculations for `newx` and `newy`, and the second part draws the lines. We chose to draw a dotted line as it gave a better impression of where the planet was. For added accuracy, the number of orbits so far (for that planet) and the time in Earth years are shown in text fields as well.

Now we come to an interesting new feature of Java. We would like the `Orbit Applet` (which we are going to develop) to be independent of the planet being shown. However, the applet needs four values which are specific to the planet in question, viz: the semi-major axis (in AU), the eccentricity (dimensionless), the orbit period (in Earth years), and the planet's name. Table 8.2 shows these values for the nine planets.

The question is how to get these values into the applet. Since the applet only wants the values for the planet whose orbit it is currently showing, the solution of connecting to a file (as in Example 8.3) is not really satisfactory. Java provides a more direct route which can be used specifically with applets running in HTML pages.

Table 8.2 *Planetary parameters*

Planet name	Axis	Eccentricity	Period
Mercury	0.39	0.21	0.24
Venus	0.72	0.007	0.62
Earth	1.0	0.02	1.0
Mars	1.52	0.09	1.88
Jupiter	5.20	0.05	11.9
Saturn	9.55	0.06	29.5
Uranus	19.2	0.05	84.0
Neptune	30.1	0.009	165.0
Pluto	39.4	0.25	248.0

The PARAM facility

Interaction between applets and web pages is achieved through the **PARAM** facility. The data is entered in a `PARAM` tag and then retrieved from the page itself via an `Applet` method called `getParameter`. Parameters are listed between the `<APPLET>` and `</APPLET>` tag brackets and each parameter must be of the form:

HTML parameter
`<PARAM NAME = "formal" VALUE = "actual">`

`NAME` indicates that the string that follows is the name of the parameter that is being sought. Within the same set of angle brackets, forming a pair, there is the `VALUE` to be assigned to that parameter. The value is also a string, but obviously it can later be parsed as a number or whatever other type is required. In the HTML page for Mars, for example, there would be tag

```
<PARAM NAME="name" VALUE="Mars">
```

and we would get the name of the planet as follows

```
planetName = getParameter("name");
```

The result in `planetName` would, of course, be the string 'Mars'.

If the value to be fetched is a number, then a conversion follows, as in:

```
<PARAM NAME="axis" VALUE="1.52">

String s = getParameter("axis");
a         = Double.valueOf(s).doubleValue();
```

because all the parameters in the PARAM tags are strings.

The full class, which follows a now familiar pattern, is:

```
import java.applet.*;
import java.net.*;
import java.util.*;
import java.awt.*;
import java.awt.event.*;

public class OrbitApplet extends Applet implements ActionListener {

/*  Applet to draw the orbit of a planet
 *  ----------------------------------- N T Bishop and
 *                                      J M Bishop Dec 1998
 *
 *    INPUT DATA to be fetched from the web page
 *
 *    NAME     DESCRIPTION      TYPE       UNITS
 *    a        semi-major axis  real       AU %(*)
 *    ep       eccentricity     real       dimensionless
 *    p        period           real       year [of Earth]
 *    planetName                string
 *
 *  1AU is 1 Astronomical Unit, and is defined as the semi-major
 *  axis of the Earth's orbit. It is approximately
 *  150 million km.
 */

  static final int    n  = 100;       // number of angular
                                      // grid-points
  static final double ddt= 0.02;      // time-step in years of
                                      // planet
  static final double pi = Math.PI;
  static final int    limitxy = 300;// n could be made larger,
                                      // and ddt could be made
                                      // smaller, if more
                                      // accuracy is needed.
  double a, ep, p, dt,
         d, t, th,
         torbit, tfrac, r;
  double tref [] = new double [2*n+1];
  int    ith, norbit, tyear, x, y, newx, newy;
  String planetName;

  private Canvas area;
  private OrbitCanvas orbit;
  private Button startButton;
  private TextField orbitBox, yearBox;
```

```java
public void init () {
  setLayout (new BorderLayout());
  initializeData();
  area = new Canvas();
  add ("Center", area);
  Panel p = new Panel ();
  startButton = new Button("Start");
    startButton.addActionListener(this);
    p.add(startButton);
    p.add(new Label ("Orbits"));
    orbitBox = new TextField(4);
    p.add(orbitBox);
    p.add (new Label("Years"));
    yearBox = new TextField(7);
    p.add(yearBox);
  add ("South", p);
}

private void initializeData() {
  // These parameters come from the web page
  String s;
  planetName = getParameter("name");
  s          = getParameter("axis");
  a          = Double.valueOf(s).doubleValue();
  s          = getParameter("eccentricity");
  ep         = Double.valueOf(s).doubleValue();
  s          = getParameter("period");
  p          = Double.valueOf(s).doubleValue();
  System.out.println(planetName+"  "+a+"  "+ep+"   "+p+"  ");
  t=0.0;
  tyear=0;
  tfrac=0.0;
  torbit=0.0;
  norbit=0;
  ith=0;
  dt=ddt*p;
  x=scalex((1-ep*ep)/(1+ep));
  y=scaley(0.0);
  d=Math.sqrt(1-ep*ep);
  tref[0]=0.0;
  tref[n]=p/2;
  tref[2*n]=p;

  for (int i=1; i< n; i++) {
    th=i*pi/n;
    tref[i]=p/(2*pi)*(2*Math.atan(Math.tan(th/2)*(1-ep)/d)
            -d*ep*Math.sin(th)/(1+ep*Math.cos(th) ) );
    tref[2*n-i]=p-tref[i];
  }
}

public void actionPerformed (ActionEvent e) {
  // There is only a StartButton
  orbit = new OrbitCanvas(area);
  orbit.start();
}
```

```
int scalex (double coord) {
   return (int) (limitxy*coord/4.0+limitxy/2.0);
}

int scaley (double coord) {
   return (int) (-limitxy*coord/4.0+limitxy/3.0);
}

The class OrbitCanvas is placed here

}
```

The table

The fourth part of the web page, the table, consists of additional facts and figures about the planet which are not needed for drawing the orbit. In the system that we are using, the table is created through the web page. In problems that follow, we look at how to gather all the information in one place rather. It is not that any of these values might change and need to be updated, but the technique of using data from files is a good one to practise.

What follows are the details of each of the planets that will be required. Remember that pictures can be obtained from NASA as well.

Mercury

Semi-major axis	0.39AU
Eccentricity	0.21
Orbital period	0.24 year
Orbital speed	48 km/s
Inclination to ecliptic	7°
Mass ($\times$ mass of Earth)	0.056
Radius ($\times$ radius of Earth)	0.38
Density	5.4×10^3 kg/m^3
Length of day	58.7 days

Mercury is the planet closest to the Sun. It is a barren world, without atmosphere or water. It is tidally bound so that the length of its year is the same as that of its day: one side of the planet always faces the Sun, and is baking hot, while on the other side it is always night and freezing cold.

Venus

Semi-major axis	0.72AU
Eccentricity	0.007
Orbital period	0.62 year
Orbital speed	35 km/s
Inclination to ecliptic	3°
Mass ($\times$ mass of Earth)	0.82

Radius ($\times$ radius of Earth)	0.95
Density	$5.3 \times 10^3 \text{ kg/m}^3$
Length of day	243 days

Always hidden behind thick clouds, Venus has had an air of mystery attached to it. Now, however, we know that Venus is a most inhospitable place, with an atmosphere that consists mainly of carbon dioxide, resulting in a runaway greenhouse effect and a surface temperature greater than that of molten lead.

Earth

Semi-major axis	1.0 AU
Eccentricity	0.02
Orbital period	1.0 year
Orbital speed	30 km/s
Inclination to ecliptic	0°
Mass ($\times$ mass of Earth)	1.0
Radius ($\times$ radius of Earth)	1.0
Density	$5.5 \times 10^3 \text{ kg/m}^3$
Length of day	23.93 hours

Our planet Earth is unique in the solar system in that it supports life in abundance. It has the necessary physical environment to support life: water, an average temperature at which the water is liquid, and significant quantities of other chemical elements.

Mars

Semi-major axis	1.52 AU
Eccentricity	0.09
Orbital period	1.88 years
Orbital speed	24 km/s
Inclination to ecliptic	2°
Mass ($\times$ mass of Earth)	0.11
Radius ($\times$ radius of Earth)	0.53
Density	$3.9 \times 10^3 \text{ kg/m}^3$
Length of day	24.6 hours

The red planet, Mars, is the planet most similar to Earth, but it is much colder, has a very thin atmosphere, and contains very little water. However, there is evidence that it had much more water in the past, and in liquid form, prompting speculation that there may have been some form of life on Mars.

Jupiter

Semi-major axis	5.20 AU
Eccentricity	0.05
Orbital period	11.9 years

Orbital speed	13 km/s
Inclination to ecliptic	1°
Mass (× mass of Earth)	318.0
Radius (× radius of Earth)	11.2
Density	1.3×10^3 kg/m^3
Length of day	9.8 hours

Jupiter is the largest planet in the solar system. It is a gas giant, and in composition is more like a small star than a planet like Earth. It is well known for its system of satellites, and a giant storm, the red spot, that has been raging for centuries.

Saturn

Semi-major axis	9.55AU
Eccentricity	0.06
Orbital period	29.5 years
Orbital speed	9.6 km/s
Inclination to ecliptic	2°
Mass (× mass of Earth)	95.0
Radius (× radius of Earth)	9.5
Density	0.69×10^3 kg/m^3
Length of day	10.2 hours

The second largest planet is Saturn. It is also a gas giant without a solid core, and has numerous satellites, including a collection of small bodies that form a system of rings around the planet.

Uranus

Semi-major axis	19.2AU
Eccentricity	0.05
Orbital period	84.0 years
Orbital speed	6.8 km/s
Inclination to ecliptic	1°
Mass (× mass of Earth)	14.5
Radius (× radius of Earth)	4.0
Density	1.2×10^3 kg/m^3
Length of day	17.3 hours

Uranus is not visible to the naked eye, and its discovery had to wait until the 18th century, well after the invention of the telescope. It is a small gas giant, and also has a system of rings.

Neptune

| Semi-major axis | 30.1AU |
| Eccentricity | 0.009 |

Orbital period	165 years
Orbital speed	5.4 km/s
Inclination to ecliptic	2°
Mass (× mass of Earth)	17
Radius (× radius of Earth)	3.8
Density	$1.7 \times 10^3 \text{ kg/m}^3$
Length of day	16 hours

The discovery of Neptune in the 19th century was something of a triumph for mathematical astronomy, because its existence and location were calculated from observations of perturbations to the orbit of Uranus.

Pluto

Semi-major axis	39.4AU
Eccentricity	0.25
Orbital period	248 years
Orbital speed	4.7 km/s
Inclination to ecliptic	17°
Mass (× mass of Earth)	0.002
Radius (× radius of Earth)	0.24
Density	$0.9 \times 10^3 \text{ kg/m}^3$
Length of day	64 days

Pluto was only discovered in the 20th century, again from observations of perturbations in the orbits of Neptune and Uranus. It is an unusual planet, with high eccentricity, that at times brings it inside the orbit of Neptune; and the largest inclination to the plane of the ecliptic.

QUIZ

8.1 What method is used instead of `println` in applets?

8.2 Compared to `awt` applications, why do applets not have `main` methods?

8.3 Applets usually have an `init` method. What is its counterpart in an application?

8.4 Give the HTML tag for running an applet for a class called `Orange.class` with a width and length of 200 pixels.

8.5 What does the `getCodeBase` method do?

8.6 What are the two image formats supported by Java?

8.7 What does the `getAppletContext` method do?

8.8 In what units of time does the `sleep` method for threads operate?

8.9 In Example 8.4, what happens each time we call `repaint()` from the `mouseMove` method?

8.10 On average, which requires more storage space: sound or images?

PROBLEMS

8.1 **Lots of dukes.** Add more dukes to the catching applet. Have each move at a different rate.

8.2 **Martian lander simulator.** Allow for horizontal motion. The spacecraft must land within 25 m of a target point, because outside this region Mars's surface is not sufficiently flat. We need to specify extra initial data, namely horizontal velocity and horizontal displacement from the target point. As well as the fuel rate, the scientist must also be able to control the angle from the vertical at which the engines thrust.

8.3 **Applications to applets.** Choose an earlier example and convert it to an applet together with some explanatory text on the first window, done in HTML.

8.4 **Bouncing balls.** A classic animation is one that has balls bouncing in a window. When they get to an edge, they ricochet off at a random angle. Write a program which shows one ball bouncing in this manner, and then extend it for several balls.

8.5 **Pets lost and found.** Based on the pet tag system devised for the Savanna Veterinary Association (Example 6.4), the *Savanna News* wants to set up an online version of its popular Lost and Found column. The idea is that owners who have lost pets will enter details and also a photograph. Those who have found pets can type in tag details as usual and get back the other data. Design and implement such a system using applets and web pages. Images of some pets are available for use on *JGES*'s web page under Other Material.

8.6 **Martian lander simulator.** The program runs faster than real time. Make a change to the program so that it runs approximately in real time.

8.7 **All nine planets.** Using the data supplied in the Case study, and images from NASA, create web pages for the other planets.

8.8 **Comparative orbits.** It would be wonderful to see all the orbits going together. Write a separate applet which has a choice box and will start up a new thread to show another orbit while existing ones are still running.

8.9 **Planet data collection.** Collect all the data in a file and create a connection to the file so that the values needed by the applet are read from there, not from the web page. Incorporate the image, HTML and table sections into the applet itself.

CHAPTER 9

Distributing

9.1 Formalities of threads

Java is a modern language and is fully network aware. We have already seen two ways in which Java can expand into more than just a single program: by connecting to resources on the Internet, and by creating additional threads within a program. In this chapter we consider threads again, looking at them more formally and at how they are used in circumstances other than animation.

In addition to threads, we shall add to our distribution repertoire by looking at Java's ports and sockets capability. In this manner, we shall be able to connect up several machines to work on a solution together, either in a very asynchronous fashion, as in the chat program (Example 9.4), or in lock-step synchrony, as in the nuclear reactor Case study (section 9.5)

Why threads?

Why do we actually need threads? Two particular situations illustrate their value:

1   **User interfacing.** If an applet or graphics application is busy drawing or displaying text, the user may wish to stop this activity. If a cancel button is provided, we can press the button, *but* the program will only detect the button press once it has reached a passive state: that is, it has finished computing or outputting and is waiting for events. However, if the button is being handled by a separate thread, the opportunity to react will come around regularly, even while the other computation is proceeding. This process has already been illustrated in the examples in Chapter 8.

2   **Many instances.** Sometimes one wants identical copies of a picture, of multiple windows or of different versions of a computation to be available simultaneously. We shall see in the nuclear reactor program below that we can set up multiple rods and watch them working together. Each would be handled by a separate thread. In the simple case, the threads will be straight copies of each other and will run independently. Java also allows the threads to communicate and synchronize their activities, as discussed in later sections.

From the user's point of view, the presence of multiple threads should be transparent. From the programmer's side, though, work has to be done to set up the threads in the first place, to keep them running and to detect when they should finish. During the lifetime of a process, threads can be created and destroyed at will. They are a cost-effective way of handling processor power and memory for non-trivial programs.

Threading a program

To 'thread' a program, we first have to identify those methods that can run independently. Usually, these are already in a class and it is the class that becomes a thread, possibly in multiple instantiations.

`Thread` is a class in the `java.lang` package, which means that it is always available and no special import is needed. Any class that wishes to be a thread class must inherit from `Thread`. Each prospective thread class must implement the `run` method. Basically, we take the executable part of the class and put it in a `run` method (allowing `run` of course to call methods to assist it as usual).

The `main` method is by default a thread, and it is from there, or from another active method such as `Applet`'s `init`, that the other threads are set in motion. As we shall see in later examples, threads can spawn their own threads as well.

The `Thread` class

Among many others, the `Thread` class has the following important methods:

```
Thread creation and methods

class classname extends Thread { ....}
classname threadname = new classname (parameters);
new classname (parameters)

start ();
run ();
stop ();
sleep (milliseconds);
yield ();
```

A class is declared as threaded by extending the `Thread` class. Thereafter each new thread is created in the same way as any other object declaration, as shown in the first line of the form. Alternatively, if there is no need to give the thread a name which its parent knows, we can use the second form, which simply creates a thread of the given class. Threads are dynamically created in Java; we do not need to state in advance how many of a certain kind of thread there will be. Every time a new thread declaration is executed, a new thread object comes into existence.

`start`, `run` and `stop` are the three important thread methods. After a thread has been created via its constructor, the creating method calls `start`, which is defined in the `Thread` class. `start` will cause `run` to be called, thus causing the thread to join the operating system's list of threads waiting to run. In a while, it will get its chance at the processor and start executing independently.

`run` will usually consist of a loop which continues until some condition is met, in which case the loop ends. At this point the `run` method meets a natural end and the thread dies as a result.

The `stop` method can be called from one thread to another and once received via the `Thread` class will cause the called thread to die. In most cases, the `stop` method is not used, and 'natural death' is more common.

`sleep` and `yield` are class methods. Both cause the thread to relinquish the processor. `sleep` will wait for the specified time, and then the thread will be ready to run again. `yield` is not needed if the operating system is sharing time between processors, but if it is not, then calling `yield` is a way for a thread to stand back and give others a chance.

Java also supports priorities for threads. These can be set as a value between 1 (low) and 10 (high) and direct the operating system as to which thread to run next, if there is a choice. Higher-priority threads that are waiting to run will always go first.

Communication between threads

Threads can be quite independent. However, it is often the case that threads need to pass information between each other, e.g. the results of subcalculations, or signals to change to another mode of working. Because threads are objects, such communication can use the normal object techniques, such as calling methods or updating non-private variables. On the face of it, there would seem to be no problem in threads communicating in either of these ways. However, conflicts can occur which would cause the program as a whole to give incorrect results.

To avoid such a possibility, Java provides means for threads to **synchronize** their activities. There are two levels of synchronization provided:

1   protection of shared resources;
2   signalling changes in conditions between threads.

Protecting shared resources

In order to protect resources such as variables that could be accessed by several threads at once, we funnel updates through a method, and mark the method with a special modifier:

Synchronized method
`synchronized` *modifiers name* `(parameters)`

Java then guarantees that once a thread has gained access to a synchronized method, it will finish the method before any other thread gains access to that or any other synchronized method in that object. Such threads are placed in a queue, awaiting their turn. The thread therefore has exclusive access to the object from within the synchronized method. An object with one or more synchronized methods acts as a **monitor** on its data. The `Display` class uses such a monitor, as we shall see in the next section.

In order not to delay the other threads unduly, synchronized methods should be kept to a minimum and only contain statements which are genuinely sensitive to interference.

EXAMPLE 9.1   Car parks for a viewpoint

Problem   There is a famous viewpoint in the winelands of Savanna that has two car parks at its two access roads. We would like to keep track of how many cars enter each car park and also how many cars in total visit the viewpoint.

Solution   Create an applet which shows a picture of the view as well as counters of the number of cars in the three places. At a later date, Savanna Conservation may decide to limit the number of cars at the viewpoint, in which case the car parks will serve as buffers. We should bear this in mind when designing the system. The choice of an applet rather than application is made to show how threads interface with applets; we shall not be using the features of a browser, and the program can run in an applet viewer.

Design   There are three different counters to consider. The main one, that of the viewpoint, 'belongs' to the applet itself. The other two are to operate independently and therefore reside in two separate additional threads. However, the threads are identical in every respect except name (West and East car parks), so we define one thread class and instantiate it twice.

Entering the viewpoint is done by calling a method which updates the total number of cars and displays it. Because the enter method can be called by two threads, potentially simultaneously, and because it updates a variable, we declare it as synchronized, thereby ensuring that the variable does not get corrupted.

Program   The program follows.

```java
import java.io.*;
import java.applet.*;
import java.awt.*;
import java.util.*;

public class CarPark extends Applet {

  /*  The Car Park applet     by J M Bishop  January 1998
   *  ====================
   *
   * Simulates a viewpoint with two car parks.
   * Reads and displays an image of the view.
   * Illustrates threads and a synchronized method.
   * Can be run simply in appletviewer.
   */

  Image im;
  ViewPoint view;
  Random delay = new Random();
  boolean stopping;

  public void init () {

    // Get the image
      im = getImage(getCodeBase(),"reserve.jpg");
    // Ensure that the image has been received before
    // the constructor returns.
      MediaTracker tracker = new MediaTracker(this);
      tracker.addImage(im, 0);
      try { tracker.waitForID(0);}
      catch (InterruptedException e) {}
      Font f = new Font ("SanSerif",Font.PLAIN,24);
      setFont(f);
      stopping = false;

      view = new ViewPoint("View",150);
      new CarThread("West",0).start();
      new CarThread("East",300).start();
  }

  public void stop () {
    stopping = true;
  }
```

```
class CarThread extends Thread {
//---------------------------

  int cars;
  int x;
  String pos;

  CarThread (String s,int n) {
    pos = s;
    x = n;
  }

  public void run () {
    while (!stopping) {
      cars++;
      display(x,cars,pos);
      view.enter();
      try {sleep (factor(x));}
      catch (InterruptedException e) {}
    }
  }
}

class ViewPoint {
//-------------

  int x;
  int cars;
  String pos;

  ViewPoint (String s,int n) {
    x = n;
    pos = s;
  }

  synchronized void enter () {
    cars++;
    display (x,cars,pos);
  }
}

// Utilities
// ---------
  public void paint (Graphics g) {
    g.drawImage(im,0,0,this);
  }

  void display(int x, int cars, String s) {
    Graphics g = getGraphics();
    g.setColor(Color.orange);
    g.fillRect(x,300,120,50);
    g.setColor(Color.black);
    g.drawString(s+" "+cars,x+5,330);
  }
```

```
int factor (int x) {
  return Math.abs(delay.nextInt()%5000+x);
}

}
```

Should `display` also be synchronized? No, `display` is a passive method, merely taking parameters and displaying them. The displays are on different parts of the screen so no conflict is possible. Suppose `display` also had statements to print values. Would the output lines become entangled? Fortunately not, because `print` and all similar methods in the `PrintWriter` class are declared as `synchronized`. Therefore only one method can be using them to affect the `System.out` object at once.

Testing   Figure 9.1 shows the output from the program, running under an applet viewer. The HTML has only the applet tag, as the image is drawn by the applet, not by the HTML.

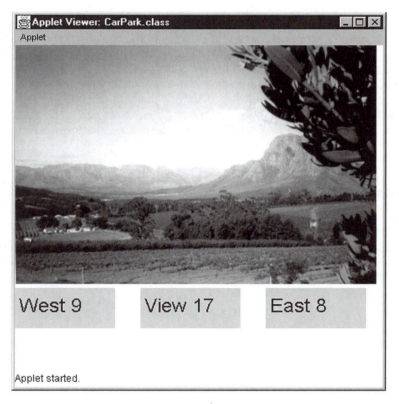

Figure 9.1 *The car parks for the viewpoint showing the counters*

Signalling between threads

Protecting shared resources is one aspect of synchronization. The other is indicating to a thread when a condition that it is waiting for has been met. The methods involved are

Synchronization methods
`wait ();` `notify ();`

If a thread finds that it cannot continue because the object it is busy with is not quite in the right state, it calls `wait` from within a synchronized method belonging to that object. The thread will then be placed on a queue associated with the object.

A thread that has altered some relevant data or conditions in an object should call `notify`. This will give all the waiting threads a chance to recheck their conditions for getting on the queue. Some of them may then be able to run at the next opportunity provided by the operating system.

In theory, threads that are waiting should eventually be notified that they can run. In practice, this depends on careful programming, considering all possible combinations. It is quite possible to construct a program where a certain condition does not get set and we find thread 1 waiting for thread 2 which is waiting for thread 1. This situation is called **deadlock** and means of detecting and preventing it are covered in courses on operating systems and concurrency. Java can detect some logical errors, particularly if `wait` and `notify` are used with unsynchronized methods. In this case an exception called `IllegalMonitorStateException` will be thrown.

9.2 Inside the `Display` class

The `Display` class has been a mainstay of our programming development throughout this book. Now at last we are going to look inside it. Although it does not have any extra threads, it does use thread methods to set up a small monitor which watches over the Ready button. Let us first look at the structure of the class, then at this and other interesting techniques used inside `Display`.

The structure of the `Display` class

The `Display` class, at 220 lines, is really a very modest utility. It consists of the eight public methods (with some extras through overloading), only three private methods, and two supporting classes. The private methods and their functions are:

- `initializeDisplay` – handles all the GUI initialization of the window, setting up a scroll pane for input and a text area for output, as well as the Ready and Close buttons;
- `getEntry` – performs the work common to the three public `get` methods;
- `insertPrompt` – does the same for the three overloaded public `prompt` methods.

The table of input values

The values which are input via the display are maintained by it in a hash table, as shown in Figure 6.2. The table has an interesting structure. The key is a string, as we have seen, and could be something quite long, such as 'Initial acceleration in m/s/s'. The values are objects of the following class:

```
private class Data {
  TextField field;
  String value;
}
```

As soon as a new input field is requested via a prompt, a field is created and added to the input section. The reference to this field forms part of the entry in the table. The other part is the value which is supplied to the `prompt` method. Notice that we retain the value as a string. This makes rewriting it in the text field more accurate from the user's point of view. If we had stored numbers, we would have been faced with the need to decide on a format for them, which may not be what the user had in mind, and could never have been general enough.

The `getEntry` method is interesting. It is used by `getInt`, `getDouble` and `getString` to check whether the label supplied is valid, and to get a copy of the current data from the table. The method with one of the gets is

```
private Data getEntry (String s) {
  if (table.containsKey(s))
    return (Data) table.get(s);
  else {
    outDisplay.append("\nERROR: No such input label: "+s+"\n");
    return null;
  }
}

public int getInt (String s) {
  Data d = getEntry(s);
  return Integer.valueOf(d.value).intValue();
}
```

Notice that the error message is sent to the output section, which is a fairly user-friendly thing to do.

When does the table get updated? Firstly, we will have noticed that it is not necessary to press <return> after making changes in a data field. However, pressing the Ready bar acts as a general 'return' and it is in response to this event that the input section is scanned. The `ready` method includes the following loop:

```
// copy all the values from the boxes to the table
for (Enumeration e = table.keys(); e.hasMoreElements();) {
  String name = (String) e.nextElement();
  Data d = (Data) table.get(name);
  d.value = d.field.getText();
  table.put(name, d);
}
```

Having stored the reference to each text field in the table, we can very easily pick off the values from the GUI.

The `ready` watcher

One of the most interesting parts of the `Display` class is its `Watcher` class. The logic behind the watcher is this. When the program reaches a `ready` call, it transfers control to the `Display` class, which prepares to read the values from the input section. However, the `Display` class must wait until such time as the user physically presses the bar. In other words, we have to synchronize with the `actionPerformed` method which responds to the bar being pressed.

The synchronization is performed in a little monitor which has the form

```
class Watcher {

  private boolean ok;

  Watcher () {
    ok = false;
  }

  synchronized void watch () { // called by ready
    while (!ok) {
      try {wait(500); }
      catch(InterruptedException e) {}
    }
    ok = false;
  }

  synchronized void ready () { // called by actionPerformed
    ok = true;
    notify();
  }
}
```

The `watch` method uses a thread `wait` to go round continuously and consider whether the boolean `ok` has been set or not. As soon as the bar is pressed and the event picked up by `actionPerformed`, the `ready` method is called, which sets `ok` and notifies anyone waiting in this monitor. `watch` comes round, re-evaluates `ok` and is then able to continue.

The full listing of `Display` follows.

The `Display` class in full

```java
package javagently;

import java.awt.*;
import java.awt.event.*;
import java.util.*;
import java.io.*;
import javagently.*;

public class Display extends Frame implements ActionListener {

  /* Display       by J M Bishop    July 1999
     **********
     is a simple class that provides facilities for
     input and output on a window.
     The data values are entered in boxes in the input section.
     Different data choices can be entered if the driving program
       asks for them.
     There is an optional integration with the Graph class

     Interface
     =========
     new Display (title)    - sets up a new Display object with a title
     println (string)       - prints a string in the output section
     prompt (label, value)  - sets a box in the input section with the
                              given label
     ready (message)        - prints a message then enables reading from
                              the boxes
     getDouble (label)      - gets the double value that was set with that
                              label
     getInt (label)         - gets the int value that was set with that
                              label
     getString (label)      - gets the string value that was set with that
                              label
     reposition (graph)     - takes a graph and places it on the bottom
                              left of the input section
  */

  private String title;

  public Display (String t) {
    /* the alternative constructor -
       has a title */
    title = t;
    initializeDisplay();
  }

  private Hashtable table = new Hashtable(10);
  private int xwidth, yheight;
  private Button okButton, closeButton;
  private TextArea outDisplay;
  private Panel inDisplay;
  private ScrollPane inPane, outPane;
  private Watcher okWatcher = new Watcher();
  private boolean graphInFront;
  private Graph graph;
```

```java
private void initializeDisplay () {
  xwidth = 640;
  yheight = 480;
  setSize(xwidth,yheight);
  setTitle(title);
  setLayout(new BorderLayout());
  Panel p = new Panel ();
    p.add(new Label("INPUT"));
    p.add(new Label("OUTPUT"));
  add(p,"North");
  p = new Panel (new FlowLayout(FlowLayout.CENTER,15,0));
    inPane = new ScrollPane(ScrollPane.SCROLLBARS_ALWAYS);
    inPane.setSize(xwidth/2 - 40, yheight - 100);
    inDisplay = new Panel(new GridLayout (0,2,10,10));
    inPane.add(inDisplay);
  p.add(inPane);
  outDisplay = new TextArea(24,40);
    p.add(outDisplay);
  add(p,"Center");
  p = new Panel(new BorderLayout());
    okButton = new Button("Ready");
    okButton.addActionListener(this);
    okButton.setEnabled(false);
    p.add("Center",okButton);
    closeButton = new Button("Close");
    closeButton.addActionListener(this);
    closeButton.setEnabled(true);
    p.add("East",closeButton);
  add("South",p);
  addWindowListener (new WindowAdapter () {
    public void windowClosing(WindowEvent e) {
      System.exit (0);
    }
  });
  setVisible(true);
  graphInFront = false;
}

public void reposition (Graph g) {
  // makes the graph smaller and puts it on the bottom
  // half of the input section
  g.setLocation (30, yheight/2-30);
  g.setSize(xwidth/2 - 40, yheight/2-15);
  graphInFront = true;
  graph = g;
}

public void actionPerformed (ActionEvent e) {
  if (e.getSource() == okButton) {
    okWatcher.ready();
  } else
  if (e.getSource() == closeButton) {
    System.exit(0);
  }
}
```

```
private class Data {
  TextField field;
  String value;
}

private Data getEntry (String s) {
  if (table.containsKey(s))
    return (Data) table.get(s);
  else {
    outDisplay.append("\nERROR: No such input label: "+s+"\n");
    return null;
  }
}

public int getInt (String s) {
  Data d = getEntry(s);
    return Integer.valueOf(d.value).intValue();
}

public double getDouble (String s) {
  Data d = getEntry(s);
    return Double.valueOf(d.value).doubleValue();
}

public String getString (String s) {
  Data d = getEntry(s);
  return d.value;
}

private void insertPrompt(Data d, String s, TextField t) {
  Panel p;
    p = new Panel(new FlowLayout(FlowLayout.RIGHT));
      p.add(new Label(s));
      inDisplay.add(p);
      t.addActionListener(this);
      t.setEditable(true);
      p = new Panel(new FlowLayout(FlowLayout.LEFT));
      p.add(t);
      inDisplay.add(p);
  d.field = t;
}

public void prompt (String s, int n) {
  Data d = new Data();
  TextField t = new TextField(10);
  insertPrompt(d, s, t);
  d.value = Text.writeInt(n,0);
  t.setText(d.value);
  table.put(s, d);
}

public void prompt (String s, double n) {
  Data d = new Data();
  TextField t = new TextField(10);
  insertPrompt(d, s, t);
```

```
      d.value = Double.toString(n);
      t.setText(d.value);
      table.put(s, d);
  }

  public void prompt (String s, String n) {
    Data d = new Data();
    TextField t = new TextField(n.length()+2);
    insertPrompt(d, s, t);
    d.value = n;
    t.setText(d.value);
    table.put(s, d);
  }

  public void ready (String s) {
    outDisplay.append(s+"\n");
    okButton.setEnabled(true);
    setVisible(true);
    if (graphInFront) graph.toFront();
    okWatcher.watch();
    // copy all the values from the boxes to the table
    for (Enumeration e = table.keys(); e.hasMoreElements();) {
      String name = (String) e.nextElement();
      Data d = (Data) table.get(name);
      d.value = d.field.getText();
      table.put(name, d);
    }
  }

  public void println (String s) {
    outDisplay.append(s+"\n");
  }

  class Watcher {

    private boolean ok;

    Watcher () {
      ok = false;
    }

    synchronized void watch () {
      while (!ok) {
        try {wait(500); }
        catch(InterruptedException e) {}
      }
      ok = false;
    }

    synchronized void ready () {
      ok = true;
      notify();
    }
  }

}
```

9.3 Ports and sockets

In Chapter 8, we concentrated on connections via high-level URLs. Java provides another level of connection: that of ports and sockets. A **port** is an abstraction of a physical place through which communication can proceed between a server and a client. The server is said to provide the port, and the client links into it.

Operating systems have processes assigned to specific ports, with server software that runs continuously, listening for anticipated messages of particular kinds. Ports are generally known by numbers. For example, under Unix, connecting to port 13 will return the date and time of the computer. Other ports provide for receiving and sending mail, checking the status of the computer, finding out who is logged on, and so on. Most of the time these ports will not be available to mere users, as security could be impaired. However, there are many vacant ports which we can use where we can create our own services.

Such a service will be a multi-threaded Java program which provides sockets on the given port. A **socket** is an abstraction of the network software that enables communication in and out of this program. A Java socket can be created if we have a valid computer Internet address and a valid port number. Several sockets can be created on a single port, enabling many clients to make use of the service provided, as shown in Figure 9.2.

Once a socket has been created, the client and server communicate in whatever way has been arranged. In Java, the simplest method is to establish an ordinary stream from the server to the client. Thereafter, the server can use read and print methods to get and send data.

If the client is a Java program then it will also have a socket and streams which match those of the server. Alternatively, the client could be an existing program such as telnet, or the server could be an existing service such as the time of day. The form associated with setting up a socket and streams is

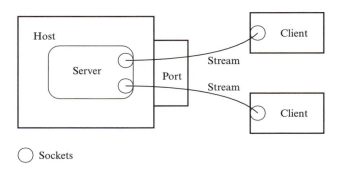

Figure 9.2 *Diagrammatic view of ports and sockets*

Creating sockets

```
ServerSocket listener = new ServerSocket (port);
Socket name = listener.accept();
Socket name = new Socket (host, port);
```

---

and the form for attaching input and output streams to it is

Streams for sockets

```
BufferedReader instreamname =
    new InputStreamReader (name.getInputStream());
PrintWriter outstreamname = new
    PrintWriter(name.getOutputStream(),true);
```

If we are creating a socket on the server side, we first set up a permanent listening socket on that port, based on the `ServerSocket` class. Then for each client that accesses the port, a separate socket of the `Socket` class is set up via the `accept` method. From the client's side, to create such a socket we instantiate the `Socket` class directly and indicate the host to which it must connect.

The two stream connections follow the same pattern as any other stream connections. The one difference is that the output stream indicates to the `PrintWriter` class that it must flush (i.e. clear the line's buffer) each line (the `true` parameter).

EXAMPLE 9.2 Opening a port

Illustration A simple program to act as a client accessing an existing server on a host is the following. In this case, we use port 13 which returns the time of the computer. The program uses the second form for creating a socket.

```
import java.io.*;
import java.net.*;
import javagently.*;

class Ports {
  public static void main(String[] args) {

    String computer;
    int port;

    if (args.length > 0) computer = args[0];
    else computer = "zeus.cs.up.ac.za";
    if (args.length > 1) port = Integer.parseInt(args[1]);
    else port = 13; // the clock port

    System.out.println("Accessing port "+port+" on "+ computer+"\n");
    try {
```

```
      // Create a socket to the given port.
      // Set up an input stream to read what the socket on that
      // side provides.

      Socket t = new Socket(computer, port);
      BufferedReader in = Text.open(t.getInputStream());

      // Read from the server until readLine
      // returns no more data
      while (true) {
        String s = in.readLine();
        if (s == null) break;
        else System.out.println(s);
      }
    }
    catch(IOException e) { System.out.println("Error" + e); }
  }
}
```

Testing   If we ran this program without parameters, it would default to the computer called `zeus.cs.up.ac.za` and to port 13. The result would be the date and time printed out, such as:

Accessing port 13 on zeus.cs.up.ac.za

Sun Jul 17 15:57:14 1999

We now consider how to create our own server program on a spare port. Ports above 8000 are usually spare, so we can use one of those.

EXAMPLE 9.3   Creating an ATM server

Problem   We would like to simulate the operation of an ATM machine connected to a bank, and handle the initial PIN number validation.

Solution   We shall set up a server on a vacant port. The service should allow multiple connections from clients representing ATM machines. The protocol between the server and a client should go something like this:

Server	**Client**
Welcome to Savanna Bank	
Please type in your PIN number or type CANCEL	
	1234
Incorrect PIN. Try again.	
	5678
Please start your transactions	

We only have a simulation here, so there is no database of clients in this service, and the PIN number will be 5678, for all clients!

Design   If there are to be multiple clients then it is certain that they will be running at different speeds and will need their own threads within the server. This is no problem, as we have fully investigated how to set up threads earlier in this chapter. The question is rather how to test the service. We could set up a Java client program similar to the one in Example 9.2, but actually there is an easier way: we can use another existing client, telnet. Telnet has a simple protocol which, in the absence of any other instructions, will read and write to a host, line by line. Thus we can telnet into our chosen port and type in lines one at a time.

Program   The program makes use of a class called `InetAddress` which represents Internet addresses, as well as their string equivalents. The server follows (with comments to explain what is happening at each stage).

```
import java.io.*;
import java.net.*;
import javagently.*;

class ATMServer {

  /* A simple server program    by J M Bishop December 1996
   * =======================
   *                             Java 1.1 revised January 1998
   * Allows multiple simultaneous connections.
   * Illustrates sockets and networking.
   */

  static final String magicPIN = "5678";

  public static void main(String[] args ) {

  // Set up the port address from the command line,
  // or default to 8190

    int port = 8190;
    InetAddress serverAddress=null;

    if (args.length > 0)
      port =Integer.parseInt(args[0]);
    try {
      serverAddress = InetAddress.getLocalHost();
    } catch (UnknownHostException e) {}

  // Initial printing on Server side only
  // using System.out

    System.out.println("******  SAVANNA BANK ********");
    System.out.println("Simulate an ATM session by "
        + "telnetting in to ");
    System.out.println(serverAddress.getHostName() +
        " on port "+port);
    System.out.println("from any number of different computers or");
    System.out.println("from different active Windows.");
```

```
    // Set up the server socket
       try {
          ServerSocket listener = new ServerSocket(port);

          int c = 0;
          while (!done) {

          // This is where the program waits for new clients
            Socket client;
            if (!done)
              //This is where the program waits
              client = listener.accept( );
            else break;
            c ++;
            System.out.println("Card inserted on " +
                 client.getInetAddress().getHostName());
            System.out.println("Starting a new client, numbered "
                 +c);
            new handler(client, c).start();
          }
          listener.close();
       }
       catch (IOException e) {
          System.out.println("Port "+port+
            " may be busy. Try another.");
       }
    }

  private static boolean done = false;

  static  void closeDown () {
    done = true;
  }
}
```

Note that we do not keep track of the handlers by name or reference: they are simply spawned off to do their own thing. The handler threads look like this:

```
import javagently.*;
import java.io.*;
import java.net.*;

class handler extends Thread {

    private Socket toClient;
    private int id;

    handler(Socket s, int i) {
    // Remember the client socket number and client id number
      toClient = s;
      id = i;
    }

    public void run() {
```

```
try {
  BufferedReader conin = Text.open
    (toClient.getInputStream());
  PrintWriter conout = new
    PrintWriter(toClient.getOutputStream(),true);

  conout.println( "Welcome to Savanna Bank");
  for (int tries = 0; tries < 3; tries++) {
    conout.println("Please type in your PIN "+
        "number or type CANCEL");
    String s = conin.readLine();
    System.out.println("Client "+id+":"+s);

    if (s.equals("SHUTDOWN")) {
      ATMServer.closeDown();
      break;
    }
    else if (s.equals("CANCEL")) {
      conout.println("Transactions halted. Goodbye.");
      break;
    }

    else if (s.equals(ATMServer.magicPIN)) {
      conout.println("Please start your transactions");
      break;
    }
    else
      conout.println("Incorrect PIN. Try again.");
  }
  System.out.println("Simulation complete. Thanks.");
}
catch (IOException e) {System.out.println("IO Error");}
  }
}
```

Each thread records its socket reference when constructed. It then asks for the input and output streams associated with that socket, which will give it access to the client that is on the other side. The handler sends an introductory message to the ATM and enters its loop, asking for a PIN number three times. The client can also type CANCEL or there is a chance to stop the server (not generally advertised). When the loop ends, the socket to the client is closed and then the thread dies naturally.

Testing   To run the server, we simply execute it as a normal Java program. If we want to telnet into the server as a client from the same machine (which is certainly possible) then we should run the server in the background using & on Unix or a separate window on a windowing environment. A typical session is shown in Figure 9.3.

The kind of server represented in this example is taken further in the next Case study.

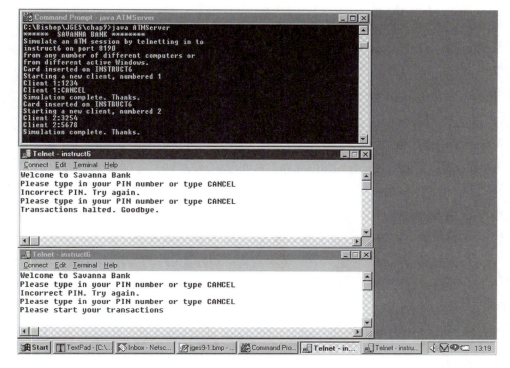

Figure 9.3 *The output from the ATM server and two simultaneous clients*

9.4 Case study 4: The chatter system

In Example 9.3, each of the clients was completely independent. It would be nice to extend the system so that the messages typed in by one are relayed to each of the others by the server. Such a server is known as a 'Chat program'.

Keeping track of clients

The first issue is how to keep track of clients within the server. Clients can sign on and leave at will, and the number of clients could be very hard to control or predict. It thus makes sense to envisage a linked list of clients rather than an array, since we know that we can add and remove from such a list without worrying about the number of elements.

  If we declare

```
private static List clientList = new List ();
```

where `List` is the class already in the `javagently` package (discussed fully in Chapter 10) then adding a new client thread's reference to the list is done by

```
clientList.reset();
clientList.add(client);
```

We have to reset the list, because it may have been left in an unsatisfactory position by some other operation. This way, the new clients are added to the front of the list each time. These statements appear in the main program, just after the launching of a new handler for the client.

Now, how do we remove a client from the list? Clearly, the client must request such removal, once a BYE has been detected. The client knows what its socket reference is, and this is unique among the current clients. Therefore, the server can look through the list, comparing socket references, and when a match is found, delete that object from the list. The extract of code is

```
Socket t;
for (clientList.reset(); !clientList.eol(); clientList.succ()) {
  t = (Socket) clientList.current();
  if (t.equals(s)) break;
}
clientList.remove();
```

Since this loop is in a method that has been called by a thread which 'owns' an existing socket, the loop will eventually detect a matching socket and reach the break-statement.

Broadcasting to all clients

Broadcasting a message to all clients is even easier than the above removal. Since the message has to be echoed to the originator as well, we do not have to differentiate between that client and the rest and we simply loop through all of them.

```
for (clientList.reset(); !clientList.eol(); clientList.succ()) {
  s = (Socket) clientList.current();
  p = new PrintStream(s.getOutputStream());
  p.println(name + ": "+message+"\r");
}
```

For each client on the list, we get the corresponding output stream and send the message there.

Synchronizing activities

The removal and broadcast operations both access the list of clients kept by the server. Given that the removal operation will make fairly drastic changes to the list, it would not be wise for both operations to be active simultaneously. Therefore they are declared as `synchronized` and Java will ensure that once one has begun, it will finish before the other is attempted.

The server

The code for the chat server therefore looks like this in full:

```java
import java.io.*;
import java.net.*;
import javagently.*;

public class ChatServer {

  /* The Chatter program    by J M Bishop  January 1997
   * ===================    Java 1.1 January 1998
   * Sets up a server for multiple conversations.
   *
   * Join in by typing
   * telnet x y
   * where x and y are the computer's name and port as
   * given when the Chatter starts.
   *
   * Illustrates sockets, streams on sockets,
   * threads, synchronization and the use of lists.
   */

  private static List clientList = new List();
  private static int id = 0;

  public static void main(String[] args) throws IOException {
    // Get the port and create a socket there.
    int port = 8190;
    if (args.length > 0)
      port = Integer.parseInt(args[0]);
    ServerSocket listener = new ServerSocket(port);
    System.out.println("The Chat Server is running on port "+port);

    // Listen for clients. Start a new handler for each.
    // Add each client to the linked list.
    while (true) {
      Socket client = listener.accept();
      new ChatHandler(client).start();
      System.out.println("New client no."+id+
          " from "+ listener.getInetAddress()+
          " on client's port "+client.getPort());
      clientList.reset();
      clientList.add(client);
      id++;
    }
  }

  static synchronized void broadcast(String message, String name)
      throws IOException {
    // Sends the message to every client including the sender.
    Socket s;
    PrintWriter p;
```

```
      for (clientList.reset(); !clientList.eol(); clientList.succ()) {
        s = (Socket)clientList.current();
        p = new PrintWriter(s.getOutputStream(), true);
        p.println(name+": "+message);
      }
    }

  static synchronized void remove(Socket s) {
  /* Finds the client on the list (by comparing socket
   * references) and removes it.
   */
    Socket t;
    for (clientList.reset(); !clientList.eol(); clientList.succ()) {
      t = (Socket)clientList.current();
      if (t.equals(s))
      break;
    }
    clientList.remove();
    id--;
  }

}

class ChatHandler extends Thread {

  /* The Chat Handler class is called from the Chat Server:
   * one thread for each client coming in to chat.
   */

  private BufferedReader in;
  private PrintWriter out;
  private Socket toClient;
  private String name;

  ChatHandler(Socket s) {
    toClient = s;
  }

  public void run() {
    try {
      /* Create i-o streams through the socket we were
       * given when the thread was instantiated
       * and welcome the new client.
       */

      in = new BufferedReader(new InputStreamReader(
        toClient.getInputStream()));
      out = new PrintWriter(toClient.getOutputStream(), true);
      out.println("*** Welcome to the Chatter ***");
      out.println("Type BYE to end");
      out.print("What is your name? ");
      out.flush();
      String name = in.readLine();
      ChatServer.broadcast(name+" has joined the discussion.",
        "Chatter");
```

```
        // Read lines and send them off for broadcasting.
      while (true) {
        String s = in.readLine().trim();
        //Check first three characters for BYE.
        //Avoids problems with different line end characters.

        if (s.length() > 2 && s.charAt(0) == 'B' &&
            s.charAt(1) == 'Y' && s.charAt(2) == 'E') {
          ChatServer.broadcast(name+" has left the discussion.",
          "Chatter");
          break;
        }
        ChatServer.broadcast(s, name);
      }
      ChatServer.remove(toClient);
      toClient.close();
    }
    catch (Exception e) {
    System.out.println("Chatter error: "+e);
  }
  }

}
```

A sample chat session

Once again. we use telnet for the clients. The following could be a sample chat session, as recorded on the server's display.

```
Chat/Chatter>java ChatServer 8191 &
[2] 5802
Chat/Chatter>The Chat Server is running on port 8191

Chat/Chatter>telnet zeus 8191
Trying 137.215.18.16 ...
Connected to zeus.cs.up.ac.za.
New client no.0 on client's port 57889
Escape character is '^]'.
*** Welcome to the Chatter ***
Type BYE to end
What is your name?
Nelson
Chatter: Nelson has joined the discussion.
Anyone out there?
Nelson: Anyone out there?
New client no.1 on client's port 1026
Chatter: Seagull has joined the discussion.
Hi Seagull
Nelson: Hi Seagull
Seagull: Hi Nelson, how's the coffee shop?
Great. Business is booming.
Nelson: Great. Business is booming.
Seagull: Oh well, bye for now
```

```
Seagull - you must type BYE to end
Nelson: Seagull - you must type BYE to end
Seagull: BYE
Try again
Nelson: Try again
Seagull: BYE
Chatter: Seagull has left the discussion.
BYE
Nelson: BYE
Chatter: Nelson has left the discussion.
Connection closed by foreign host.
```

Notice that we told telnet to look for the host called 'zeus' and it translated this to a numeric Internet address, 137.215.18.16. The server, once it accepts the client, can get this Internet address and translate it back to its full string equivalent, in this case 'zeus.cs.up.ac.za'. You can also use the special Internet address '127.0.0.1' to telnet into your own machine.

When running the chat server using telnet, some oddities may emerge when trying to say goodbye, or with the echoing or non-echoing of lines locally. It is worth experimenting to find out how your computers react.

9.5 Case Study 5: The nuclear reactor

Computer processor power has increased dramatically over the last few years, and doubtless the improvement will continue. Even so, there will always be problems that are just too big for a single processor – as computer power grows, so too does user demand for even better performance.

An obvious way to speed up computation is to have several computers, instead of just one, working on the same problem. This is called parallel processing. As we shall see, it is fairly straightforward to implement in Java. However, the way in which parallel processing is implemented is crucial in determining whether or not the expected speed-up in code performance actually occurs.

An in-depth discussion of the principles of efficient parallel program design is beyond the scope of this book. Instead, we give a short discussion of the principles of parallel processing, as well as the major factors that affect the successful parallelization of a code.

Principles of parallel processing

In what follows we use the term 'code' to mean 'program'. Let us suppose that a particular code has been parallelized, so that there are two versions of the code: sequential and parallel. The parallel code has n_T different threads, and suppose that these threads run on n_P different processors; since each processor must have at least one thread, this means that $n_T \geq n_P$.

The usual objective of parallelization is that the total running time for the parallel version of the code (T_P) should be substantially shorter than that of the sequential version (T_S). The speed-up of the code is the ratio

$$\frac{T_s}{T_p}$$

and ideally the speed-up should equal the number of processors, n_P. As we shall see, there are a number of overheads that make it almost impossible to achieve this target. Nevertheless, an efficient parallelization of a code should have a speed-up that is comparable to n_P.

An important concept to look at is **balance**. It may happen that one or more of the processors is idle for a lot of the time that the program is being run. The workload is not being evenly distributed amongst the processors, and it is said to be unbalanced. A lack of balance in a parallel code is a symptom of inefficient coding. The nature of parallel programming is such that one can have a situation where a processor has to wait for input from elsewhere before it can continue. Thus it is very rare for the total idle time (i.e the idle time summed over all processors) to be zero, but the total idle time should be small in comparison to the total computer time spent running the program ($= n_P T_P$).

Another important concept is the **communication–computation ratio**. In parallel programming there is an overhead that does not occur in the sequential version, namely communication between processors. (There is even an overhead that occurs when two threads on the same processor communicate, but usually this is small and we will not consider it.) So, in an efficient parallel program the time spent in communication is much less than the time spent in computation. We would like to express this in a precise way, in terms of byte/flop, with byte representing the total data transfer, and flop representing the total number of floating point operations in the program. The communication time is very much hardware dependent, and to a lesser extent so is the time of computation. Thus a suitable byte/flop ratio depends crucially on the hardware configuration. For example, suppose that the same parallel program is being run on

1   a dedicated parallel machine, with the various processors all in the same box and hard-wired together;

2   a number of machines in a computer laboratory, linked together on a local area network; and

3   a number of computers all over the world, with communication over the Internet.

Clearly, the amount of time spent on communication increases dramatically as one moves from case 1 through 3, and an efficient parallel program running under configuration 3 will have a much smaller byte/flop ratio than would be possible if running under configuration 1.

So far we have been discussing efficiency, but there can be other reasons for going parallel, and the issue of efficiency would then be less important. One such reason is memory. Suppose a user has a program whose total memory requirement is 1 Gbyte, but that the available resource is just a number of machines each with 64 Mbytes of RAM. One possibility is to run the program on one machine, and regularly swop data between RAM and a hard disk; however, this would be very slow. A better option, although it would involve a certain amount of recoding, is to go parallel and distribute the memory requirements over, say, 20 machines.

All programs should have a clear, logical structure, and this is particularly important in parallel programming. If there are a number of threads working in parallel, it can be very difficult to work out why a program is not doing something that it is expected to do. One way to bring some control into a parallel program is to use the master/worker model. There is one master thread that gives tasks to other threads (the workers), and the workers report back to the master. It may be necessary for the worker threads to communicate with each other, but where possible input–output should be routed through the master thread.

Finally, there can be some confusion between parallel processing and vector processing. The idea of vector processing is that many scientific programs involve manipulation of vectors, e.g. $\sum a_i b_i$. When the vector is long, this type of operation can be piped and implemented much faster than the same number of ordinary multiplications and additions. However, Java does not implement vector processing, so we do not discuss this topic further.

Heat flow in a nuclear reactor

The safe design of a nuclear reactor requires a full understanding of the heat flow within the reactor, and the ability to predict what is going to happen to the temperature at different places in the reactor, under a variety of situations. In particular, if the temperature inside any fuel rod gets so high that it melts, then a major disaster could occur. The accurate modelling of this process is very complex, and depends on the specific design of the reactor. The model given here illustrates some of the features of the real problem, but our primary purpose is to illustrate parallel programming in Java, and our model is much simplified.

A nuclear reactor consists of a number of fuel rods, say about 1 cm in diameter by about 50 cm long. There are also channels between the rods for coolant to flow, as well as spaces to insert damper rods. The power output of the reactor is controlled by the damper rods. When they are fully removed, spontaneous nuclear reactions in the fuel rods produce neutrons that cause further reactions in the reactor, which produce even more neutrons, and the process accelerates yielding large quantities of heat. The coolant takes the heat to an exchanger where it is transferred to heat water into steam and so drive a turbine that generates electricity.

On the other hand, when the damper rods are fully inserted many of the neutrons are absorbed and the chain reaction does not occur; only a small amount of heat is produced by the reactor. These features are illustrated in Figure 9.4. In reality the rods are cylindrical in a cylindrical tank, but in the simple model that is used here, we suppose that the rods form a square array and that each rod has a square cross-section. There is a (square) channel for coolant between the faces of each rod, and the remaining space is available for damper rods.

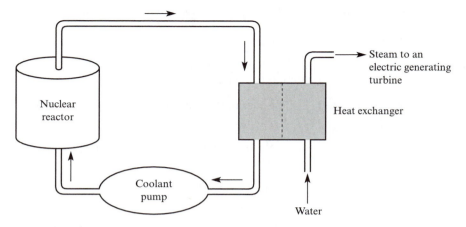

Figure 9.4 *Diagram of a nuclear reactor*

Our model of the reactor uses the variables listed in Table 9.1, where the name of the identifier in the program is also given. We also use a number of parameters and constants (the mathematical formulation of the problem is that parameters and constants are regarded as given, and the variables are the quantities that we wish to find). We give the usual symbol for each of these parameters, the name of the identifier used in the program that follows, as well as its default value.

In our simplified model, the temperature within each rod obeys the heat flow equation

$$\frac{\partial T}{\partial t} = \frac{k}{\rho_R c_R} \nabla^2 T + \frac{h}{\rho_R c_R}$$

subject to the boundary condition that the temperature on the surface of the rod is equal to that in the coolant channel that it touches. Because we work with a simple two-dimensional model of the reactor (whereas the reactor is three-dimensional), we take this boundary condition to be constant along the length of the rod, and to be the average of the coolant's inflow and exit temperatures. In each channel the coolant's average temperature evolves according to

$$\frac{\partial T_C}{\partial t} = \frac{k}{c_C \rho_C w_C}(\nabla T_{f1} + \nabla T_{f2}) + \frac{2v}{\ell}(T_{in} - T_C)$$

where $f1$ and $f2$ are the two rod faces that have a common interface with the channel. The coolant's temperature as it exits the channel is $2T_C - T_{in}$.

The numerical coding of the problem is straightforward. Each rod is represented on a grid of n_g by n_g points, with the default value for n_g being 10. The numerical formula for $\nabla^2 T$ is

$$\nabla^2 T_{i,j} = \frac{T_{i,j+1} + T_{i,j-1} + T_{i+1,j} + T_{i-1,j} - 4T_{i,j}}{dx^2}$$

Table 9.1 *Parameters for the nuclear reactor program and their default values*

Symbol	Parameter	Default value
$T(x,y,t)$	temp[][]	The temperature in a fuel rod at time t at the point (x, y) in the rod
$T_C(t)$	coolant[][][]	The average temperature of the coolant, at time t, in a channel
v	cvel	4 m/s: the velocity of the coolant through each channel
h	heatin	5×10^8 W/m^3: the quantity of heat generated, per unit volume per unit time, in each fuel rod
T_{in}	tempin	400 K: the temperature of the coolant as it enters the reactor
k	diffuse	2.2 W/m/K: the heat diffusion constant of a fuel rod
s_R	rspheat	220 J/kg/K: the specific heat of a fuel rod
s_C	cspheat	698 J/kg/K: the specific heat of the coolant
ρ_R	rdensity	10^4 kg/m^3: the density of a fuel rod
ρ_C	cdensity	800 kg/m^3: the density of the coolant
ℓ	rlength	0.5 m: the length of a fuel rod or coolant channel
w_R	rwidth	0.01 m: each rod has cross-section $w_R \times w_R$
w_C	cwidth	0.02 m: each coolant channel has cross-section $w_C \times w_R$
T_{melt}	Tmeltdown	2800 K: the temperature at which a fuel rod will melt
$\nabla T_{fi}(t)$	rodface[][][]	The outward temperature gradient at face fi of a rod at time t

where dx is the distance between the grid points. The time step is dt and the default value is 0.1; for reasons that are beyond the scope of this book, dt must be small otherwise a numerical instability occurs. The rods are regarded as being in a square array of size n_r so that there are $(n_r)^2$ rods in the array. We suppose that there are n_p processors available for the problem, and require that $(n_r)^2$ should be exactly divisible by n_p so that the rods can be evenly distributed among the processors.

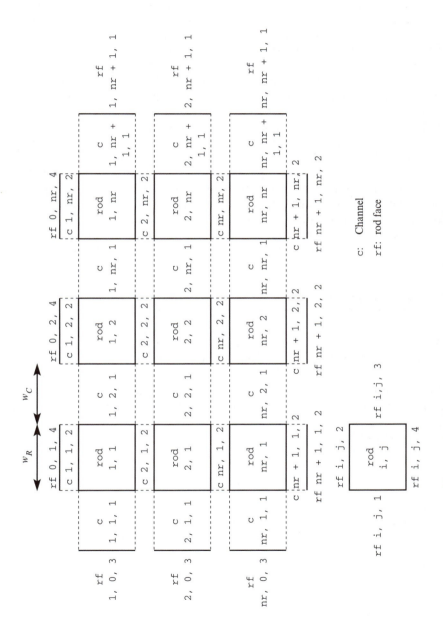

Figure 9.5   *Cross-section of the nuclear reactor in the case $n_r = 3$*

Parallelization using threads

The parallelization strategy is to place each rod on a different thread, and to distribute these threads evenly amongst the available processors. This is because the evolution of the heat equation in each rod is computationally intensive. The coolant channel computations are each very short, and all of them are placed on the master thread, which also handles all the input–output. The master thread reads in the various parameters for the problem, and then passes this data to each worker thread. The master thread also distributes the initial data: the temperature throughout each rod and the coolant is constant, at the coolant inflow temperature. Also the temperature gradients on the rod faces are initially set to zero. Now each worker thread evolves the temperature in its rod for one time step, and reports the new temperature gradients on the rod faces (as well as the maximum temperature in the rod) to the master thread. The master thread uses this information to find the temperature of the coolant as it exits each channel; this information is now passed to the appropriate worker thread and the whole process is repeated. At regular time intervals, data is written onto the graphical display. The computation ends at a time determined by the user, or if the temperature of any rod exceeds its melting point (which event would cause a nuclear disaster).

Different coordinates are used for the rods, rod faces and coolant channels, and it is essential that these are correctly applied in the program. Figure 9.5 shows the situation in the case $n_r = 3$.

Running the reactor

The program consists of two classes: `Reactor.java`, which contains the master thread; and `Rods.java`, which contains the worker thread. At present, the program runs with the various threads on the same processor. In order to run the program, first run `reactor.java`. If necessary, adjust the data parameter in the display window and press the Ready bar. Once the reactor diagram appears, press the Start button, then start up n_p command windows (the default for n_p is 3) and in each window run `Rods.java`.

In order for the threads to run on different processors, the address 127.0.0.1 in the statement

```
Socket connection = new Socket ("127.0.0.1");
```

in `Rods.java` must be changed to the Internet address of the processor that is running `Reactor.java`. In order to make this process more flexible, the address can be submitted as a string in the arguments to `main` (see Problem 9.8).

Reactor.java

```
import java.awt.*;
import java.awt.event.*;
import java.io.*;
import java.util.*;
import java.net.*;
import javagently.*;
```

```java
public class Reactor extends Frame implements ActionListener {

  /* Simulation of the temperature in a nuclear reactor
   * ==================================================
   * by N T Bishop & J M Bishop, December 1998
   *
   * The program uses this file, Reactor.java, as well as Rods.java.
   * It illustrates parallel processing in Java.
   */

  static int nr;
  Display display =new Display("Temperature in a nuclear reactor");
  double rlength,rwidth,cwidth,rdensity,cdensity,rspheat;
  double cspheat,cvel,diffuse;



  double tempin,Tmeltdown,heatin,t,dt,dx,k3,TTmax;
  int ng,ntotal,nreport,face;
  int np;        // no of processors
  int rodsperp; // rods per processor

  double coolant [] [] [];
  double rodface [] [] [];
  double Tmax [] [];

  Handler handler []= new Handler[10]; // estimated maximum processors

  private Button startButton;
  private TextField coolantField [][][];
  private TextField tempMaxField [][];
  private TextField tField;
  private TextField TTmaxField;

  // The next two methods set up the graphical displays
  Reactor () {
    int gridx, gridy;

    initialize();
    Label el= new Label("Nuclear Reactor");
    add("North",el);
    Panel p = new Panel();
      startButton = new Button("Start");
        startButton.addActionListener(this);
        p.add(startButton);
      p.add(new Label("t"));
        tField = new TextField("",6);
        p.add(tField);
      p.add(new Label("TTMax"));
        TTmaxField = new TextField("",6);
        p.add(TTmaxField);
    add("South",p);

    p = setupDisplay();
    add("Center",p);
  }
```

```
Panel setupDisplay() {
  Panel p = new Panel();
  int i,j;
  coolantField = new TextField [nr+2][nr+2][3];
  tempMaxField = new TextField [nr+1][nr+1];
  GridLayout layout = new GridLayout(2*nr+1,2*nr+1);
  p.setLayout(layout);

  for (int row = 0; row<=2*nr; ) {
    for (int col = 1; col<=2*nr; col+=2) {
      p.add(new TextField("",6));
      i = row/2+1;
      j = (col+1)/2;
      coolantField[i][j][2]=new TextField("C"+i+","+j+",2",6);
      coolantField[i][j][2].setBackground(Color.green);
      p.add(coolantField[i][j][2]);
    }
    p.add(new TextField("",6));
    row++;
    if (row<2*nr) {
      for (int col = 0; col<=2*nr;) {
        i = (row+1)/2;
        j = col/2+1;
        coolantField[i][j][1]=new TextField("C"+i+","+j+",1",6);
        coolantField[i][j][1].setBackground(Color.cyan);
        p.add(coolantField[i][j][1]);
        col++;
        if (col<2*nr) {
          i=(row+1)/2;
          j=(col+1)/2;
          tempMaxField[i][j]=new TextField("T"+i+","+j,6);
          tempMaxField[i][j].setBackground(Color.red);
          p.add(tempMaxField[i][j]);
        }
        col++;
      }
    }
    row++;
  }
  return p;
}

public void actionPerformed (ActionEvent e) {
  // must be a StartButton
  startRods();
  master();
}

void initialize() {
  display.prompt("Grid points, ng", 10);
  display.prompt("Number of reports, ntotal", 100);
  display.prompt("Iterations between reports, nreport", 5);
  display.prompt("Rod length, rlength", 0.5);
  display.prompt("Rod width, rwidth", 0.01);
```

```
display.prompt("Coolant channel width, cwidth", 0.02);
display.prompt("Rod density, rdensity", 10000);
display.prompt("Coolant density, cdensity", 800);
display.prompt("Rod specific heat, rspheat", 220);
display.prompt("Coolant specific heat, cspheat", 698);
display.prompt("Coolant speed, cvel", 4);
display.prompt("Rod diffusion coefficient, diffuse", 2.2);
display.prompt("Coolant temperature on input, tempin", 400);
display.prompt("Rod melting temperature, Tmeltdown", 2800);
display.prompt("Heat generated in rod, heatin", 5e8);
display.prompt("Start time, t", 0);
display.prompt("Time step, dt", 0.1);
display.prompt("Number of processors, np", 3);
display.prompt("Number of rows of rods, nr", 3);

display.println("The Nuclear Reactor Simulator");
display.println("=============================\n");
display.ready("Press the button when values are ready");

ng=display.getInt("Grid points, ng");
ntotal=display.getInt("Number of reports, ntotal");
nreport=display.getInt("Iterations between reports, nreport");
rlength=display.getDouble("Rod length, rlength");
rwidth=display.getDouble("Rod width, rwidth");
cwidth=display.getDouble("Coolant channel width, cwidth");
rdensity=display.getDouble("Rod density, rdensity");
cdensity=display.getDouble("Coolant density, cdensity");
rspheat=display.getDouble("Rod specific heat, rspheat");
cspheat=display.getDouble("Coolant specific heat, cspheat");
cvel=display.getDouble("Coolant speed, cvel");
diffuse=display.getDouble("Rod diffusion coefficient, diffuse");
tempin=display.getDouble("Coolant temperature on input, tempin");
Tmeltdown=display.getDouble("Rod melting temperature, Tmeltdown");
heatin=display.getDouble("Heat generated in rod, heatin");
t=display.getDouble("Start time, t");
dt=display.getDouble("Time step, dt");
np=display.getInt("Number of processors, np");
nr=display.getInt("Number of rows of rods, nr");
// Must have  dt < (rwidth/(ng-1))^2 /2 *rspheat*rdensity/diffuse
// otherwise the program will be numerically unstable
dx=rwidth/(ng-1);

coolant = new double [nr+2] [nr+2] [3];
rodface = new double [nr+2] [nr+2] [5];
Tmax    = new double [nr+1] [nr+1];

display.println("\nWhen the reactor diagram appears, press");
display.println("the 'Start' button; then start "+np+" windows");
display.println("running the Worker program.");
display.println("(The number of windows must divide into "+nr*nr);
display.println("which is the number of rods: the program");
display.println("will allocate the rods among the worker");
display.println("windows.)");
```

```
      // Initialize the temperature gradients of the rod-faces
      for (int i = 0; i < (nr+2); i++)
        for (int j = 0; j < (nr+2); j++)
          for (int k = 0; k < 5; k++)
            rodface[i][j][k] = 0.0;

      // Initialize the temperature of the coolant
      for (int i = 0; i < (nr+2); i++)
        for (int j = 0; j < (nr+2); j++)
          for (int k = 0; k < 3; k++)
            coolant[i][j][k] = tempin;

    k3=diffuse/(cspheat*cdensity*cwidth);
  }

  void startRods () {

    //Instantiate a handler for each processor
    rodsperp = nr*nr/np;
    display.println("There will be "+rodsperp+" rods for"+
      " each worker.\n");

    try {
      ServerSocket listener = new ServerSocket(8190);

      for (int p = 0; p < np; p++) {
        display.println("Waiting for a worker ");
        Socket processorAddress = listener.accept();
        display.println("Processor joined from "+
          processorAddress.getInetAddress().getHostName());
        display.println("Starting processor "+p+" with "+
          rodsperp + " rods");
        handler[p] = new Handler(processorAddress, p);
      }

      for (int p = 0; p < np; p++) {
       handler[p].start();
       handler[p].connectUp();
       }

      listener.close();
    }
    catch (IOException e) {
      display.println("This port "+
        " may be busy. Try another.");
    }
  }

  void master() {

    for (int it=1; it<=ntotal; it++) {
      for (int jt=1; jt <=nreport; jt++) {
        t=t+dt;
        createCoolants();
```

```
        // Send coolant data to the appropriate rod
        for (int h = 0; h<np; h++) {
          handler[h].send();
        }

        // Receive temperature gradients of each rod-face, as
        // well as the maximum temperature in each rod
        for (int h = 0; h<np; h++) {
          handler[h].receive();
        }
   // Find the maximum temperature throughout all the rods
        TTmax = 0;
        for (int i = 1; i<=nr; i++)
          for (int j = 1; j<=nr; j++)
            if (Tmax[i][j]> TTmax) TTmax = Tmax[i][j];

      }//jt

      report();
      if (TTmax > Tmeltdown) {
         display.println("\nEMERGENCY - Meltdown predicted. ");
         display.println("Shut down reactor immediately");
         break;
      }

   }//it
}

void createCoolants() {
// Evolve the coolant temperatures by one time-step
  for (int ic=1; ic <= nr+1; ic++) {
    for (int jc=1; jc <= nr+1; jc++) {
      face=1;
      coolant[ic][jc][face]+= dt*(
        2*cvel/rlength*(-coolant[ic][jc][face]+tempin) +
        k3*(rodface[ic][jc-1][face+2]+rodface[ic][jc][face] )
      );
      face=2;
      coolant[ic][jc][face]+= dt*(
        2*cvel/rlength*(-coolant[ic][jc][face]+tempin) +
        k3*(rodface[ic-1][jc][face+2]+rodface[ic][jc][face] )
      );
    }//jc
  }//ic
}

void report() {
// Output data to the reactor display
  int i,j;
  tField.setText(""+t);
  TTmaxField.setText(""+TTmax);
  for (int row = 0; row<=2*nr; ) {
    for (int col = 1; col<=2*nr; col+=2) {
      i = row/2+1;
      j = (col+1)/2;
```

```
          coolantField[i][j][2].setText(""+coolant[i][j][2]);
      }
      row++;
      if (row<2*nr) {
        for (int col = 0; col<=2*nr;) {
          i = (row+1)/2;
          j = col/2+1;
          coolantField[i][j][1].setText(""+coolant[i][j][1]);
          col++;
          if (col<2*nr) {
            i=(row+1)/2;
            j=(col+1)/2;
            tempMaxField[i][j].setText(""+Tmax[i][j]);
          }
          col++;
        } //col
      }
      row++;
    }//row
  }

  public static void main (String args []) {
    Frame f = new Reactor();
    f.setSize(600,400);
    f.setVisible(true);
    f.addWindowListener (new WindowAdapter() {
      public void windowClosing (WindowEvent e) {
        System.exit (0);
      }
    });
  }
/*--------------------------------------*/
  class Handler extends Thread {

    private Socket processor;
    private int id;
    private BufferedReader conin;
    private PrintWriter conout;

    Handler (Socket s, int i) {
      processor = s;
      id = i;
    }

    synchronized void send() {
      // send coolant temperatures to appropriate rods
      for (int rod = 0; rod < rodsperp; rod++) {
        int ic = (id*np+rod)/nr + 1;
        int jc = ((id*np+rod) % nr) + 1;
        conout.println(rod+"  "+
        coolant[ic][jc][1]+"  "+coolant[ic][jc][2]+"  "+
        coolant[ic][jc+1][1]+"  "+coolant[ic+1][jc][2]);
      }
    }
```

```
    synchronized void receive () {
      // receive temperature gradients at all the rod faces
      // r is only a counter, not a rod number, because
      // responses could come in any order

      for (int r = 0; r < rodsperp; r++) {
        try {
          String s = conin.readLine().trim();
          StringTokenizer T = new StringTokenizer(s);
          int rod = Integer.parseInt(T.nextToken());
          int ic = (id*np+rod)/nr + 1;
          int jc = ((id*np+rod) % nr) + 1;
          rodface[ic][jc][1] = extractDouble(T);
          rodface[ic][jc][2] = extractDouble(T);
          rodface[ic][jc][3] = extractDouble(T);
          rodface[ic][jc][4] = extractDouble(T);
          Tmax[ic][jc] = extractDouble(T);
        } catch (IOException e) {
          System.out.println(e);
        }
      }
    }

    double extractDouble (StringTokenizer T) {
      String item = T.nextToken();
      return Double.valueOf (item.trim()).doubleValue();
    }

    synchronized void connectUp() {
      // open connection with rods and send start-up data
      try {
        conin = Text.open(processor.getInputStream());
        conout = new PrintWriter(
                 processor.getOutputStream(),true);
        conout.println(id+"  "+rodsperp+"  "+ng+"  "+
               ntotal+"  "+ nreport+"  "+
               rdensity+"  "+rspheat+"  "+diffuse+"  "+
               tempin+"  "+heatin+"  "+dt+"  "+dx);
      } catch(IOException e) {
        System.out.println(e);
        System.exit(0);
      }
      display.println("Handler "+id+" operating");
    }

    public void run () {
      while (true)
        try {sleep(500);}
        catch (InterruptedException e) {}
    }//run

  }//Handler
  /*------------------------*/

}//ReactMaster
```

Rods.java

```
import java.io.*;
import java.net.*;
import javagently.*;
import java.util.*;

class Rods {

  /* This is the worker program for Reactor.java
  */

  public static void main (String args[]) throws IOException {

    int ng,ntotal,nreport;

    double rdensity,rspheat,k1,k2;
    double diffuse,tempin,heatin,dt,dx;
    double coolant [] = new double [5];

    int id, nrods;

    RodWorker rod [];

    // Change the following statement if Reactor.java is on
    // another processor
    Socket connection = new Socket("127.0.0.1",8190);

    // Get initialization data
    try {
      BufferedReader conin =
        Text.open(connection.getInputStream());
      PrintWriter conout =
        new PrintWriter(connection.getOutputStream(),true);

      String s = conin.readLine().trim();
      System.out.println("Received start up data");
      StringTokenizer T = new StringTokenizer(s);
      id = Integer.parseInt (T.nextToken());
      nrods = Integer.parseInt (T.nextToken());
      ng = Integer.parseInt (T.nextToken());
      ntotal = Integer.parseInt (T.nextToken());
      nreport = Integer.parseInt (T.nextToken());
      rdensity = extractDouble(T);
      rspheat = extractDouble(T);
      diffuse = extractDouble(T);
      tempin = extractDouble(T);
      heatin = extractDouble(T);
      dt = extractDouble(T);
      dx = extractDouble(T);

      k1=diffuse/(rdensity*rspheat);
      k2=heatin/(rdensity*rspheat);

      rod = new RodWorker[nrods];
```

```
        for (int i = 0; i<nrods; i++) {
          rod[i] = new RodWorker (i, ng, ntotal, nreport,
                     tempin, k1, k2,
                     dt, dx, conout);
          rod[i].start();
        }

        while (true) {
        // receive coolant temperature data and pass to the
        // thread for the appropriate rod
          for (int i = 0; i<nrods; i++) {
            s = conin.readLine();
            T = new StringTokenizer(s);
            int nrod = Integer.parseInt(T.nextToken());
            coolant[1] = extractDouble(T);
            coolant[2] = extractDouble(T);
            coolant[3] = extractDouble(T);
            coolant[4] = extractDouble(T);
            rod[nrod].send(coolant);
          }
        }

    } catch(IOException e) {
      System.out.println(e);
      System.exit(0);
    }
  }

  static double extractDouble (StringTokenizer T) {
    String item = T.nextToken();
    return Double.valueOf (item.trim()).doubleValue();
  }

}

class RodWorker extends Thread {

  int ng,ntotal,nreport;

  int id;

  double rdensity, rspheat, diffuse, heatin;
  double k1, k2, tempin, dt, dx, Tmax;

  double temp [] [];
  double tempold [] [];
  double coolant [] = new double [5];
  double rodface [] = new double [5];

  PrintWriter conout;
  private boolean ready;
```

```
RodWorker (int id_, int ng_, int ntotal_, int nreport_,
          double tempin_,double k1_, double k2_,
     double dt_, double dx_, PrintWriter conout_) {
  id = id_;
  ng = ng_;
  ntotal = ntotal_;
  nreport = nreport_;
  tempin = tempin_;
  k1 = k1_;
  k2 = k2_;
  dt = dt_;
  dx = dx_;
  conout = conout_;

  temp = new double [ng+1] [ng+1];
  tempold = new double [ng+1] [ng+1];

  for (int i=0; i<ng+1; i++)
    for (int j=0; j<ng+1; j++)
      temp[i][j] = tempin;
      for (int i=0; i<=4; i++)
        coolant[i] = tempin;
}

// Receive coolant data from method main above
synchronized void send (double c []) {
  for (int i=1; i<5; i++)
    coolant[i]=c[i];
  ready=true;
}

public void run() {
  System.out.println("Rod "+id+" starting up");
  for (int it=1; it<=ntotal; it++) {
    for (int jt=1; jt<=nreport; jt++) {
      // Evolve the rod temperatures and find the temperature
      // gradients in the rod-faces
      for (int i=0; i<ng+1; i++)
        for (int j=0; j<ng+1; j++)
          tempold[i][j]=temp[i][j];
      for (int ic=2; ic<=ng-1; ic++)
        for (int jc=2; jc<=ng-1; jc++)
          temp[ic][jc]=tempold[ic][jc]+dt*
              (k1*(tempold[ic+1][jc]+tempold[ic-1][jc]+
              tempold[ic][jc+1]+
              tempold[ic][jc-1]-4*tempold[ic][jc] )/(dx*dx) +k2);
      for (int ic=1; ic<=4; ic++)
        rodface[ic]=0.0;
      for (int ic=2; ic<=ng-1; ic++) {
        temp[ic][1]=coolant[1];
        temp[ic][ng]=coolant[3];
        rodface[1]+=(temp[ic][2]-temp[ic][1])/((ng-2)*dx);
        rodface[3]+=(temp[ic][ng-1]-temp[ic][ng])/((ng-2)*dx);
      }//ic
```

```
for (int jc=2; jc<=ng-1; jc++) {
  temp[1][jc]=coolant[2];
  temp[ng][jc]=coolant[4];
  rodface[2]+=(temp[2][jc]-temp[1][jc])/((ng-2)*dx);
  rodface[4]+=(temp[ng-1][jc]-temp[ng][jc])/((ng-2)*dx);
}//jc

// Find the maximum temperature in the rod
Tmax = 0;
for (int i=1; i<=ng; i++)
  for (int j=1; j<=ng; j++)
    if (Tmax < temp[i][j]) Tmax = temp[i][j];
  // The main program should have passed
  // on the coolant values.
  while (!ready) {
    try{sleep(50);
    }
    catch(InterruptedException e) {}
  }//i
  ready = false;
  // send the rod-face temperature gradients and
  // the highest temperature in the rod
  conout.println(id+"  "+
    rodface[1]+"  "+rodface[2]+"  "+
    rodface[3]+"  "+rodface[4]+"  "+Tmax);
    }//jt
  }//it
  }
}
```

Testing   We have now come to a case where there is no analytic solution for the problem computed. Even so, there are a number of tests that can be made:

1   Vary the physical parameters of the problem, and check that the results scale as would be expected, e.g. the temperatures should be proportional to the heat generation constant for the rod material, h.

2   Do an approximate heat balance calculation: the heat generated in the rods, the heat flow across the rod/coolant interface, and the heat being carried away from the reactor by the coolant should all be the same when the reactor has reached a steady state.

We have checked the scaling properties for the parameters v, h, T_{in}, ℓ, w_R, w_C. Also, we have used the program output to find the various heat flows in test 2. For the default case, these all work out to be about 2×10^5 W.

Results of running the program are given in Figures 9.6 and 9.7. These are for the default case, except that we have changed the coolant velocity from 4 m/s to 0.01 m/s to simulate a reactor that has a problem with its coolant flow. In this case, the reactor becomes critical after 18.5 s.

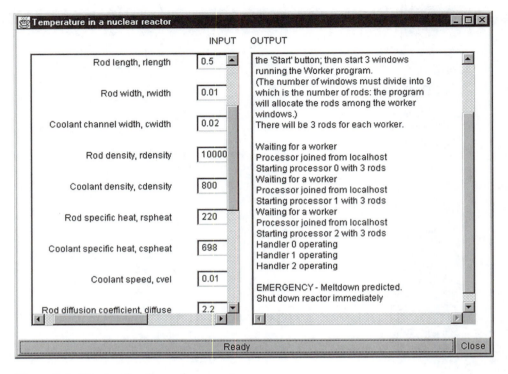

Figure 9.6 *Display for the nuclear reactor*

9.1 In which package is the `Thread` class declared?

9.2 Give a statement to create a new thread called `x` of class `T`.

9.3 In multi-threaded programs, does `start` call `run` or the other way round?

9.4 Do all methods in a monitor class have to be synchronized? Explain your answer.

9.5 Explain why the `ViewPoint` class in Example 9.1 was not made into a thread.

9.6 Give a statement to create a new car park thread called `North`, with a counter to be displayed at position 450.

9.7 The following class is being turned into a thread:

```
class Picture extends Canvas {
public void paint (Graphics g) {
  g.drawImage (i,50,50,this);
  }
}
```

Complete the transformation.

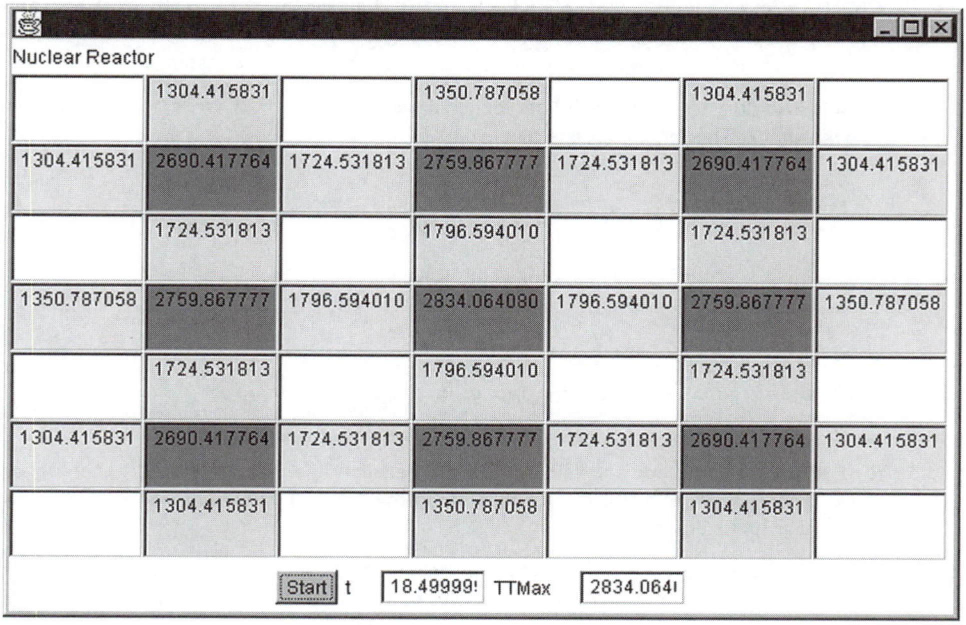

Figure 9.7 *Nuclear reactor program output showing the temperature in the rods and coolant channels*

9.8   In Case study 4, the handler thread can call

```
Server.closeDown()
```

if a special message is received. When will the server react to the message?

9.9   What is the difference between a socket and a server socket in Java's APIs?

9.10   In the reactor program, what would happen if fewer than the requested worker windows started?

PROBLEMS

9.1   **Working watch.** In Problem 7.5, we designed the face of a digital watch. Now, using a thread, make it actually work, with the digits clicking over and the buttons for resetting and displaying being active at the same time.

9.2   **Viewpoint full!** Savanna Conservation is concerned about the number of cars going up to the viewpoint in Example 9.1. See if you can extend the program so that the viewpoint has a maximum number of places and cars can only enter from the car parks if there is space. If not, they use the wait synchronization method to queue. When a car leaves (after a random time spent looking at the view), the car parks are notified that another car can come in.

9.3   **Chatting clients.** The Chat program (Case study 4) provides a server only. Using the ports program in section 9.3 as a basis, create a Java program which can be started up on the client side and provide similar facilities to telnet.

9.4 **Chatting on the web.** Even after Problem 9.3, the user interface to the Chat program is pretty basic. Try making the server into an applet and embody it in an HTML page which provides instructions, displays the output, and has a separate line for typing in input.

9.5 **Knock knock!** Using the ATM server as a basis (Example 9.3) write a server to play Knock! Knock! The game goes like this:

```
Client                    Server
Knock knock
                          Who's there?
Amos
                          Amos who?
Amos Quito.
```

Use telnet for the client again.

9.6 **Nuclear reactor.** Adapt the program to investigate the following:

(a) If one of the coolant channels gets blocked, will there be a meltdown?

(b) For $t < 60$ s, the coolant velocity has the default value, but for $t \geq 60$ s the coolant velocity is zero (to simulate a coolant pump breakdown). How long will it be until the reactor melts down?

9.7 **Nuclear reactor.** Perform an empirical analysis of the numerical stability of the system. Increase dt, and see what happens. Then, with dt at the default value (0.1), increase n_g and see what happens.

9.8 **Distribution.** Adjust Rods.java so that, while the local host remains the default site for Reactor, Reactor's Internet address can be given as a parameter when each Rod is run.

9.9 **Parallelism.** With all the threads on a single processor, measure how long it takes for the nuclear reactor program to run. In the measurement, ignore all start-up time, so measure wall clock time between $t = 1$ s and $t = 51$ s (say). Now repeat the experiment with four computers (one master and three workers). What speed-up do you get?

CHAPTER 10

Additional topics

10.1 Strings and string handling

Strings were the first data items that we introduced in this book and they have been used extensively since. It is now time to take a formal look at what they really are and what facilities are available for them. Strings are special in Java for several reasons:

- `String` is a class so that strings are objects and not variables.
- There is a special notation for string constants which is a shorthand for creating string objects with known contents.
- Strings, unlike other objects, have an operator defined for them, i.e. the + for concatenation.
- Once created, the contents of a string object cannot be changed.
- Another class, `StringBuffer`, enables changes to the contents of a string.
- There is a difference between an empty (but initialized) string and a null (i.e. not initialized) string.

So, for example, if we make the declaration

```
String filename = "rates.data";
```

an object will automatically be created and initialized (without us using new) and will contain a reference called filename. Compare this declaration with a similar one for Dates (as postulated in section 6.1):

```
Dates graduation = new Dates (4,12,2002);
```

Here the constant is given in brackets and new is used.

Regarding empty and null strings, consider the following two statements:

```
String s1;
String s2 = "";
```

s1 will have the special value called null until it is given some other string value. Such a string is not valid for string manipulation methods, and if an attempt is made to access it, a NullPointerException will be thrown by the system. s2, on the other hand, can be used in string manipulation: it just has no contents and a length of zero. The difference between the two is brought out in Example 10.1.

The strings created in quotes or read into objects of the String class cannot be altered. There is another Java class, StringBuffer, which allows for this sort of thing. The String class has several constructors, some of which are shown in the next form:

Creating a string

```
String ();
String (String value);
String (char value[]);
String (char value[], int offset, int count)
String (StringBuffer buffer)
```

Thus we can create a string from another string, or from a character array or from a StringBuffer.

There are many methods available in the String class, and the next form shows a selection of them:

Manipulating strings

```
// class methods
  String    valueOf (int i)
  String    valueOf (double d)
  ... and 9 others
  // instance methods
  char      charAt (int index)
  int       compareTo (String s)
```

```
boolean    equals (Object obj)
int        indexOf (String s)
int        indexOf (String s, int fromindex)
int        length ()
String     substring (int begin, int end)
boolean    startsWith (String prefix)
char []    toCharArray ()
String     toLowerCase ();
String     trim ();
... and 33 others
```

`length` will give the length of the string. Note that unlike for an array, this is a method call, so the brackets are required. Although a string cannot be indexed directly, it is made up of characters and the character at any index position can be obtained via `charAt`. The whole string can also be transformed into a character array if required. For example,

```
char study [];
study = filename.toCharArray();
```

produces an array of length 10 with each character from the original string (i.e. `"rates.data"`). `indexOf` operates as a searching mechanism, enabling one to find a substring in a string. So, for example,

```
int dotpos = filename.indexOf('.');
```

will produce 5 in `dotpos`. Similarly, a substring can be extracted, as in

```
String name = filename.substring(0,dotpos-1);
```

which would give `"rates"` in `name`.

     `compareTo` and `equals` enable whole strings to be compared. The comparison operators <, > and == should not be used for this purpose. The reason is connected with the fact that strings are objects, the full implications of which were carefully discussed in section 6.1. The difference between assigning string values and their references was also covered in section 6.1. For `compareTo`, the comparison works as follows:

```
a.compareTo(b)      a less than b        result will be negative
                    a same as b          result will be 0
                    a greater than b     result will be positive
```

The comparison is a straight alphabetical one. So, for example,

```
String filename = "rates.data";
String filename2 = "dates.data";
System.out.println (filename.compareTo(filename2));
```

will produce 1. In other words, `"rates.data"` does come alphabetically after `"dates.data"`.

One of the common operations in programming is to convert strings to numbers and back again. The `valueOf` methods can take any of the primitive types and produce a string from it. We would only want to use `valueOf` if we wanted to keep the string in the program for a while, rather than print it out immediately.

EXAMPLE 10.1   Removing double spaces

Problem   Standards have been set up which indicate that in typed paragraphs, there should only ever be single spaces. We would like to process existing text and replace any double spaces by single ones.

Solution   We can read a file a line at a time, looking for double spaces using the string method `indexOf` and proceed accordingly.

Algorithm   String manipulation algorithms can be very tricky. This one is best taken in stages. Let us start by reading one line of text and printing out the line together with the position of the first occurrence of a double space. The Java would be

```
s = fin.readLine();
System.out.println(s.indexOf("  ",s) + "  " + s);
```

If we enclosed this in a program to process a whole file, we could get output such as

```
0     Algorithm String manipulation algorithms can be very tricky.
33    This one is best taken in stages.  Let us start by reading one
-1    line of text and printing out the line together with the
52    position of the first occurrence of a double space.  The Java
10    would be
```

which indicates that the first line has a double space at the beginning; the second and third lines have doubles somewhere in the middle; the third line has no double space, so `indexOf` returns –1; and the last line has a double space at the end, i.e. after the last word.

To find more than one occurrence of double space in a string we shall have to loop round, checking from where we left off each time. The basic loop looks like this:

```
startingFrom = 0;
while (true) {
  spaceAt = s.indexOf("  ",startingFrom);
  if (spaceAt==-1) break;
  s = s.substring(0,spaceAt)+" "
    + s.substring(spaceAt+2,s.length());
  startingFrom = spaceAt+2;
}
System.out.println(s);
```

In other words, we recreate s each time from the part from 0 to the double space, plus a single space, plus the remainder of the string. We know we have finished processing the string when the `indexOf` method returns –1.

Program   The full program incorporates these sections, and also checks for the end of the file. It does so by looking for a null string. For testing purposes, the program is set up to read from the keyboard, but the `fin` stream could just as easily be directed to a file of the user's choice using `Text.open`.

```java
import java.io.*;
import javagently.*;

class Spaces {

  /* Removing spaces program    by J M Bishop  Dec 1997
   * ----------------------    Java 1.1
   *
   * Replaces double spaces by single.
   * Illustrates use of string handling methods.
   */

  public static void main (String args []) throws IOException {

    System.out.println("Program to convert double spaces");
    System.out.println("to single ones.");
    BufferedReader fin = Text.open(System.in);

    String s = "";
    int spaceAt, startingFrom;
    try {
      while (true) {
        s = fin.readLine();
        if (s==null) throw new EOFException();

        startingFrom = 0;
        while (true) {
        spaceAt = s.indexOf("  ",startingFrom);
          if (spaceAt==-1) break;
          else if (spaceAt==0)
              s = s.substring(1,s.length());
          else s = s.substring(0,spaceAt)+" "
                + s.substring(spaceAt+2,s.length());
          startingFrom = spaceAt+2;
        }
        System.out.println(s);

      }
    }
    catch (EOFException e) {}
  }
}
```

Testing   The following shows some simple test data entered interactively.

```
Program to convert double spaces
to single ones.
Line one  with one double.
Line one with one double.
```

```
Line one  with  two.
Line two with two.
Line three ends with one.
Line three ends with one.
  Line four starts with one.
 Line four starts with one.
Line five has a   triple.
Line five has a   triple.
```

Obviously, there are many improvements that could be made to this program, and they are picked up in the problems at the end of the chapter.

The `StringBuffer` class

As we have mentioned, strings themselves are immutable. If we want to change the length or contents of a string, we basically have to break it up into bits and rejoin them, making a new string, as explained in Example 10.1. `StringBuffer` is an alternative class which provides methods such as `append`, `insert` and `setcharAt`, all of which enable efficient alterations to existing strings.

10.2 Inside the `Text` class

We mentioned in Chapter 2 that reading numbers was somewhat awkward in Java, and introduced the `Text` class as a means for providing these simple facilities. In this section we now look at the inside of that class, to see how it actually performs its task. But first we have to examine an important Java feature: the tokenizer.

Tokenizers

We have already mentioned that Java is slightly deficient in the input arena, and that the `Text` class was created to make up for the problem. Java's approach is to read strings, and to provide a very efficient means of breaking a string up into tokens and then convert the token to the required type. Tokens are substrings separated by characters such as a comma, a space or a tab. In this way we can pick off substrings from the input and pass them to the string versions of the envelope class routines for conversion in order to get the values we want. Envelopes were covered in section 6.1.

The methods provided by the `StringTokenizer` class, which is in `java.util`, are

StringTokenizer declaration and access

```
StringTokenizer (String s);
StringTokenizer (String s, String delimiters);
StringTokenizer (String s, String delimiters, boolean returnasTokens));
```

```
String   nextToken ();
String   nextToken (String delimiter);
boolean hasMoreTokens ();
int      countTokens ();
```

Having read in a string, we delare a tokenizer on it, as in

```
StringTokenizer T = new StringTokenizer (S);
```

We then look through the tokens, checking for the end, as follows:

```
while (T.hasMoreTokens()) {
  System.out.println(T.nextToken());
}
```

Changing the delimiter set

We can also change the default delimiters from the usual space, tab and end-of-line, to something else. For example, if we were analyzing a program, we would want semi-colon, brackets and so on also to be delimiters; otherwise, they will be part of the tokens. Suppose we have the line

```
spaceAt = s.indexOf(" ",startingFrom);
```

With default delimiters, the tokens would be

```
spaceAt
=
s.indexOf(" ",startingFrom);
```

which probably is not what we wanted. We could get a better effect by declaring

```
StringTokenizer T = new StringTokenizer (S," .(,);)=:",false);
```

which increases the delimiter set and excludes delimiters from the tokens. That is,

```
spaceAt
s
indexOf
" "
startingFrom
```

which is more like it. We now consider how envelopes and tokenizers are used in the Text class.

The Text class methods

We have now covered enough of the language to explain this useful addition to our programming repertoire. The class is not long, but it does make use of tokenizers and envelopes. The methods provided by the class were given in Chapter 3, and are repeated here:

The `Text` class methods

void	prompt (String *s*)
int	readInt (BufferedReader *in*)
double	readDouble (BufferedReader *in*)
String	readString (BufferedReader *in*)
char	readChar (BufferedReader *in*)
String	format (**int** *number*, **int** *align*)
String	format (**double** *number*, **int** *align*, **int** *frac*)
BufferedReader	open (InputStream in)
BufferedReader	open (String *filename*)
PrintWriter	create (String *filename*)

The `Text` class is composed of a set of methods which can be called in any order. There is no initializing to be done, so the methods must be sure to initialize themselves. The methods are static, and the class is not intended to be instantiated. It operates as a service provider in the same way as the `Math` class.

The general algorithm for each of the reading methods is illustrated by that for reading an integer, `readInt`. The routine can initialize itself by detecting a null token. If this is the case, it reads a line and generates the tokenizer. It then calls `nextToken`, to get a token, and tries to convert the token to a number. Both statements can go wrong:

- The call to `nextToken` can fail if there are no more tokens. The appropriate action is therefore to read another line.
- The conversion can fail if the substring forming the token does not represent a number of the proper kind. Again an exception is raised. Here we just print a message and try again.

If both statements complete successfully, the method exits.

The class also has a `prompt` method for writing out a short message and staying on the same line, as well as `format` and `open` methods (discussed in section 4.1). The class contains interesting statements in each of the numeric conversion methods. The `readInt` method uses the `parseInt` method from the `Integer` envelope class as follows:

```
return Integer.parseInt(item);
```

However, the `Double` class does not have a corresponding parse method, and the conversion is a bit more complex:

```
return Double.valueOf(item.trim()).doubleValue();
```

Let us consider what this does. `item` is a string returned from the tokenizer. Working from the inside outwards, we first trim it of spaces, using a method from the `String` class. Then we call the `Double.valueOf` method to convert the string to an object of type `Double`. Finally, we take the object out of its envelope and turn it into a `double` type. This statement is certainly worth putting into a typed method!

Listing of the `Text` class

```java
package javagently;

import java.io.*;
import java.util.*;
import java.text.*;

public class Text {

  public Text () {};

  /* The All New Famous Text class      by J M Bishop  Aug 1996
   *              revised for Java 1.1 by Alwyn Moolman Aug 1997
   *              revised for efficiency by J M Bishop Dec 1997
   *              revised with renamed output methods
   *              by J M Bishop in July 1999
   *
   * Provides simple input from the keyboard and files.
   * Now also has simple output formatting methods
   * and file opening facilities.
   *
   * public static void    prompt (String s)
   * public static int     readInt (BufferedReader in)
   * public static double  readDouble (BufferedReader in)
   * public static String  readString (BufferedReader in)
   * public static char    readChar (BufferedReader in)
   * public static String  format (int number, int align)
   * public static String  format
   *                   (double number, int align, int frac)
   * public static BufferedReader open (InputStream in)
   * public static BufferedReader open (String filename)
   * public static PrintWriter create (String filename)
   */

  private static StringTokenizer T;
  private static String S;

  public static BufferedReader open (InputStream in)  {
    return new BufferedReader(new InputStreamReader(in));
  }

  public static BufferedReader open (String filename)
                    throws FileNotFoundException {
    return new BufferedReader (new FileReader (filename));
  }

  public static PrintWriter create
                   (String filename) throws IOException {
    return new PrintWriter (new FileWriter (filename));
  }
```

```java
public static void prompt (String s) {
  System.out.print(s + " ");
  System.out.flush();
}

public static int readInt (BufferedReader in) throws IOException {
  if (T==null) refresh(in);
  while (true) {
    try {
      return Integer.parseInt(T.nextToken());
    }
    catch (NoSuchElementException e1) {
      refresh (in);
    }
    catch (NumberFormatException e2) {
      System.out.println("Error in number, try again.");
    }
  }
}

public static char readChar (BufferedReader in) throws IOException {
  if (T==null) refresh(in);
  while (true) {
    try {
      return T.nextToken().trim().charAt(0);
    }
    catch (NoSuchElementException e1) {
      refresh (in);
    }
  }
}

public static double readDouble (BufferedReader in) throws IOException {
  if (T==null) refresh(in);
  while (true) {
    try {
      String item = T.nextToken();
      return Double.valueOf(item.trim()).doubleValue();
    }
    catch (NoSuchElementException e1) {
      refresh (in);
    }
    catch (NumberFormatException e2) {
      System.out.println("Error in number, try again.");
    }
  }
}

public static String readString (BufferedReader in) throws IOException {
  if (T==null) refresh (in);
  while (true) {
    try {
      return T.nextToken();
    }
```

```
      catch (NoSuchElementException e1) {
        refresh (in);
      }
    }
  }

  private static void refresh (BufferedReader in) throws IOException {
    S = in.readLine ();
    if (S==null) throw new EOFException();
    T = new StringTokenizer (S);
  }

  //  Format methods
  //  --------------

  private static DecimalFormat N = new DecimalFormat();
  private static final String spaces = "                    ";

  public static String format(double number, int align, int frac) {
    N.setGroupingUsed(false);
    N.setMaximumFractionDigits(frac);
    N.setMinimumFractionDigits(frac);
    String num = N.format(number);
    if (num.length() < align)
      num = spaces.substring(0,align-num.length()) + num;
    return num;
  }

  public static String format(int number, int align) {
    N.setGroupingUsed(false);
    N.setMaximumFractionDigits(0);
    String num = N.format(number);
    if (num.length() < align)
        num = spaces.substring(0,align-num.length()) + num;
    return num;
  }

  public static String writeDouble (double number, int align, int frac) {
    // Deprecated in July 1999 but retained for compatability
    return format (number, align, frac);
  }

  public static String writeInt (int number, int align) {
    // Deprecated in July 1999 but retained for compatability
  return format (number, align);
  }
}
```

The writing methods makes use of the `java.text` package, which is the subject of the next section.

10.3 Formatting with the `java.text` package

In this chapter we consider the various ways that Java provides for formatting text, both internally and externally. Initially, Java did not have much in this regard, but Java 1.2 has extensive facilities for handling data in a manner which is locale dependent. This means that programs can present themselves in the most appropriate style for the country in which they run. In many ways, such presentation details could be regarded as not essential in a first course, but we give them here to show how different Java is to languages that precede it. In the format methods of our own Text class, we made use of features of the `java.text` package. In this section we describe and assess this approach to writing numbers.

The concept of a formatter

Java differs from other languages in that the formatting for numbers is not given in the print-statements, but in a separate object altogether. Then in the print-statement, the relevant format object is joined up with the item to be printed. Several format objects can exist together in a program at any one time, and they can be used and reused at will.

The formatters that are available in `java.text` are DateFormat, Simple DateFormat, NumberFormat, DecimalFormat and a somewhat different one called MessageFormat. We discuss the date formatters in the next section and concentrate on number formatters here.

NumberFormat and its subclass DecimalFormat provide facilities for formatting all kinds of numbers, including percentages and currencies, in various forms. First we create a format, and then we can customize it in two ways:

1   for particular formatting requirements, such as the number of fractional digits to be printed for a real number;

2   for different locales around the world, which have different conventions for decimals, currency symbols, thousand groups and so on.

The latter is a very powerful aspect of Java and puts the language in a class of its own for worldwide computing.

Since NumberFormat is an abstract class, creating a format is done by class methods, as given in the form:

Creating number formatters

`NumberFormat getInstance ()`
`NumberFormat getCurrencyInstance ()`
`NumberFormat getNumberInstance ()`
`NumberFormat getPercentInstance ()`

Each of the four creation methods has a corresponding version which mentions a new locale, other than the default one, that should be used. Perhaps a better way of handling locales is actually to switch between them. We shall discuss this further later on in the section.

To use a formatter, the following instance methods apply. Since all the other numeric types can operate within `long` and `double`, only two methods are needed.

Using number formatters

```
String format (double number);
String format (long number);
```

So, for example, to compare the default writing of numbers to the default settings of the formatter, consider

```
NumberFormat N = NumberFormat.getInstance ();

system.out.println(Math.PI + "   " + 10000);
system.out.println(N.format(Math.PI) + "   " + N.format(10000));
```

which would print out

```
3.141592653589793  10000
3.141  10,000
```

The printing out of numbers with commas is not very common, except in financial matters, so we would want to customize the format in most cases. To do so, we make use of the following instance methods:

Customizing a number formatter

```
void setMaximumIntegerDigits (int newvalue);
void setMinimumIntegerDigits (int newvalue);
void setMaximumFractionDigits (int newvalue);
void setMinimumFractionDigits (int newvalue);
void setGroupingUsed (boolean newvalue);
```

For each of the set methods, there is a corresponding get method which can, if needed, provide the current settings.

Note that it is a good idea to use short identifiers for formatter objects, because together with `format` they tend to clutter up print-statements.

Formatting real numbers

To see the effect of changing the various settings for real numbers, the best example is to dissect the `Text.writeDouble` method. It is as follows:

```
public static String format
                (double number, int align, int frac) {
  N.setGroupingUsed(false);
  N.setMaximumFractionDigits(frac);
  N.setMinimumFractionDigits(frac);
  String num = N.format(number);
  if (num.length() < align)
    num = spaces.substring(0,align-num.length()) + num;
  return num;
}
```

The three set calls establish that there must be no grouping of thousands and that the number of fractional digits is fixed. If we set the minimum but not the maximum then we would get spaces as padding on the right, whereas usually we want zeros. The number is then formatted and put into a local string, because there is one adjustment to be made. The number formatter has a default setting of 1 for the minimum integer digits, so we will always get a number such as 0.567 rather than .567. If we set the maximum to (`align-frac`) then we will get numbers of fixed width, but there will be leading zeros, not spaces. Therefore we add the extra spaces by means of string manipulation instead.

Setting the maximum integer digits has another danger: Java will truncate anything else. Thus with a maximum digits of 3, 1000 will be printed as 0. In general, therefore, the old `Text` class is still a useful tool.

In the `DecimalFormat` class there is a facility to set up a pattern to be used in formatting. However, creating a pattern such as ###0.### requires string handling as well if the number of hashes is a variable. We shall consider patterns again when customizing dates.

Currencies

As part of the number formatting facilities, we can get currencies printed out nicely. To print a number as a currency, we use

```
NumberFormat C = NumberFormat.getCurrencyInstance();

System.out.println (C.format(10000));
```

which could give in return:

```
$10,000.00
```

Currencies are fun because Java will pick up the correct currency formatting and currency symbol from the computer and use it. Example 10.2 illustrates what happens.

EXAMPLE 10.2   Currency conversion table

Problem   We would like to investigate the effect of local changes on the printing of currencies.

Solution   We set up a small test program which gets five exchange rates and then prints out a table with the amount converted from rand.

Program   The program is very simple. A currency format is created for each of the locales that are involved. The rates are read in and then the converted amounts printed.

```
import java.text.*;
import javagently.*;
import java.util.*;
import java.io.*;

class Currency {

  /* Testing currency formatting    by J M Bishop Dec 1997
   * ---------------------------
   *                                  Java 1.1
   * Illustrates the very useful features of the
   * Numberformat class in java.text.
   * Expects five exchange rates in a file
   * called rates.data.
   */

  public static void main (String args []) throws IOException {

    BufferedReader in = Text.open ("rates.data");
    PrintWriter out   = Text.create ("currency.out");

    System.out.println("The output goes to currency.out so it ");
    System.out.println("can be viewed properly. On the screen, ");
    System.out.println("the tabs may not line the columns up");
    System.out.println("neatly, and the special characters");
    System.out.println("might not show up correctly. ");
    System.out.println("All looks fine in a file in courier.");

    out.println("Currency conversion table");
    out.println("=========================");
    out.println();
    out.println("The exchange rates are:");
    out.println("Rand\tDollars\tPounds\tYen\t\tMarks\t\tFrancs");
    double d = Text.readDouble(in);
    double p = Text.readDouble(in);
    double y = Text.readDouble(in);
    double m = Text.readDouble(in);
    double f = Text.readDouble(in);
    out.println("1\t"+d+"\t\t"+p+"\t\t"+ y+"\t\t"+ m+"\t\t"+ f);
    out.println();

    NumberFormat Nr =
                NumberFormat.getCurrencyInstance(Locale.getDefault());
    NumberFormat Nd = NumberFormat.getCurrencyInstance(Locale.US);
    NumberFormat Np = NumberFormat.getCurrencyInstance(Locale.UK);
    NumberFormat Ny = NumberFormat.getCurrencyInstance(Locale.JAPAN);
    NumberFormat Nm = NumberFormat.getCurrencyInstance(Locale.GERMANY);
    NumberFormat Nf = NumberFormat.getCurrencyInstance(Locale.FRANCE);
```

```
      for (int rand = 1000; rand < 10000; rand+=1000)
        out.println(
          Nr.format(rand)    + '\t' +
          Nd.format(rand/d)  + '\t' +
          Np.format(rand/p)  + '\t' +
          Ny.format(rand/y)  + '\t' +
          Nm.format(rand/m)  + '\t' +
          Nf.format(rand/f));
      out.close();
    }
  }
```

Testing   The output from the program will be

```
Currency conversion table
=========================
The exchange rates are:

rand          dollars       pounds       yen              marks            francs
1             4.8845        8.047        0.0378           2.7361           0.8174

R1 000.00     $204.73       £124.27      ¥26,455.03       365,48 DM        1 223,39 F
R2 000.00     $409.46       £248.54      ¥52,910.05       730,97 DM        2 446,78 F
R3 000.00     $614.19       £372.81      ¥79,365.08       1.096,45 DM      3 670,17 F
R4 000.00     $818.92       £497.08      ¥105,820.11      1.461,93 DM      4 893,56 F
R5 000.00     $1,023.65     £621.35      ¥132,275.13      1.827,42 DM      6 116,96 F
R6 000.00     $1,228.38     £745.62      ¥158,730.16      2.192,90 DM      7 340,35 F
R7 000.00     $1,433.10     £869.89      ¥185,185.19      2.558,39 DM      8 563,74 F
R8 000.00     $1,637.83     £994.16      ¥211,640.21      2.923,87 DM      9 787,13 F
R9 000.00     $1,842.56     £1,118.43    ¥238,095.24      3.289,35 DM      11 010,52 F
```

The output is very interesting, considering that we did no work ourselves! The fomatting for rand is picked up from the machine's default setting (our computer). Your computer might be set differently, so the program will have a slightly different output.

Inputting formatted data

We have concentrated up to now on outputting data. The `java.text` package also provides for inputting formatted data in each of its classes. Formatted data is distinguished from unformatted data in that the items need not be delimited by spaces and so on, but must appear in particular columns in the input line. They may even abut each other as in the following:

```
76 89123 45 10   6100
```

If this data is interpreted with a format of maximum and minimum digits as 3, then the resulting numbers are 76, 89, 123, 45, 10, 6 and 100.

The general term for getting input data in Java is **parsing**, which is analogous to formatting for output. However, data these days is very seldom presented without delimiters of some sort, and in general tokenizers, as discussed in section 10.2, are adequate for most needs. A distinct disadvantage of parsing via the formatters is that the results are presented as objects, so one still has to do the conversion to primitive types.

10.4 Dates, calendars and times

Originally in Java 1.0, there was a useful `Date` class which included methods for getting and setting parts of the date, among others. These functions have now been taken over by another, much more complex class, `Calendar`. Rather than itemize `Calendar`, we just list here the parts we shall need for the next example:

- constants indicating the various fields, e.g. `YEAR` or `MINUTE`;
- constants for the days and months, e.g. `MONDAY` or `DECEMBER`;
- a class method that creates an object, i.e. `getInstance`;
- instance methods for getting and setting parts of the date, i.e. `get` and `set`.

`get` and `set` require field parts to be specified, for example

```
int y = get(Calendar.YEAR);
set (Calendar.YEAR, 2001);
```

In addition, `set` can be given three values – year, month and day – but note that it is best to use the constant names provided for the months, e.g. `Calendar.MAY` not 5.

Date formatting

In the same way as we can format numbers and currencies, we can also format dates. From the `DateFormat` class of `java.text` we create a formatter with a specific style, being one of `DEFAULT`, `FULL`, `LONG`, `MEDIUM` or `SHORT`. Thus instead of the simple

```
System.out.println("Today is "+ today.getTime());
```

in the above program, we can be more specific and say

```
DateFormat D = DateFormat.getDateInstance(DateFormat.FULL);
System.out.println("Today is "+ D.format(today));
```

which would print out the more user-friendly version of

Tuesday, December 07, 1999

The various options are explored in the next example.

Similarly, we can select a time formatter and print the time in a variety of ways. The method here is `getTimeInstance`.

Date parsing

A useful feature of the `DateFormat` class is the method to parse a date from a string. It enables us to read dates. For example, if we declare an ordinary date formatter as

```
DateFormat DF = DateFormat.getDateInstance();
```

and have data such as

```
1999-Aug-15
```

we can read it with

```
Date D = DF.parse(Text.readString(in));
```

`parse` can raise an exception, so it is necessary to catch it here or mention it in all the methods associated with the call. Catching it could look like this:

```
DateFormat DF = DateFormat.getDateInstance();
Date D = new Date();
String s = Text.readString(in);
try {
 D = DF.parse(s);
} catch (ParseException e) {
   System.out.println("Error in date " + s);
}
```

The default date format is the simple one shown above. Of course, other date formats can be insisted upon by changing the style of the formatter, as shown in the next example.

EXAMPLE 10.3 Formatting and parsing dates

Problem Illustrate the various options for input and output of dates in Java.

Solution The solution, as always, is to set up a test program. The one that follows is carefully crafted not only to give the necessary illustrative output, but also to exercise some of the other interesting aspects of date formatting in Java. Specifically:

- date formats can be sent as parameters;
- the parse method throws a `ParseException` which indicates a date in the wrong form.

Program Notice that we have set the program up for the US locale which will put the month before the day. It is easy to change this statement. A locale of UK would put the day number before the month and skip the day name.

```java
import java.text.*;
import java.util.*;
import javagently.*;
import java.io.*;

class CustomDates {

  /* Testing date formatting   by J M Bishop Dec 1997
   * ----------------------   Java 1.1
   *
   * Writes dates in multiple formats and
   * prompts for dates back in the same form.
   */

  CustomDates () {
  }

  static BufferedReader in = Text.open(System.in);
  static Date d = new Date ();
  static Date my = new Date();

  static void echoDate(String style, DateFormat Din,DateFormat Dout)
                    throws IOException {
    System.out.println(style+"\t"+Din.format(d));
    String s = in.readLine();
    System.out.println("\t\t\t"+s);
    try {
      my = Din.parse(s);
    }
    catch (ParseException e) {
      System.out.println("Invalid date "+s);
    }
    System.out.println("\t\t\t"+Dout.format(my));
  }


  public static void main (String args []) throws IOException {

    Locale.setDefault(Locale.US);
    DateFormat DS = DateFormat.getDateInstance(DateFormat.SHORT);
    DateFormat DM = DateFormat.getDateInstance(DateFormat.MEDIUM);
    DateFormat DL = DateFormat.getDateInstance(DateFormat.LONG);
    DateFormat DF = DateFormat.getDateInstance(DateFormat.FULL);
    DateFormat DD = DateFormat.getDateInstance(DateFormat.DEFAULT);

    echoDate("SHORT",DS,DF);
    echoDate("MEDIUM",DM,DF);
    echoDate("LONG",DL,DF);
    echoDate("FULL",DF,DF);
    echoDate("DEFAULT",DD,DF);
  }
}
```

Testing

```
SHORT    10/25/99
         10/20/04
         Wednesday, October 20, 2004
MEDIUM   Oct 25, 1999
         Oct 20, 2004
         Wednesday, October 20, 2004
LONG     October 25, 1999
         October 20, 2004
         Wednesday, October 20, 2004
FULL     Monday, October 25, 1999
         Saturday, October 20, 2004
         Wednesday, October 20, 2004
DEFAULT  Oct 25, 1999
         Okt 20, 2004
Invalid date Okt 20, 2004
         Wednesday, October 20, 2004
```

We notice two points from this output:

1   Java has decided that two-digit years such as 04, belong in the 21st century, i.e., 2004, not 1904.

2   In FULL style, if an invalid day is entered, the formatter ignores it and presents the correct one.

Time zones

In its mission to be a truly worldwide and web-oriented language, Java provides for detecting the time zone of the computer running the program. From the time zone, the zone code, the offset from UT (Universal Time, also known as Greenwich Mean Time) and information about daylight saving can be established.

EXAMPLE 10.4   Testing time zones

What follows is a small test program to show the information that can be deduced about the computer's time zone.

```
import java.util.*;

class WorldTime {

    /* Time Zone program    by J M Bishop December 1997
     *                         Java 1.1
     * Uses the Java libraries to display
     * time anywhere in the world.
     */
```

```
      public static void main (String [ ] args) {
        TimeZone here = TimeZone.getDefault();
        Date today = new Date();

        System.out.println(today);
        System.out.println("We are in " + here.getID() + " time zone");
        System.out.println("with " + here.getRawOffset()/3600000 +
                           " offset from UT");
        System.out.println("Daylight Savings Time used here is " +
                           here.useDaylightTime());
        System.out.println("and being now in Daylight Savings Time is "
                           + here.inDaylightTime(today));

      }
    }
```

Sat Dec 06 17:11:54 EST 1997
We are in EST time zone
with -5 offset from UT
Daylight Savings Time used here is true
and being now in Daylight Savings Time is false

Once you have run the `WorldTime` program, it is quite fun to change your time zone and run it again. On a Windows NT system, you do this by going into Help, selecting time zones and clicking the arrow. You are shown a map of the world and can select any time zone from the menu. On Windows 95 systems, the time zone slice is shown on the map as well. Figure 10.1 shows this screen.

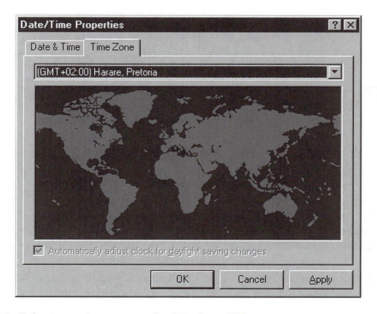

Figure 10.1 *Selecting a time zone under Windows NT*

Localized date formatting

Java has a useful class called `locale` which we can use to switch to different countries and their accompanying date and currency formats. We can even create our own, if the language is not one known to the Java `Locale` class. Examples of using locales are given in the companion text to this one, *Java Gently (2nd edition)*.

10.5 Lists of objects

We observed in Chapter 5 that one of the problems with arrays is that they are rigid, both in size and arrangement. One cannot remove an element without pushing all the later elements up, and this takes time and effort. Hash tables, discussed in section 6.2, get away from both of these restrictions, but they store the data in a somewhat unconventional way ('hashed'). The classical alternative to an array is the **linked list**, and we shall spend this section looking at how one can be defined in Java. We have already used lists in the `Graph` class (section 7.4) and the chatter program (section 9.4).

In an array, items are stored sequentially, and we know that item $i + 1$ follows item i. In a linked list, the items are regarded as self-standing, but connected together by **links**. These links can be made and broken, and thus we can have a structure that, unlike an array, can grow and shrink at will while the program is executing.

Suppose we have some string objects already created in a linked list as in

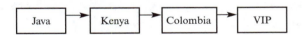

If the object with 'Colombia' in it needs to be removed, then we can just arrange to redirect the links as in

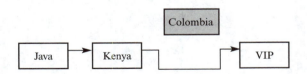

Java will then **garbage collect**[†] the space that the unwanted object occupied and it will be no more. The question is: what are the links? They are nothing more complicated than the references that we introduced in Chapter 7. So in order to establish a chain of objects like this, we just need to declare an object inside itself and space for a reference – the link – will be reserved. We shall call the objects forming a linked list **nodes**.

---

† Garbage collection is the process of reclaiming storage. Java does it automatically when objects are no longer in use.

Creating a list

The Java for a general sort of node is

```
class Node {
/* The Node class for storing objects that are linked
 *together.
 */

// The constructor copies in the data
// and the link to the given node
// (which may be null).
Node (Object d, Node n)) {
  link = n;
  data = d;
}

Node link;
Object data;
}
```

To create such a node, we must supply a value for its data and the node it is going to be linked to. Initially, the list will have nowhere to link to, so the following will work:

```
Node list = new Node ("VIP",null);
```

which gives us

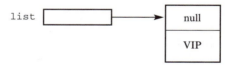

To link the next node to the list, the statement is

```
list = new Node ("Colombia", list);
```

Consider this statement a step at a time. new Node creates the space for a node. The data item is filled with "Colombia". The link item is filled with a reference to where list is currently referring. Then the list object is made to refer to this new one, shown in

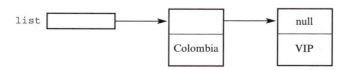

And so the creation of the list can continue. To add the next two nodes, we could use

```
list = new Node ("Kenya", list);
list = new Node ("Java", list);
```

Notice that we have taken the shortcut of drawing the strings inside the nodes themselves. As objects in their own rights, they should of course be represented with references, so that the Colombia node, for instance, would actually look like this:

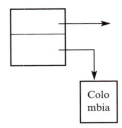

Removing from a list

Having created a list which has nice dynamic properties, we must consider the Java for removing an item from it. Let us start with the list of four coffees shown above. Assume that x, referring to Colombia, has been identified as the object to be removed. What we want to do is take the link that is referring to Colombia – that is, Kenya – and make it refer to what Colombia is presently referring to – that is, VIP.

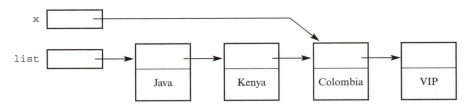

The assignment should be

```
Kenya's link = x.link;
```

However, there is a problem with the left hand side of this assignment. We do not have a name or reference for the Kenyan node. Objects in a linked list are essentially anonymous, except for the first one, unless we travel through the list and establish temporary names for nodes. That is of course exactly what we did in order to find Colombia and have x refer to it. The answer to the problem is to keep track of *two* objects as we look for something, one running behind the other. Let us assume that this has been done, and that xPrevious refers to Kenya. The assignment then can be

```
xPrevious.link = x.link;
```

and the resulting diagram is

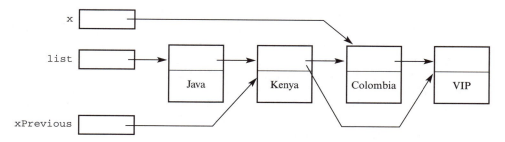

It does not matter that Colombia is still referring to VIP as it is no longer linked into the list. However, since another object, x, is still referring to Colombia, it is not garbage collected yet.

However, there is a problem: if x refers to the first node, Java, then what is the meaning of xPrevious? It will start at null. If xPrevious is null, it will not be possible to use the assignment above. This possibility must therefore be taken care of in the remove method as follows:

```
if (xPrevious == null)
   list = x.link;
else
   xPrevious.link = x.link;
```

Searching a list

Finally, we consider how x was found in the first place. Now that we know we have to keep track of the previous node as well as the current one, we can devise the general loop for finding a sought-after value in a list as follows:

```
Node x = list;
Node xprev = null;
do {
   if (x.data.equals(soughtAfter)) break;
   xprev = x;
   x = x.link
   }
while (x != null);
```

We assume that data is an object, rather than a variable, and will therefore need to be compared using its equals method.

A class for lists

Given that lists are going to be useful in many circumstances, it makes sense to define them as a class and put the class in a package. A classic list class is somewhat more sophisticated than this book allows. However the differences are in performance rather than functionality. In keeping with our 'Gently' approach, we shall present a simple list class here.

What are the members of such a class? The data will be three objects referring to the start of the list and the items we are at now and previously. We shall declare them private to prevent untoward access, and provide all legitimate access to the list through methods.

What methods should the class include? We have already explored add and remove. In addition to these, a list must be able to return its current element – that is, where the user is currently in the list – and also to indicate whether the list is empty or not.

In order to scan through the list for various reasons, such as searching or displaying the items, we provide a trio of methods which mirror the parts of a for-loop. These are reset, succ (for successor) and eol (for end-of-list). The proposed List class makes use of the Node class, as discussed above. It is

```java
package javagently;

public class List  {

    /* The List class      by J M Bishop October 1997
     *                      no change for Java 1.1
     * Maintains a list of objects in
     * last in first out order and provides simple
     * iterator methods.
     */

    private Node start, now, prev;

    public List() {
        now = null;
        start = null;
        prev = null;
    }

    public void add(Object x) {
        prev = now;
        if (start == null) {
            start = new Node(x, null);
            now = start;
        } else {
            Node T = new Node(x, now.link);
            now.link = T;
            now = T;
        }
    }

    public void remove() {
        if (isempty() || eol()) {
            return;
        } else {
            if (prev == null) {
                start = now.link;
```

```
        } else {
            prev.link = now.link;
            now = now.link;
        }
    }
}

public boolean isempty() {
    return start == null;
}

public Object current() {
    return now.data;
}

public void reset() {
    now = start;
    prev = null;
}

public boolean eol() {
    return now.link == null;
}

public void succ() {
    now = now.link;
    if (prev == null)
        prev = start;
    else
        prev = prev.link;
}

class Node {

    /* The Node class for storing objects that
     * are linked together.
     */

    Node link;
    Object data;

    /* The constructor copies in the data
     * and the link to the given node
     * (which may be null).
     */

    Node(Object d, Node n) {
        link = n;
        data = d;
    }

}

}
```

10.6 Other object properties

Classes, objects and members of objects can be given a modifier which indicates how they can be used. Not all modifiers apply to classes: some are for objects and other members of classes (methods, variables) only. Table 10.1 gives a summary of the meaning of some of Java's main modifiers. Several of these modifiers have already been covered in earlier chapters, and can be looked up in the index for full details.

Protection in objects

Like many object-oriented languages, Java recognizes that objects are an encapsulation mechanism that provides both a public and a private face. In Java, there is a choice of four levels of protection: private, protected, package (the default) and public. The meaning of these levels is defined in Table 10.1, and illustrated using Figure 10.2.

The diagram shows four classes A, B, C and E, each having one variable field, and E having an object as well, instantiated from B. A and B are in the same package, but C and E are not specifically in any package. They are therefore in what is known as the default package, which is where most of our test programs to date have been created. Java does not require that classes be in named packages, although we have made extensive use of this facility with `javagently` and `jgeslib`. The classes also have inheritance relationships, which can stay within packages or cross package boundaries. So E inherits from B which inherits from A, although E is in a different package.

Table 10.1 *The meaning of some of the modifiers applicable to classes and members*

Modifier	Class	Member
No modifier	Accessible only within its package	Accessible only within its package
public	Accessible anywhere its package is	Accessible anywhere its class is
private	n/a	Accessible only within its own class
protected	n/a	Accessible within its package and its subclasses
abstract	May not be instantiated	A method is not implemented here but in a subclass
final	May not be subclassed	A field may not be changed; a method may not be overridden
static	A top-level class, not an inner one	Class member accessed through its class name

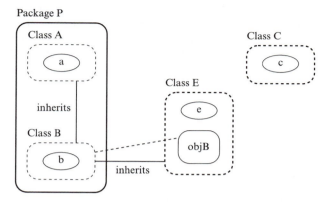

Figure 10.2 *Class diagram for illustrating protection*

Now we can explain the accessibility modifiers as follows, working from the least to the most accessible.

- **private.** Applies only to members (not classes) and restricts access to the class that defines it. Therefore if all the variables were declared as private in the example they could only be seen in their own classes, e.g. a in A, b in B and so on.

- **package.** In the absence of any other modifier, classes and members have package-wide visibility. Thus a would be seen from B and b from A. Of course, they will need to be suitably qualified in their naming, in the sense that B cannot just ask for a: it must refer to A.a (if a is static) or AObj.a if AObj is an object of class A. By the same token, A and B can see each other, but they cannot be seen outside of P. According to this definition, B could not in fact have package accessibility, because the diagram shows that it is used in an inheritance relationship by E outside the package. What package accessibility says is that the import-statement has no effect on classes such as B: it still cannot be seen outside its package.

  What about C and E that are not in a named package? In order to be visible to each other, they would have to be stored in the same physical directory, and therefore comprise a virtual package. Then c would be accessible from E and e from C. Once classes are in packages, though, to cross the boundaries requires an import statement.

- **protected.** If we want members to be visible outside of a package, but only to those inheriting their class (as E does from B) then we change the modifier to protected. In this way we could tighten up on a in A so that only B could see it. Protected members are therefore just like default ones, and their accessibility does not extend outside a package, even in the case of inheritance.

- **public.** The most expansive level says visibility is everywhere, provided the correct connections have been set up. What this means is that if B is public, objects of class B can be created in E or in C provided they import the package P. If C and E are in the same directory, then E can also create objects of class C (without importing). With `public`, an interesting point arises: making a class public does not automatically make all its members public. Everything keeps its package accessibility unless specifically changed to something else.

Inner classes

In Java classes have 'first class' status in that they can be declared anywhere, used as parameters, and as local members to other classes, methods and blocks. Table 10.2 summarizes the four kinds of inner classes that can be used.

A nested class is just like any other class, but it is grouped inside another class for ease of development and handling. Often it is not convenient to have every class in a different file, and, with nested classes, we can keep them together. By declaring the class as static, we indicate that it is to have the same top-level status as the enclosing class. Nested classes can be imported from within their enclosing class. In a way, they are similar in effect to Java's package concept. Our `DataHandler` classes were frequently nested in one file, as were the classes we used in early programs for structuring purposes.

Table 10.2 *Types of inner classes*

Inner class type	Defined as	Used for	Comment
Nested top level	Static member of another class	Grouping classes	Name includes enclosing class name
Member	Ordinary member of another class	Helper class, sharing members among classes	Access to enclosing instance of other class. Special syntax for `this`, `new` and `super`. Cannot have static members
Local	Member of a method or block	Adapter class to be passed as a call-back, e.g. in event handling	Same as for member
Anonymous	Unnamed member of a method or block	One-off class defined where needed	Same as for member: no name or constructor; it can only be instantiated once; defined in an expression

Member classes are typically helper classes for the enclosing class. They are not visible outside of it, but can make use of all its members, private or not. While an inner class may not have the same name as its enclosing class, it can have the same name as other member classes of other enclosing classes, thus cutting down on the number of names one has to invent in a big system. Member classes are regarded as elegant and worth using.

Because of the ability to use one's own members and those of an enclosing class, member classes can distinguish two versions of `this`. An unqualified `this` refers to the member class, whereas to refer to the enclosing class we preface `this` with its name. Similar extensions are made for `new` and `super`. A notable restriction of member classes is that they may not have static members. Any static members required must be grouped in the top-level class.

Anonymous classes perform the same function as local classes with the restriction that they do not have a name and therefore can only be instantiated once, at the point where they are defined. They are very useful with Java's event handlers, which we studied in Chapter 7. To give the flavour of such a class, here is a typical usage:

```
f.addWindowListener(new WindowAdapter () {
  public void windowClosing(WindowEvent e) {
    System.exit(0);
  }
});
```

`WindowAdapter` is an interface (see section 7.2) which needs to have a `window Closing` method defined, so that it can be called at the appropriate moment for the window called `f` here. So we create a new anonymous class as a parameter to the `addWindowListener` method. The whole class is passed as a parameter and at the appropriate moment, `windowClosing`, as defined here, will be called. Anonymous classes are used often in Chapter 7.

Local classes are much the same as anonymous ones, except that we give them names and can have more than one instantiation. The choice as to which to use is mostly a matter of taste.

10.7 Interfaces for generality

The third technique that Java provides for abstraction is interfaces. An **interface** is a special kind of class which defines the specification of a set of methods, and that is all. The methods together encapsulate a guarantee: any class which implements this interface is guaranteed to provide these methods. We can think of an interface as defining a set of standards, and a class that implements them gets a 'stamp of approval' as having conformed to those standards. Objects of the class can therefore gain access to any methods that need an object with those standards.

The forms for an interface and for a class that implements it are as follows:

Interface declaration

```
interface interfacename {
  method specifications
}
```

Interface implementation

```
class classname implements interfacename {
  Bodies for the interface methods
  Own data and methods
}
```

The application of interfaces that we shall consider is that of sorting anything. Firstly, we must examine how to sort.

Sorting and searching

Sorting and searching are very common operations in computing, and many systems provide high-level commands which enable data to be sorted or searched in any specified way. These commands rely on one of a number of algorithms, and every programmer should know at least one sorting algorithm and one searching algorithm by heart. In this text we introduce simple ones: selection sort, which performs in a time proportional to the square of the number of items being sorted, and linear search which is proportional to the number of items, as its name suggests. Other algorithms (e.g. Quicksort and binary search) perform faster, but are perhaps more difficult to understand and remember and are beyond the scope of this book. Consult *Java Gently (2nd edition)* for the full treatment.

Selection sort

Sorting items means moving them around in a methodical way until they are all in order. A method used by some card players is to sort cards by holding them in the right hand, finding the lowest one and taking it out into the left hand, then finding the next lowest and taking it out, until all the cards have been selected, and the left hand holds the cards in order. The following sequence illustrates how this method works.

Left hand	Right hand
	7 3 9 0 2 5
0	7 3 9 – 2 5
0 2	7 3 9 – – 5
0 2 3	7 – 9 – – 5
0 2 3 5	7 – 9 – – –
0 2 3 5 7	– – 9 – – –
0 2 3 5 7 9	– – – – – –

We could implement this by having two arrays and picking the numbers out of one, adding them to the other. However, there is a way of keeping both lists in the same array, the one growing as the other shrinks. Each time an element is picked out, the gap it leaves is moved to one end, thus creating a contiguous area, which is used to hold the new list. The move is done by a simple swap with the leftmost element of the right hand. So, the example would proceed as follows:

```
Left hand     Right hand
              7 3 9 0 2 5
0                 3 9 7 2 5
0 2                 9 7 3 5
0 2 3                 7 9 5
0 2 3 5                 9 7
0 2 3 5 7                 9
0 2 3 5 7 9
```

The underlined digits are those that moved at each phase. Each time, a reduced list is considered, until only one element is left.

Because sorting is clearly going to be useful in many contexts, it makes sense to put it in a method from the beginning. The parameters would be the array to be sorted and the number of items that are active in it. Initially, we shall say in the formal parameter what type of items are being sorted, and then see how, by using interfaces, we can relax this requirement.

```java
static void selectionSort (double a [], int n) {
  double temp;
  int chosen;

  for (int leftmost = 0; leftmost < n-1; leftmost++) {
    chosen = leftmost;
    for (int j = leftmost+1; j < n; j++)
      if (a[j] < a[chosen]) chosen = j;
    temp = a[chosen];
    a[chosen] = a[leftmost];
    a[leftmost] = temp;
  }
}
```

Sorting is a frequent requirement in computing, and it is useful to have a sorting algorithm handy. The above algorithm can be applied to arrays of any size, and can be used to sort in ascending order just by changing the comparison from < to >. Note, however, that if we wish to sort from highest to lowest, then the value that moves to the left each time will be the largest, not the smallest. The example sort given here sorts an array of doubles, and uses the < operator for the comparison. If the items being sorted are objects, then < won't work and will need to be replaced by a method, typically called lessThan or compareTo.

Searching

A simple linear search involves proceeding through an array until an item is found or until the end of the array is reached. If we only want to return whether or not the item is there, then a boolean method does the trick, as in

```
boolean search (double[] a, int n, double x) {
  for (int i = 0; i < n; i++)
    if (x == a[i]) return true;
  return false;
}
```

However, if we also want to return where in the array the item was found (so that we can update it, perhaps) then a more complex method is needed.

EXAMPLE 10.5   Sorting anything

Problem   The sort we developed is obviously extremely useful and we would like to adapt it so that it is independent of what we are sorting. Then, in particular, we would like to apply this new general sorting class to the Veterinary Association system (Example 6.4) so that we can produce a sorted list of the pets. The solution to the problem falls into two parts: generalizing the sort, and connecting the program to it.

Generalizing the sort   We consider what makes a class of objects sortable, and encapsulate this operation (or operations) in an interface called `Sortable`. Then we change the `selectionSort` method so that it works with sortable objects only. Thereafter any class that needs sorting must just implement the `Sortable` interface, and it can call the methods of the `Sort` class.

Now what makes objects sortable? What makes sorting one class different from another? It is not the assignment of the objects, since this is defined for all types and classes. The answer is that it is the comparison between two items. The comparison triggers the interchange of items, which is how all sorts work. How this comparison is done will differ from class to class.

Interface design   Sorting is obviously a common utility so we shall put it in the `jgeslib` package. First we set up the sortable interface as follows:

```
package jgeslib;

public interface Sortable {
  boolean lessThan (Sortable a);
}
```

Then we adapt `selectionSort` to use `Sortable` and encompass it in a class as follows:

```
package jgeslib;

public class Sort {

    /* The Sort class    by J M Bishop  Feb 1997
     *                      revised October 1997
     * Provides one sorting method
     * for arrays of objects of any length,
     * where the objects' class implements the
     * Sortable interface.
     */

  public static void selectionSort(Sortable a [], int n) {
    Sortable temp;
    int chosen;

    for (int leftmost = 0; leftmost < n-1; leftmost++) {
      chosen = leftmost;
      for (int j = leftmost+1; j < n; j++)
        if (a[j].lessThan(a[chosen])) chosen = j;
        temp = a[chosen];
        a[chosen] = a[leftmost];
        a[leftmost] = temp;
    }
  }
}
```

The array parameter and the temporary variable are both now declared as `Sortable`. Also the comparison which used the boolean relation < now calls the `lessThan` method on one of the objects, giving the other as a parameter.

Sorting the register The next step is to make our tags register sortable, which essentially means making objects of the `Tags` class sortable. The first question is: what field do we want to sort on? We could simply sort on pet names, in which case a `lessThan` method would look like this:

```
public boolean lessThan (Sortable secondTag) {
  Tags temp = (Tags) secondTag;
  return (name.compareTo(temp.name) < 0);
}
```

The local object `temp` is needed because we have to cast the parameter (which is of the general interface type) to the specific type `Tags` before we can pick up fields belonging to `Tags`. If we did this, then only `Tags` would implement `Sortable`, and any `XTags` would go back in the inheritance hierarchy to use `lessThan`. There is nothing in an `XTag` which alters the way in which sorting would be performed.

Suppose, however, the association would like to sort on phone numbers, since this will group together pets for a given owner; that is, under the old tags system. But with `XTags`, they would like the vet's phone number to be considered instead. Now sorting for `XTags` is different to that for `Tags`. Moreover, how do we define `lessThan` when one of the operands is a `Tag` and the other an `XTag`?

We start by realizing that selectionSort will call the method in the class of the first operand. So at a particular place in the sort, if the first operand to be compared is a Tags object, we shall arrive at the lessThan method for Tags. At this stage, the parameter could be either type. Here is what the lessThan method will look like, and then we discuss it:

```
public boolean lessThan (Sortable secondTag) {
  Tags temp = (Tags) secondTag;
  // temp may be a tag or an xTag, so we get
  // the relevant phone field by calling a method
  String secondString = temp.getPhone();
  return (phone.compareTo(secondString) < 0);
}
```

Having got the second operand from the parameter, we are not sure what type it is. So we employ the technique of dynamic binding, and extract via a method the phone number we want. If the second operand is a Tag, then getPhone for Tags will be called, which is

```
String getPhone () {
  return phone;
}
```

If, however, the second operand is an Xtag, Java will direct getPhone to that class, which returns the vet's phone number as follows:

```
String getPhone () {
  return vet;
}
```

The lessThan method in Xtags is exactly like the above except that the last line refers to vet, as in

```
return (vet.compareTo(secondString) < 0);
```

As already explained, the second operand will pick up an owner's phone number or a vet's phone number, depending on the type of the object at run time. For completion's sake, here is the full Tags class again:

```
import jgeslib.*;

class Tags implements Sortable {

    /* The Tags class          by J M Bishop January 1997
     * --------------          adapted July 1999
     * for keeping data on a pet.
     */

    String name, phone;

    public Tags(String n, String p) {
        name = n;
        phone = p;
    }
```

```
    String getPhone () {
      return phone;
    }

    public boolean lessThan (Sortable secondTag) {
      Tags temp = (Tags) secondTag;
      // temp may be a tag or an xTag, so we get
      // the relevant phone field by calling a method
      String secondString = temp.getPhone();
      return (phone.compareTo(secondString) < 0);
    }

    public String toString() {
        return "Owner: "+phone+"   "+name;
    }

}
```

The XTags class has similar changes. We also switched around in the toString
method the order of the displaying of the vet and owner, so that it will be obvious that
the sort is being done on different fields.

```
import jgeslib.*;

public class XTags extends Tags implements Sortable {

    /* The XTags class            by J M Bishop  January 1997
     * ---------------            Sorting July 1999
     * for extended vet tags with vet numbers.
     * Uses inheritance and interfaces */

    String vet;

    public XTags(String n, String p, String v) {
        super(n, p);
        vet = v;
    }

    String getPhone () {
      return vet;
    }

    public boolean lessThan (Sortable secondTag) {
      // The firstTag is an xTag because we are here
      Tags temp = (Tags) secondTag;
      // temp may be a tag or an xTag, so we get
      // the relevant phone field by calling a method
      String secondString = temp.getPhone();
      // This next line differs from Tag's in that it
      // uses vet as the first operand
      return (vet.compareTo(secondString) < 0);
    }

    public String toString() {
        return "Vet: "+vet+" "+name+"  Owner: "+phone;
    }
)
```

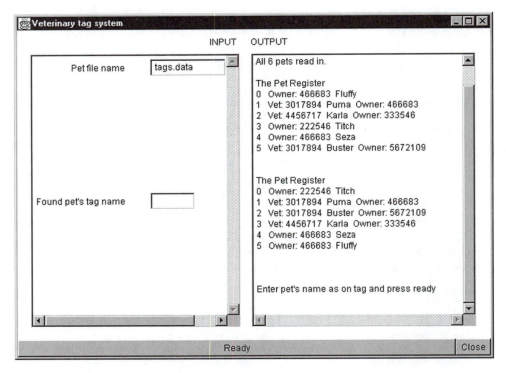

Figure 10.3 *The sorted pets register*

Finally, the main program needs minor adjustment. It does not implement `Sortable`. It does not mention `Sortable`: all this is handled by the tag classes. All it has to do is call

```
Sort.selectionSort (register,index);
```

The main program is based on `VeterinaryTags.java` from Chapter 6, and this version is called `VeterinaryTagsSorted.java`. The changes that have been made are:

1   Add a statement `import jgeslib.*;`

2   Inside the `TagDataHandler` class, there is a new method `sortTags`

```
void sortTags() {
  Sort.selectionSort(register, index);
}
```

3   Two statements have been added to the main method:

```
public static void main (String args[]) throws IOException {
  TagDataHandler vetAssoc = new TagDataHandler();
  vetAssoc.initialize();
```

```
      vetAssoc.makeTags();
      vetAssoc.showTags();
      vetAssoc.sortTags();    //NEW
      vetAssoc.showTags();    //NEW
      while (true)
         // ends when close button is pressed on display
         vetAssoc.checkTags();
   }
```

The ouput from the program after the register is sorted on these phone numbers is given in Figure 10.3. We have altered the way in which each line is printed to emphasize how the sorting is achieved.

Before we leave interfaces, we stress that they can only have method specifications in them and no completed methods or variables. However, they can include constants if necessary. Interfaces can also be subclassed.

QUIZ

10.1 Write a loop to go through an array of names and print out the first position of the letter 'e' in each name, if it exists.

10.2 Write statements to convert the word JAVA to small letters, then capitalize the J.

10.3 If s is a string holding an integer number, give statements to (a) store the integer as a variable and (b) print the integer without first storing it.

10.4 Give two reasons why the `NumberFormat` class of `java.text` is not as useful as it could be for outputting numbers reasonably simply.

10.5 If `tragic` is a `Calendar` object, use the set method to give it the date 31 August 1997.

10.6 How would Java print your birthday this year in `FULL` style?

10.7 Draw a diagram showing how the list at the end of section 10.5 would look if another coffee, say Kona, was added. Use the `add` method of the `List` class.

10.8 What is the essential difference between a nested class and a member class?

10.9 In Figure 10.2 how would we declare e if we wanted it to be visible from C?

10.10 If we decided to sort the pets register on the pet names instead, what would we need to change in Example 10.5?

PROBLEMS

10.1 **Birthdays.** The `after` and `before` methods of the `Calendar` class in the `util` package will return true or false depending on the relationship between the instance object and the parameter. For example,

```
      new Calendar (1999,Calendar.DECEMBER,25).before
                (new Calendar (1999,Calendar.DECEMBER,1))
```

will be false. Write a program which sets up your birthday and the day of Easter this year and displays the result of each of the three relations – before, equals and after – between the two dates.

10.2 **Typing improvements.** There are different schools of thought for typing spaces after full stops. It used to be that one entered two spaces, but now the fashion seems to be one. Adapt Example 10.1 so that the user can choose one of these styles, and the program will standardize an input file accordingly.

10.3 **Validating codes.** Course codes at Savanna University have a precise form: four capital letters followed immediately by three digits. Write a class for such codes, and include methods to create, convert to a string and check a code for validity. Test the class with a small test program.

10.4 **Palindromes.** A palindrome is a word or sentence that reads the same forwards as backwards, disregarding punctuation. Famous palindromes are

> Madam, I'm Adam
> Able was I ere I saw Elba.

Write a boolean method which will check whether a given string is a palindrome or not. Call the method from a test program.

10.5 **Concordance.** A concordance is a list of words similar to an index, where the position of each word – its page number and line number – in a piece of text is indicated. The difference between a concordance and an index is that a concordance considers all words except common ones such as 'and', 'the' and 'is'. Write a Java program to create a concordance from a piece of text at your disposal. Use hash tables.
Hint: The hash table will have the words as keys and the page/line numbers as values. Since the words could occur more than once, the value will have to be an array of numbers, and will have to have an upper limit, say ten occurrences, recorded.

10.6 **Multiple word names.** A problem we detected earlier (e.g. in the converter program in Example 7.4) is that we cannot have names with spaces in them. The reason is that a space delimits the whole name, so it cannot be *in* the name. We solved the problem by changing the data so that names like United.States were written with a full stop in the middle.

Now that we know more about formatting, what would be the best approach to employ for a method that could read such names? Assume that the names are lined up in columns of a fixed size and that no other data items will be in that column.

Write a suitable method to read multi-word and use it to remove the data restriction from the converter program.

10.7 **Your own dates.** Choose another country not supported by the standard locales and customize Java to reflect the language and conventions of that country. Investigate the APIs via Java's Help and try to customize the currency formatting as well. The approach is very similar to that for dates.

10.8 **Egalitarian minutes.** The Council of Savanna University has decreed that in future all minutes of meetings will omit titles of those speaking. Instead of Prof Brown, committees may choose between John Brown, Brown, JB or John, depending on circumstances. However, in any one document, only one convention should be used. Your task is to process a document, looking for titles, i.e. Prof Dr Mr Ms Miss Rev, remove them, and replace the name that follows with the selected form.

To solve this problem, the program will need information regarding the names of the people. For example, if the John Brown format is chosen, and the program encounters Prof Brown, then it must be able to find John from somewhere. There are two options:

(a) Interact with the secretary or whoever is running the program and get the information that way. This is simple to set up, but could be tedious and error prone when running.

(b) From the attendance and apologies lists at the beginning of the document, construct a hash table with the necessary information. Assume that these lists give everyone's details in full, e.g. Prof John Brown (JB). Make use of the string method `startsWith` to find the lists.

You will have to decide how the hash table is to be arranged, i.e. what is the key, but remember that we can search the keys and the values, and various customized searching can also be added.

Answers to quizzes

Chapter 1

1.1 A compiler translates a program written in a humanly-readable computer language into a computer-readable machine language.

1.2 A compilation error occurs if the language is used incorrectly, e.g. with incorrect spelling or grammar. A logic error results from a program that is asked to perform an invalid action, such as division by zero, or to take a sequence of steps that do not produce the desired result.

1.3 Clock speeds are going up all the time. They are measured in hundreds of megahertz.

1.4 Computers that run Java would start at 32 megabytes, but more likely 64.

1.5 Removable diskettes are fairly standard at 1.44 Mbytes. Hard disk drives start from 1 gigabyte upwards.

1.6 This text book fits nicely on one or two 1.44 Mbyte diskettes (Macintoshes seem to write smaller files than PCs and we use both).

Chapter 2

2.1 `args`

2.2 They would all produce the answer 6.

2.3 A year contains 31 536 000 seconds. From Table 2.1, we can see that an `int` variable will not hold 1000 times this value. We would have to use `long` as the type for the variable.

2.4
```
System.out.println(
  "----------------------\n" +
  "|     Peter Piper     \n" +
  "|     16 Beach Drive  \n" +
  "|     Sunnywood       \n" +
  "----------------------");
```

```
System.out.println("------------------------");
System.out.println("|    Peter Piper        ");
System.out.println("|    16 Beach Drive     ");
System.out.println("|    Sunnywood          ");
System.out.println("------------------------");
```

In the first example, the five lines of the address do not fit on one program line, and so are split into separate strings, concatenated together.

2.5
```
        2
9000009
64
3
3
2
```

2.6   `x = Math.sqrt ((b*b-4*a*c)/(2*a))`

2.7   2

2.8
```
int distance;
double flour;
int age;
int minutes;
double balance;
```

2.9
main	method
newArrive	variable
Math	class
round	method
final	keyword
NewFleet	class
class	keyword
100	constant
System	class
out	object
println	method
arrive	constant

2.10   Java compilers work in several passes. They find certain easy errors, like the following:

```
quiz2.java:3: Identifier expected
max = 10;
  ^

quiz2.java:5: Identifier expected
double K = 1,000;
          ^

quiz2.java:7: Identifier expected
int 2ndPrize = G25;
  ^
```

```
quiz2.java:7: Invalid character in number
int 2ndPrize = G25;
    ^
```

```
quiz2.java:9: Duplicate variable declaration: double x was double x
double x = 6;
       ^
```

Then if we comment out the lines above, these next errors appear:

```
quiz2.java:2: Class integer not found.
integer I, j, k;
```

```
quiz2.java:6: Undefined variable
int Prize = G50;
       ^
```

```
quiz2.java:8 Incompatible type for double. Explicit cast needed to
convert double to integer.
int homeTime = 4.30;
       ^
```

Chapter 3

3.1 None

3.2
```
for (int century = 1900; century < 2000; century +=10)
   System.out.print(century+" ");
System.out.println();
```

3.3
```
display.ready("Press the ready bar to continue");
double x = display.getDouble("Starting value in Ohms");
```

3.4 The values that were given as the defaults in the prompts will be read.

3.5
```
double euros (double dollars, double dollarspereuro) {
   return dollars / dollarspereuro;
}
```

3.6 `g.nextGraph();`

3.7 We probably forgot to call `g.showGraph();`

3.8
```
g.setColor(g.magenta);
g.setLine(false);
g.setTitle("Readings");
```

3.9 The solve method contains a predictor–corrector which is specific to the dbydt function and the current and other values set up by the class. To emphasize that the class can only work on this specific function, we gave it the qualified name.

3.10 `CurrentEulerSolver euler = new CurrentEulerSolver();`

Chapter 4

4.1 `String countryName = fin.readLine();`

4.2   `System.out.println("Checked is "+checked+"thisMonth is"+thisMonth);`

4.3
```
int i = 0;
while (i < 10) {
  ch = Text.readchar(in);
  if (ch <='0' | ch >= '9') break;
  i++;
}
```

4.4   It will give an error message and request that the number be retyped. The message is:

`Error in number. Try again.`

4.5   EOFException could occur while reading (it will get thrown by the Text class) and DivideByZeroException could occur during division.

4.6
```
if (pre == 'm') System.out.print("milli");
if (pre == 'c') System.out.print("centi");
if (pre == 'K') System.out.print("kilo");
System.out.println("metre");
```

4.7   Yes, they are all the same.

4.8
```
switch (i) {
    case 0 : System.out.println("Sunday"); break;
    case 1 : System.out.println("Monday"); break;
    case 2 : System.out.println("Tuesday"); break;
    case 3 : System.out.println("Wednesday"); break;
    case 4 : System.out.println("Thursday"); break;
    case 5 : System.out.println("Friday"); break;
    case 6 : System.out.println("Saturday"); break;
}
```

4.9   We would get 999 500 000

4.10   The bisection method is slower because it has to evaluate the function more times than the Newton–Raphson.

Chapter 5

5.1
```
String daysOfWeek [] = {"Sunday", "Monday","Tuesday",
            "Wednesday", "Thursday", "Friday", "Saturday"};
```

5.2   There are several errors:

(a) The declaration of A should only have A mentioned once, on the left hand side, i.e.

`int A [] = new int [10];`

(b) The length of the array is given by the property length, not a method, so there should be no brackets.

(c) A.length returns 10 but the last index for A is 9, so A[A.length] does not exist.

5.3 Yes, we could say:

```
mean (B,100);
```

5.4 The rows come first.

5.5 `java.lang.ArrayIndexOutOfBoundsException`

5.6 No.

5.7 Yes, a row can be passed as a parameter.

5.8 Yes.

5.9 The number of elements must be mentioned first in the data file. We read it and then do the delaration of the array.

```
int n = Text.readInt(fin);
double A [ ] = new double[n];
```

5.10
```
double highest (double A [], int n) {
    double top = Double.MIN_VALUE;
    for (int i; i<A.length; i++)
      if (a[i] > top) top = a[i];
    return top;
}
```

Chapter 6

6.1
```
class Giraffe extends Herbivore {
    private double neck;
    Giraffe (String name, int grass, double n) {
      super (name, grass);
      neck = n;
    }
}
```

6.2 If s has been created with `s = " ";` then it is no longer a null object and has a reference (albeit to an empty space). In order to compare s to the empty string, we must use `equalTo`, as in

```
System.out.println
        ("s is an empty string is " + (s.equalTo("")));
```

6.3 The last line contains an `Object` which has to be converted into an object of the class `Dates` before it can be assigned. The correct line is

```
Dates d = (Dates) holiday.get ("Foundation Day");
```

6.4 If the display is to be used by an inner class, then it must be declared as static so that both the main method of the outer class, and the methods of the inner class may use it. If it is wholly for use by one class, then it can be declared as an ordinary instance object of that class.

6.5   It depends on how the constructors for `Elephant` are arranged. If there is a constructor which defaults the upper fields and only requires a tusk's length, then the declaration is valid.

6.6   `patient = (Elephant) jumbo.clone();`

6.7   `toString`

6.8   Depending on whether the object stored in `register[i]` is a `Tag` or an `XTag`, different versions of `toString` will be called. The one returns a string made up of two values, and the other a string made up of three values.

6.9   The Close button on the display can be pressed to close down the program. The program itself runs in an endless loop calling `checkTags` from the `main` method.

6.10 ```
a = n;   // incorrect - assigning to a lower class
e = r;   // incorrect - classes at the same level
```

# Chapter 7

7.1   ```
double getField (TextField t) {
   return Double.valueOf (t.getText()).doubleValue();
}
```

7.2   ```
TextField school = new TextField(8);
p.add (new Label ("SCHOOL"));
p.add(school);
```

7.3   `TextArea` specifies an area in which text can be displayed and scrolled. Text can also be selected and a cut-and-paste effect obtained. `ScrollPane` creates a scrollable viewing area for graphics and text.

7.4   Typing into a `TextField` gives a normal `ActionEvent` which is the same as for `Button`. There is another event called `TextEvent` which can also be used, since a `TextField` is a `TextComponent` by inheritance (refer to Table 7.1).

7.5   `event.getSource()`

7.6   ```
Choice c = new Choice ();
c.addItem("Monday");
c.addItem("Tuesday");
c.addItem("Wednesday");
c.addItem("Thursday");
c.addItem("Friday");
c.addItem("Saturday");
c.addItem("Sunday");
```

7.7   Component is an abstract class and therefore cannot be directly instantiated as an object.

7.8   Once the frame `f` has been declared and set visible, the Java Runtime System looks for a `paint` method for `f` and calls it.

7.9   `BorderLayout`

7.10   `Font mine = new Font ("Serif", Font.BOLD, 24);`

Chapter 8

8.1   `drawString`

8.2   The applet takes over the function of setting up the program and defining the window size.

8.3   A constructor

8.4   `APPLET code = "Orange.class" width=200 height=200>`
      `</APPLET>`

8.5   `getCodeBase` finds out where the applet came from so that the browser's Java runtime can fetch other information from the same source.

8.6   GIF and JPEG

8.7   `getAppletContext` finds out where the applet is running so that the applet can perform operations on that machine. An example is writing to the status bar.

8.8   milliseconds

8.9   The `paint` method is called. It is supplied with new coordinates for the duke, who therefore seems to move.

8.10   Images generally require more space.

Chapter 9

9.1   `java.lang`

9.2   `T x = new T();`

9.3   `start` does indeed call `run`.

9.4   No, only those methods that access data items at potentially the same time as other methods must be declared as synchronized.

9.5   The `ViewPoint` class is an inner class of the main program and therefore runs with `main`'s thread of control. As `main` has no buttons to watch or other actions to attend to, it can provide all the necessary computing power that `ViewPoint` needs.

9.6   `new CarThread ("North",450).start();`

9.7
```
class Picture extends Thread {
  private Canvas a;
  Picture (Canvas a) {
    area = a;
  }
```

```
public void paint (Canvas a) {
  Graphics g = area.getGraphics ();
  g.drawImage (i,50,50,this);
  }
}
```

9.8 A handler that detects a SHUTDOWN message called closeDown in the server. closeDown sets the boolean done to true. However, the server will not detect that done is true until it comes round its loop to start a new client. So it needs another new client to start up before it can shut down! It is, however, polite enough to service the new client until they both end together.

9.9 A ServerSocket object resides on the server and its function is to listen for new clients. A Socket object resides on the server, but there is one created for each client to handle its requests.

9.10 The system will carry on waiting for a further worker and will not proceed with the simulation.

Chapter 10

10.1
```
for (int i = 0; i<names.length; i++) {
  int epos = names[i].indexOf('e');
  if (epos >= 0)
    System.out.println(names[i] + " e at " + epos);
}
```

10.2
```
word = word.charAt[0] +
       word.toLowerCase().subString(1,word.length()-1);
```

10.3 (a) `int i = Integer.parseInt (s);`

(b) `System.out.println(s);`

10.4 (a) The default for printing numbers larger than 999 arranges them with commas, e.g. 1,000. Such a format is not easy to read back in again.

(b) Numbers are truncated if the space allowed is not sufficient, e.g. printing 1000 in a space of 3 will give 0. (*Java Gently*'s text class will rather expand the space in such a case.)

10.5
```
tragic.set (Calendar.YEAR, 1997);
tragic.set (Calendar.MONTH, Calendar.AUGUST);
tragic.set (Calendar.DAY, 31);
```

10.6 The answer depends, of course. For a UK locale, it would be:

Wednesday, 7 October 1967

but for a US locale it would be

Wednesday, October 7, 1967

10.7

10.8 Nested classes can be accessed outside of their enclosing class; member classes may not.

10.9 C is in the same package as E so package accessibility is available. Declare e as:

```
int e;
```

10.10 Both the less than methods would change. In fact, we can remove `lessThan` from `XTags` and just have it in the upper class, `Tags`. It will do a comparison on names and return the boolean which is used by the sort.

Index

What follows in a comprehensive index which contains not only references into the text in the normal manner, but also several sub-indices of important categories in the book. These are:

- applets
- exceptions
- forms
- graphs
- numerical methods
- packages
- programs
- problems

In addition, the entry for each Java method or class gives the class or package that contains it, for example:

isEditable method in TextField class   259